Sociology

FOURTH EDITION

Christopher Townroe

George Yates

 LONGMAN

ADDISON WESLEY LONGMAN LIMITED
Edinburgh Gate,
Harlow, Essex CM20 2JE, England
and Associated Companies throughout the world

First published 1987
Second edition 1990
Third edition 1995
Fourth edition 1999

Set in 10.75/12 pt Times New Roman

A catalogue record for this book is available from the British Library

ISBN 0-582-25730-1

Printed in Singapore

The publisher's policy is to use paper manufactured from sustainable forests.

For Jenny and Georgina; Paul, Jackson, Susannah, Kate, Tom and Amy

Contents

CHAPTER 1

Introducing sociology

Socialisation – are we brain-washed to conform?

1 Sociology and social groups

The word sociology was first used in English in 1843 and it means the study of human societies. This book is an introduction to the ways in which sociology can help us to understand modern British society.

Society is made up of social groups, ranging from families and local darts teams to large social institutions such as the Roman Catholic Church in Britain. The following case study shows how we belong to a range of social groups. Note that in each group we have a position which carries with it certain obligations and expectations – this is often called a person's **role**. For example, the role of parent involves the obligation to care for one's children.

Case study: Mrs Catherine Wyatt, 28 years old

Types of social groups	*The groups to which Mrs Wyatt belongs*	*Her positions or roles in the group*
Family	The Wyatts	Daughter, mother, wife, sister, etc.
Occupational group	Data Processing Department	Computer programmer
Trade union	UNISON	Health and Safety Representative
Recreational club	'The Dog and Duck' Darts Team	Treasurer
Church	The Church of England	Member of choir at St Peter's Church
Educational group	Thursday evening class on furniture restoration	Student
Parents' group	Hillview Estate Baby-sitting Circle	Organiser

Activities

1   Construct similar charts for (a) yourself and (b) an adult you know well.

2   Find out what is studied in the following social sciences: psychology and economics.

Imagine that your sociology class became marooned on a desert island and lived there for many years. After a while you might develop common rules, values, social arrangements and so on. One of the rules might be that food is distributed equally. In the interests of survival, a common value system might peacefully emerge concerning the best way to settle disputes. You might all value the judgements of the wisest islander. Also, in the interests of survival, social arrangements might come into being, such as regular meetings at which group decisions are made. The common way of life that emerged would then exert a powerful influence on your attitudes and behaviour. Your offspring, presuming there are any, would be brought up to fit in with your shared way of life.

It follows, therefore, that to understand these islanders it is necessary to examine the social world they have created which is influencing their behaviour and their thoughts. Of course, these islanders, in common with all human beings, are not only influenced by their society but also exert an influence upon it. In other words, society makes us but we make society as well. If some sociologists appeared on your island, they would be intrigued by your way of life and society and they would want to understand it. Sociology is, then, concerned with understanding the way of life that is shared by a group of people. This way of life is made up of so many things: institutions, economic activity, customs and beliefs, the distribution of wealth

Some people, such as travellers, live in minority social groups.

and property, the exercise of power. What the sociologist tries to do is make sense of these aspects of group life by:

- examining their character;
- showing how they are connected to each other;
- showing how they affect and are affected by the individual;
- identifying how they have changed;
- analysing the nature and causes of social problems.

Understanding the social world is a valuable activity in itself. But the value of sociology also consists of its attempt to suggest ways in which the quality of our lives could be improved.

2   Viewpoints on human behaviour

Sociologists are interested in the *social* aspects of human behaviour; that is, the ways humans behave in relation to others, in relation to social groups. When biologists look at human behaviour they are concerned with how the body works while psychologists focus on the workings of the mind. Let us illustrate this by asking three different specialists for some interesting facts on two common human activities: eating and sleeping.

Viewpoints on eating

Mrs A. Crania, a biologist, on eating: 'Did you know that the transit times vary between an average adult and a vegetarian? The time taken from eating to elimination by the body is on average forty-three hours but for a vegetarian it is thirty-seven hours. And even when no food is eaten about 7 to 8 grams of faeces are excreted daily.'

Mrs P. Brain, a psychologist, on eating: 'Have you heard of anorexia nervosa, the "slimmers' disease" where patients virtually stop eating altogether? Well, very often they are teenage girls of above average ability; hard-working high achievers under pressure to succeed from their parents. They have a negative self-image, thinking themselves to be fat and ugly when they are really just average in appearance. They are often frightened of growing up and in a way they can go back to girl-hood by starving themselves because this stops their monthly periods.'

Mrs B. Snoop, a sociologist, on eating: 'Did you know that Orthodox Jews observe dietary laws which are delivered from chapter 11 of Leviticus in the Old Testament of the Bible? These laws are extremely strict regarding which food may be eaten and how food is to be prepared. For example, pork is forbidden, and milk and meat products may not be prepared or eaten together. One social consequence of following these laws is that Orthodox Jews have been able to retain their identity as a group.'

The biologist has concentrated on the workings of the digestive system, the psychologist has discussed neurotic obsessions arising from unconscious fears in the mind, and the sociologist has looked at the custom or culture of a particular social group.

Viewpoints on sleeping

Mrs A. Crania, the biologist, on sleeping: 'A person loses from 28 to 42 grams in weight per hour of sleep or 300 grams per night; less urine is produced per hour of sleep and body temperature falls during normal sleeping time whether we are awake or not.'

Mrs P. Brain, the psychologist, on sleeping: 'The average new-born baby sleeps sixteen to seventeen hours a day but most adults have seven and a half hours' sleep which breaks down into 100-minute-long cycles. During each cycle we go through four distinct stages, each with different brain wave patterns. During the fourth stage we enter a period with rapid eye movements and if woken then, we will almost always report a dream.

'Sleep deprivation is a form of torture and can cause hallucinations. When a New York disc jockey, Peter Tripp, stayed awake for 201 hours for charity he was assessed by doctors. At one stage he ran away from them because he believed that they were undertakers who had come to bury him. After the "wakathon" he became fairly seriously depressed for some time.'

Mrs B. Snoop, the sociologist, on sleeping: 'Did you know that most rock musicians are "night owls"? They often stay up all night in recording studios or night clubs and then they sleep all day. Sleep patterns also

Many rock stars are 'night owls' and spend their leisure hours in night clubs.

varied between occupational groups in Ancient Greece. Plato describes how upper-class Athenians would spend hours during the night discussing ideas and enjoying entertainment by female dancers and musicians. Productive work was done by the slave. He would labour in the fields from the early hours of daylight, before it got hot. Not for him nights of revelry and discussion followed by lazy mornings, then afternoons in the gymnasium.'

Once again we see how the sociologist has concentrated on human behaviour in the context of a social group. Sociologists emphasise the way that patterns of behaviour are learned from society while biologists and psychologists often argue that we inherit many of our characteristics and abilities. These differences of outlook are reflected in the 'nature versus nurture' debate.

3   Nature versus nurture

The **nature** versus **nurture** debate concentrates on the question of how far our ability is fixed at birth by our inborn 'nature':

There once was a man who said, 'Damn,
I suddenly see what I am.
I'm a creature that moves
In predestined grooves,
I'm not even a bus, I'm a tram!'

The following case study suggests that the course of our lives is, to a certain extent, determined at birth; that is, we move in 'predestined grooves'.

Case study: the 'Jim Twins'

James Lewis and James Springer were identical twins who were separated in the first year of life and brought up separately. They never met again until they were reunited as adults by Thomas Bouchard, the professor of psychology at Minnesota University. Bouchard traced them as part of the Minnesota Study of Twins Reared Apart and he discovered an amazing number of coincidences about the separate lives that the 'Jim Twins' had led:

– both had married women called Linda,

– both had been divorced and had then married women called Betty,

– one twin had called his first son James Allan and the other had called his James Alan,

– both had had a dog that they had named Toy,

– both had spent their holidays on the same small beach in Florida,

– both drove a Chevrolet,

– both built white benches round the trunk of a tree in their gardens,

– both bit their fingernails to the quick.

Identical twins

An important point about the Jim Twins is that they are identical or monozygotic twins. In other words, they first became separate entities when a zygote or fertilised ovum divided in their mother's womb.

Most twins are dizygotic or fraternal and they result when two ova are discharged simultaneously into the fallopian tube and then fertilised independently by different spermatozoa. All cells contain **chromosomes** which control the characters of living things. Since each ovum and each sperm contain a unique, randomly determined selection of twenty-three single chromosomes, fraternal twins are therefore as different as any brothers and sisters.

We are all genetically unique apart from identical twins who have the same genetic inheritance. But it must be recognised that identical twins normally lead very different adult lives. The differences between the Jim Twins no doubt outnumbered the similarities.

Married identical twins.

Genes

All cellular organisms inherit characteristics from their parents through the **genes** which are contained in chromosomes. This applies to microbes, insects, cabbages and kings. In human beings the genes inherited from parents determine:

1   physical features such as colour of eyes, hair and skin and shape of facial features;
2   certain genetic diseases such as haemophilia, muscular dystrophy, thalassemia and sickle-cell anaemia;
3   anatomical traits such as height and weight – to a certain extent!

In the last case we must sound a note of caution and say that body form and structure are also shaped by non-hereditary influences: your friends might be tall and heavy because they have inherited this from their parents or because of the diet and exercise they have had during their upbringing.

Nature and nurture

The idea that humans are determined by these two influences dates back to the Ancient Greek philosopher Protagorus who, in the fifth century BC, compared 'physis' (nature) and 'nomos' (tradition). *Nature* refers to a person's genetic inheritance or inherited characteristics. *Nurture* refers to the ways in which upbringing and environment influence our development as individuals. It is, however, difficult to unravel the separate influences of nature and nurture. If the children of musically talented parents are themselves musically gifted, is it because of genetic inheritance (nature) or because they grew up in a musical environment (nurture)?

To ask which of these two factors is most important is a bit like asking which is the more important ingredient in an omelette: is it the eggs, or the filling and flavouring, or the skill of the cook, or the heat in the pan? Clearly the eggs are essential but it is arguable whether they are more important than anything else.

In 1969, an American psychologist, Jensen, claimed that only 20 per cent of the variation between people's intelligence is due to their environment and experience while 80 per cent is fixed from birth by genetic inheritance. The case of the Jim Twins might lead us to agree that genes are more influential but this matter is very controversial. Sociologists emphasise the importance of nurture rather than nature.

Case study: the Skeels experiment

The importance of nurture was shown in a famous experiment by H. M. Skeels on two groups of orphans who were thought to be of low intelligence.

The first group

These were thirteen 2-year-old orphans who were transferred to an institution where they were paired with older, subnormal girls who acted as 'substitute mothers', loving them and playing with them.

The second group

These were twelve 2-year-olds who were left in the unstimulating environment of the orphanage until adoption.

The result

After two years the first group were returned to the orphanage or were adopted; their average IQ (intelligence quotient) had risen from 64.3 to 92.8. In other words, their measured intelligence had risen from the level of 'mentally retarded' to not far off the average score for all 4-year-olds which is 100. In contrast, the second group's average IQ scores had fallen from 86.7 to 60.5. These gains and losses in IQ were found to have persisted when both groups were tested again at the age of 22.

Activities

1 Can you suggest why the intelligence of the first group improved while that of the second group deteriorated?

2 Why do you think that some would see the Skeels experiment as morally wrong?

Genetics and social policy

Most modern social scientists emphasise the importance of nurture but in the nineteenth century many believed that genetic inheritance effectively shaped the course of our lives and these beliefs led to a number of proposals:

1 In nineteenth-century Italy, Lombroso claimed that criminality was shown by certain physical features and was inherited. This idea led to the proposal that the population should be examined to track down all criminal types. (We discuss Lombroso's discredited idea in Chapter 12.)

2 In 1934, the British psychologist Cyril Burt concluded that intelligence 'is inherited, or at least **innate**, not due to teaching or training' and he proceeded to develop the IQ tests used in the 11+ examination. (The controversy that surrounded the 11+ examination is discussed in Chapter 10.)

3 In 1883, Galton invented the idea of **eugenics**. He was greatly influenced by Darwin's theory of evolution and Mendel's science of genetics. Eugenics means studying methods to improve the human race by selective breeding. By the 1930s this idea had led many states in the USA to adopt laws for the compulsory sterilisation of 'defective' humans. In Nazi Germany the idea of breeding a pure Aryan master-race led to the gas chambers of Hitler's death camps.

4   Socialisation and social control

What we inherit from our parents may or may not have a great effect on our characters and abilities. But what cannot be sensibly denied is the crucial effect that our upbringing has on us. This is dramatically shown by the following case study.

Case study: the Portuguese 'chicken girl'

Isabel Quaresma is ten, but cannot talk, and is only now learning to eat with a spoon. She is a 'wild child' who has only recently been brought into regular contact with human beings. ... Since birth the child has lived in a chicken coop. Her mother is a mentally deficient rural worker living in poverty. ... The mother works in the fields all day and soon after Isabel's birth confined her to the chicken coop, where she was thrown pieces of bread and shared the chicken-feed with the fowls. Neighbours had gossiped about this scandal for years but had done nothing, not wanting to interfere with a family matter. At last, however, a district hospital radiographer at Torres Vedras Hospital approached local institutions to accept Isabel. After a string of refusals, the radiographer took her into her own home, but could not cope. Isabel's contact with humans had been minimal and she could neither talk nor was she toilet trained – in the chicken coop she had lived in her own excrement. Her gestures and sounds resembled those of the fowls she had lived with since infancy. She scratched food up with her hands.

Isabel is now at a private clinic for severely handicapped children in Lisbon. ... The most striking thing about her appearance is her severely stunted body. She has a tiny head, and the stature of an infant. X-rays have shown her skull structure to be sound. Her dwarfed form is almost certainly due to a life of malnutrition. One eye is clouded with a cataract, thought to be the result of a scratch from the hens she lived with. She communicates in repetitive calls and beats her arms and drums her feet to express emotion – actions probably imitative of her only living companions.

Dr João dos Santos is optimistic about her chances of social awakening. But, he explains: 'It all depends on whether we can built warm human contacts which will move her to want to speak and communicate with us.'

(Source: Jill Joliffe in the *Guardian*, 12 June 1980)

Activities

1   Describe the ways in which Isabel Quaresma differed from a normal 10-year-old.
2   Imagine that immediately after your birth you were raised by apes in the forest. If this had happened you would lack certain skills necessary for !iving in human society, such as the ability to talk a human language and the knowledge of customs like queuing for buses.
    (a)   List some other social skills that you would lack.
    (b)   What skills might you have gained?

Culture, norms and socialisation

All communities have a **culture**, or common way of life. A society's culture includes language, customs, norms and values.

- An example of a **custom** is the way we celebrate birthdays with gifts, cakes and parties.

Isabel Quaresma and her mother in 1980.

- Social **norms** are expected patterns of behaviour: the rules which regulate our actions by defining what is acceptable. Norms affect what we think, such as who might make a suitable marriage partner; what we say, such as the way we greet colleagues at work; and what we do, such as how we queue for a bus. Social **deviance** occurs when we break social norms: when we disobey norms or deviate from them.
- Norms are based on a **value system**. Our shared moral code might stress the sanctity of human life. Our society might place great value on economic growth and material success. Or we might value greatly the conservation of our environment. Our system of values might emphasise the importance of generosity to distant relatives.

During our lives we learn the culture of a social group. That is, we learn to think and behave in ways that are acceptable to a particular group. This learning process is called **socialisation**.

There are three stages of socialisation:

1   Primary socialisation   This stage involves the socialisation of the young child in the home. For example, a child may be taught by its parents always to say 'please' and 'thank you'.

2   Secondary socialisation   This describes the influences outside the home that shape our behaviour. Children may learn how to behave from formal organisations such as the Church and the Cubs or the Brownies. We are also subject to informal influences, such as our **peer group**, that is our friends of the same age. Other agencies of socialisation are schools and the **mass media**, meaning TV, radio, magazines and books. The next chapter looks at how these influence our ideas of what is considered to be appropriate masculine and feminine behaviour.

3   Adult socialisation   Primary and secondary socialisation may teach us that it is wrong to tell lies or to use foul language, but we cannot be fully prepared during childhood for adult roles such as being a parent or a doctor. Medical students are gradually taught how doctors should behave by, for example, joining senior consultants on their rounds of the hospital wards. From their observations the students may learn what is thought to be a good bedside manner with patients.

Social control and social change

Social control refers to the means used by society to maintain order and stability. One way we learn norms of behaviour is through the sanctions and punishments reserved for those who deviate from the norms of society. A clear example is theft. This may be dealt with in one of two ways:

1   Formal social control refers to the methods of controlling behaviour which involve the laws and official punishments of a society. Thus, for example, burglars are dealt with by formal agencies of social control, such as the police, the courts and the prisons.

2   Informal social control is exercised by informal agencies of social control, such as the family, friends and neighbours. If, as children, we try stealing apples from next-door's garden, our playmates might express disapproval and refuse to join in, the owner might threaten and chase us, or our parents might declare us 'grounded' and stop us going out to play.

The formal institutions would have immense difficulties in imposing the law on a community if there was not a widespread willingness to obey the law in the first place. This willingness or consent is brought about by informal agencies of social control. As we have seen, the family teaches the values of a society to the young and trains them to act in socially acceptable ways.
    Our next case study describes a situation in which disagreement arose concerning norms of behaviour. Changing attitudes about standards of behaviour can lead to a change in the law.

Case study: bathing on Spanish beaches

From 1939 to 1975 Spain was ruled by General Franco, a dictator, who controlled Spanish life very strictly. In the 1960s Spain developed numerous Mediterranean resorts for foreign tourists. Many foreigners were surprised to find that bikinis were banned on Spanish beaches. In this instance Spain's strict religious traditions coincided with Franco's dislike of modern fashions. Since the death of Franco, Spain has become a more relaxed society. This has been partly due to the influence of ideas and fashions portrayed on TV. Spain now allows not only bikinis but also topless sunbathing.

A teenage Spanish girl who has had a strict religious upbringing and who then bathes topless on the beaches is no longer committing an illegal act and will no longer incur the penalties of the law. But, although she is not punished by the official agencies of social control, she may have performed a deviant act according to the standards of her family. If this is the case, her parents can punish her with a number of informal sanctions such as refusing to allow her to visit the beach again and by withdrawing their affection for her.

Activities

1 Why do you think that the laws about swimwear on Spanish beaches have been relaxed?

2 Give three examples of norms in other societies which differ from norms in British society.

3 Give three examples of norms in British society which have changed since the nineteenth century.

4 Describe the norms that direct behaviour in the following situations:
  (a) a doctor's waiting room;
  (b) a school assembly;
  (c) an 18th birthday party.

---

5   The work of sociologists

This section introduces two examples of the type of research undertaken by British sociologists. Further details of sociological research methods can be found in Chapter 17 of this book.

A truancy survey

In 1993 the Department for Education paid for a national survey to be undertaken by Dennis O'Keeffe, a sociology lecturer at the University of North London, in which 38,000 15- and 16-year-olds completed questionnaires. These asked if they had played truant during the previous six weeks. One in three pupils admitted to at least one act of truancy and 10 per cent of 16-year-olds said that they truanted at least once a week.

Sociologists must be prepared for their findings to challenge common-sense assumptions. Most people might assume that those who truant (a) do so because they hate school; (b) are mainly at very large schools; (c) roam the streets and commit petty crimes. In fact, most of the truants said that they liked school. They approved of most of their subjects and wanted to stay on after the minimum school-leaving age. They were just as likely to come from small schools as from large ones. And many never left the school site but just bunked off the odd lesson after registering with their form tutor.

Research into drugtaking

If a sociologist hangs around with a group of drugtakers and watches how they lead their lives, this is called **participant observation**. If the researcher studies a particular couple of drugtakers, this is a **case study** (which may or may not be typical of most drugtakers in the area). If relaxed, taped conversations are chosen rather than questionnaires, this is known as **informal, unstructured** or **in-depth interviewing**.

Lee Young is a lecturer at Liverpool University. In October 1992, he got to know Janice and Owen when he called at their council-house squat. Aged 23 and 26 respectively, they had been addicted to heroin, cocaine and crack since they were 16 or 17. Janice, who had a baby son, was earning over £1,000 a week as a prostitute and they spent most of this on crack and heroin.

When Lee Young saw them sharing a syringe with the 'runner' who delivered heroin from a 'dealer', he asked them if they were aware of the risks of HIV infection. They replied that they only shared injecting equipment with people that they knew well.

Janice had been waiting for over two years to enter a detoxification and long-term rehabilitation unit. In the meantime, she was registered at a drug clinic and was receiving methadone (a synthetic opiate substitute).

In December 1993, Lee Young called on Janice and Owen to deliver a Christmas card and some bedding. He found another couple decorating the flat. Janice and Owen had left their squat, leaving no forwarding address.

Preparing for a 'fix' of heroin.

Activities

1   What problems might you have if you tried to carry out a survey of pupils to discover the extent of truancy and its causes?

2   Why might health authorities pay for the sort of research carried out by Lee Young?

3   'Sociologists need curiosity and patience when collecting data. They must evaluate their evidence in a critical way. And they must be objective, neutral and unbiased.' What is meant by 'objective, neutral and unbiased'?

GCSE question from Southern Examining Group 1996

Study Item A. Then answer *all* parts of the question which follow.

Item A
Distribution of time taken on police activities

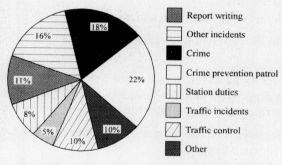

- Report writing
- Other incidents
- Crime
- Crime prevention patrol
- Station duties
- Traffic incidents
- Traffic control
- Other

From *In Focus; Sociology Review* (September 1994)

(a) (i)   According to the information in Item A, what percentage of police time is spent on crime?   (1)

(ii)   According to the information in Item A, on which police activity is the largest amount of time spent?   (1)

(iii)   Why might the police carry out this activity?   (1)

(b) (i)   Give *one* example of a punishment used in formal social control. Describe how it might control people's social behaviour.   (2)

(ii)   Identify *one* group of people who are more likely to experience formal social control than others. Suggest a reason for this.   (2)

(c) (i)   Explain what is meant by 'social deviance'.   (2)

(ii)   Identify and describe *one* informal way of controlling social deviance.   (2)

(d) (i)   The mass media are said to play an important role in the process of socialisation. Describe *one* way in which the mass media do this.   (3)

(ii)   Identify *one* other agent of socialisation.   (1)

CHAPTER 2

Sex role stereotyping

1 Traditional gender roles

There are two sorts of difference between men and women:

1 **Sex differences** refer to the different biological attributes of men and women.

2 **Gender differences** refer to the different masculine and feminine roles which men and women are expected to perform in society. Sociologists stress the extent to which gender roles are learned rather than inborn.

In British society, tradition gives us fixed images of the characteristics and the roles that are suitable for each gender.

Traditional gender characteristics

Some of the characteristics traditionally associated with masculinity and feminity are:

- *Masculine*   hard   logical   brave   aggressive   unemotional independent

- *Feminine*   soft   illogical   timid   passive   emotional   dependent

Traditional gender roles

The roles in life that have in the past been set aside for the two sexes follow on from the qualities of character that each sex is supposed to possess. Men have been expected to fulfil the 'important' positions of life such as business-man, lawyer, surgeon, government minister, general: the type of position that requires resourcefulness, skill, expertise, coolheadedness and courage. Also, men have been expected to take up those occupations such as builder, miner or firefighter that require strength and the willingness to face danger.

Women, on the other hand, have traditionally been expected to play a different part in society. Essentially, what has been required of women is not that they lead or build or create but that they serve others. Thus an important job for a woman has been that of housewife and mother. Typical female occupations, such as nurse, typist or junior school teacher, have also involved serving others.

Sexism: prejudice and discrimination

Some people use these traditional ideas of masculinity and femininity to pre-judge the abilities of women and to argue that women should remain unequal because they are inferior to men. This type of **prejudice** is 'sexism' and when it leads to unfair treatment for women we would call that **sexist discrimination**. The following experiment will show you how far the traditional ideas of gender roles are changing.

Activities: sex role experiment

This experiment requires the co-operation of an English teacher and some male and female pupils. You ask the teacher to set the following homework: Write an essay beginning 'Today is my eightieth birthday and I look back to the day I left school ...'

You then compare the male and female pupils' answers. When this exercise was tried with grammar school girls in 1968, most described lives in which their roles were limited to being housewives.

In 1983 the experiment was repeated with 190 third-year pupils and 50 sixth-formers, half boys and half girls. The following differences emerged:

Girls

Eighty-seven per cent described marriage (compared to 60 per cent of the boys) and most saw marriage and motherhood as the main focus of their lives. Many spelt out the number of children they imagined having, their sex, names, age gaps between them and *their* future lives. Thirty-three per cent even wrote about grand- and greatgrandchildren.

Boys

They saw marriage as providing a backdrop against which to play out the drama of their careers. Eight times as many boys as girls referred to world events (rather than personal events) such as nuclear war or political changes.

You could also look at two studies which have investigated the ambitions of teenage girls: '*Just Like a Girl': How Girls Learn to be Women* by Sue Sharpe and *Losing Out: Sexuality and Adolescent Girls* by Sue Lees.

Nature, nurture and stereotypes

Male and female pupils might explain their different views of their future lives by stressing the importance of *nature* and saying that a woman's womb naturally equips her for a life centred on the home and focused on child-rearing.

Sociologists, however, point to the importance of *nurture* or the process of socialisation. They stress how our upbringing prepares us for our sex roles and how the portrayal of these roles in comics and on TV offers us **stereotypes**.

A stereotype is an over-simplified image which distorts reality. For example, we might hold the view that all young football supporters are hooligans.

In 1996, Jane Couch, right, 'the Fleetwood Assassin', won the women's world welter-weight title in Copenhagen. In 1998, an industrial tribunal ruled that the British Boxing Board of Control had no valid reasons for refusing her a professional licence.

'Big boys should never cry' is a sex role stereotype. When stereotypes of social groups are exaggerated, they can easily lead to blind prejudice.

Breaking down gender barriers

The next three parts of this chapter look at some of the ways in which the different agencies of socialisation mould us into traditional sex roles. Although we are largely steered toward narrowly defined masculine or feminine categories, we do have some choice in this matter. We can only belong to one of the two biological sex categories, but we can choose from a wide spectrum of gender attributes for different activities.

If enough fathers push prams then it no longer deviates from masculine norms and eventually our culture will be rewritten so that pram-pushing becomes a masculine, or at least a 'gender-neutral', activity. One example

These two sex symbols were teenage pin-ups in the mid-1980s. Were they also gender models for teenagers to copy?

of the way that traditional gender barriers have broken down is the 'unisex' fashions dating from the 1960s, such as both sexes wearing denim jeans and T-shirts. And the mid-1980s saw the 'gender-bender' phenomenon: for example, women competing at body-building and male pop stars such as Boy George and Marilyn wearing female make-up.

While a person's sex is biologically determined, their gender is socially constructed. That is to say, our ideas of what is feminine and what is masculine depend on our culture. In many cultures women perform activities that our society would traditionally see as masculine or unfeminine. For example, women are not allowed to serve as active combat troops in Britain but women have joined in front-line fighting in many societies, such as modern Israel.

10

Peter likes to help.

He sees Daddy go up.

He wants to help Daddy.

I want to help you,
he says.

Please can I help you?

Yes, says Daddy, you can
help me.

help   sees   Daddy

20

Here we are at home,
says Daddy.

Peter helps Daddy with
the car, and Jane helps
Mummy get the tea.

Good girl, says Mummy
to Jane.

You are a good girl to
help me like this.

Good   good   girl

Some pages from Boys and Girls (*Book 3b in the Ladybird Key Words Reading Scheme*) – *published in 1964 but still being purchased by some schools and libraries in the 1980s.*

2   Sex role stereotyping in the home

Many customs that surround the birth of a child express the different gender roles that girls and boys are expected to fulfil. Elena Belotti gives this example from Italy:

> In Lucania, when a boy is born, a pitcher of water is poured into the road to symbolise that the newborn baby's destiny is to travel the road of the world. When a girl is born, water is thrown on to the hearth to show that she will lead her life within the confines of the home.

From birth we start to learn the appropriate gender roles for both sexes in our culture. Our primary socialisation (see page 9) gives us our first lessons in sex roles in the following ways:

- parents' role models;
- the way we are dressed as toddlers;
- games and toys;
- rules about appropriate behaviour.

Parents' role models

One of our main lessons in sex roles comes from the example that our parents set us in the way they divide up tasks around the house. Even when wives are going out to work, they still tend to find that their husbands leave most of the domestic chores to them. This is shown in the following survey:

The domestic division of labour in households with working women. (Source: British Social Attitudes.)

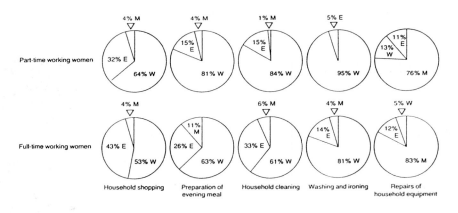

Key
M = mainly man
W = mainly woman
E = shared equally

Data-response exercise: the domestic division of labour

1   When wives are working full-time, in what percentage of households do husbands equally share household cleaning?

2   Which domestic task is most likely to be done by men?

3   Which domestic task is most likely to be equally shared between men and full-time working women?

4   Using the figures above, explain the following statement: 'When young children notice who cooks each day, they are learning a role model.'

5   How far do the figures support the claim that domestic chores are now jointly shared, especially when wives are working full-time?

Clothes, games and toys for toddlers

When researchers from the State University of New York observed babies at shopping centres, they guessed the babies' sex and then checked by asking the parents. The pairs of observers rarely disagreed and mistakes in guessing the babies' sex were even rarer. It turned out that 77 per cent of the girls wore pink and 79 per cent of the boys wore blue.

Toys and games are an important aspect of socialisation because they teach skills and develop patterns of behaviour. The toys and games considered suitable for girls often prepare them for their expected roles in life as housewives and carers. In contrast, the toys and games designed for boys prepared them for their expected roles as achievers in the competitive world outside the home.

Case study: survey of girls aged 7 to 10

In 1996, Clark's, the shoemakers, conducted a survey of 600 girls aged between 7 and 10. The best toy, nominated by half the girls, was traditional rollerskates. Next in popularity came soft animals and Sindy dolls. 20 per cent said that their TV remote control was their favourite toy.

The favourite play activity was dressing up as a bride, followed by acting like a princess, a pop star or the Disney character Pocohontas. They rated the caring professions highly: 17 per cent wanted to be a vet, 13 per cent a nurse and 10 per cent a teacher.

Art and maths were both rated top subject at school by 27 per cent of the girls; only 7 per cent put science at the top of their list. Computing was nominated by only 2 per cent and French, technology and RE were each rated top by only 1 per cent.

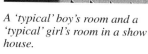
A 'typical' boy's room and a 'typical' girl's room in a show house.

Activities

1   An interesting piece of research is to look through the toddlers section of a clothing catalogue and count the number of items which are clearly designed (a) for girls, (b) for boys, in comparison with those that are (c) 'unisex' and suitable for either.
2   Look at a sample of advertisements for children's toys in a toy catalogue or on children's TV. Make three lists for toys which are shown (a) mainly used by girls, (b) mainly used by boys, (c) for either sex.
3   Describe the personality characteristics and the expectations of life that are likely to be developed by (a) toys for boys, and (b) toys for girls.

Rules about appropriate behaviour

The Equal Opportunities Commission has produced a booklet called *An Equal Start ... Guidelines for those working with the Under-Fives* which says:

> There is a time in every child's life for tranquillity and a time to release aggression and let off steam; there is a time to be docile and a time to be assertive; a time to cry and a time to shout. None of these characteristics is determined by the sex of the child and none should be regarded as inappropriate for either a girl or a boy.

Some of the ways that parents tend to lay down different rules for girls have been described in a survey of children in Nottingham called *Seven Years Old in the Home Environment*. This survey found that in comparison with boys, 7-year-old girls were:

- twice as likely to be fetched from school;
- more likely to be told that they must say where they are going before going out;
- much more likely to be stopped from 'brawling in public' with their brothers and sisters, although fighting in the home was often tolerated;
- more likely to be given the responsibility of looking after a younger brother or sister;
- far less likely to object to displaying affection in public, such as kissing their parents goodbye at the garden gate as they set off for school. The book describes how Bartholemew sits on his mother's lap in the evening and insists on his bedtime kiss; but he refuses even to wave her goodbye in the morning if anyone is watching. The **taboo** on male tenderness is thus enforced by the peer group: Bartholemew is afraid to appear a 'cissy' in front of his friends.

Activity

What rules, laid down (a) by parents and (b) by peer groups, affect what is considered to be suitable behaviour for teenagers of either sex?

3 Media images

The mass media, which include comics, magazines, television and radio, present us with a picture of the world. The images of men and women that they portray are generally stereotyped ones. These images encourage us to have very limited ideas of masculinity and femininity. This can be seen from an examination of various media.

Children's magazines

These tend to present two worlds. One is a feminine world of home, family, personal relationships and personal appearance. The other is a masculine world of national and international affairs, industry and technology. Research by Hartley, Goulden and O'Sullivan into six weekly magazines (*Bunty, Mandy, Princess, Champ, Spike* and *Tiger*) shows how story settings reflect these two worlds:

Setting	154 Girls' stories	122 Boys' stories
Home	54	16
School	54	16
Local community	38	32
National community	4	0
International community	0	53
Fantasy world	4	5

Women in textbooks

A 1983 report called *'Pour Out the Cocoa, Jane': Sexism in Children's Books* describes the following analysis of science textbooks: 23 popular chemistry books contained 258 pictures of males and only 26 pictures of females; 80 per cent of illustrations in physics books showed only men and when women did appear they were 'in a bathing suit, in a bath, as a nurse, with a vacuum cleaner'. With increased awareness of gender stereotyping in the 1990s, publishing companies must take care to represent women fairly in their textbooks.

Women in TV advertisements

During 1992, a group called Feminist Forum launched a scheme to celebrate advertisements that took a positive, non-stereotypical view of women. After monitoring commercials throughout the year, the only award given was a booby prize for an advertisement for a mobile telephone. This featured a frightened woman alone at night at a bus stop, calling her husband to rescue her.

The continuing sexism in TV commercials was confirmed by sociologists at Aston University when they analysed the content of 500 prime-time TV advertisements. Their study found that:

- men outnumbered women by almost two to one;
- 89 per cent of the advertisements had male voice-overs;
- men were more than twice as likely to be shown in paid employment;

- 64 per cent of women were 'attractive' ('the kind of people who might appear in a clothes magazine') compared to 22 per cent of men;
- female characters were twice as likely as males to receive sexual advances.

Referring to incidental characters, the researchers noted that:

There were many more male than female 'sportspeople'. In an advertisement for Mars Bars, a 'team' of attractive young people prepare for and go on a sailing trip. Male characters perform active, physical tasks, such as hoisting the mast and sails and steering the boat. The women perform light tasks, such as loading boxes of Mars Bars, and passing them around, or sit decoratively and watch the men.

In contrast to the above examples of sex role stereotypes, more men than women were shown cooking, but usually for a special event, such as a candle-lit dinner.

Activities

1   Carefully watch two commercial breaks, such as the advertisements before and after the early evening news. List the products advertised and for each advertisement where women appear, describe their roles. How far are they portrayed as either (a) housewives, or (b) sex objects, to interest men in products aimed at males?

2   Meryl Streep, the leading American film actress, said in an interview in 1993 that sexism in American films is not decreasing but increasing. She claimed that there was a growing trend for women to be depicted as the objects of brutal treatment by men. Describe the portrayal of women in five recent films.

---

4   Gender and education

The education system reflects the society of which it is a part. Thus, the gender inequalities of wider society can be found in schools, colleges and universities. The situation is changing. There may be fewer gender differences in classroom experiences and in courses followed in higher education. But gender inequalities also persist. For example, in 1994, only 5 per cent of professors at Oxford University and only 7 per cent of professors at Cambridge University were women.

Girls outperform boys

Statistics released in 1998 showed girls outperforming boys in national curriculum tests at 7, 11 and 14. Girls also beat boys at GCSE level in all but one local education authority. In terms of the proportion of pupils gaining 5 A to C grades at GCSE, the gap between boys and girls has widened nationally to 9 per cent in just 10 years. In some areas, 15 per cent more girls are achieving this academic benchmark. The gap is widest in English, where 59 per cent of girls achieve grade C or above compared to 41

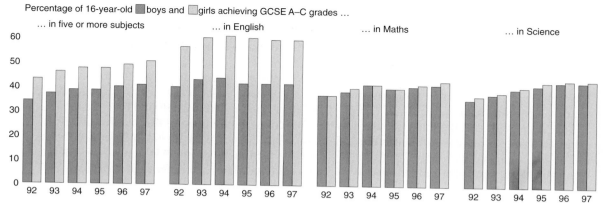

Percentage of 16-year-old ■ boys and □ girls achieving GCSE A–C grades ...

... in five or more subjects　... in English　... in Maths　... in Science

(Source: The Observer,
4 January 1998)

per cent of boys. But boys are also behind in 'boys' subjects', such as maths, science and technology.

Girls are more successful. They are also less likely to fail: only 21,500 girls left school without any exam passes, compared to 28,500 boys. With A levels and degrees, boys seem to take more risks. This means that they are both more likely to get top grades and more likely to fail, whereas girls are more likely to get average grades.

A number of reasons have been suggested for boys' underachievement:

- In many areas traditional male manual jobs have been lost (e.g. coal, steel, shipbuilding) and new service sector jobs (e.g. office work) may seem to be for women; this limits the ambitions and prospects of many boys.
- Boys see reading as a feminine activity since it is largely taught by mothers and women teachers in first schools.
- There is a decreasing proportion of male teachers in secondary schools. This alienates boys from education since boys need male role models.
- The coursework component in GCSE exams favours girls because they are more conscientious.
- Boys have a less serious approach to school work in general due to 'laddish culture' – encouraged by TV programmes such as *Men Behaving Badly* and enforced by peer pressure: the average boy hates to appear to be a swot or a boffin.
- Boys are more restless and get bored with lessons more easily.
- Girls have a new-found assertive confidence born of feminism, 'girl power' and economic opportunities (more women than men are now qualifying as doctors and solicitors).
- Harris *et al.* have identified 'gender regimes' both at home and in the wider community. Girls see women who are organisers, mothers who go out to work and also manage the home and family. So girls grow up with the idea that being a woman involves being highly organised and productive. This encourages them to adopt a thorough and determined approach to school work. They spend longer on homework and are more likely to meet deadlines than boys. The male gender regime in working-class communities encourages male chumminess and a hostility to authority. Boys thus grow up less motivated, less determined and less organised than girls.

Case study: women fall behind in degrees of excellence

Men are outstripping women in competition for the best degree results in nearly every field of study at Britain's universities. Fewer than one in fourteen women achieve firsts compared with nearly one in nine men.

The gap is widest in the most popular arts subjects. Some 17 per cent of men achieve firsts in English compared with only 7 per cent of women. The picture is the same in history, where 10 per cent of men get firsts against 5 per cent of women. In French, 10 per cent of men gain top honours compared with 6 per cent of women.

One reason could be subjectivity in marking, according to Laurie Taylor, Professor of Sociology at York University. 'Academics hang on to their subjective evaluation of students way beyond the point at which they should,' he said.

Any suggestion of discrimination was, however, dismissed by Baroness Warnock. She put it down to the inherent caution of women. Their more conscientious approach meant that they were more likely to achieve good second-class degrees and avoid thirds.

'Men are slightly more adventurous. They are prepared to chance their arms. They may make fools of themselves and get thirds, but, on the other hand, it may turn out to be very impressive,' said Warnock, former mistress of Girton College, Cambridge.

Science, however, is one area where women have succeeded in confounding stereotypes. Across all engineering and mathematical subjects, they were less than 2 per cent behind the men in the proportion of first-class degrees awarded. They were ahead in statistics, computer studies and mechanical engineering.

Academics argue that such achievements can be explained by the fact that it is the most committed and brightest girls who opt for science courses. Women who opt for theoretical physics are very serious about it, so they go on to do better than some of the men.

(adapted from an article by Charles Hyams, *The Sunday Times*, 23 May 1993)

We might find that within a generation there is no longer a tendency for women undergraduates to show caution and timidity in their finals exams. They may become just as intellectually adventurous and reckless as men. This would demonstrate that such differences are culturally determined, rather than being natural and innate.

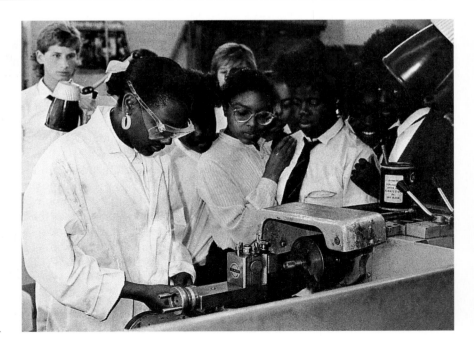

Girls enjoying a craft lesson.

5   Women in 'his-story'

An important point to realise in any discussion of sex role stereotyping is how far things have changed in recent years. For example:

- Many publishers and librarians now give priority to children's stories with girls in active and adventurous roles.
- Many advertisements now feature 'liberated women' such as career women who drink Guinness.
- Many schools campaign against sexism. This new philosophy can be found in PE departments which encourage mixed sports, with girls joining in football games and boys joining modern dance classes.
- In 1972 women were allowed to run in races further than 400 metres in the Olympic Games.
- In 1970 General Motors in the USA introduced an **affirmative action programme** to promote greater opportunities for women. The company increased the proportion of female students at its engineering college from 0.6 per cent in 1970 to 32 per cent in 1977.
- A few similar attempts, called **positive discrimination**, have been tried in Britain. For example, some Labour councils actively recruit women into manual jobs with trade apprenticeships, such as electrician or carpenter. Also, the Equal Opportunities Commission has launched a programme called WISE (Women into Science and Engineering).

Activities

1   Carry out a survey to compare the career ambitions of males and females.
2   Time how long it takes you to list twelve famous men, excluding royalty, from British history before 1900. Now time yourself again, this time listing twelve famous women, excluding royalty, from British history before 1900.

If we look back in British history, we find that few women had influential roles in society. Very few women ever became political leaders or famous writers, artists or scientists. A useful book on this topic is *Hidden from History* by S. Rowbotham.

The progress towards greater freedom for women and more equality between the sexes has taken many years. Some of the landmarks are shown in the following date chart.

Steps on the road towards equality between the sexes

1792   Mary Wollstonecraft wrote *A Vindication of the Rights of Women*, inspired by Tom Paine's *Rights of Man*.

1849   Queen's and Bedford Colleges were established for women at the University of London.

1874   Girton College for women was set up at Cambridge, but they were not allowed full degrees until 1948.

1888   The TUC passed its first resolution for equal pay and women were given the vote in county council elections.

1889   Annie Besant led the Bryant and May match-girl strikers to victory.

1905   Annie Kenney, a trade unionist and **suffragette** (a woman campaigning for women's right to vote), submitted a written question on behalf of 96,000 female cotton workers asking 'Will the Liberal Government give votes to women?' at an election rally. Winston Churchill, candidate for North-West Manchester, chose to ignore the question and, after she had heckled him, she was dragged from the meeting with Christabel Pankhurst who spat at a policeman to get herself arrested. After refusing to pay fines, they became the first suffragettes to be imprisoned.

1914   500,000 women went to work in the 'war effort', for example in munitions factories.

1918   Women over 30 were given the vote in general elections and the first women joined the police.

1919   Nancy Astor became the first woman MP and the Sex Disqualification (Removal) Act opened up the professions to women.

1928   Women over 21 were given the vote. They now had the same entitlement to vote as men.

1941   Britain became the only country to introduce conscription for women (if they were unmarried and aged 20 to 30).

1958   The first women peers were allowed in the House of Lords.

1969   The Women's Liberation Movement held its first demonstration, disrupting the 'Miss World' contest at the Albert Hall with smoke bombs and bags of flour.

Women and men demonstrating against the Mecca Miss World Contest in 1971.

1970 The Equal Pay Act gave women the right to the same wages as men if they were doing broadly similar work for the same employer, and the Matrimonial Proceedings Act gave wives the right to an equal share of a couple's assets (e.g. the value of their house) on divorce.

1972 The feminist magazine *Spare Rib* was launched. Erin Pizzey set up the first refuge for battered wives. By 1980 there were 99 Women's Aid Groups and 200 refuges.

1975 The Sex Discrimination Act was passed and the Equal Opportunities Commission was set up to help enforce this law against treating women less favourably than men in areas such as: education and training; recruitment advertising and getting a job; buying a house and getting a loan.

1976 The first Rape Crisis Centre was opened by feminists in London. The Domestic Violence Act allowed victims of marital violence to get their spouse excluded from the marital home by court order.

1980 Women Against Violence Against Women held their first national conference in Leeds – where the Yorkshire Ripper had just murdered his thirteenth female victim.

1982 NALGO, the union for council office workers, printed and distributed 250,000 pamphlets against sexual harassment at work.

1984 The Equal Pay Act was amended so that either sex could now ask an industrial tribunal to award equal pay if their work was of 'equal value' in terms of effort, skill, decision-making and other demands.

1984 Scotland Yard set up an Equal Opportunities Unit after it was disclosed that it had been running an illegal quota system which restricted recruitment of women to 10 per cent. (In 1988, 30 per cent of Metropolitan Police recruits were women.)

1986 The 1975 Sex Discrimination Act was amended with an equality clause which relates to retirement, dismissal and demotion as well as access to opportunities for promotion, transfer and training.

1987 Dame Elizabeth Butler-Sloss was the first woman judge to be appointed to the Court of Appeal.

1990 Independent taxation for husband and wife was introduced.

1991 Stella Rimington became the first woman head of M15.

1992 Betty Boothroyd became the first woman speaker of the House of Commons. Barbara Mills became the first woman Director of Public Prosecutions.

1993 The Labour Party adopted the positive discrimination policy of having all-women shortlists when selecting candidates in half of all seats.

A woman priest in the Church of England.

1994   The first women priests were ordained in the Church of England.

1995   The proportion of women managers rose from 9.5 to 10.7 per cent (in a sample of 300 companies surveyed by the Institute of Management). Women were found to be the main or only breadwinner in 30 per cent of families.

1996   A survey of more than 4,500 companies in 17 countries showed that 63 per cent of small and medium-sized British companies employ women in senior management (compared with an EU average of 50 per cent). But another survey of 2,300 big companies found only 4 per cent of directors and top managers were women. 6 per cent of barristers and 6 per cent of circuit judges were women. There was only one woman Lord Justice of Appeal out of 33, 7 female High Court judges out of 89 and just one woman chief constable. Of 292 countries in the world only 6 had female prime ministers and only 2 had women as both heads of state and government.

1997   The number of women MPs doubled from 63 to 120 (18 per cent, compared to 40 per cent in Sweden). Five of the new cabinet ministers were women. But there has never been a female Chancellor of the Exchequer, Home Secretary, Foreign Secretary or Defence Secretary.

2000   It is predicted that 50 per cent of small businesses in the USA will be owned by women, compared with just 3 per cent in 1960.

Activity: do you agree with this feminist conclusion?

The important question is not how and why women come to mother our children, but how and why men do not. The issue is not just 'nature' or socialisation experiences, but social control and power. Men don't rear children because they don't WANT to rear children. By leaving childcare to women, men are free for activities outside the home which bring status and power. Parenting is a time-consuming and unpaid occupation. This explains why parenting brings lower status, less power and less control of resources.

(adapted from 'Women in the Family: Companions or Caretakers' by Diana Leonard and Mary Anne Speakman in *Women in Britain Today*, 1986)

6   Men in crisis

In 1998, there was a call for a Royal Commission on the position of men in society. British men are seen to be in crisis for a number of reasons. Different people have made the following observations:

- Girls are increasingly outperforming boys at school.
- The future is female: the changing structure of the economy means less manual jobs, while most new jobs are in the service sector. Men are losing traditional jobs and women are more likely to gain from new occupational opportunities. (In *After Success* (1995), Ray Pahl argues that, since the eighteenth century, men have developed as masculine providers. They have become power-seekers who have learned to control their emotions. Their emotional reticence makes it difficult for them to relate to their children and grandchildren. It also makes it more difficult for them to relate to the more interactive demands of the new, people-related jobs in customer-oriented service industries.)
- Young men have a higher suicide rate than young women and it is on the increase (see page 356).
- On divorce, men's pension entitlements are now counted as a joint financial asset, of which the ex-wife can claim a large share. So divorced men may not only lose their wife, children and house but also savings and future pension payments earmarked for their ex-partner.
- Doting mothers allow sons to be naughty. Men then look for a mother-lover combination in a partner. Post-feminist young women refuse just to be providers of sexual and domestic services. Men then get confused, angry and often violent.
- There has been a male backlash against discrimination and equal pay laws and against positive discrimination policies. In the USA, the National Coalition of Free Men claims that men are now more discriminated against than women.
- In Britain, the men's rights movement includes Fathers Need Families and campaigns against the Child Support Agency.
- The progress of the gay movement in gaining acceptance of homosexual lifestyles has left many insecure men feeling that their masculinity has been 'feminised'.

- The 1990s was supposed to be the decade of the caring, sharing 'New Man' (epitomised in car ads featuring fathers with children) but has ended up being the decade of the 'New Lad' (epitomised by magazines such as *GQ* and TV shows about 'fantasy football').
- In the USA the publication of Robert Bly's *Iron John* marked the emergence of the men's rights movement in 1990. Bly has said 'Men are really tired of being told they should be women. Someone said that in the last 30 years, a woman can be anything she wants, but a man has to be a woman. Now a lot of women are unhappy with this, but they should have thought of that before they asked men to get rid of their aggression and maleness.' Bly offers men a third way. Rather than replace 1950s macho man with 1980s feminised man, he suggests that men rediscover their mythical, animal, wildman natures. Fathers must teach their sons to be real men.
- The Christian right-wing 'Promise Keepers' staged a Million Man March on Washington in 1997. They are men who promise to live up to traditional responsibilities as husband, father, breadwinner and head of the household.
- 1997 saw the publication of *Man Enough, Embodying Masculinities* by Victor Seidler, the professor of Social Theory at Goldsmiths College, the University of London. He argues that men must engage in debate about sexuality and spirituality. They must open up their emotions and discuss the feelings involved in relationships: feelings such as guilt, loss and grief.
- 1997 also saw a spate of 'girl power' ads. Posters for Lee Jeans showed a woman's stiletto on the buttocks of a naked, prostrate man under the heading 'Put the Boot In'. Wallis clothes had a 'Dress to Kill' campaign in which men were so distracted by beautiful women that they put themselves into life-threatening situations (e.g. a guard at the end of a tube train about to be decapitated on entering a tunnel, because he looks back at a woman on the platform who is wearing Wallis clothes). The Nissan Micra was promoted with the slogan 'Ask Before You Borrow It'. A man was shown holding his crotch in agony after being attacked by the female owner of the car he had borrowed. These ads caused a spate of protests to the Advertising Standards Authority.

Research on young middle-class men

John Galilee is a sociologist at Lancaster University. His qualitative research is on the daily life experiences of middle-class young men in their twenties. He has found that they still have the same privileges that they have had for generations. It is taking them a bit longer than before to enter traditional professional jobs, but they do still enter such jobs in a relatively short period of time. Rather than fearing women entering such jobs, their responses showed that they actively embraced working with the opposite sex on equal terms.

The global woman

Anne Crocker has said that we should look at the wider perspective. From looking around the world it is difficult to sustain the argument that men are now somehow losing out to women. This is her 'CV of the global woman' in 1998:

As a result of embryo sex testing she is quite likely to be aborted (China and India), or abandoned and murdered for being a girl (China). She will be fed less than her male siblings and be more likely to be malnourished (anywhere that food is scarce).

She may have her genitals mutilated in unsanitary conditions (Africa). She might be married-off to a middle-aged man at the age of 9 or 10 (Indian sub-continent) or be sold to a brothel (South-east Asia). If she declines the chosen man, she is likely to be murdered for 'dishonouring' her family (Gulf states).

She may be burned to death by her in-laws (India) or routinely beaten by her husband (almost anywhere). She will be constantly pregnant as contraception is unavailable (most of the world, especially Catholic countries) and she will take second place when it comes to healthcare. She is likely to have few legal rights and fewer job prospects, making it almost impossible to be independent.

GCSE question from Southern Examining Group 1996

How far can it be argued that the mass media contribute significantly towards gender socialisation? (10)

GCSE question from Southern Examining Group 1997

Study Item A. Then answer *all* parts of the question which follows.

Item A

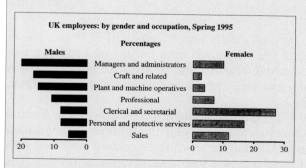

UK employees: by gender and occupation, Spring 1995

Adapted from *Social Trends*, 1996

(a) According to the information given, which occupation had the lowest percentage of female employees? (1)

(b) According to the information given,

   (i) what percentage of male employees were managers and administrators? (1)

   (ii) state whether males or females were more likely to be employed in Sales. (1)

(c) Explain what sociologists mean by 'the underclass', giving *one* example of a social group whose members might be said to belong to it. (3)

(d) (i) What is meant by 'social status'? (1)

   (ii) Identify and explain *one* problem that sociologists face when allocating individuals to social classes on the basis of their occupations. (3)

(e) (i) Identify *one* form of wealth. (1)

   (ii) Governments in the United Kingdom have sometimes attempted to redistribute income and wealth in society. Identify and explain *one* method they have used to bring about such a change. (3)

CHAPTER 3

Childhood and youth culture

Introduction: the evolution of childhood

When a class of 6-year-olds in a London infant school were asked to draw pictures of adults and children, their pictures showed adults working and children playing. This separation of the adult world of work and the childhood world of play has only occurred in the last few hundred years.

During the Middle Ages children were dressed exactly like adults and joined in grown-up activities. In 1212, 20,000 French children and 30,000 German boys and girls were led by two 12-year-olds to go to and fight in the Holy Land. This Children's Crusade is not so surprising when you realise that children were allowed to wear a sword from the age of 5 and join the army from the age of 11.

As late as the 1600s, Heroard's diary about Louis XIII of France shows how he joined in dances at the royal court from the age of 3 and at 5 was practising archery and watching bear-baiting. By the time little Louis was 7, he was riding, hunting and enjoying entertainments such as wrestling, jousting and bull-fighting.

Daniel Defoe said, in 1724, that all children over the age of 4 or 5 could earn their own bread. Apprenticeships, teaching the skills of a craft, started between the ages of 7 and 12. But in the seventeenth century (1600 to 1700) an increasing number of merchants sent their sons to grammar schools. The development of schooling was one of the factors that reflected the changing status of childhood.

This painting by François-Hubert Drouais shows how children in the eighteenth century were dressed as 'mini adults'.

1   The changing status of children and teenagers

Three important factors which have helped to give childhood its modern character are:

1   schooling;
2   exclusion from adult paid work; and
3   laws which protect children and define their status.

Schooling

This was made compulsory up to the age of 10 in 1880 and the school-leaving age was raised as follows:

1880	10 years old
1893	11 years old
1899	12 years old
1902	13 years old
1914	14 years old
1947	15 years old
1972	16 years old

Exclusion from adult paid work

During much of British history the rich arranged the marriages of their children to create alliances between powerful families while the poor exploited the labour of their children by making them work. In 1761, a woman called Anne Martin was sentenced to two years in Newgate Prison for blinding children so that she could use them for begging. More commonly, children in the early nineteenth century were forced to work the same eleven- or twelve-hour day as their parents.

In 1842 the First Report of the Commission on the Employment of Children and Young Persons in Mines was presented to Parliament. This report quoted an 8-year-old girl, Sarah Goodber, who described her working day operating 'the trap', a lever to control the air supply, in a Yorkshire coal mine:

> I'm a trapper in the Gauber Pit, I have to trap without light, and I'm scared. I go at four and sometimes half-past three in the morning and come out at five and half past. I never go to sleep. Sometimes I sing when I've light, but not in the dark: I dare not sing then.

This report resulted in Lord Shaftesbury's Mine Act of 1842 which stopped underground working in pits for all girls and for boys under the age of 10. Numerous Factories Acts have restricted the hours that young people can work. Under the 1973 Employment of Children Act, paid work is not allowed under the age of 13 except for doing light farm work for one's parents or taking part in films or stage shows with a special licence. Pupils aged between 13 and 16 may only work for two hours on a school day, between 7 and 9 a.m. and 4.30 and 7 p.m.

Laws that protect children and define their status

Crime   Up to 1780 there were 200 offences that carried the penalty of death by hanging and children were held by law and custom to be adult, and therefore responsible for their crimes, over the age of 7. For example, a 7-year-old girl was hanged in Norwich for stealing a petticoat, and in one day alone, in February 1814, five children were condemned to death at the Old Bailey courts. Their crimes were burglary and theft and they were aged between 8 and 12.

Today, the age of criminal responsibility in England and Wales is 10. Below this age you cannot be charged with a criminal offence, although you can be arrested, cautioned and held under a 'place of safety' order. Between the ages of 10 and 14 the prosecution has to prove that a child knows the difference between right and wrong.

When teenagers under the age of 17 are arrested, the police must inform their parents or guardians and they should not be interviewed without them, or another adult such as a social worker, being present.

Crimes involving young people under 17 are normally dealt with in a juvenile court. If you are found guilty of an offence for which an adult could be sent to prison, then at 14 you can be sent to a detention centre, at 15 you can be sent to a borstal and at 17 you can be sent to an adult prison.

Sex and marriage   A girl cannot legally consent to sexual intercourse with a man until she is 16. Before 1885 the age of consent was 12 and it was raised to 16 in 1929. In the event of 'under-age sex' between a man and a girl aged 15 or under, it is the man rather than the girl who can be prosecuted for an offence.

Between the ages of 16 and 18 a girl (or should we call her a young woman?) may only marry with her parents' consent. A girl under 17 who goes to live with her boyfriend may be given a supervision order or a care order by a juvenile court if her parents, the police or the social services regard her as in 'moral danger'.

It is unlawful for two consenting males to commit homosexual acts in private unless they are both over 18. MPs are debating whether to lower the age of consent to 16.

The 1989 Children Act   This law gave children certain new rights. It threw out the notion of children as the property of their parents and gave them the right to be heard and have their views taken into account, particularly in custody cases. Children now have the right to independent legal representation and a number of highly publicised cases have given rise to the idea of children 'divorcing' their parents.

Corporal punishment   Guidelines in the 1989 Children Act say that physical punishment has no place in the child-care environment. Corporal punishment in state schools was outlawed by the 1986 Education Act and the 1989 Children Act guidelines state that 'smacking, slapping or shaking' are banned in all children's homes and foster care and 'should not be used' in nurseries, playgroups and childminding. But:

- In 1992 the European Court of Human Rights, considering the case of a boy who was 'slippered', ruled that moderate corporal punishment was not unlawful in private schools.
- In 1994 the High Court ruled that a childminder had the right to smack boys and girls in her care, 'only if and to the extent' that the child's parents wished her to do so.
- A Nottingham University survey has found that 83 per cent of mothers believe in the value of a smack.

In 1991, Britain ratified the United Nations Convention on the Rights of the Child. Article 19 of the Convention obliges governments to prevent physical violence to a child by parents or carers.

Other age limits   In Britain you have these rights and obligations at the following ages.

Age	Activity
5	You can see a U or PG film unaccompanied.
	You can drink alcohol in private.
	You must attend school.
	You must pay fares on buses and trains.
7	You can open, and draw money from a National Savings account.
10	You can be convicted of a criminal offence (if it is proved that, at the time, you knew your actions were seriously wrong) (age 8 in Scotland).
	You can receive an indefinite jail sentence for murder.
12	You can buy a pet.
	You can get a job (no more than two hours on a school day or a Sunday).
14	You can enter a pub.
	You have full adult responsibility for criminal actions.
	You can ride a horse on a road without protective headgear.
15	You may see a 15 film.
	You may be sent to prison.
16	You can leave school.
	You can pay tax (but not vote on how it is spent!).
	You can buy cigarettes (may be raised to 18).
	You can drive a moped.
	You can work down a mine.
	You can have beer or cider with a restaurant meal.
	You can marry without parental consent in Scotland.
	You can marry with parental consent in the rest of Britain (for women: age 15 in France and Denmark, 14 in Greece, 12 in Ireland and Spain).
	A girl can consent to heterosexual intercourse (17 in Ireland, 15 in France, Greece and Sweden, 14 in Iceland, 12 in Spain).
	A boy can join the armed forces (with parental consent).
17	A girl can join the armed forces (without parental consent).
	You can drive most vehicles (age 14 in some states of the USA).
	You can buy any firearm or crossbow.
18	You are an adult.
	You can vote.
	You can do jury service.
	You can buy and drink alcohol (age 14 in France and 21 in the USA).
	You can get a mortgage.
	You can be tattooed.
	You can place a bet.
	You can give your body to science.
	A man can consent to a homosexual act with another adult man in private (may be lowered to 16). (Gay sex is legal at 17 in Ireland, 15 in France, Greece and Sweden, 14 in Iceland, 12 in Spain.)
19	You are entitled to free full-time education up to this age.
21	You can become an MP.
	You can adopt a child.
	You can rent a car.
	You can drive heavy vehicles.
	You can apply for a licence to sell alcohol.

These laws change from time to time. You can check them in the reference section at your local library. A good book is *First Rights* published by the National Council for Civil Liberties.

Would it be simpler and better if there was just one age, 17, at which adult activities were allowed?

Case study: adolescence in a hunting and gathering society – initiation to adulthood among the !Kung

The !Kung were traditionally a hunting and gathering people in the Kalahari Desert of Namibia in southern Africa. Girls were often married at the age of 7 or 8 to young men at least twice their age. But they were not expected to live with their husbands until after their first menstruation. This landmark called for far greater ritual celebration than the actual marriage ceremony.

Initiation to adulthood for a !Kung boy came at about 14 once he had proved himself as a hunter by killing a large antelope on his own. As Van der Post and Taylor have described,

> On his return to the camp he must stay apart from everyone else, especially women. The animal, once killed, must be cooked on a special fire which the women must avoid; and he himself must not partake of the meat. After this he was scarified by his male relatives with a series of short, vertical incisions on his face, arms, chest and back.

After this ritual the boy would be regarded as a man and a hunter, ready for marriage.

Activities: test yourself on some legal age limits

1 How old do you have to be to:
   (a) buy cigarettes and smoke in public?
   (b) claim Income Support?
   (c) enter a betting shop and place bets?
   (d) enter a pub?
   (e) buy fireworks?
   (f) change your name without your parents' consent?
   (g) work your own market stall?
   (h) choose your own doctor and give consent for treatment?
   (i) use a pawn shop?
   (j) make a will?
   (The answers to this quiz are at the end of the chapter.)

2 Describe any celebrations, ceremonies or rituals in modern British society which you think mark the end of childhood or the start of adulthood.

(Answer on p. 52)

---

2   The ideas of youth and youth culture

Youth

Young people's legal rights vary as they go through their teenage years. There is a gradual transition to adulthood between the ages of 14, when young people start paying full fares on public transport, and 18, when they can give blood and sit on a jury. At 18 parents no longer have custody over their children who are no longer 'minors' but have reached the age of 'majority'.

The raising of the school-leaving age could be seen as extending childhood further into adulthood. Or one might argue that a recent social category has arisen called youth, meaning the period between childhood and adulthood.

Youth has expanded in both directions

1   Youth starts earlier than in the past because young people are reaching sexual maturity at a lower age. In 1840, the average age for girls to have their first menstrual period was sixteen and a half. In 1993, this average age of 'menarche' had fallen to twelve and a half, because of better nutrition and health.

2   Youth also ends later than before because an increasing proportion of those in their twenties are still partly dependent on their parents. Many are at college or university and many remain living at home due to housing and job shortages. These young people are extending their youth into their twenties before becoming fully independent adults.

We now turn to the question of how far young people have a distinct culture of their own. Many adults find it difficult to understand features of the teenage world, such as GCSE and GNVQs, rapping and raves, which never existed when *they* were young. Teenyboppers' 'flavour of the month' pop idols and fast-changing fashions seem to give young people a way of life that is alien and closed to most adults. While most teenagers enjoy this **youth culture**, some join particular youth groups with distinct lifestyles.

What is meant by youth subcultures?

In looking at post-war youth cults such as teddyboys and punks, sociologists have asked whether such groups are **subcultures**. For sociologists, culture means a way of life of a society. A subculture therefore refers to a way of life shared by a minority which is different in important respects from the life pursued by the majority of the population. For example, travellers have a subculture because they have their own distinctive patterns of behaviour and different values and beliefs from the rest of society. Therefore, the term **youth subculture** is used to refer to a group of young people who lead a distinctive way of life with their own attitudes, values and modes of behaviour.

Hippies at a 1967 'Flower Power' gathering in Hyde Park.

Case study of a youth subculture: the hippies

In the late 1960s some young people developed a 'hippy' lifestyle which, by our definition, would qualify as a youth subculture. Their **alternative value system** can be seen in some of their well-known slogans. 'Peace and Love' shows a rejection of militarism and violence. The message 'Tune In, Turn On and Drop Out' means take 'mind-expanding' drugs and reject the 'rat-race' of the conventional career ladder.

One approach to understanding youth cults is called **semiology** or **semiotics**. This means the study of signs and symbols. If we look at the outward styles of the hippies we can interpret their meanings and so try to 'read' their subculture:

1   Long hair for men indicated a rejection of the discipline of school, work and the army which dictated 'short back and sides' haircuts. Long hair also expressed a rejection of traditional ideas of masculinity in favour of the freedom of 'unisex' hairstyles.

2   Wide, flared trousers indicated a rejection of the narrow trousers with turn-ups of the 'straight' world of office workers.

3   Necklaces of beads with bells and loose, smock-like shirts called kaftans indicated an identification with Eastern mysticism; and, like the bell-bottomed trousers, this loose clothing symbolised a free-and-easy, casual approach to life.

Reasons for post-war youth cults

Some sociologists have suggested that youth cults are a post-war phenomenon. As well as the raising of the school-leaving age, the following reasons are usually given for the emergence of youth culture:

1   Affluence: in the 1950s teenagers had more money to spend than previous generations. Industry began to respond to the growing spending power of this age group by producing goods specifically aimed at the youth market.

2   Leisure: modern teenagers not only have more money to spend than previous generations but they also have more free time in which to enjoy discos, films, records, fashions and so on.

3   The mass media: two sorts of influence can be seen:
(a) the record industry, TV, radio and magazine publishers have expanded to cater for the teenage market;
(b) the mass media as a whole have stimulated interest in new youth groups. The popular press often seem obsessed with the new, 'way-out' styles of the young.

It is undoubtedly the case that these factors have had an effect on young people's lives and since the 1950s a series of youth cults has emerged with their own styles of dress and music. However, it is a mistake to think that youth culture only arrived after the Second World War. The next two parts of this chapter look at two youth groups: one from the 1890s and the other from the 1930s.

3   The Edelweiss Pirates in Hitler's Germany

The Hitler Youth

Nazi Germany was a **totalitarian state**. In other words, Hitler's Nazi Party tried to control, by persuasion and terror, all the important areas of an individual's life. The Nazis demanded total loyalty and service from the German people and the young were trained to become good Nazi citizens by the Hitler Youth organisation. The activities of the Hitler Youth took place after school or work and at weekends. These activities included hiking and camping, along with military drill and instruction in Nazi beliefs.

The Edelweiss Pirates

In 1939 the Hitler Youth was made compulsory up to the age of 18. This was by no means popular and a number of alternative, anti-Nazi youth cults spontaneously appeared. Upper-middle-class youth in Germany formed the Swing Movement and upset the Nazis by dancing the 'jitter-bug' to the music of American jazz bands. Also, a working-class youth subculture arose around the Edelweiss Pirates who took their name from their badges. These metal badges were worn on their collars and were the shape of edelweiss flowers or the skull and crossbones. The Edelweiss Pirates started in the west of Germany but groups, such as the 'Roving Dudes' of Essen, sprang up across the country and all saw themselves as 'pirates' – rebels outside the law.

The activities of the Pirate groups

The Edelweiss Pirates usually wore checked shirts, dark short trousers and white socks. Although it was wartime, the different Pirate groups were able to enjoy a wide range of similar activities. The sexes were segregated in the Hitler Youth but the Pirates took girls along on their weekend camping trips into the country and girls joined them when they met in parks in the evenings. They wanted freedom and their resentment of the Nazi system was shown in two of their activities: beating up members of the Hitler Youth and singing Nazi tunes with anti-Nazi lyrics.

The Nazi crackdown on the Edelweiss Pirates

The Pirates were mainly youths who had left school at 14 for fairly well-paid factory jobs and who resented having to belong to the Hitler Youth up to the age of 18. They were also joined by conscript soldiers on leave and by 1944 their activities had escalated from defacing Nazi posters to hiding army deserters and escaped prisoners. In Cologne, they even killed the local chief of the Gestapo. The Nazis stepped up their response from warnings, arrests and shaving the heads of Pirates to rounding up thousands, sending many to concentration camps and hanging their 'ringleaders'. In fact they had no real leaders.

The Edelweiss Pirates are a good example of a youth subculture. They were rebels with their own values and styles of dress and music which were alternatives to those of the dominant, official Nazi way of life.

Group hanging of twelve Edelweiss Pirates, Cologne-Ehrenfeld, 1944, for taking part in underground anti-Nazi activities such as sabotage and arms raids.

4   The original hooligans of the 1890s

Violent youth in Victorian London

In 1974, the Conservative cabinet minister, Sir Keith Joseph, said: 'For the first time in a century and a half, since the great Tory reformer Robert Peel set up the Metropolitan Police, areas of our cities are becoming unsafe for peaceful citizens by night and some even by day.' This issue of law and order was a key part of Mrs Thatcher's election campaign of 1979. In fact, nineteenth-century Londoners going through their badly lit streets at night were frequent prey to young ruffians armed with cudgels. It has been estimated that a Briton in the early 1980s had a 25 per cent lower chance of being murdered than in the 1860s.

Flogging, which had been abolished in 1861, was reintroduced in the 1863 Garotters' Act after a wave of street robberies in which victims were choked. *The Times* of 10 June 1863 observed that this new peril of the streets had created 'something like a reign of terror' in which 'whole sections of a peaceable city community were on the verge of arming themselves against sudden attack'.

The first 'Hooligans'

In 1899 there were 3,444 cases of assault on London's 13,213 police constables and *The Times* complained: 'The pickpocket is dying out, the Hooligan replaces him.' As Pearson has noted,

The word 'hooligan' made an abrupt entrance into common English usage, as a term to describe gangs of rowdy youths, during the hot summer of 1898. 'Hooligans' and 'Hooliganism' were thrust into the headlines in the wake of turbulent August Bank Holiday celebrations in London which had resulted in unusually large numbers of people being brought before the courts for disorderly behaviour, drunkenness, assaults on the police, street robberies and fighting.

Various new recreations of working-class youth were blamed at the time. These developments in popular culture which were condemned included the music halls, professional football, the 'penny dreadful' comics, bank holiday excursions to seaside resorts and then the moving-pictures of the early cinema. One solution was seen to be the growing Christian boys' organisations, such as the Boys' Brigade, the Church Lads' Brigade and, after 1908, the Boy Scouts. Baden-Powell, the founder of the Boy Scouts, called the Hooligan 'the best class of boy'.

The uniform of the hooligan: 'All of them have a peculiar muffler twisted round the neck, a cap set rakishly forward, well over the eyes, and trousers very tight at the knee and very loose over the foot.'

Summary

We can note four aspects of the late nineteenth-century urban delinquents:

1   Affluence   As was noted at the time, the Hooligans were not the very poorest slum-dwellers. They were well-shod and often had enough money in their pockets to pay their fines as well as afford their own special styles of clothing. Their money came from their job as 'handy lads' in factories, errand boys, messenger boys or delivery van boys.

2   Leisure   Groups such as the 'Peaky Blinders' or 'Sloggers' in Manchester and the 'Somers Town Gang' or 'Chelsea Boys' in London had enough free time to hang around the streets and create their own gang subcultures.

3   The temporary delinquent career   A correspondent in the *Daily Graphic* of 1900 noted: 'It is a mistake to confuse the Hooligan with the habitual criminal – the man whose living is crime. The Hooligan works ... The Hooligan, as he gets older, generally settles down into a respectable, if a humble, member of society.'

4   The mass media   J. Davis has shown that the London Garotting Panic of 1862 resulted in increased arrests because a media panic led to greater police vigilance. Thus the 'crime wave', such as it was, can be seen as having been created by the actions and reactions of the press, the public and various government agencies. It did not reflect any significant increase in actual criminal activity in the streets.

Policing the Crisis by S. Hall and others has similarly concluded that the Mugging Panic in 1973 was stirred up by the press. It is to the effects of the media on post-war youth culture that we now turn.

Activities

1   Interview some teenagers of different ages and find out whether they belong to any youth organisations. If they do, ask them to describe the aims and activities of their organisations.

2   What does the Hooligan phenomenon at the turn of the century have in common with any of the post-war youth cults?

5   Youth culture and the media

Some observers argue that youth culture has emerged because of post-war affluence, extended schooling and the unclear position in which modern youth find themselves. But sociologists such as Stan Cohen have drawn attention to the extent to which youth subcultures are the creation of the mass media.

Mods and rockers and moral panics

Cohen has looked at how the press reported events at Clacton on Easter Sunday 1964. On this particular bank holiday, it was very cold and wet and there was some fighting between young people who had gone to the coast for a day of fun. A few youths ended up throwing stones at each other and breaking windows and some of these belonged to groups of motorbike riders called rockers or scooter riders called mods. The papers chose to report these disturbances as 'riots' and battles'. Cohen argues that they exaggerated events for two reasons:

1 The press often have little news to report over a bank holiday and there is also a natural tendency for reporters to overdramatise events in the sensationalist, popular papers.
2 The press tend to take the same view as the police, magistrates and parents when there is seen to be a threat from gangs of youths. They overreact and amplify people's fears.

When a society is undergoing rapid change, many people may feel anxious that their basic institutions and values are being undermined. They may focus their fears onto groups that can be blamed for society's ills. These groups often have three characteristics:

1 The groups selected for the role of scapegoats are usually weak, such as New Age travellers or one-parent families. It is safe to attack such groups because they lack the power to retaliate.
2 They can be demonised as **folk devils** because they can be condemned for their supposedly deviant way of life.
3 They may have a subculture that, while relatively harmless, is distinctive, so that the effects of their activities can be blown out of all proportion.

This phenomenon of a group becoming the object of exaggerated concern and fears has been termed a **moral panic** by sociologists. Cohen drew attention to the role of the media in creating and sustaining the moral panic about the mods and rockers.

The media amplification spiral

Each of the seven stages in the **media amplification spiral** leads on to the next:

1 **Initial problem**   Bored youths seek excitement.

2 **Initial solution**   Youths go in groups to the seaside on bank holidays looking for fun.

3 **Reaction from the media**   Media exaggerate the activities and appearances of the gangs. They create popular stereotypes of mods and rockers and they predict more trouble.

Daily Mirror

Scooter gangs 'beat up' Clacton

3d.   Monday, March 30, 1964   No. 18,746

'WILD ONES' INVADE SEASIDE—97 ARRESTS

By PAUL HUGHES

THE Wild Ones invaded a seaside town yesterday—1,000 fighting, drinking, roaring, rampaging teenagers on scooters and motor-cycles. By last night, after a day of riots and battles with police, ninety-seven of them had been arrested.

A desperate S O S went out from police at Clacton, Essex, as leather-jacketed youths and girls attacked people in the streets, turned over parked cars, broke into beach huts, smashed windows, and fought with rival gangs.

Police reinforcements from other Essex towns raced to the shattered resort, where fearful residents had locked themselves indoors

By this time the centre of Clacton was jammed with screaming teenagers. Traffic was at a standstill

Fought

The crowd was broken up by police and police dogs. Several policemen were injured as the teenagers fought them.

A number of arrests had already been made. Addresses had been taken, and messages sent to parents.

And worried mothers and fathers were beginning to arrive from the London area to bail out their sons and daughters.

The harassed police were glad to see them go. For the cells at Clacton police station were crammed with youngsters under arrest.

By last night the score of arrests and charges — still incomplete — included:

Thirty for assault on police and civilians; thirty for creating disturbances and fighting; ten for theft; and at least twenty for other offences, including drunk and disorderly, malicious damage and using obscene language.

Rough

Police said the court hearings would begin on April 27.

The Wild Ones—this was the title of a Marlon Brando film in which teenaged motor-cyclists terrorised a town—have caused trouble in Clacton before. But not on this scale.

They began arriving on Friday and Saturday and many slept rough on the beach, under the pier, in promenade shelters, and in beach huts they broke open.

Others spent the night roaring round the town on their scooters and motorcycles.

Youths in leather jackets help a police officer making inquiries last night into the rampage by gangs of teenagers at the seaside resort of Clacton. A police dog stands by.

This report of the 'riots and battles' of the mods and rockers, in Clacton on Easter Sunday in 1964, was typical of the press.

4   Moral panic   The public become increasingly anxious about the aggressive mods (short hair and parka coats) and rockers (greasy hair and leather jackets).

5   Reaction from the forces of law and order   More police are drafted in to bank holiday resorts; confrontations with youths lead to more arrests; courts give out stiffer sentences.

6 Isolation of the deviant groups   Those young people who identify with the 'folk devil' groups feel persecuted and anti-police. They become more isolated from the rest of society and develop more cohesive subcultures.

7 Confirmation of stereotype   Members of youth cults see themselves as troublemakers and live up to their label or media image.

The further reaction of the media ensures that the process then continues by a repetition of stages 3 to 7. This spiral can be described as a **self-fulfilling prophecy**: that is, a prediction that leads people to act in such a way that their actions make the prediction come true. In this case the media's original moral panic creates troublemakers who may try to live up to their sensationalised reputation.

6   Youth subcultures in the 1990s

We now look at two youth subcultures. Both have partly developed from earlier movements. Ravers have been inspired by the hippies of the 1960s and Goths arose from the punks of the 1970s. The media have created a considerable moral panic about ravers. In 1994, the Essex police deployed a helicopter, as well as roadblocks, to try to prevent all-night acid house parties or raves; six-month prison sentences were proposed for organisers, for breaking the licensing laws which govern the holding of public entertainments.

The Goths

Tristan Hoare, a student of youth subculture, gives the following description of Goths. The Goths have their own style of dress, music and values. The style of dress reflects their outlook: just as Goths are doggedly independent of other youth subcultures, their dress is independent of mainstream fashion. Nobody mistakes a Goth for a raver or an indie-kid. The title 'Goth' was given to this group by the media due to their vampire style of dress; a style that brings to mind the Gothic world of writers such as Shelley, Stoker and Poe. The works of these writers are to be found on the shelves of Goths, alongside their modern-day equivalents, such as Stephen King, Clive Barker, James Herbert and Ian Watson. The Gothic by-word is black. So Goths tend to wear black clothes and black shoes (never trainers), to have black hair and to wear black make-up. The Gothic physical ideal is athletically slim with a deathly pale complexion.

The subculture revolves, as with most youth subcultures, around its music. This veers between grinding aggressive rock (Sisters of Mercy, Fields of the Nephilim and Creaming Jesus) through post-punk morbidity (Siouxsie and the Banshees, Bauhaus and Alien Sex Fiend) to industrial dance music (Nine Inch Nails, Cubanate and Sheep on Drugs). These bands are influenced by Andrew Eldrich, Carl Macoy, Peter Murphy and David Vanian, etc., while the females look towards Patricia Morrison, Siouxsie Sioux and Danielle Dax.

Samantha Baldi, a Goth.

Hardcore Nosebleed ravers.

The social outlook of Goths in general is one of hatred for the norms of society, which is partly the result of the negative response they tend to receive from non-Goths, in particular from the older generation. Goths have a passion for the arts – music, poetry and painting – and expend massive amounts of time and effort on their own appearance, treating themselves as canvases for their creativity. A certain degree of rivalry exists among a group of Goths over who looks the most impressive.

Some people mistakenly think that Goths are Satanists (devil worshippers), possibly because of their style of dress. They are, however, interested in earlier non-Christian religions and ways of life, especially in Celtic Britain. This interest in the Celts is shown by their preference for the Celtic style of jewellery. Given these interests, it is not surprising that very few Goths are Christians.

In conclusion, the Goths are a flamboyant and distinctive youth sub-culture, but not an aggressive one. It is probably their distinctiveness and independence that has helped to keep them going for so long.

Case study: raves and the 'new tribes' of the 1990s

In 1993 Alix Sharkey investigated some of the latest trends in youth culture. Sharkey went to an all-night rave held during the summer in a field in Hertfordshire. Among the 15,000-strong crowd she reckoned that there were five 'tribes', each with their own style of dress and music, as well as their own manners and customs:

- The Hardcore Nosebleed people wore baggy jeans, colourful tops and 'mental' accessories (floppy hats, dummies, industrial face masks, hand-held luminous bands).
- The Trendy-Trance tribe had a sharper look: short, well-cut hair; hot pants and tank tops; label jeans and Caterpillar boots.
- The Eurotechno-Ambient crowd had a dark and mysterious image: slinky, sexy clothes with lots of black and silver.
- The Young Crusties had a recycled, patch-work look that was part raver, part punk and part New Age traveller.
- The Hippy Nouveau tribe had the latest, fashionable version of the Seattle 'grunge' look: flared loons, Afghan coats and cheese-cloth shirts, with lank shoulder-length hair and a distinct odour of patchouli.

Here are the 'new tribes' of 1993 according to Camilla Berens, the editor of *Pod* magazine:

- Those involved in social protest. An example is the Dongas, environmental activists who lived in teepees on Twyford Down to prevent the bulldozing of this beauty spot for the M3 extension.
- 'Permaculture' tribes, such as Newcastle's Flowerpot tribe, who set up self-sufficient ecologically sound alternative communities.
- The younger sound-system and art tribes, who come together for large-scale alternative dance parties, like DIY, Sugarlump, Tonka, Mega Dog, Fundamental, LSDiesel, Slack and Tribal Energy.

The tribes described by Berens perhaps demand more of a full-time commitment than the ravers described by Sharkey. Those who have jobs and live at home or are students, may be weekend ravers. Jobless ravers living in squats and joining New Age traveller festivals in the summer-time may be more committed to an alternative lifestyle.

(adapted from 'New Tribes of England' by Alix Sharkey, *The Guardian*, 1993)

7   Youth and gender

Gender differences among youth adults in Great Britain may be seen in the following findings of the government's 1990 *General Household Survey*:

Participation in active sports, games and physical activities reported by 16- to 19-year-olds for the twelve months before interview

	Females	*Males*
Swimming	74%	66%
Keep fit/Yoga	50%	11%
Cycling	31%	53%
Tenpin bowls/Skittles	27%	25%
Snooker/Pool/Billiards	41%	72%
Badminton	32%	33%
Darts	18%	42%
Tennis	27%	31%
Running (jogging, etc.)	24%	35%
Weight lifting/training	18%	37%
Ice skating	26%	14%
Horse riding	14%	3%
Table tennis	15%	27%
Squash	12%	19%
Skiing	6%	9%
Sailing	4%	7%
Other water sports	12%	18%
Hockey	17%	12%
Fishing	4%	20%
Netball	20%	–
Basketball	11%	22%
Athletics	12%	20%
Self-defence	4%	8%
Gymnastics	6%	–
Soccer	7%	62%
Golf	8%	34%
Cricket	–	24%
Rugby	–	11%
Motor sports	–	6%

Elliot Dempsey (Oxford United) and Dominic Brindley (Stoke City) compete in the Table Football Championship in London, in 1998.

Case stydy: from Madonna to the Spice Girls

1998 saw the publication of *Youth in Britain since 1945* by Bill Osgerby. In this book he discusses how female pop singers have engineered assertive and rebellious forms of feminine identity:

> In the late 1970s the rise of punk rock provided a fertile space for the politicization of sexuality and female identity, brash female artists like the Slits and Siouxsie Sioux enacting transgressive forms of femininity in their unconventional hair and clothing styles and their assertive stage performances.
>
> During the eighties the erotic videos and stage-shows of artists like Madonna further challenged traditional, passive notions of female identity, while in the early nineties the American underground rock scene saw the emergence of the 'Riot Girrl' movement – a loose alliance of all-women bands and individual women artists who made loud, confrontational music that self-consciously developed a feminist critique of the patriarchal power structures of the rock establishment ... mainstream British pop also saw moves by young women into highly visible, confident and often defiant musical styles.

The late nineties, for example, saw an all-girl fivesome, the Spice Girls, spring to the forefront of pop stardom. In many respects the Spice Girls were a perfectly conventional vehicle of mainstream pop. Recruited, modelled and marketed by a team of producers and record company moguls, their album, 'Spice', sold over three million copies in 1996 while their single, 'Wannabe', reached number one in twenty-seven countries. The Spice Girls' image, however, recast many of the qualities conventionally associated with female pop artists. Although their dictum of 'Girl Power' amounted to little more than an advertising slogan, the Spice Girls' strident, fiesty stage personas embodied many of the changes that had taken place in the possibilities for women's public self-expression over the preceeding twenty years. The Spice Girls' blend of brazen cheek, fun-seeking energy and confident sexuality elaborated a version of feminine identity which, in some respects at least, transgressed traditional norms and conventions, laying claim to a cultural visibility and assertiveness which had previously been the province of male-dominated youth subcultures.

(Source: *Youth in Britain since 1945*, by B. Osgerby, Blackwell, 1998)

Activity

It is claimed that girls do not enjoy the same freedom from parental control as boys and that this explains why girls are far less prominent in youth groups. Compose a questionnaire on parental supervision and give it to a sample of male and female teenagers.

Conclusion

Childhood and youth are social categories. They are defined differently in different societies and at different stages in history. Most young people generally follow the conventions of their parents and for those who do have contact with a youth subculture, it is usually a brief flirtation. Many sociologists conclude that youth culture has a positive function. It helps adolescents through a period of uncertainty and stress when they are searching for their own identity.

The continuing strength of traditional youth organisations is shown in the following figures from the Office for National Statistics' *Social Trends:*

UK membership	1971	1991
Cub Scouts	265,000	349,000
Brownie Guides	376,000	385,000
Scouts	215,000	192,000
Girl Guides	316,000	225,000
Duke of Edinburgh's Award Scheme	122,000	200,000
Youth Club UK – boys	179,000	310,000
– girls	140,000	290,000

Answers to the test on legal age limits on page 38

(a)	16	(d)	14	(g)	17	(i)	14
(b)	18	(e)	16	(h)	16	(j)	18
(c)	17	(f)	18				

GCSE question from Southern Examining Group 1993

Why have changes taken place in the relationship between parents and children during the twentieth century?   (10)

GCSE question from Southern Examining Group 1998

Study Item A. Then answer *all* parts of the question which follows.

Item A

In January 1993, under-fives in Gloucestershire had no opportunity to attend nursery schools or classes, although 32 per cent of them got into school before the legal starting age. In Cleveland 57 per cent of under-fives were in nursery schools or classes in primary schools. 60 per cent of under-fives in Walsall were in nursery schools or classes, while in Bromley only 2 per cent had the chance of a nursery school or class.

Adapted from *Department for Education, Statistical Bulletin*, June 1994

(a) According to Item A,

   (i) what percentage of under-fives in Cleveland were in nursery schools or primary school classes?   (1)

  (ii) where did under-fives have no opportunity of attending nursery schools or classes?   (1)

 (iii) in which area did the under-fives have the highest chance of attending nursery schools or classes?   (1)

(b) (i) Identify *two* ways in which schools themselves might put some ethnic minority groups at a disadvantage.   (2)

  (ii) Identify *two* ways in which schools could make educational opportunities more equal for all ethnic groups.   (2)

(c) (i) What is meant by 'peer group'?   (2)

  (ii) State *one advantage* and *one disadvantage* of educating pupils in single sex schools.   (2)

(d) (i) Identify *one* way in which schools prepare pupils for employment.   (1)

  (ii) There have been many changes to the education system since 1975. Identify *one* such change and explain how it has, or has not, increased equality of opportunity in education.   (3)

CHAPTER 4

The family as a social institution

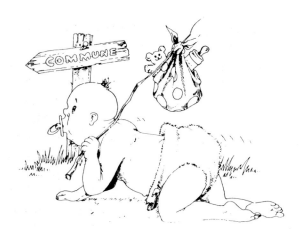

Do we need families?

1 The universal functions of the family

Many sociologists argue that the family is the most basic and enduring of all social arrangements because it satisfies basic and enduring needs. We begin this chapter by identifying these needs. Next, we look at family life in a Kenyan tribe and in an Israeli kibbutz. Finally, we examine the development of the British family.

The three basic needs that the family fulfils

1   A society must have new members to replace those that have died, otherwise it will become extinct. **Procreation**, having children, is the obvious method of acquiring new members. Producing babies is not, however, enough; the children need to be cared for after birth. It is possible, of course, for birth to take place outside a family grouping. Babies could be produced by a couple who were not united in any way and then be looked after by one parent alone or by an institution that society had created for that purpose. But the family seems to have always been a natural grouping to meet the basic need of procreation and child-rearing.

2   A society needs its new members to be socialised into its values and patterns of behaviour. This job of **socialisation** could be left entirely to professional childminders, but throughout history the family has had the essential responsibility of preparing the young for membership of society. The natural bonds of affection between parents and children make the family unit an effective and readily available agency of socialisation. This, then, is the second basic need that the family fulfils.

A toddler's play is part of the process of socialisation.

3   Most of us have a need for stable and intimate relationships with another person or a small group of people. The family makes this possible and so provides us with **emotional support** and psychological satisfaction.

These are the three basic functions that the family performs and they explain why the family is a grouping that has persisted throughout history. We now look at an example of a **pre-industrial society** where the family had a wide variety of functions.

2   The family in a pre-industrial society

In the 1930s Jomo Kenyatta was an African student in London. Within thirty years he was the first president of the independent republic of Kenya. His book, *Facing Mount Kenya: The Tribal Life of the Gikuyu* (1938), describes, from first-hand experience, his people's traditional way of life before it was disrupted by European missionaries, white farmers and colonial administrators. It gives us a clear picture, from the inside, of a pre-industrial society in which the family had a wide range of important functions. Some of these are described below.

The functions of the traditional Gikuyu family

1   Procreational functions   The Gikuyu tribal custom requires that a married couple should have at least four children, two male and two female. The first male is regarded as perpetuating the existence of the man's father, the second as perpetuating that of the woman's father. The

first and second female children fulfil the same ritual duty to the souls of
their grandmothers on both sides. The children are given the names of the
persons whose soul they represent.

2   Religious functions   The Gikuyu have ceremonies for communing
with the spirits of their ancestors. They also worship the god Ngai, who is
the creator and giver of all things.

> ... religion is interwoven with traditions and social customs of the people.
> Thus all members of the community are automatically considered to have
> acquired, during their childhood teachings, all that is necessary to know
> about religion and custom. The duty of imparting this knowledge to the
> children is entrusted to the parents.

So the parents act as both priests and teachers.

3   Educational functions

> The education of very small babies is ... carried on through the medium
> of lullabies. In these the whole history and tradition of the family and
> clan are embodied and, by hearing these lullabies daily, it is easy for the
> children to assimilate this early teaching.
>
> When the child is able to speak, he can answer many questions which
> are asked gently and naturally to test how much he has learnt. Such
> questions as these might be asked: What is your name? Who is your
> father? What is your age-group? What is the name of your grandfather?
> And your great-grandfather? ... Why are they given such-and-such names
> for their age-groups?
>
> Peer groups are named after events, such as battles and droughts,
> which occur at the time of their initiation into adulthood. In the late 19th
> century one age-group was called 'gatego' meaning Syphilis. This enables
> a tribe with no written records to remember historical events such as the
> arrival of European illnesses.
>
> When the children are very young they are left at home minding small
> babies, or are taken to the field where they are allowed to play in the
> corner of the cultivated field. ... As soon as they are able to handle a
> digging-stick they are given small allotments to practise on. ... Parents
> help them to plant seeds and teach them how to distinguish crops from
> the wild plants or weeds.
>
> To test the boy's power of observation and memory, two or three
> herds from different homesteads are mixed, and the boy is asked to
> separate them by picking out all that belong to his herd.
>
> The girl's training in agriculture is the same as that of the boy. The
> mother is in charge of the co-education of her children. In the evening
> she teaches both boy and girl the laws and customs, especially those
> governing the moral code and general rules of etiquette in the com-
> munity. The teaching is carried on in the form of folklore and tribal
> legends. At the same time the children are given mental exercises through
> amusing riddles and puzzles which are told only in the evenings after
> meals, or while food is being cooked.

It can be seen that the family is the major unit of socialisation and social
control in Gikuyu society.

Women preparing food in an African village.

4   Economic functions

The chief occupations among the Gikuyu are agriculture and the rearing of livestock, such as cattle, sheep and goats. Each family, i.e. a man, his wife and their children, constitute an economic unit.

Children join in farming work from an early age and tasks that are shared equally between the sexes include planting, weeding, harvesting, beer-brewing and trading at the markets. Everyone's life is based on agriculture and the ownership of farms is organised according to bonds of kinship: the family is the basis of land tenure.

5   Political functions   Organisation of the tribe is clearly based on the family unit:

The Gikuyu customary law of marriage provides that a man may have as many wives as he can support, and that the larger one's family the better it is for him and the tribe. ... In Gikuyu the qualification for a status to hold high office in the tribal organisation is based on family. ... It is held that if a man can control and manage effectively the affairs of a large family, this is an excellent testimonial of his capacity to look after the interests of the tribe.

In the Gikuyu system of government elders are linked through village and district councils where judges are elected. In all this 'the starting point was the family. From the governmental point of view members of one family group were considered as forming a family council, with the father as the president.'

Conclusion

A number of further functions are to be found within the family or within the grouping of several families known as a **clan**. These functions include care of the old and sick and recreational activities such as dances. Kenyatta concludes that a Gikuyu's personal needs, physical and psychological, are satisfied 'while he plays his part as a member of a family group, and cannot be fully satisfied in any other way'. The family in pre-industrial Britain was similar to the traditional Gikuyu family in so far as it carried out a similarly broad range of functions.

Activity

The modern **welfare state** includes payments from central government such as pensions and unemployment or sickness benefits. It also includes local government services such as council housing, schools and social workers.

List those functions of the typical pre-industrial family which have been partly or completely taken over by the welfare state in modern Britain.

---

3 An alternative to the family: communal living on a kibbutz

Zionism was a movement founded in 1897 to re-establish a Jewish nation in Palestine. In 1909 seven young Jewish pioneers, recently arrived in Palestine from Europe, set up a farm in which they each had an equal say in making decisions. Living in tents with few resources, it made sense to share all that they had. Collective settlements also offered defence against hostility from local Arabs. There was a great need for labour because large tracts of land had to be reclaimed from the malarial swamps in the Jordan Valley. For this reason, women came to work alongside men, while the children were raised in large groups by childminders.

This was the beginning of the kibbutz movement. By 1990 there were about 270 kibbutz villages (**kibbutzim**) in Israel. Some were inspired by socialist ideas of equality of income and equality between the sexes. A guiding principle has been that property is shared and work is organised collectively.

Life in the average modern British family compared with collective life on a typical kibbutz

1   The average British family is supported by one or both parents earning a living and the family is a unit of consumption with the family budget determining a family's standard of living. On a kibbutz the community as a whole is the unit of consumption; there is no family budget, only a community budget. This offers collective provision for individual needs; members are equally rewarded for their labour not with wages but with housing, food, clothing and all the necessities of life as well as some pocket money.

2   The members of an average British family are dependent on one another. In a kibbutz wives are not dependent on husbands, husbands are not dependent on wives and children are not dependent on parents: all are dependent on the community.

3   Mothers in average British families are often full-time housewives. In the economy of the kibbutz wives share an equal role with their husbands.

4   Average British families eat, sleep and live together in self-contained units with parents having almost sole responsibility for their children. Kibbutzniks eat in a communal dining room. Their children are weaned at six months and then live in separate children's houses where they are looked after by **metapelets** ('metapel' means 'to take care'). The children visit their parents in their bungalows or flatlets for about two hours in the early evening each day and for longer periods on the Sabbath.

Communal upbringing on the Kabri Kibbutz in Israel.

The Children of the Dream

This was the title of a study published in 1969 by Dr Bruno Bettelheim, an American expert in child psychology, who visited many kibbutzim. In comparing upbringing on the kibbutz with conventional family life he came to the following conclusions:

Advantages

1   All children are given opportunities and no child has better clothes or more pocket money than any other.

2   There are no signs of problems such as battered babies, bullying, serious mental illness or sex crimes.

3   There is little jealousy, rivalry or possessiveness.

4   No one feels neglected, lonely or abandoned.

5   There are few educational failures and pupils are not plagued by the pressures of ambitious parents.

6   Kibbutzniks are hard workers renowned for their loyalty and bravery. Although they were less than 4 per cent of Israel's population in 1967, they constituted 25 per cent of the casualties in the Six-Day War and many of the army's heroes.

Disadvantages

1   The same kibbutznik officers were said to lack flexibility in making rapid, spontaneous decisions on the battle-field. During socialisation, the pressure to conform stifles the adventurous individuality and originality which is needed for creative intellect. Bettelheim observed that if a kibbutznik expressed a personal opinion and then found that others were not supporting him, he always either backed down immediately or else pretended that he was only joking.

2   Because they are deprived of warm, close, intimate contact with others, kibbutzniks tend to be shy outside their group, emotionally undemonstrative and unable to establish really deep, loving relationships.

3   One major advantage of family life is that it offers children the chance to be themselves, to rebel against their parents and to explore negative feelings. But while outbursts of temper offer relief to adolescent confusions and frustrations in normal homes, teenagers on the kibbutz are expected to suppress any anger.

4   They also have to suppress any sexual arousal while sharing mixed dormitories up to the age of 18. And they dare not question the doctrines of the system. As one kibbutz psychiatrist told Bettelheim, 'The result of all this repression is that our children are ashamed to be ashamed, are afraid to be afraid. They are afraid to love, are afraid to give of themselves.'

It should be recognised that other social scientists have come to different conclusions about kibbutz life and so have criticised Bettelheim's study.

Recent developments

In the first kibbutzim, shared child-rearing was seen as a key part of creating collective loyalty. There was a strong tendency to emphasise the community and so to downgrade the importance of the family. In recent years, however, there has been a reaction to this and many parents want to play a greater part in bringing up their own children. It used to be the custom that parents did not visit their babies in the kindergarten during the day, but now parents tend to visit whenever they like and many mothers resent the influence that the childminders have over their children.

When kibbutzim were being set up, personal housing was given low priority and a couple often only had a two-room flatlet (a bit like at a Butlin's holiday camp). Most would watch TV or read the papers in the kibbutz club rather than in private. But families on more modern kibbutzim are likely to have bungalows with their own kitchens and in 1974 children slept in their parents' quarters in 10 per cent of kibbutzim.

This re-emergence of the traditional family unit perhaps shows that the communal way of life on the kibbutz is not a real alternative to the family. There seems to be a vital need for family affiliation and it seems that close relations between members of a community, as exists in a kibbutz, are perhaps not an adequate substitute for family ties.

Activity

Bearing in mind the conclusions of Bettelheim's research, give reasons for why you would or would not like to experience living in one of the following social units:

(a) an Israeli kibbutz,
(b) a boarding school,
(c) a hippy commune,
(d) an oil rig or a battleship,
(e) a monastery or a convent.

---

4   Extended and nuclear families

Before we look at family life in Britain, we need to make clear the distinction between the **nuclear** and the **extended family**.

The nuclear family

A nuclear family consists of the unit with just two generations: parents and their children. For example, Tony Blair grew up in a nuclear family consisting of mother, father and children. Following his own marriage he formed his own nuclear family with his wife and children.

The extended family

This term was originally used to describe a social unit living under the same roof in which a nuclear family is joined by other relatives. An example would be J. R. Ewing living at Southfork Ranch (just outside Dallas in Texas) with his wife Sue Ellen, his mother Miss Ellie, his brother Bobby, his sister-in-law Pam and his niece Lucy. Since such as arrangement involves several nuclear families living together, it is also called a joint family. Another example from a TV series is *The Waltons* household.

In describing the evolution of the typical British family, sociologists have stressed the way in which **industrialisation** and **urbanisation** (the movement of people to large towns) in the nineteenth century led to widespread poverty among the urban working class. Since there were few of today's welfare services, people needed help from their extended families who often lived in nearby streets. If we use the term in this sense then we can say that most of us have an extended family because most of us have relatives outside our immediate nuclear family.

The term 'extended family' does not therefore refer only to a situation in which a nuclear family lives with other relatives in the same household. It refers to all the relatives of a nuclear family. There are, of course, wide variations in the closeness of contact between relatives and sociologists are interested in identifying the reasons for these variations.

Four generations of the British royal family on the occasion of Prince Harry's christening in December 1984.

A four-level classification of kin involvement

In two classic studies of kinship in 1956 and 1970, J. Firth and his colleagues developed the following way to survey involvement with kin:

1   Universe of kin refers to all the 'recognised kin' which a person acknowledges as existing.

2   Unnamed kin are those recognised kin a person cannot name. The assumption here is that if you do not know the name of a grandmother's sister or a cousin's child, then these relatives are unlikely to be of any consequence in your life.

3   Named kin can be split into 'non-effective kin', with whom you rarely or never interact, and 'effective kin' with whom you have some form of social contact.

4   Effective kin can be separated into 'peripheral kin' and 'intimate kin'. Those who we see regularly, and who play a significant part in our lives, can be seen as our close, intimate kin.

A two-level classification of kin

Primary kin are those to whom we are connected by just one link on the family tree, such as parent, sibling, spouse and children. They are most likely to be our intimate kin.

   Secondary kin are not directly connected to us. They are only connected through primary kin. For example, aunts and uncles are only connected through our parents, and nieces and nephews are only connected through our brothers and sisters.

In his 1970 study of middle-class families, Firth found:

- 40 per cent of adult respondents had no contact with their first cousins;
- 45 per cent only saw cousins rarely, at family ceremonies, such as weddings and funerals;
- 98 per cent of parents kept in contact with their adult child.

Involvement with primary kin may be lifelong but, if parents divorce, up to one-half of non-residential parents (usually fathers) lose effective contact with their children within a few years of separation.

Activities

1 Draw a family tree for the main characters in your favourite TV soap opera such as *EastEnders* or *Coronation Street* OR draw your own family tree and show the two nuclear families to which your mother or father belong.

2 Contacts within the extended family often bring mutual support. For example, grandparents might regularly babysit with their grandchildren and grandchildren might often do the shopping or the gardening for their grandparents.

   (a) Which relatives in your extended family have you seen during the last twelve months?

   (b) How often do you usually see each of these relations?

   (c) What are the different reasons for your contact with them?

   (d) In what ways do you maintain indirect, rather than face-to-face, contact with them?

3 Imagine that you are married with two children. Your parents propose that they join you in buying a large house so that you can all live together. What would be the main advantages and disadvantages of this arrangement to all involved?

Case study: the extended family in the East End of London in the 1950s

In 1954 and 1955, Peter Townsend and Peter Marris studied *The Family Life of Old People* in Bethnal Green by interviewing a random sample of 203 pensioners. They found that:

> ... fifty-eight per cent of the old people belonged to a three-generation extended family in the sense that they saw relatives of the two succeeding generations every day or nearly every day and shared much of their lives with them. The group of relatives varied in size from six to over twenty. Generally it was built around grandmother, daughter, and grandchild, but variations were introduced by the sex and number of surviving children, the marital status and degree of incapacity of old people, and the distances at which the relatives lived.

Mrs Knock, aged sixty-four, lived with her husband, a single son, and a granddaughter of eight years old. Her eldest daughter lived in the next street and her youngest daughter in the same street. She saw them and their children every day. They helped her with the shopping and she looked after the grandchildren when they were at work. Money was exchanged for these services. Her youngest son, recently married, lived two streets away and called every evening. Her two daughters had the midday meal with her and she sent a meal to her youngest son because his wife was at work in the day.

(Source: *The Family Life of Old People* by P. Townsend, Penguin, 1963)

5   The evolution of the 'typical' British family

In *The Symmetrical Family* Michael Young and Peter Willmott have argued that the family in Britain has gone through four stages of development:

1 the pre-industrial nuclear family;
2 the industrial extended family;
3 the modern nuclear family;
4 the managing director family.

Stage 1: the pre-industrial nuclear family

Before the Industrial Revolution and the introduction of the factory system, a typical family operated as a **unit of economic production**. This means that husband, wife and children all worked together, for example, in farming or a cottage industry such as manufacturing textiles in the home. The average family lived as a small nuclear unit, like many modern families. This occurred because couples often married late (in their late twenties) and their own parents often died early (in their early forties), with only a few years between the two events. This meant that few families had surviving grandparents to join those few children who survived infancy and so create three-generation extended family households. Laslett has estimated that from 1564 to 1821 only 10 per cent or so of homes contained kin beyond the basic nuclear family; this figure was about the same in 1966.

Stage 2: the industrial extended family

The factory bell and compulsory education split up the family which had previously worked together as an economic unit. By the end of the nineteenth century adults were commonly earning wages outside the home while children had to attend school.

The lack of welfare provision by the government meant that the extended family offered important support to the poor. Anderson has studied the 1851 census statistics for Preston, in Lancashire, which at that time was a rapidly growing town of textile mills. The figures show that 23 per cent of households contained extended kin such as grandparents or orphaned nephews and nieces who needed to be cared for.

Family units became larger because (a) five or six children often survived in the Victorian family, (b) adult life expectancy also increased so that more grandparents survived, (c) relatives often lived nearby or in the same household. Willmott and Young's study of Bethnal Green, in East London, in the 1950s showed how the extended family of the nineteenth century had continued in traditional, urban, working-class communities. They found that many young couples started their married lives in one of their parents' homes; the generations then stayed in close contact.

The Demeter tie

In one of the Greek myths Demeter searches for years for her lost daughter, Persephone. The mother is tied to her daughter by a strong bond. In traditional working-class communities this tie is recognised in this rhyme:

A son's a son until he gets him a wife,
but a daughter's a daughter all her life.

In stable communities such as pit villages, where sons followed fathers down the coal mine, there was little **social mobility** between the 1850s and the 1950s. Few sons moved up in the world to non-manual jobs and few moved away to other areas. Male relatives could 'put in a good word' with employers and landlords to help young men get jobs and homes, but it was often young wives who were most in need of help from the extended family.

Tunstall's survey of the fishermen of Hull found that trawlermen would leave their wives while they went on month-long voyages but they would forbid their wives to go out to work. Isolated with their children, the wives would turn to their female relatives for companionship. Since the burden of raising families in poverty has usually been shouldered by women, they have often depended on the support of relatives. And so the extended family has been called an informal trade union of women.

The Bethnal Green survey found that the households of mothers and their married daughters were in many ways merged: 60 per cent lived within two or three miles of each other, 80 per cent had seen each other within the previous week and 50 per cent visited daily.

Marital roles

The industrial extended family was partly **patriarchal**, which means that the father was the dominant authority. Yet it was also **matriarchal** in the sense that wives often organised all the practical aspects of family life, such as putting money by in different jars to pay the bills and equipping children for school or work.

Willmott and Young have talked of husbands being squeezed out of the warmth of the female circle and taking to the pub in their defence. One could also say that the women defended themselves from poverty while their husbands spent a lot of their incomes on alcohol. The late Victorian working man's home was often cold, damp, gloomy and overcrowded; many men preferred to spend their evenings in the welcoming comfort of the Victorian pub with the luxury of its engraved glass windows, upholstered seats, gas lamps and coal fires.

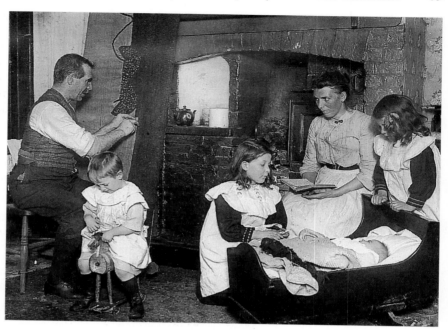

A miner's family at home in 1912.

Stage 3: the modern nuclear family

In this stage the family has the following characteristics:

1   **Conjugal roles** are joint rather than segregated. This means that marital roles and family decisions are more equally shared. Therefore there is greater symmetry or balance between husband and wife than in the stage 2 family.

2   The husband's leisure is more **privatised** and **home-centred** with activities such as DIY and watching TV.

3   Smaller nuclear families (with only two or three children, like stage 1) operate as self-contained **units of economic consumption**; with **child-centred** recreation, such as outings to the Alton Towers theme park.

4   There is more isolation from the extended kinship network because families are more geographically and socially mobile, moving house and changing job. They are also more self-reliant as a result of affluence and the welfare state.

The process of transition to stage 3 family life is vividly illustrated by the young East Enders who left the close-knit communities of the Bethnal Green slums in the 1950s. They moved out to the overspill estates and the Essex new towns such as Basildon and Harlow. Here husbands could dig the garden of their new 'semi' and could dare to push the pram down the street.

In considering family life in the 1990s, Graham Allan warns against viewing modern families as cut off and isolated. The home used to be seen as the place for just the family, especially in working-class culture. Now-adays, it is increasingly accepted as a setting for sociability with friends, for entertaining non-kin. In this sense, the home can be seen as an increasingly socialised (rather than privatised) space which has been opened up to those outside the family.

The principle of stratified diffusion

Willmott and Young use the idea of stratified diffusion to explain the process by which family life has evolved. The idea means that patterns or styles of life filter down from the upper to the lower classes. Here are four examples:

1   Foreign holidays were once only for the upper classes but by the 1970s cheap package holiday flights allowed many working-class families to enjoy Mediterranean holidays.

2   Female education and ideas of equality in marriage enabled the working class of the 1930s to follow the middle class of the 1880s in using birth control to plan for smaller families.

3   By the 1960s many working-class homes were enjoying the luxuries of consumer durable goods such as TVs, washing machines and refrigerators as well as telephones and central heating.

4   More and more working-class families have also copied the middle class in switching to stage 3 nuclear patterns of family life.

The idea of stratified diffusion implies that we can predict the next stage for the average family of the future by looking at the upper-middle-class family of today. As far as the material aspects of home life go, we might expect that continued economic growth will allow more families to enjoy wall-to-wall carpets, double-glazing, patio doors, dishwashers and second telephones, second TVs, second cars and second toilets.

Stage 4: the managing director family

Young and Willmott predict a shift from the stage 3 family which is centred on the home to a future where life is centred on work and on leisure based outside the home. In this family of the future (which is claimed to be already spreading from the professional classes) both husband and wife have interesting technical careers and a range of leisure pursuits such as sailing, squash, golf, jogging, riding and hang-gliding. Such activities are not necessarily shared: on a Tuesday evening father goes straight from a conference to the badminton club, mother dashes from a business appointment to her evening class in car maintenance, while teenage son and daughter fix meals in the microwave oven before heading off to the roller-disco and the sub-aqua club.

Young and Willmott found signs of this new type of **work-centred** and less cohesive family life in their survey of London in the early 1970s. Signs included:

- more work satisfaction and a decline in unrewarding, low-skill jobs;
- more shiftwork;
- more women leading independent lives alongside their roles of wife and mother;

- new trends such as flexi-time and home-working via computer terminals;
- men and women increasing their commitments outside the home, in both work and leisure, as their education and standards of living rise.

Case study: Now the office is where the heart is

1997 saw the publication of the *The Time Bind* by A. R. Hochschild. The author notes that Americans take hardly any holiday (12 days a year compared to the German average of 30) and that, over the past two decades, the average American has added an extra 164 hours – a full month of work – to their working year. Why do Americans stay so late at the office? Hochschild argues that they do so because they want to. They have switched allegiances and now regard work as home and home as work. No longer do frazzled employees look forward to home as a sanctuary, a place to get away from the stresses of the workplace. Instead, jobs provide a refuge from the demands of increasingly fractured family life.

Hochschild's interviewees told her that the office was simply more interesting than home. Work 'offered a natural theatre in which one could follow the progress of jealousies, sexual attractions, simmering angers. Home, on the other hand, offered fewer actors on an increasingly cramped stage'. Paid work also brings more status, as countless mothers who have opted to stay at home can testify. But work is also becoming more like home. New, progressive management techniques have made the firm feel like a family, with informal and supportive relations between staff. There are picnics, outings and birthday cakes for employees. They can wear their own clothes on Dress-Down Friday and call their bosses by their first names. They have more of their best friends at the office than anywhere else, certainly more than the neighbourhood where they live.

Home, meanwhile, has become more like work. With both partners working, couples say that home has become a place of pressure, requiring discipline and deadlines: playing with the kids for half an hour, bathing them for 20 minutes, an hour of quality time, a rushed dinner, then finally collapse in a heap. Women are discovering what men have known for decades: that the office can be an island of calm, an escape from the agonies of domesticity.

(adapted from 'Commentary' by Jonathon Freedland, the *Guardian*, 29 October 1997)

Conclusion

Young and Willmott try to encompass all family life in Britain over the last few hundred years in just four stages or patterns. While it is useful to identify broad trends in the development of the family, it would be misleading to fail to recognise the diversity of family life in modern Britain. Some indication of this variety is given in the next chapter, together with a more detailed account of changes such as falling birth rates and rising divorce rates.

GCSE question from Southern Examining Group 1996

Study Item A. Then answer *all* parts of the question which follow.

Item A

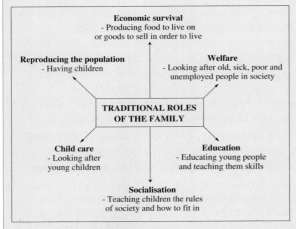

(a) (i)   According to Item A, what is 'socialisation'?   (1)

(ii)   State an example from Item A of how the traditional family carries out its welfare role.   (1)

(iii)   Choose *one* of the roles from Item A and give an example of how it has changed in modern Britain.   (1)

(b) (i)   Give an example of how parents teach their children to 'fit in' with society.   (1)

(ii)   Identify and explain *one* way in which childhood has changed this century.   (3)

(c) (i)   State *two* reasons for the increase in the divorce rate in Britain this century.   (2)

(ii)   Identify *two* types of family unit in which people might live as a result of divorce.   (2)

(d) (i)   Identify and describe *one* way in which being responsible for an elderly relative might affect family life.   (3)

(ii)   Give an example of *one* kind of help that might be provided for families looking after elderly relatives.   (1)

CHAPTER 5

Recent patterns of family life

1 Has family life become better or worse?

Recent changes in family life have provoked both optimistic and pessimistic responses. Some believe that the family in modern Britain is declining and that the centuries-old social arrangement called 'marriage' is no longer working. The opposite view is that family life is in many ways better than ever before. A number of points in this debate are listed below.

1 The loss of functions A negative view of the modern nuclear family sees it as stripped of many of the functions that it used to fulfil in the past. The positive view argues that the welfare state now offers support, ranging from child benefit payments to leisure centres, which enables the family to make a better job of its different basic functions.

2 Mobility and isolation Does family life suffer if the mobile nuclear family moves away from the warmth of stable local kinship networks and a friendly community? Family life is not necessarily worse on a new housing estate or in a tower block of flats. Many families now enjoy increased choice about where to live and which neighbours or relatives to visit. The 1996 British Social Attitudes survey found that 48 per cent of adults (with living mothers with whom they do not live) see their mothers at least once a week. Only three per cent never see their mothers. 75 per cent of parents with adult children speak to them on the phone at least once a week. Almost three-quarters of respondents believed that close relatives should keep in contact even if they do not have much in common.

3 Child abuse and 'latch-key children' There has been some concern over the neglect of children who return home from school to an empty home because parents are at work. The media have also highlighted recurring cases of severe cruelty to children. But standards of child care are far higher than, say, 150 years ago. Also families with working mothers may be materially and emotionally better off than those with housebound 'captive wives'. Housewives without paid jobs may be depressed by money worries and by the isolation of being trapped at home all day with toddlers.

4 The decline in popularity of marriage? In 1995, 40 per cent of marriages were remarriages for one or both partners. This shows that marriage remains popular. But the total number of marriages in 1995 was the lowest figure recorded since 1926 and the number of first marriages in 1995 was half the number in 1970. The decline in the proportion of young people marrying has been accompanied by a marked rise in cohabitation (couples living together without getting married).

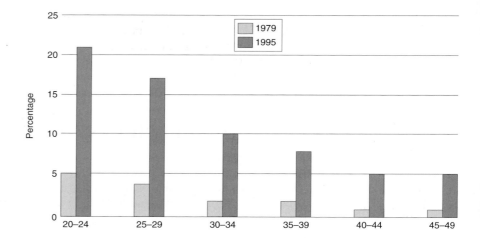

Percentages of all women aged 20–49 cohabiting: by age, 1979 and 1995 (Source: 'Living in Britain 1995', General Household Survey.)

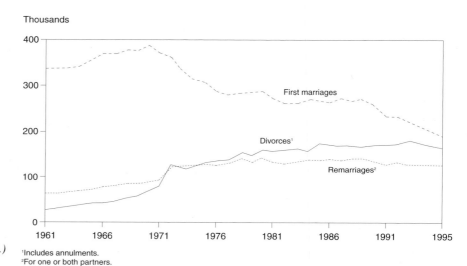

Marriages and divorces in the United Kingdom (Source: Social Trends, 1998.)

[1]Includes annulments.
[2]For one or both partners.

5   The increase in divorce and broken homes   We cannot conclude that the rise in divorce means that there has been an increase in marital breakdown. In the past many **empty-shell marriages** continued, long after any loving relationship had died, merely because divorce was so difficult to obtain. Broken homes and orphans were more common in the last century when families were often disrupted by the early death of a parent due to illness or an accident at work, or by the disappearance of fathers due to desertion, migration or war.

6   Domestic violence and mental illness   Ronald Fletcher has argued that higher rates of divorce show that partners have higher expectations of married life and that therefore marriage is in a 'healthier condition' than in the past. We have higher standards and are less prepared to put up with unsatisfactory marital relationships than married couples in former years. But many women stay married to unsupportive husbands and those with three children under 10 are the single group in the population most likely to suffer from persistent depression. Many wives also live with husbands who are violent as well as unsupportive. A campaign against domestic violence in 1994, called Zero Tolerance, estimated that in London alone almost 100,000 women a year seek treatment for violent injuries inflicted by their partners. Also, the NSPCC estimates that every week three children are killed by their parents.

This chapter focuses on some of these issues, such as the rise in divorce and the increase in mothers going out to work. We also go in search of that elusive phenomenon: 'the typical British family'.

2   The roles of working mothers

The rise in the proportions of children with mothers who go to work has been one of the major changes affecting family life since the war.

The increase in mothers going out to work

In the stage 1 pre-industrial family, wives were economic partners in home-based production. After the Industrial Revolution, wives were far less likely than their husbands to join factory-based work. Out of 1,382,000 factory workers in the 1841 census only 8,789 were women. The 1851 census shows that only 25 per cent of married women went out to work. Very few of these were middle-class wives and those working-class mothers who were employed in places like textile mills were increasingly 'squeezed out' by men protecting scarce jobs and by new laws which regulated women's hours and conditions at work. The result was that only 10 per cent of married women went out to work in 1911.

The two world wars temporarily brought women back into the labour force but the dramatic increase in mothers at work has occurred since the 1950s. In 1961 30 per cent of married women were 'economically active' and by 1987 this had risen to 66 per cent. Much of this increase has been due to the recent trend for mothers to return to work more quickly after having a baby. In the early 1950s the average time of return was 7.5 years after the latest birth but by the 1980s it was an average of 3.5 years. Also, many women are now returning to work between births.

In 1994, government projections showed that 80 per cent of new jobs would be filled by women 'returners', going back to work after having children.

Reasons for the increase in working mothers

We can list some of these reasons under two headings: motivating factors and enabling factors.

Motivating factors

1   A mother's income can be essential for financial survival. The 1978 DHSS Report *Wives as Sole and Joint Breadwinners* estimated that three or four times as many families would be in poverty if it were not for the

earnings of working mothers. The 1990s have seen economic recession with more fathers out of work and with husbands on low wages finding fewer opportunities of boosting their pay by working overtime. There has also been an increase in one-parent families, 90 per cent of them with mothers rather than fathers.

2   A mother's motivation for returning to work might be to raise the family's standard of living so that they can afford a bigger mortgage in order to buy a better house, or so that they can afford foreign holidays.

3   If you lack a waged occupation then society gives you a comparatively low status. This is true of housewives in the same way as it applies to pensioners, children, students and the unemployed. More women want a separate identify apart from the roles of wife and mother. Margaret Thatcher is an example of a career-minded woman who saw motherhood as a threat to her independence and ambitions. In 1953 she had gained a chemistry degree at Oxford and was studying law when her twins, Carol and Mark, were born. Her own mother helped to look after them so that, four mothers later, she was able to pass her final law exams. She has since said: 'I thought that if I didn't do something quite definite then, there was a real possibility that I'd never return to work again.'

4   Many mothers are attracted by the sociable adult company of the workplace as well as the satisfactions of involvement in interesting jobs.

CONSERVATIVE WINNER

MARGARET THATCHER FOR WESTMINSTER

Margaret Thatcher's twin children did not prevent her from starting a political career.

They are keen to escape from the boredom and depression of being an isolated *Captive Wife* – the title of Hannah Gavron's study of mothers who were housebound with small children.

Enabling factors

1   Industry has increased its demand for female labour which is often employed at low wages and on a part-time basis. (Only 31 per cent of working mothers are in full-time jobs.) Vacancies have expanded particularly in **service sector jobs** such as catering, cleaning, shops and offices. A number of employers have developed flexi-time and job-sharing schemes as well as workplace crèches (nurseries for toddlers).

2   Women now have better educational opportunities as well as a fairer deal at work due to the Equal Pay Act and the Sex Discrimination Act.

3   Mothers now have smaller families than previous generations.

4   Husbands are far less disapproving of their wives going out to work and modern research has argued against Bowlby's 1951 report which suggested that children of working mothers suffered from maternal deprivation.

5   Household gadgets such as tumble-dryers, freezers, microwave ovens and food processors as well as convenience foods have helped to reduce the time and labour of housework and child care. Sue Sharpe's research in *Double Identity: The Lives of Working Mothers* also found that sons, as well as daughters, were fairly often given generous pocket money for helping around the home.

A few employers provide workplace crèches for the children of their employees.

Average hours spent: (per week, in 1988)	in paid employment	doing household chores
Women in part-time jobs	20	37.5
Women in full-time jobs	39.7	27.5
Men in full-time jobs	44.5	12

The parenting deficit

There is growing concern, especially in the United States, that children are being neglected in families in which both parents have full-time jobs. According to Demos, an American think-tank, the number of hours that the average parent spends with his or her children has nearly halved in the past twenty-five years. Americans call this shortfall a 'parenting deficit'. Professor Etzioni of the Demos think-tank claims that this decline has arisen because parents are putting their careers and the achievement of a high standard of living above the well-being of their children. He states, 'Now that we have seen the result of decades of neglect of children, the time has come for both parents to revalue children and for the community to support and recognise their efforts.' Parents with little time available for parenting sometimes aim for 'quality time' when they share activities with their children.

Some commentators claim that the same pattern of a parenting deficit has emerged in Britain. Children are left alone for long periods in which the television and the video act as a substitute for parental company and guidance. The extent of this problem is not yet well established by research. What is well established, however, is that in two-career households British fathers are still not meeting their responsibilities in the home. Thus the problem of a parenting deficit is caused by this deficiency on the part of men and not just by mothers working outside the home.

Activities

1   Conduct a survey of a number of mothers to find out how many have full-time or part-time jobs and how many pay their children for help around the home.
2   Interview four working mothers and ask them for their reasons for returning to work. Then see how far the reasons that they have given match the motivating factors given above.
3   Interview some full-time housewives and ask them why they do not go out to work.
4   Ask some men about their attitudes to wives going out to work and young mothers pursuing full-time careers.

3   Are conjugal roles fairly shared?

With so many women going out to work, are men now doing their fair share of chores around the home, including child care? Surveys on the domestic division of labour, such as the findings on page 18, show that conclusions about joint or symmetrical conjugal roles in the modern, stage 3 family have been overstated.

In 1993 and 1994, the Mintel market research group produced two survey reports, called *Women 2000* and *Men 2000*. Here are some of the findings:

- Eighty per cent of women said that they take, or share equally, big financial decisions with their male partners. Yet fewer than 40 per cent have their own bank accounts.
- Forty-two per cent of married men claimed to share at least one domestic task equally with their wives but only 26 per cent of women thought that this was the case.
- Eighty-five per cent of working women said that they almost always do all the laundry and ironing. A similar proportion said that they are entirely responsible for cooking the main meal (80% had a microwave oven and half said that they used it every day). Twenty-five per cent of husbands were 'happy cookers' who preferred entertaining and experimenting rather than cooking everyday meals.
- Fifty per cent of husbands admitted to being 'sloths' over housework. They were more likely to be in the 35–54 age group.
- 'Newish man' or the 'semi-sharer' was most likely to be middle class and young. Men under 34 without children were best at sharing jobs in the home: 'Men seem to set out with good intentions to share domestic chores but the catalyst appears to be the arrival of children. At this stage, the man appears to abdicate his responsibility for his share, regardless of whether his partner is working.'

These findings may be compared with the modest improvements discovered among the 3,000-strong sample of the *British Social Attitudes* survey:

Percentage agreeing that:	1984	1991
Household shopping is shared equally	39	47
Making the evening meal is shared equally	16	20
Washing and ironing is shared equally	9	12

Conclusion

The rest of this chapter explores the ways in which we now have a wide diversity of 'family households'. An increasing number of these households split and reform. For example, a woman may leave her male partner and then live with a new partner. But the woman is the primary carer who is the constant factor at the heart of most 'family households'.

When mothers go out to work, they are responsible for the child-care arrangements. When children are sick, they are usually cared for by the woman. Men may 'help', but they generally only assume responsibility for the more enjoyable aspects of child care, such as the Sunday morning trip to the park while mum slaves away over the dinner! The burden of care for disabled children or elderly relatives also tends to fall on the woman's shoulders. Most informal, unpaid carers are women.

Traditional sociology sees the nuclear family as the core of the family. But the above examples all support the argument that the universal core to the 'family household' is the **female-carer core unit**: the woman.

4   What is the typical family like?

The 'cereal packet norm'

Next time you watch the advertisements on TV, see how far this picture is true: the typical advertiser's family shows mother seeing off her two children to school and her husband to work in the morning and then getting on with cleaning the floor and putting the dirty clothes in the washing machine. Her two children are ideally one of each sex and the boy is preferably the eldest. They return home to find her cutting sandwiches or getting in her brilliant white washing from the line.

Advertisements for products such as breakfast cereals and washing powders have for many years featured such stereotypes and sociologists have asked how far this 'cereal packet norm' really applies to the average family. The first part of this chapter has already shown that the typical modern mother goes out to work. We now look at some of the ways that families and households vary.

The four phases of the family life-cycle

1   'Nest-building'   The average length of time between a couple's marriage and the birth of their first baby is just under three years and about 90 per cent of couples in their first marriage have children. This first, home-making stage of the new family is shorter for the 30 per cent or so of teenager mothers who get pregnant while single and then get married before their first child is born.

2   Child-rearing   This 'whole families' phase lasts from the birth of the first child to when the first child leaves home. During the nineteenth century many women died in early middle age, in their forties or early fifties. Since the average number of children was six, this meant that the typical wife in the nineteenth century spent most of her married life rearing children.

3   Dispersal   In 1993, the average age of marrying for the first time was 28 for men and 26 for women. The average 26-year-old bride is 29 when her first child is born and so will be only 47 when this child becomes an adult. With her offspring 'leaving the nest' and dispersing to set up their own households and families, our average mother can now look forward to another 34 years of life in a shrinking family unit.

4   Elderly couple   With their children grown up and 'dispersed', our average couple now approach retirement in a two-person household – like the nest-building phase. The average wife can expect to spend her last years alone as a widow. This is because the average wife has a husband who is two years older than herself and because the average male life expectancy is some six years less than that of females.

Changing patterns of life for typical women in Britain

	Year of marriage		Phase in family life-cycle
	1870	*1996*	
Age at marriage	25	26	
			Nest-building
Age at first birth	27	29	
(Number of children)	(6)	(2)	Child-bearing
Age at last birth	40	33	
			Child-rearing
Age when last child 18	58	51	
Age at death	68	81	
(Years after dispersal)	(10)	(30)	

Figures from the census reveal that families in the second, child-rearing phase are outnumbered by the families in the other phases of the family lifecycle.

Types of households

	1961	*1997*
	(%)	*(%)*
No family		
One person under retirement age	4	12
One person over retirement age	7	15
Two or more unrelated adults	5	2
One family		
Married couple only	26	28
Married couple with one or two dependent children	30	21
Married couple with three or more dependent children	8	5
Married couple with independent child(ren) only*	10	6
Lone parent with at least one dependent child	2	7
Lone parent with independent child(ren) only	4	3
Two or more families (joint family household)	3	1

* An 'independent child' is a son or daughter who is over 16 and no longer in full-time education but who is still living at home.
(Source: Office of Population Censuses and Surveys)

The diversity of family patterns can be seen in the breakdown of all types of households. This shows that one of the most common household types in an average street is the single-person household (27 per cent of all homes). There are more homes containing couples without children (28 per cent of all households) than there are homes with couples in the child-rearing stage, fitting the advertisers' dream, the cereal packet norm (married couples with one or two dependent children are only 21 per cent of all homes).

The marital biography of Julie Brown

The four phases of the family life-cycle, described above, are a traditional stereotype. They apply to an 'average couple'. But this case study of Julie Brown shows how one person may have a succession of different marital identities. This creates a 'pluralism (variety) of marriage patterns'.

Age 18 Julie moves into a flat with her boyfriend, Gary.

Age 19 Julie has a son, Barry.

Age 20 Julie splits up with Gary and takes Barry to live with her parents.

Age 22 Julie and Barry move in with the new man in her life, Greg.

Age 23 Julie marries Greg.

Age 25 Julie and Greg have a daughter, Sharon.

Age 29 Greg leaves Julie. She moves into bed-and-breakfast accommodation.

Age 30 Julie divorces Grey and moves in with another divorcee, Tony. Tony is quite a bit older than Julie and his teenage children live with his ex-wife.

Age 32 Julie's children, Barry and Sharon, are joined by one of Tony's teenage children, Michael.

Age 45 All three children have now left home. After a heart attack, Tony says 'Isn't it about time we got married?'

Age 47 Julie marries Tony.

Age 54 Tony dies and Julie becomes a widow.

Age 84 Julie dies.

5   Single-parent families

Unmarried mothers

A recent study of a Dorset village shows that around 80 per cent of all the children living there in the 1870s and 1880s were illegitimate. Births outside wedlock are again becoming common, rising from less than 10 per cent of all births in 1971 to over 30 per cent in 1992.

In 1996, around four-fifths of births outside marriage were jointly registered by both parents. Of these, three-quarters were living at the same address, cohabiting. Only about 8 per cent of all live births were solely registered outside marriage in 1996, almost three-quarters more than in 1971.

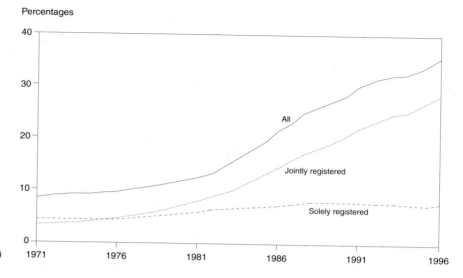

Percentages

*Births outside marriage as a percentage of all live births, England and Wales (Source:*Social Trends, *1998.)*

Lone-parent families

In 1996, lone parents headed 21 per cent of all families with dependent children, nearly 3 times the proportion in 1971. Of all female lone parents, 38 per cent had been single since the birth of the children, 33 per cent were divorced, 24 per cent were separated and 6 per cent were widowed. On average, each year around 15 per cent of lone mothers cease to be lone parents, usually as a result of forming a new partnership. This suggests that for half of all lone mothers their lone parenthood lasts for 4 years or less.

Lone parent families as a percentage of all families with dependent children: 1971 to 1995 (Source:'Living in Britain 1995', *General Household Survey.)*

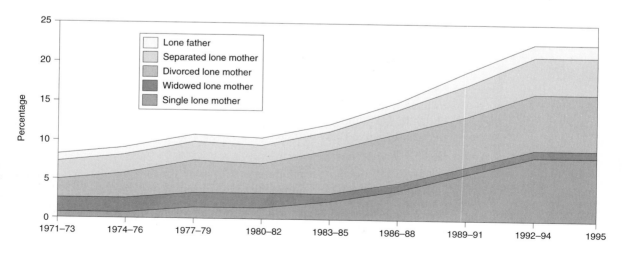

In 1993, the Daily Mirror *launched a 'Fight for Single Mums' to defend them against proposed cuts in their Social Security benefits.*

The moral panic over single-parent families

In the 1992 American presidential election, the Vice-president, Dan Quayle, condemned the unmarried TV sitcom character, Murphy Brown, for deciding to have a baby as a 'lifestyle choice', without a husband to help raise the child. In the same year, Peter Lilley, the Minister for Social Security, told the Conservative Party conference 'I've got a little list' of benefit scroungers, including

> Young ladies who get pregnant just to jump the housing list,
> And dads who won't support the kids of ladies they have ... kissed.

By 1994, with John Major's 'Back to Basics' slogan and the tabloid press hounding single mums who had left their children 'Home Alone', there was a moral panic over single-parent families. Concerns focused on the cost to the welfare state, teenage single mothers and the effects on the up-bringing of children.

The costs to the welfare state

By 1994, over 21 per cent of families with children were headed by a lone parent. The 1992 *General Household Survey* found the following employment rates:

	Employment rates of mothers with children under 5	
	Lone mothers	Married or cohabiting mothers
Part-time job	14%	34%
Full-time job	8%	13%

The number of lone parents relying largely on Income Support benefits rose from 245,000 in 1971 to 985,000 in 1992 and is predicted to rise to 1.4 million (out of 1.7 million lone parents) by the year 2000. One way to cut the expense to the welfare state is to chase the absent fathers who are failing to pay regular maintenance for their children. When this task was given to the new **Child Support Agency**, in 1993, less than 25 per cent of lone mothers were receiving maintenance payments.

Another way to cut expenditure on benefits to lone parents would be to encourage and enable more of them to find jobs. Possible policies would be cutting benefits and providing training and child-care facilities.

Teenage single mothers

A confidential Cabinet Paper on single parents was leaked to the press in 1993. Findings included the following:

- Only 5 per cent of single mothers in 1992 were teenagers (although 25 per cent of single mothers started as teenage mothers).
- In 1992 there were only 42,000 16–19-year-old single mothers claiming Income Support.
- Only 2.4 per cent of new council lettings in 1992 were to lone parents under 19.
- Most teenage mothers have little or no idea of the benefits to which they are entitled – there is 'no evidence' that they get pregnant in order to obtain a council flat.

In 1993, the Minister for Wales, John Redwood, visited the St Mellon's council estate in Cardiff. He then made a speech claiming that 'over half' the houses were occupied by single parents and arguing that their benefits should be cut. The BBC's *Panorama* then filmed teenage mothers on the estate who said that they got pregnant to get council housing.

The effects on children's upbringing

The 1993 Cabinet Paper found that there does not appear to be a link between lone-parent families and criminality and that it is poverty, rather than the absence of a second parent, that is associated with young offenders. But the American sociologist, Charles Murray, has argued that, even after taking the effects of poverty into account, the children of lone parents fare worse at school and in finding jobs and are more criminal than children from two-parent families (in the USA they are twice as likely to be imprisoned).

After the 1991 riots on the North Tyneside Meadow Well estate, a sociologist from Newcastle University, Norman Dennis, argued that the disappearance of lifetime male employment had created a generation of thieving and loutish young men. They had grown up without the discipline and role model of fathers and without the traditional expectation that they themselves would become responsible fathers, with the 'project for life' of responsibility for their own wife and children.

Case study: the effects of broken homes

In 1994, Exeter University's Department of Child Health published the results of research on 152 children, aged 9–10 and 13–14. These children consisted of 76 who lived with both parents and 76 whose parents had split up. The children from the two groups were paired on factors such as age and social class. In the second group, 31 were in lone-parent households, 26 had become part of a step-family and 19 had experienced multiple disruption through at least three different homes.

Of the 76 children in 'reordered' families, only a third had frequent, regular contact with the parent who had left the family home. In terms of problems of health, behaviour and school work:

- Those with both parents, whose parents' relationship was good, had the least problems.
- Those with both parents, whose parents' relationship was in difficulties, had more problems.
- Those in reordered families had twice as many problems.

- The 19 who had experienced multiple family disruption were ten times more likely than those in intact families to have a low opinion of themselves and eight times as likely to need extra help with school work and to have health problems, such as stomach aches, nausea, bed-wetting and psychosomatic illnesses.

The reordered families were more likely to be living on Social Security but poverty was not found to be a major cause of suffering. Children in poor, intact families fared better than those in equally poor, single-parent or step-families.

Of the children whose parents had split up, hardly any had been given the chance to discuss preparations for the change and 21 per cent had received no explanation, from either parent. Children from broken homes seem to fare best if they have a chance to discuss their distress, if mediation services minimise post-separation conflict between parents and if regular contact is maintained with the absent parent.

---

6   The rise in divorce and the reconstituted family

	1961	1971	1981	1991
Total marriages in the UK	397,000	459,000	398,000	375,000
Total divorces in the UK	27,000	80,000	157,000	168,000

The proportion of marriages ending in divorce has risen from 2 per cent in 1926 to 33 per cent in 1991 and is forecast to rise to 40 per cent by the year

2000. We can attempt to explain this increase by looking, first, at general factors that have affected most couples and, second, at factors affecting particular groups who get married.

General reasons for the rise in divorce

1   Changes in the law   In the 150 years before the 1857 Matrimonial Causes Act there were only about 250 divorces granted: in other words, less than two per year. Divorce did not really become accessible to the average couple until the 1949 Legal Aid Act. In the 1960s the law still obstructed the easy termination of unhappy, 'empty-shell' marriages. This was partly because the partner petitioning for divorce had to prove the other partner's guilty conduct. It has been estimated that less than half of all marital breakdowns appeared in the divorce statistics.

The 1969 Divorce Reform Act has, since 1971, simplified procedures so that divorce is now obtainable on the grounds of **irretrievable breakdown of marriage** which can be due to separation, desertion, adultery or 'unreasonable behaviour'. In 1984 the law was changed to permit divorce after one year of marriage (not three years as before).

2   Changing attitudes   Reform of the divorce laws reflects society's changing norms. Some believe that the declining influence of the church (**secularisation**) means that people attach less value to marriage; so it has become another disposable item in our 'throwaway culture'. Others maintain that the media's emphasis on romance and personal happiness gives us all higher ideals than our grandparents had: we expect higher standards in our marriages and so it is perhaps inevitable that an increasing number of marriages will fail to come up to the mark.

An increasing number of children grow up in one-parent families: this father is bringing up his son on his own.

In Eire, strong religious values have made divorce a prominent political issue.

3   Other 'opportunity-increasing' factors   Even if unhappy wives in the past had not faced an uphill struggle against obstructive divorce laws and **social stigma** (disapproval and condemnation of divorcees), they would still have faced practical problems such as finding work, finding new housing and finding new partners. Women today are more likely to be independent: with a decent education, fewer children and a job where they can meet new partners. The 1970 Matrimonial Proceedings Act gives wives an equal right to ownership of the home and the development of the welfare state has made council flats and Income Support available.

Particular groups who are more divorce-prone

1   Teenage marriages   In 1901 only 1.6 per cent of men married as teenagers. In 1971 the figure was 10 per cent of men and 30 per cent of women. On current trends, 50 per cent of these teenage brides and almost 60 per cent of these teenage husbands will see their marriages end in divorce. Apart from immaturity, a number of factors can be listed: many teenage brides are pregnant, many face housing difficulties and financial problems, many are married to unskilled manual husbands who are five times more likely to get divorced than husbands with professional occupations.

2   Mismatched partners   It could be argued that all partners who get divorced were mismatched but sociologists tend to concentrate on conflict generated by social factors such as mobility. If a husband receives rapid promotion at work, he may feel that he has 'left his wife behind', even though they both have the same social origins. Difficulties can also arise when a person marries someone outside his or her social group, for example a partner from a different ethnic or religious group.

3   Groups with a reduced commitment to marriage   Partners who have failed to have children, or spouses in the dispersal phase of the family's life-cycle, may be less committed to their marriages than those in the honeymoon stage of home-building. Those who have parents or close relatives who are divorced also tend to be more prone than average to get divorced.

4   Certain occupational groups   Some jobs carry a higher risk of divorce. Obvious examples are long-distance lorry drivers, sailors and professional criminals. In 1983 the divorce rate for husbands in classes 1 and 3 was 7 per 1,000 compared to 28 per 1,000 among classes 6 and 7 and 34 per 1,000 for the unemployed. (These categories of social class are explained in Chapter 9.)

Serial monogamy and the blended family

Polygamy means marriage between a member of one sex and two or more members of the opposite sex. Our laws restrict us to **monogamy**: marrying only one partner. The traditional Christian wedding ceremony unites bride and groom 'til death us do part' but in America divorce and remarriage have become so common that a new pattern of marriage has been called **serial monogamy**. This means that each spouse marries a series of partners.

The Family Policy Studies Centre predicts that, by the year 2000, 40 per cent of marriages will be ending in divorce. It is increasingly common for children to see their parents' marriage break up. Since two-thirds of divorcees remarry, many of these children will only temporarily belong to one-parent families. They can usually expect to gain a step-father from their mother's remarriage and they may also gain step-brothers and step-sisters (step-siblings). This **reconstituted family**, created from two previous marriages, has been called a **blended family**. One of the characteristics of such a step-sibling family is that it is unplanned so that all of the children may be of similar ages or, by contrast, they may be separated by an unusually large number of years.

The last section of this chapter looks at the way that families in three ethnic minorities also diverge from the nuclear family of the 'cereal packet norm'.

Activity

The American anthropologist George Murdock has estimated that there have been 4,000 separate societies since the dawn of humankind. In examining studies of a sample of 250 societies, he found the family to be a universal institution and 75 per cent of these societies practised **polygyny**. This is the form of polygamy in which each man has more than one wife.

Among societies such as the Gikuyu, men (a) had a life expectancy little beyond their thirties, (b) set great store by having sons and (c) married late, after they had accumulated the necessary cattle to pay the brideprice (the opposite of a dowry).

Why do these factors make polygyny a sensible arrangement?

7   Family life in ethnic minority cultures

The pattern of household types varies between ethnic groups. Pakistanis and Bangladeshis tend to live in large households – in 1997 their average household sizes were 4.4 and 5.0 respectively compared with 2.4 for the general population. In 1991, nearly one in 10 of both Indian and Pakistani/Bangladeshi households contained two or more families compared with only 1 in 100 of households from white or black ethnic groups. *Ethnic Minorities in Britain* (1997) found the following pattern of contact between adults and their aunts and uncles who lived in Britain: 70 per cent of Indians had seen an aunt or uncle in the previous 4 weeks compared to a figure of 66 per cent for Pakistanis and Bangladeshis, 51 per cent for Caribbeans and 37 per cent for whites.

The Asian family

The cultural differences between Punjabis, Tamils, Pakistanis and Bangladeshis are as great as their similarities. Sikhs, for example, have freer attitudes to the social position of women than Muslims. Nevertheless, Asian families in Britain tend to follow a common pattern of maintaining traditional loyalties with multi-generation, extended networks of kin. The strengths and flexibilities of the Bengali kinship system are symbolised by the fact that in Bengali there are fifty-three different terms for a relative while in English we use a basic dozen terms.

In 1994, Sean Newsom interviewed Soyful Alom, a 35-year-old Bengali, married with three children and living in Tower Hamlets. He lived just along the street from his parents and his brothers lived nearby. Soyful saw all seventeen members of these households as living together. They ate together in the evening and Soyful's father decided how much each earner should contribute to joint costs and large expenditures, such as financing Soyful's brother to start a restaurant.

A Hindu family in Bradford.

Ethnic Minorities in Britain (1997) found that the traditional parentally organised marriage is in decline. Consultation and negotiation are now prevalent. Most young Hindus and Sikhs are now, at least in their own estimation, the final arbiters in the choice of their marriage partner. Muslims are the group most likely to marry a cousin. Among younger, married Pakistanis, 64 per cent were married to a cousin.

Case study: the Biraderi and Pakistani families in Britain

The word 'Biraderi' is derived from Biradar, brother, and it means the clan of men who can trace their relationship to a common ancestor. As Muhammad Anwar has written, in *The Myth of Return: Pakistanis in Britain* (1979):

> From the point of view of residence, job selection, reciprocal services and other related matters in Pakistani families, the Biraderi networks play an important role. In fact the whole way of life of Pakistanis is directly or indirectly related to this institution.

In his survey of Pakistanis in Rochdale, Lancashire, Anwar was told by Mr M.S. how he was 'sponsored', or helped, by his relatives:

> 'I did not do anything, my relative Mr A.A. arranged my ticket through agents in Pakistan. He arranged my accommodation, food and job in the mill where he had worked for three years. Later my brother came to join us along with other relatives. We live like a Biraderi, as an extension of our Biraderi in Pakistan. This is the only way to be safe, successful and happy in this strange country.'

Almost 90 per cent of the Pakistanis interviewed in Anwar's survey had found their jobs with the help of a friend or relative.

Almost 80 per cent had obtained help from friends or relatives either to pay the whole price of a house or to pay a substantial deposit to bring down the size of the monthly mortgage repayments. Relatives have an obligation to help in order to maintain the *izzet* (prestige) of their Biraderi. Further examples of the way that the kinship network of the Biraderi offers support are also given by Anwar:

> ... a daughter of one person in the Biraderi is treated as a daughter of the whole Biraderi and this feeling is shown particularly at the time of marriage ceremonies. ...

> In Pakistanis communities, there appears to be an order of preference for appeal for help: family, Biraderi, fellow villagers, friends, neighbours, other Pakistanis and the rest of society. For example, if one needed to fill in an official form or go to an office for some reason, one would look to one's family first. If nobody was able to help, one would consider the Biraderi members, and so on.

When a Kenyan Asian and a Pakistani stood as Labour and Liberal candidates in the 1972 local elections in Rochdale, both candidates used the Biraderi organisation to mobilise support.

The Greek Cypriot family

Greek Cypriot families in Britain also tend to show a closeness within the extended kinship network. When a daughter marries in Cyprus, her parents traditionally provide accommodation for the newly-weds, often by building a flat above the parents' bungalow. A second daughter can be provided for by building a second storey. This wedding gift is not quite like a dowry since the property is owned by the daughter.

Many Greek Cypriots in Britain continue the pattern of married daughters living near their parents. And, although relatives do not always live nearby or work in the same businesses, close contact is often maintained by grandparents looking after the children of working mothers. Life in the Greek

Orthodox Church also keeps extended families in regular contact. Apart from meeting at weekly worship and festivals like Christmas, Easter and the Feast of the Assumption, families often meet at annual memorial services for close relatives. Also, they usually have 'open house' for aunts, uncles and cousins on 'name days' – the saint's day of the saint after whom a person has been named is as important as that person's birthday.

Even if Greek Cypriots in Britain have not returned to Cyprus for many years, they will almost certainly find many relatives eager to offer generous hospitality when they visit. It would bring dishonour on the family if anyone was reluctant to fulfil the obligation to entertain even quite distant relatives. The honour of the family's name can also be threatened if there is a hint of a daughter getting a bad reputation. Although marriages are not exactly 'arranged', suitors are often carefully selected from 'good Greek families'.

The West Indian family

In 1991, just over 50 per cent of mothers in the West Indian ethnic group in Britain were lone mothers. Fifty-nine per cent of Afro-Caribbean lone parents had paid work compared to 38 per cent of lone parents in the general population. There is a tradition of vigorous, active and self-supporting single mothers in the West Indian community. The 1984 *Black and White Britain* survey found that:

> West Indians tend to wait longer in life before setting up married or cohabiting partnerships: this is evidenced by the fact that overall 40 per cent of West Indian households contain a single adult alone or a lone parent with children under 16. It is not uncommon for West Indian women to have children in their late teens and twenties and to wait until much later to establish a marital or cohabiting household. It would be wrong, however, to characterise lone parents as predominantly young. Four-fifths of West Indian lone parents are aged 25 or over.

This pattern of family life is common in Jamaica where in 1960 the average age at marriage was 31 for women and 25 for men. Studies of Jamaica in the 1950s found only a quarter of households based on a formal marriage with another quarter consisting of common-law marriages or **consensual unions** where the partners live together without being legally united by a formal marriage. This leaves half of all households falling into a third category, called **female-dominated**. Here children may live with their mother in a single-parent family or, while mother goes out to work, female relatives may take on the roles of both missing parents.

Four factors have been suggested to explain the Caribbean tradition of families with absentee fathers:

1   The African slaves brought to work on the plantations in the West Indies were usually forbidden to marry. A slave's children automatically became the property of the mother's owner.

2   These slaves brought West African cultural traditions of **matrifocal extended families** in which family life was focused on the mother.

3   Since the ending of slavery, men in the West Indies have often lacked stable and regular employment. They have been unable to offer adequate economic support to their partners and many have had to migrate to find work. This has made them reluctant to enter into settled marriages and so

adult males have been 'marginal' to the family. In Barbados in 1921 male migration meant that there were only 526 males for every 1,000 females.

Suzanne Lyn-Cook has pointed out that when young West Indian men in Britain look at the discrimination they face, 'it doesn't give them the feeling that they have got a secure future, and that doesn't encourage them to rush into setting up conventional family units'.

4   A fourth factor is the way that our welfare system works. If an unmarried mother cohabits with her child's father, or any other man, then he is assumed to be supporting her and she loses her entitlement to Income Support payments. This same pattern in the USA, where 36 per cent of the black population is in poverty, has led Farley to talk of the 'feminisation of poverty'. His 1984 figures show that black Americans have a 56 per cent illegitimacy rate with 47 per cent of US black households headed by females. He concludes that the welfare payments of the Aid to Families with Dependent Children actually encourage desertion by fathers.

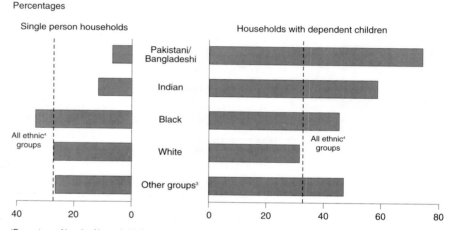

Households: by ethnic group of head of household[1], 1997[2] (Source: Social Trends, 1998.)

[1]Percentage of heads of households in each ethnic group living in each household type.
[2]Combined quarters: Spring 1996 to Winter 1996–97.
[3]Includes those of mixed origin.
[4]Includes ethnic group not stated.

Conclusion

The family persists. But when we look more closely at this enduring social institution we find a diversity of family types. For example, a special minority of families not so far mentioned are those with fostered or adopted children: over 20,000 children are adopted each year and over 20,000 are temporarily placed with foster parents.

Among the many types of family, the extended family is by no means dead. Mutual support between generations at times of birth, marriage or death, or when raising funds for a first mortgage, is so common that the modern family has been described as a **modified extended family**.

Smaller families mean fewer uncles and aunts. Greater life expectancy and younger marriage mean that young grandparents, in their late forties or early fifties when their first grandchildren are born, can expect to live to see their great-grandchildren. These four-generation families mean that **kinship networks** become 'narrower but deeper'.

Reconstituted families offer the chance to widen this narrow kinship network. Remarriage creates a form of blended family so that an additional extended family can appear overnight with the arrival of a step-parent.

In 1991, 36 per cent of all marriages involved partners who had been married before. This popularity of remarriage supports the numerous surveys that show that marriage generally increases one's happiness. Married people are much more likely to say that they are happy than single people.

GCSE question from Southern Examining Group 1996

Study Item A and B. Then answer *all* parts of the question which follow.

Item A

Distribution of domestic duties between partners

Have conjugal roles really changed in the last 20 years?

From Ken Browne, *An Introduction to Sociology* (Polity Press)

Item B

Sharing home/child duties with spouse

Married women managers were asked the question:
'How do you share the home/child duties with your husband?'

The table below lists their responses.

	Percentage giving response
I do more and it bothers me.	42
I do more and it does not bother me.	16
We share 50:50	39
He does more.	3

From C Cooper and M Davidson, *High Pressure: Working Lives of Women Managers* (Polity Press)

(a) According to the information in Item A,

   (i) name *one* traditionally female domestic role that the woman is carrying out; (1)

   (ii) name the traditionally male domestic role to which the man is referring. (1)

(b) According to the information in Item B,

   (i) what percentage of women managers said they were bothered that they did more home/child duties than their husbands? (1)

   (ii) what percentage of husbands carried out more home/child duties than their manager wives? (1)

(c) Name *two* different types of family structure found in Britain today. (2)

(d) (i) What is meant by the term, 'segregated conjugal roles'? (1)

   (ii) Explain why conjugal role relationships in Britain have changed this century. (3)

(e) (i) Identify *one* reason why there are more divorced people in Britain today than there were at the beginning of this century. (1)

   (ii) Explain the possible effects of divorce on family life. (3)

GCSE question from Southern Examining Group 1997

To what extent have the roles of husbands and wives changed in the last 40 years? (10)

CHAPTER 6

Population

Changes in the population.

Definitions

This chapter is about **demography**: the study of the size, structure and development of human populations. Before we focus on the ways that Britain's population has changed, we need to define some important terms:

Birth rate   The number of live births per 1,000 persons of all ages in one year.

Fertility rate   The number of births per year per 1,000 women of child-bearing age (15–44).

Death rate   The number of deaths per 1,000 living members of a population per year.

Rate of natural increase   The birth rate minus the death rate.

Infant mortality rate   The number of deaths of infants under 1 year old per 1,000 live births per year.

Burden of dependency   This refers to the total numbers in non-working age groups compared to the numbers in working age groups.

Emigration   People leaving the country to live in another country.

Immigration   People coming to live in the country from another country.

Net migration   The number of people immigrating minus the number of people emigrating.

1   Population growth and the census

It took from 'the beginning' until about 1830 for the human population of the world to reach its first thousand million. The following figures show the years taken to add each extra billion, with UN projections for future years:

World population	Year	Number of years taken to add extra billion
1,000 million	1830	
2,000 million	1925	95
3,000 million	1960	35
4,000 million	1974	14
5,000 million	1987	13
6,000 million	Est. 1999	12
7,000 million	Est. 2010	11
8,000 million	Est. 2022	12

The growth of the world's population may slow down in the second decade of the twenty-first century. Britain's population growth slowed down over a century earlier, due to a decrease in birth rates.

The four stages of Britain's population growth

Stage	Years	Birth rate	Death rate	Population growth
1	to 1750	High	High	Slow, to 8 million
2	1750–1880	Stable	Falling	Fast, to 26 million
3	1880–1930	Falling	Falling	Slower, to 40 million
4	1930–1990	Low	Low	Slow, to 57 million

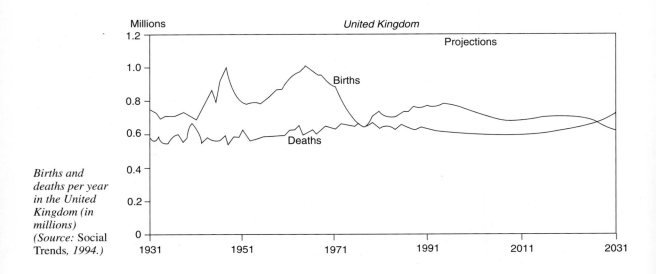

Births and deaths per year in the United Kingdom (in millions) (Source: Social Trends, 1994.)

Changes in the UK's total population size are caused by three factors: numbers of births, numbers of deaths and net migration. The numbers entering and leaving the country are monitored and all births and deaths have to be registered. This creates a running total of the size of the population. A further check is made every ten years when the whole population is counted in the census.

The census

The 1991 UK population figure of 57,801,000 is the number who were present when the 1991 census was conducted. This survey has been held every ten years since 1801 (except 1941) and since 1951 it has been taken on a Sunday evening in April. This time of year has been chosen because few people are away on holiday in April, yet the weather is not too bad for those who have to walk from door to door collecting the census forms. Each household has to fill in a form giving details about those in the house that night. Those in hospitals, hotels, prisons and boarding schools are also counted and the police try to find all those sleeping rough out of doors.

The figures are very useful to the government which has to forecast how much will need to be spent in the future on providing benefits such as pensions and facilities such as maternity hospitals. The pages of past census returns can also give us a good picture of changes in family size and patterns of **geographical mobility** (internal migration from one part of the country to another).

A page from the 1871 census.

Case study: the 1871 census

The following transcript is taken from the 1871 census for Osborne Road in Hornsey, North London (at that time part of Middlesex):

House number	Name and surname of each person	Relation to head of family	Age	Rank, profession or occupation	Where born
9	Charles Walkden	Head	27	Rail Clerk	Wiltshire
	Harriet Walkden	Wife	30		Hertfordshire
	Percy Walkden	Son	2		Middx
	Harriet Walkden	Daughter	1		Middx
	George Hunt	Boarder	22	Rail Clerk	Hampshire
	Eliza Parker	Servant	15	General Servant	Hertfordshire
11	John McMillan	Head	31	Tea Merchant	Scotland
	Elizabeth McMillan	Wife	29		London
	Arthur McMillan	Son	8 m		London
13	Richard Bullimore	Head	39	Accountant	Lincolnshire
	Louisa Bullimore	Wife	25		Middx
	Richard Bullimore	Son	8	Scholar	Middx
	William Bullimore	Son	6	Scholar	Middx
	Marion Bullimore	Daughter	5	Scholar	Middx
	Annie Bullimore	Sister	28	Farmer's daughter	Lincolnshire
	Mary Hayward	Servant	26	Domestic Servant	Hampshire
15	John Davison	Head	27	Commercial Clerk	Middx
	Alice M. Davison	Wife	21		Middx
	Alice S. Davison	Daughter	1		Herts
	Amy Richardson	Servant	22	Nursery Governess	Essex
	Elizabeth Dowdell	Servant	21	General Servant	Wiltshire

Data-response exercise: the 1871 census

1 How old was Harriet Walkden senior at the time of the 1871 census?

2 How many children lived at 13, Osborne Road, Hornsey?

3 How old was Louisa Bullimore when she gave birth to her first child?

4 What evidence is there that middle-class people lived in Osborne Road?

5 What evidence is there to show the extent of migration to London from other parts of the country?

2 Reasons for the fall in average family size

From 1871 to 1931, the birth rate more than halved from thirty-three to sixteen. In the 1970s it fell to twelve. The average number of children per family fell as follows:

1860s	6.16
1880s	4.81
1900s	3.30
1930s	2.06

By 1944 there was anxiety that the birth rate had fallen too low and so a Royal Commission on Population was set up. One of its recommendations was to encourage more births by giving mothers a family allowance, now called child benefit. The Commission's 1949 report included the following survey figures which clearly show how family size fell first among the middle classes:

Husband's occupation	Number of live births per woman first married in:	
	1900–9	1920–24
Professional	2.33	1.75
All groups combined average	3.53	2.42
Unskilled labourers	4.45	3.35

We now look at four of the major reasons for the fall of the birth rate in Britain over the last hundred years.

The availability of birth control

The intra-uterine device was invented in ancient times when pregnancy in camels was prevented by placing pebbles in their wombs. The ancient Egyptians described many methods of contraception and in the seventeenth century Cassanova used sheaths or condoms made from the intestinal membrane of the cow.

In the nineteenth century, the new discipline of economics was christened 'the dismal science' because of the gloomy predictions of *Essay on the Principle of Population*. This was written by Thomas Malthus in 1798 and claimed that population grows by **geometric progression** (that is 2, 4, 8, 16, 32) while food production can only increase by **arithmetic progression** (that is, 2, 4, 6, 8, 10). One effect of the ideas of Malthus was the ending of Parish Relief. These handouts to the destitute dated from the Elizabethan Poor Laws but they were seen as encouraging large families and so they were replaced by Victorian workhouses. In these institutions husbands were separated from their wives and children and forced to work.

Malthus only recommended later marriage as a means to avoid over-population but during the 1820s and 1830s a number of leaflets and books were published advocating pessaries (vaginal sponges) and douching (flush-

Eleven children were not uncommon in a Victorian family.

ing of the vagina) with mixtures of chemicals such as salt, zinc, sulphate, vinegar, alum, quinine, tannin, opium, prussic acid, iodine, alcohol, carbolic acid and strychnine.

Some of the landmarks in the history of birth control are:

1843   Vulcanised rubber was introduced for the sheath and cervical cap.

1877   A banned contraceptive advice pamphlet was republished by two radical reformers, Annie Besant and Charles Bradlaugh, MP. They deliberately invited prosecution to create publicity about birth control and they succeeded. Their trial and appeal attracted national press coverage with public donations paying their £1,000 legal costs.

1880s   The vaginal diaphragm, or Dutch cap, was given wide circulation in clinics in Holland.

1914   Marie Stopes wrote the first of several family planning booklets. Called *Married Love*, half a million copies were sold by 1924 and Stopes went on to set up the first birth control clinics in Britain.

1950s   The oral contraceptive, 'the pill', and the modern intra-uterine device, the IUD or 'coil', were introduced.

1974   Contraceptives became free on the National Health Service (NHS) to all women, married or single.

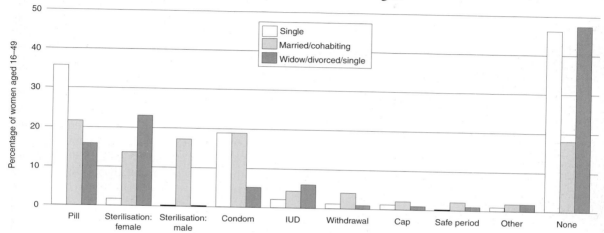

Current use of contraception by marital status: Great Britain, 1995 (Source: 'Living in Britain 1995', General Household Survey.)

The falling infant mortality rate

The infant mortality rate is the number of deaths per 1,000 live births before the age of one. It has fallen from 154 in 1851 to below seven in the 1990s.

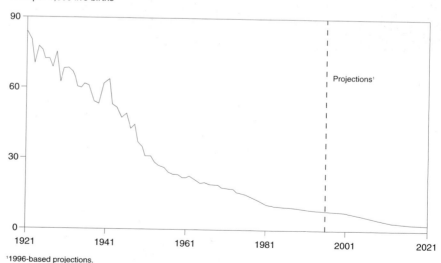

UK infant mortality rate per 1,000 live births (Source: Social Trends, 1998.)

Between the 1840s and the 1890s, the mortality rate for children aged five to nine halved from 9 to 4.3. There was less risk that a child in each family would fail to survive to adulthood and so parents no longer needed to allow for such risks by having 'extra' births.

Economic motivations

Early pioneers, such as Annie Besant, tried to popularise birth control among working-class women as a means of reducing poverty. However, before compulsory education, child labour meant that each additional child could bring in extra income to the household. And, before the development of pension schemes and welfare services for the elderly, children were seen as an insurance policy: a means to provide for their parents' old age.

Children are now an economic liability rather than an asset to their parents. A study in 1985 estimated that the typical mother can expect to lose £49,000 in life-time earnings as a result of raising two children. This figure is based on the average mother who loses nine years of full-time work, partially offset by three years of part-time earnings, and who also falls behind in promotion prospects.

In *Prosperity and Parenthood*, J. A. Banks has argued that the middle classes were first to adopt widespread family limitation in the 1880s because of economic factors such as the rising costs of school fees and servants combined with an economic depression. The next big slump occurred between the wars when unemployment rose to 20 per cent and by the 1930s working-class families had also adopted similar habits so that over 60 per cent of the population was using birth control.

This 1996 UK population pyramid shows how the economic slump in 1976 contributed to the small number of 20-year-olds in 1996, whereas the economic boom of 1964 helped to produce the large numbers of 32-year-olds. (The peak numbers of 50-year-olds is the result of the post-war 'baby boom' of 1946.) (Source: Social Trends, 1998.)

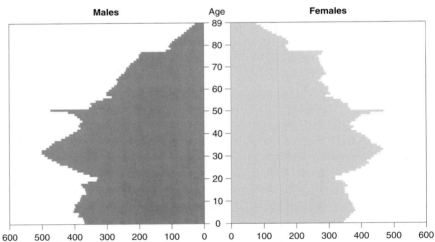

Social movitations

Changing social attitudes and norms that have affected couples' decisions on family size include secularisation, the child-centred family and **feminism**, the belief in equal rights for women. Feminism has meant that wives are better educated and more likely to want a career. Secularisation means that the Church has a declining influence. When over 60 per cent of couples were using birth control in the 1930s, this was despite the disapproval of the Churches: the Methodists did not approve of contraception until 1939; the Church of England finally sanctioned its use in 1958 and in 1968 Pope Paul VI firmly restated the Catholic opposition to artificial birth control.

If increasing numbers no longer believe in religion, then what do they believe in? Many parents see the whole point of their lives revolving around doing their best for their children and improving their standard of living. These child-centred and materialist values motivate couples to want only two or three children. After all, what's the point in having a nice new car and a smart, three-bedroomed semi-detached house if neither is big enough for all the family?

3   Britain's ageing population

Expectation of life at birth, in the UK, by sex

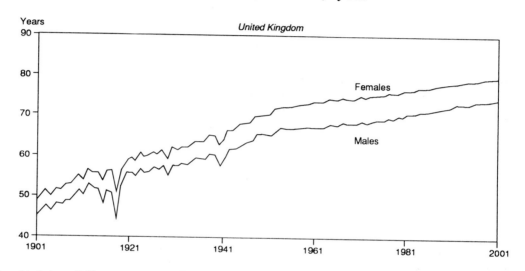

Expectation of life at birth, in the UK, by sex (Source: Social Trends, *1994.)*

Life expectancy figures show the average future life-span that new-born babies can expect to have if the death rates at the time of their birth continue. The average age of a population will rise if death rates fall (and/or birth rates fall): this produces an ageing population, with an age structure characterised by increasing proportions in older age groups. Between 1861 and 1961 the death rate in Britain halved from twenty-four to twelve.

The twentieth century saw the introduction of penicillin and antibiotics, the development of vaccines and immunisation as well as dramatic improvements in diagnostic and surgical techniques. Free personal health services for all started in 1948 through the NHS. However, the death rate had already taken its most dramatic fall during the Victorian era of public, rather than personal, health measures. Environmental health was improved by better drains and water supplies and better conditions at work, while ill-health in the home was also prevented by higher standards of diet, housing, hygiene and education.

The burden of dependency

The figures on page 100 show that the proportions of the population who were of working age were the same in 1871 and 1971. This 58 per cent had to provide the income tax, national insurance contributions and growth in economic output to support the 42 per cent of children and pensioners. Three further points need to be made:

1   The actual number employed, out of a working-age population of 35 million in 1987, was only 25 million. This is because 10 million 16- to 65-year-olds were not earning: these include full-time housewives and students, the sick and disabled, the unemployed and the early retired.

2   An increasing proportion of the dependent population are pensioners rather than children and an increasing proportion of these pensioners are very elderly. Between 1951 and 1991, the proportion of the total population who were aged 80 and over rose from 1.4 to 3.7 per cent. The over-80s are forecast to rise to 4.5 per cent by 2021. Future trends are very important for planning government spending: provision of health and social services for a person over 75 costs seven times more than for the average person of working age.

3   The number of children and pensioners per 100 people of working age was 63 in 1992. If women were to continue to retire at the age of 60, government projections are that there would be 80 children and pensioners for every 100 people of working age by 2032. But this figure drops to 71 in 2032 if the proposed common pension age of 65 is phased in from 2010.

These pie charts show that, over the last 125 years, there has been an increase in the percentage of people over retirement age.

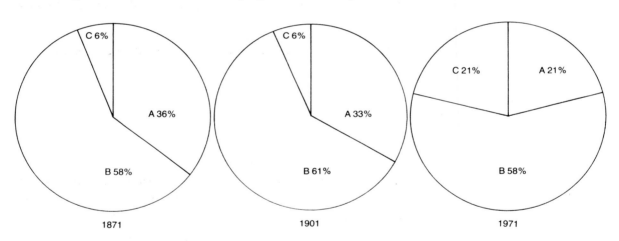

Key
A = 0 to school-leaving age
B = Working age to 60 for women and 65 for men
C = Over retirement age

The Four Ages

- The **First Age** is a period of socialisation and dependent status: childhood.
- The **Second Age** involves adult responsibility, family building and full-time employment.
- The **Third Age** may be a time of active independent life for the 'young old' (aged 50 to 74), no longer working and parenting.
- The **Fourth Age** may, for the 'old old' over 75, be a time of dependence on others. These ideas help us to avoid stereotyping all the elderly as dependent on others, as a burden on society. The experience of ageing varies according to class and gender and according to age and health. Figures on page 104 show the extent to which the 'old old' may need help from carers. The case study on page 336 describes 9 ways that the 'young old' spend their time after early retirement. In talking of the over-60s, the key word to remember is 'diversity'.

Employment in old age

We do not need to go back many generations in British society to find that most people carried on working into their old age. It is very common for the old to remain economically active in pre-industrial and early industrial societies.

Percentage of British men aged over 65 still in paid employment

Year	Percentage
1891	66
1952	33
1975	16
1992	7

It is mainly only among those in very high-status occupations that we now find the few who continue working into old age. Here are three examples:

- In 1998, 77-year-old Sir Frank Rogers went daily to his office as chairman of Reuters and director of the Telegraph Group.
- In 1998, 87-year-old Lady Barbara Castle regularly travelled from her home in Buckinghamshire to attend the House of Lords and prepare evidence for the Pensions Review Body.
- In 1997, 90-year-old Lord Eric Roll had business trips to Tokyo, Hong Kong, Boston, Paris, Vienna, Frankfurt and Rome as senior adviser to the investment bank SBC Warburg.

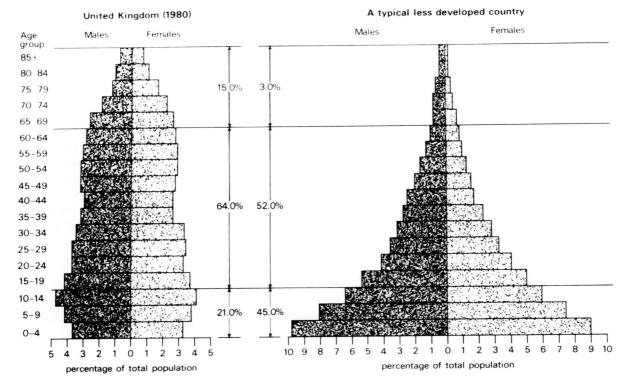

United Kingdom (1980)   A typical less developed country

A nation's age distribution changes from fir-tree-shaped to barrel-shaped as an economy matures.

The effects of divorce on the elderly

The Family Policy Studies Centre has predicted that older people will increasingly be isolated and lonely due to the rise in divorce. The following figures show that an increasing proportion of pensioners will be living alone. One result will be that fewer disabled old people will have a spouse to be their carer and so there may be increasing reliance on middle-aged daughters to be carers.

	Men		Women	
Reasons for being single	*1990*	*2025*	*1990*	*2025*
Over-65s divorced and not remarried (rising due to the increase in divorce)	2.3%	8.6%	2.6%	12.0%
Over-65s widowed (falling due to increased life expectancy)	31.0%	27.3%	58.7%	50.9%
Over-65s once married, now single (widowed plus divorced, not remarried)	33.3%	35.9%	61.3%	62.9%

Case study: the housing and health of the older population

Among the elderly, women are far more likely to live alone than men:

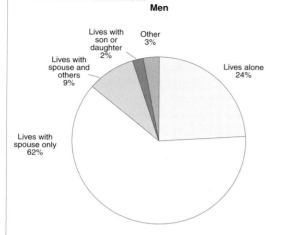

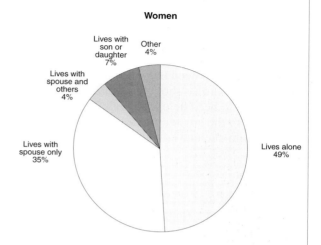

Elderly household type by sex: Great Britain, 1994 (Source: 'Living in Britain 1994', General Household Survey.*)*

Housing tenure

Despite claims made regarding the increasing wealth of retired people, the elderly in Britain are still less likely to be home-owners than the rest of the population. In 1991, 47 per cent of over-80s were in rented accommodation compared to only 25 per cent of those aged 45–59.

Residential care

The 1980s saw some big changes in the numbers of elderly people living in different types of residential and nursing homes in England:

	1980	*1992*
Local authority homes	102,890	71,369
Voluntary homes	25,449	31,483
Private homes	28,854	132,063
Total	157,193	234,915

Although there were nearly a quarter of a million people over the age of 65 in residential care in England in 1991, this was only 3 per cent of the 7.6 million elderly people in England.

Informal carers

In 1991, over 70 per cent of over-80s were women and of these over 60 per cent were living on their own. The **1990 Community Care Act**, implemented in 1993, aims to enable older and disabled people to carry on living in their own homes as long as possible. Formal domiciliary care may come in the form of home helps, district nurses or meals on wheels, provided by the local authority, the health authority or voluntary groups. But the role of unpaid carers, such as family and friends, is particularly important. Most informal carers of the elderly are women, either middle-aged daughters or pensioner wives.

The 1990 *General Household Survey* found:

- In Britain there are almost 7 million informal carers (defined as people whose lives are restricted because they have to look after someone with unusual needs).
- Seventy-nine per cent (5.4 million) are looking after someone aged 65 or over.
- Eighteen per cent (1.2 million) are themselves over 65.

A 1992 survey of members of the Carers National Association found:

- Sixty-five per cent felt that their health had suffered as a result of caring.
- Forty-seven per cent of carers had suffered financial difficulties.
- Twenty per cent had never had a break, yet 38 per cent had been caring for over ten years.

- Seventy-two per cent of carers were women and 66 per cent were over 55.

The Family Policy Studies Centre estimated, in 1992, that carers were saving the government £15–24 billion in residential home and community care costs.

The charts below show that the over-80s are far more likely to need help than the 'young old'. The charts also show that women are more likely to need help than men. This is partly due to the greater prevalence of mobility and musculo-skeletal conditions among women.

Conclusion

It is important to recognise the diversity among the 11 million or so pensioners in Britain. The

Help the Aged charity makes the following points about the above data:

The information given on the health of older people may result in a rather negative view of later life. Statistics do tend to show how many older people cannot manage a particular task, but it is worth considering how many more could manage with a little help and given an appropriately designed environment.

Older people may be more likely than the rest of the population to suffer from disability and be heavier consumers of medical services. Nevertheless, with support from community services, voluntary organisations, friends and neighbours, the majority of older people can remain independent and experience a good quality of life.

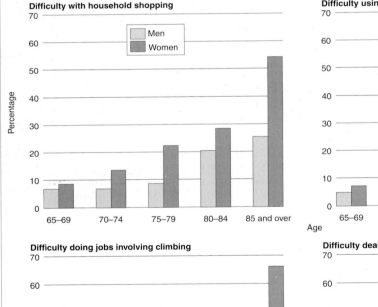
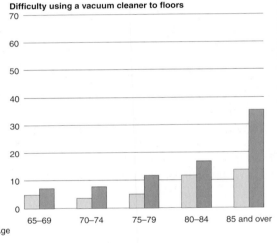
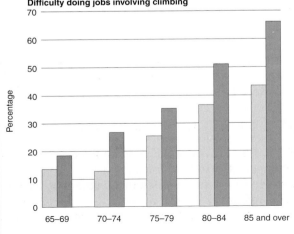
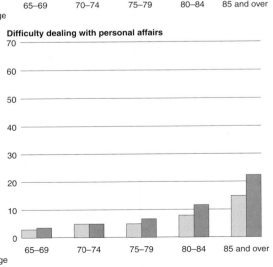

Percentage of elderly people unable to perform various tasks without help by age and sex: Great Britain, 1994 (Source: 'Living in Britain 1994', General Household Survey.)

Pensioners' get-together.

4   Internal migration patterns: urbanisation

The main reason for changes in the **geographical distribution** of the population is migration from one part of the country to another. The main shifts since 1851 can be described in three phases:

1851–1911: Rural depopulation – the drift to the cities

In 1851, 9 million people, or 54 per cent of the population of England and Wales, lived in towns and cities. By 1911, 28 million, or 80 per cent of the population, were concentrated in urban areas. The mechanisation of farm work meant a fall in demand for agricultural workers. To escape unemployment or low wages, many people left villages and moved to industrial areas.

The main parts of the country to lose population in the second half of the nineteenth century were all rural areas: the northern Pennines, the Yorkshire Wolds and the Vale of York, most of Wales outside the coalfields and a belt across the middle of England from the South-West, through the South Midlands, to East Anglia.

Apart from London and the ports of Humberside and Merseyside, the main urban areas to attract rural migrants were in South Wales, the West Midlands, South Lancashire, West and South Yorkshire, Northumberland and Durham: all fast-growing industrial areas based on coalfields.

1911–51: The growth of suburbs and the drift to the South

Some rural areas continued to lose population in the first half of this century. These included Exmoor, central Wales, northern East Anglia, the Fens, rural Lincolnshire, the Vale of Pickering, the North York Moors and the northern Pennines. But other rural areas, close to **conurbations** (or sprawling cities), gained population with the development of **dormitory suburbs** for commuters.

Areas of traditional heavy industry were hardest hit by the high unemployment of the 1930s slump. Many people left areas such as South Wales, Lancashire and North-East England as jobs disappeared in industries such as textiles, coalmining, shipbuilding and heavy engineering. Those who moved from these declining regions headed for the Midlands and the South where the growth industries between the wars included electrical engineering; the manufacture of cars, aircraft and consumer durables such as radios and refrigerators; paper making and printing; and food processing, as well as banking, finance and insurance. It has been estimated that 80 per cent of the new manufacturing plant in Britain between the wars was built around London, such as the factories of Heinz and Hoover, Firestone and Ford.

1951 onwards

The South-East's population rose from 7 million in the 1930s to 17 million in 1985. Government **regional policy** has tried to reverse the drift to the South by encouraging industry to locate in the northern and western **Celtic Fringe** and other areas of high unemployment. This can be seen if one looks at the car industry. Between the wars this was based in the Midlands and the South. But when Ford wanted to expand close to their Dagenham plant near London, the government persuaded them to build new factories in Halewood, Liverpool and Bridge End, South Wales instead. Similarly, Rootes Motors were persuaded to build a plant at Linwood in Scotland and Leyland at Bathgate in Scotland. More recently, governments have given millions of pounds to attract Delorean Cars to Belfast and Nissan to North-East England. When Nissan advertised 420 vacancies for production-line jobs at their new factory at Washington, Tyne and Wear in 1985, they received 15,000 applications.

Government policy has also encouraged **de-urbanisation** from major cities by the post-war development of new towns, such as Stevenage, Crawley, Bracknell and Harlow beyond London's Green Belt.

During the 1980s, the counties with the fastest growing populations were Buckinghamshire, Cambridgeshire, Cornwall and Dorset. All four of these counties had a population growth of more than 1 per cent a year on average between 1981 and 1991. During the same 10 years, the largest fall in population, 9 per cent, occurred in Belfast. The main areas with falling population tend to be metropolitan areas (areas dominated by a large city or cities). The urban-to-rural shift, also termed **counter-urbanisation**, is shown in the following figures:

Population changes in England and Wales, 1971–91

	1971–81	*1981–91*
Greater London Boroughs	−10.1%	−4.8%
Major cities outside London	−10.0%	−7.4%
Districts containing new towns	+15.1%	+6.1%
Resort and retirement areas	+4.9%	+5.2%
Smaller urban and mixed urban/ rural districts	+7.6%	+3.4%
Remoter, mainly rural districts	+10.2%	+6.4%

(Source: School of Urban and Regional Studies, Sheffield Hallam University, from the 1991 Census of Population)

Activities

Half of all families in the USA move house every five years. Conduct a small-scale suvey to find out how frequently a group, such as fellow students, have moved house. Ask the respondents to list their reasons for moving and the disadvantages that they have experienced as a result of moving.

Case study: rural stress

It is sometimes said that London is made up of lots of urban villages. This may be particularly true of the more settled traditional working-class areas where community life may involve frequent contact among extended kin, as depicted in the TV soap *EastEnders*. The urban-to-rural shift in population is partly due to those looking for friendly village life who think that it only exists in rural villages. In fact, rural life may be more likely than urban life to involve isolation, loneliness and stress.

Farmers are twice as likely as the general population to kill themselves. Malcom Whitaker is a volunteer for the helpline called Farming Friends. In the three villages near his Gloucestershire farm there are only 6 farmworkers, whereas at one time there were 60. Incomers have bought the farm cottages. They are fairly wealthy retired people, commuters or weekenders. Whitaker describes the loss of community life: 'There's no shop and no post office and just one pub for passing trade on the main road. One of my neighbours died 2 years ago, and it was 6 months before I heard about it. He was a stockbroker.'

In 1998, 71 per cent of English villages had no daily bus service, 93 per cent had no rail service, 83 per cent lacked a permanent GP and only half had a post office and a school.

Some of the men who had spent all their working life at the East Moors steelworks in Cardiff were also employed to help demolish it.

5   External migration patterns

What is meant by 'the English'?

For many centuries the population of England has included numerous surnames of Irish, Welsh and Scottish origin. The earliest English towns attracted migrants from the north and west, from the Celtic Fringes of the British Isles. Successive waves of settlers also came from the south and east, from across the Channel and the North Sea.

The last time that English was successfully invaded was in 1066 by the French led by William the Conqueror, Duke of Normandy. But before the Normans, invaders included Saxons from Germany; Vikings and Danes from Scandinavia; and soldiers from all over the Roman Empire, including most of the countries around the Mediterranean.

Many people would consider that the royal family is one of the most English of institutions. But the 'English' monarchy has included kings and queens from France, Scotland, Holland and Germany. Queen Victoria's husband was German and the present Queen's husband was born in Greece. It is sometimes said that Richard III, who lost his throne to the Welsh Tudors, was the last English king.

Push and pull factors and refugees

It could be argued that all English people have immigrant ancestors since everyone left England around 70,000 BC, at the start of the Ice Age, leaving no population at all until seasonal hunting groups 'immigrated' around

40,000 BC. Settlers have continued to arrive over the centuries. Most have been attracted by economic prospects – the chance to improve their standard of living (**pull factors**); some have been refugees escaping from economic desolation, such as famines, or driven from their homes by religious and political persecution (**push factors**).

In the 1990s, refugees, such as Bosnians and Somalis, have come to Britain from a number of countries torn apart by civil war. Another refugee group, over many different years, has been the Jews.

Jewish immigrants

Most of the Jewish community in medieval England followed the Norman invaders from France. After terrible persecution, all 16,000 Jews were expelled from England in 1290. The first to return in the seventeenth century were Sephardic Jews escaping from the Catholic Inquisition in Spain and Portugal. By 1800, 4,000 or so of these had been joined by some 20,000 Ashkenazi Jews from Eastern Europe who were mainly poorer and spoke Yiddish – a mixture of Hebrew and German.

At this time Britain provided a haven for nearly 80,000 refugees from the civil war in France which followed the French Revolution. This began a tradition, which continued throughout Victorian times, of Britain providing a safe refuge for many political exiles, such as the German revolutionary, Karl Marx. This reputation for providing asylum for victims of persecution was severely tested when Jewish refugees arrived again in 1882. By 1914 120,000 destitute Jews had arrived from the Russian Empire where they had been the victims of anti-semitic pogroms – campaigns of terror against Jewish communities. Many of these settled in the slums of London's East End where, in the 1930s, they were to face street battles with the 'black-shirts' of Oswald Mosley's British Union of Fascists Party.

Britain's tolerant 'open door' policy began to change with the Aliens Acts of 1905 and 1920. These restrictive laws meant that a special case had to be made to allow in 4,000 Basque children in 1937 (victims of the Spanish Civil War) and 10,000 Jewish children in 1938 (victims of the German Nazis). Many of these children left behind parents who perished in Fascist atrocities.

The history of Jewish immigration to Britain illustrates the combination of push and pull factors which can cause migration. Many were 'pulled' by Britain's 'open door' and most were 'pushed' by persecution – like the 50,000 Huguenots (French Protestants) who sought refuge from Catholic victim-isation in the 1680s and like the 5 million Irish (half the population of Ireland) who were forced by starvation to emigrate, mainly to England, Scotland or America, between 1820 and 1920.

Emigration from Britain

Despite the thousands of arrivals mentioned above, nineteenth-century Britain had an outward flow of net migration (immigration minus emigration). Between 1881 and 1921, for instance, there was a net loss of population of between 2 and 3 per cent a year. Most of the 2,278,000 British emigrants who left between 1861 and 1911 went to the USA, South Africa and the **Old Commonwealth** colonies which became self-governing dominions in 1931, such as Canada, Australia and New Zealand.

In these countries the white settlers often took the lands of the native peoples such as the Inuit, Zulus, Aborigines, Maoris and Native Americans. Except in South Africa, the whites came to form the majorities in these lands. One Maori has estimated that if the white descendants of these British emigrants were suddenly 'repatriated' and sent back to the British Isles, then 20 million people would arrive at Heathrow airport. (In the USA alone, 40 million Americans give their ethnic origin as Irish.)

The larger part of the British Empire developed into the **New Commonwealth**: the colonies mainly in Africa, the West Indies and the Indian sub-continent where the white soldiers, missionaries and plantation owners only formed a small part of the population. After bitter struggles, these nations gained independence following the Second World War – many not until the 1960s.

'The Last of England' by Ford Madox Brown (City Art Gallery and Museum, Birmingham). The subject of this painting, for which the artist used himself, his wife Emma and their child as models, was suggested by the departure of Thomas Wooler as an emigrant to Australia in 1852.

The net outward flow of the nineteenth century continued into the twentieth, as these figures for net civilian migration show:

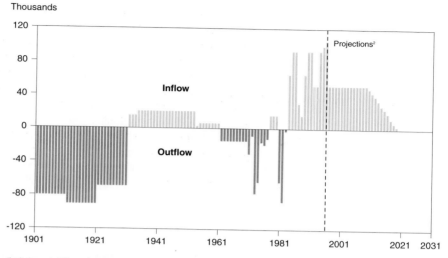

Net international migration[1]
(*Source:* Social Trends, 1997.)

[1]Includes net civilian migration and other adjustments. Ten year averages are used before 1931 and between 1951 and 1971. A twenty year average is used between 1931 and 1950. Data prior to 1971 are for calendar years, data after 1971 are mid-year estimates and projections.
[2]1994-based projections.

Post-war immigration from the New Commonwealth

Immigrants from the New Commonwealth have included refugees from Cyprus and students from West Africa, but the largest groups have come from the West Indies and India and Pakistan. The pattern of immigration of these largest groups can be described in three phases:

1 Push and pull factors in the 1950s   The obvious push factors were the poverty and unemployment that many people experienced in the Caribbean and the Indian sub-continent, while a strong pull factor was the large number of unfilled job vacancies in Britain. Additional factors included the following:

(a)   West Indian emigrants were restricted from their first choice of destination, the USA, after 1952.

(b)   The partition of India in 1947 split border areas, such as Punjab, with Pakistan. This disruption encouraged many to leave.

(c)   In the heyday of the British Empire, a quarter of the world's population were British subjects and so, automatically, were also British citizens. The 1948 Nationality Act confirmed that Commonwealth citizens remained British.

(d)   Very low enemployment in Britain in the 1950s created a labour shortage so that recruiting teams were sent to Jamaica, Barbados and Pakistan from London Transport, hospitals, textile mills, restaurants and hotels.

2 The peak in the early 1960s   By the 1960s, British politicians began to decide that they could no longer welcome unlimited immigration to the 'Mother Country' from the coloured New (rather than white Old) Commonwealth. While Acts were passed outlawing racial discrimination

Immigrants from the West Indies arriving in Britain in 1962.

in 1965, 1968 and 1976, many claim that British governments were, at the same time, blatantly racist themselves: they introduced Immigration Acts in 1962, 1968, 1971 and 1981 which were basically designed to take away the rights of British passport holders if they were black rather than white. It was the rush to enter before the first restrictions were imposed in 1962 which caused the peak in the immigration figures in 1961.

3   The falling flow of dependants   Entry vouchers for workers coming to Britain, introduced by the 1962 Commonwealth Immigration Act, were reduced so much in the 1960s that, by 1973, 90 per cent of New Commonwealth immigrants were wives, children and older parents joining men already here. This flow of dependants has since fallen.

Recent patterns of net migration

Migration between the UK and other members of the European Union (EU) has become increasingly important. In 1990, 876,000 citizens of other EU countries were resident in the UK. Over two-thirds were Irish. On the other hand, 392,000 UK citizens were living in other EU countries. The most popular EU nations were Germany (86,000) and Spain (78,000).

Another increasingly important pattern of international migration is the number of applicants seeking asylum, a safe haven to escape from persecution in their own lands. The UK received 44,840 applications for asylum in 1991. Sixty per cent of the applicants were from Africa and 30 per cent from Asia. Only 4,680 applicants were deemed to have a well-founded fear of persecution and were granted asylum.

Consider the pros and cons of the following proposals. In 1994, an organisation of different churches in Europe proposed that the member nations of the European Union should rethink their attitude to the large numbers of people wanting to migrate to EU countries, mainly from Eastern Europe and Africa. Rather than costly operations to halt illegal immigration, it was proposed that the EU should put resources into planning for a million new immigrants every year. The population of the USA is less than that of the EU and the USA absorbs around a million immigrants a year.

In 1994 the Institute for Public Policy Research report, *Strangers and Citizens*, argued that Britain's strict controls on immigration were 'disproportionate' to the harm they were intended to address. The report suggested that the controls created unnecessary barriers to income-generating overseas students, tourists and skilled entrepreneurs.

Some people have referred to 'the problem of coloured immigrants'. It is more accurate to refer to the problems created by the racial prejudice of the host population. We take a closer look at the ethnic minorities within the UK and the issue of racism in our next chapter.

GCSE question from Southern Examining Group 1997

Read Item A. Then answer *all* parts of the question which follow.

Item A

The villages in farming areas are dying. Shops that once served the farming communities are closing. The people who live in these villages work in the towns. They do their shopping in supermarkets on the way home.

There are no buses or a very limited (poor) service. When the people who work in the cities start their families and stay at home more, they realise how few facilities there are.

Adapted from an article by Louise Auty, *Wharfedale Newspapers* (November 1993)

(a) (i)   According to Item A, why are the village shops closing?   (1)

   (ii)   According to Item A, when do the people who work in the towns and cities realise that there are so few facilities?   (1)

   (iii)   Suggest *one* reason why people who work in towns and cities might choose to live in rural villages.   (1)

(b) (i)   Suggest *two* reasons for the growth in the population of towns and cities in the nineteenth century.   (2)

   (ii)   Identify and describe *one* way in which this growth affected the social relationships of people living in towns.   (2)

(c) (i)   Explain what is meant by 'urbanisation'.   (2)

   (ii)   State *two* problems caused by people leaving the inner cities to live elsewhere.   (2)

(d) (i)   What kind of age structure is likely to be found in a seaside town on the south coast of England? Explain why this is.   (3)

   (ii)   State *one* problem that such an age structure may cause for a community.   (1)

CHAPTER 7 | Ethnic minorities and racism

The spectre of prejudice is lying in wait.

Throughout history societies have been divided and human beings have persecuted and oppressed each other for a variety of reasons. Religion, sex, social class, age, nationality and race have all been, and indeed still are, the grounds upon which one group inflicts suffering on another.

One might be tempted to think that human beings are cursed with the inability to get on with one another and that the desire to persecute others simply because they are different in some way is a fixed part of human nature. Such a conclusion would, however, be mistaken for human nature is not something which is fixed, that does not allow for growth and change. Thus, some forms of persecution and oppression that existed in the past have to a certain extent been eliminated from our society. For example, the idea that women are inferior has been challenged. And homosexuals are another group that now experience far less persecution than in the past.

One type of persecution and oppression which is still the cause of tremendous suffering is racism. We begin this chapter by attempting to define racism and explain its causes.

1 What is racism?

We can define **racism** as prejudice or discrimination which is determined by the belief that one race is superior to other races. We now look more closely at three aspects of this definition.

Prejudice

Prejudices are pre-judgements which people will not modify in the light of new experience. For example, someone might hold a mentally rigid view that all young football supporters are hooligans. If this person then met a large number of polite, well-behaved young football fans but was unwilling to shift from his or her original view, then we could call this person prejudiced. A typical prejudiced viewpoint is that 'all women are awful drivers'.

Discrimination

When people, such as club doormen, are racially prejudiced and use their power to the detriment of particular groups, for example refusing admission to black youths, then they are discriminating. **Racial discrimination** occurs when a racist idea becomes a racist action. **Racial prejudice** is sometimes called 'passive racism'. Active discrimination may be on an open, individual level or it may operate on a hidden institutional level.

Institutional racism

The 1985 Swann Report defined institutional racism as 'a range of long established systems, practices and procedures which have the effect, if not the intention, of depriving ethnic minority groups of equality of opportunity and access to society's resources'. Institutional racism may be found in the following aspects of school life: admissions, setting, subject choice, curriculum, assessment, exam entries, career advice, staff appointments and provision for pupils with English as their second language.

Another example of institutional racism is the administration of justice. Research by a leading criminologist, Dr Roger Hood, of Oxford University, has found that in some courts black male defendants receive heavier sentences than whites found guilty of the same offence. Although black people make up only 5 per cent of the general population, they comprise 16 per cent of the male prison population. One reason may be because probation officers are less willing to offer to courts that they will supervise black clients on non-custodial sentences.

Racism and Nazi Germany

To understand fully the meaning of racism it is helpful to look at an historical example of a society which was openly racist and which took racism to an extreme conclusion.

The racial doctrines of the Nazi Party   Nazi ideas rested on the belief that races are fundamentally unequal and that superior races have the right to oppress and enslave inferior races. They believed that the Jews were one of the lowest races while the Germans were part of the Aryan master race. As is the case with racists, the Nazis created physical and cultural stereotypes of races. The Northern European Aryans were supposed to be tall, blond-haired and blue-eyed. It was claimed that they were superior because they were responsible for all the great cultural achievements of humankind.

The Jews, on the other hand, were stereotyped in a completely negative and unappealing manner. Physically, they were caricatured as deformed, dirty and ugly. Culturally, they were presented as destroyers of civilisation. The Nazis believed that the Aryan race would only retain its superiority if it avoided intermarriage with other races and if it conquered the inferior races.

In 1998, 6,000 extreme right-wing German neo-Nazis paraded in Leipzig.

The racist laws of the Nazi Government   When the Nazi Party, led by Hitler, took over the government of Germany in 1933, it immediately set about the systematic persecution of the Jewish people. Jews were banned from government jobs and all Jews were made to wear badges. Jewish shops and businesses had the Star of David painted on them and Germans were encouraged to boycott them.

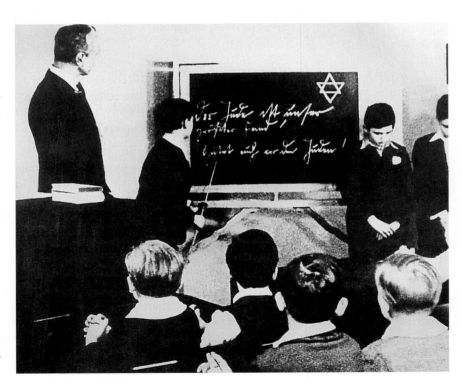

A classroom in Nazi Germany. While two Jewish boys face their class, another pupil reads from the blackboard: 'The Jew is our greatest enemy. Beware of the Jew!'

In 1935 the Nuremberg laws were passed which took away all the rights of the Jews in Germany. They were deprived of German citizenship, forbidden to marry non-Jews, banned from serving in the army or practising medicine. Jews could not be teachers, farmers, journalists, lawyers or artists. By 1938, 20,000 Jews had been placed in concentration camps.

The 'Final Solution' The next and last step in the persecution of the Jews was what Hitler called the 'Final Solution'. This took place during the Second World War and involved the extermination not only of German Jews but of Jews living in all the countries that the Nazis had conquered. The intention was genocide, the deliberate destruction of a people, and 6 million Jews died in the Nazi 'Holocaust'.

It must also be remembered that the Nazi invasion of Russia, which led to the death of at least 10 million Russian soldiers and a further 10 million Russian civilians, was partly prompted by the Nazi belief that the Slavic races were inferior and ought to be enslaved by the Aryans. The Nazi experience horrifically illustrates what racism can lead to.

Case study: declining racial prejudice in Britain

The following findings come from the *British Social Attitudes* surveys.

How would you describe yourself ... as very prejudiced against people of other races, a little prejudiced or not prejudiced at all?

	1983 (%)	1991 (%)
Very prejudiced	4	2
A little prejudiced	31	29
Not prejudiced at all	64	68

% of respondents minding 'a little' or 'a lot':

	1983	1991
Person of West Indian origin:		
... as boss	20	12
... in the family	57	44
Person of Asian origin:		
... as boss	19	14
... in the family	51	43

(Source: *British Social Attitudes, the 9th Report*)

Mixed unions

Further evidence for a decline in racial prejudice may be found in the large increase in the incidence of mixed marriages, especially among Afro-Caribbeans. The 1990 *Labour Force Survey* found that 27 per cent of Afro-Caribbean married or cohabiting family heads are in a mixed union with a white person, compared to 15 per cent in 1982 and 8 per cent in 1974.

By 1997, this figure had jumped to 40 per cent, according to a national survey of 5,200 members of ethnic minorities, conducted for the Policy Studies Institute report 'Ethnic Minorities in Britain: Diversity and Disadvantage'. The report found: 'It is striking that for two out of five children with a Caribbean mother or father, their other parent was white. This was more often a black father and a white mother than the other way round.'

2   Four causes of racism

Different groups have suffered from racism for different reasons and this makes it difficult to generalise about the causes of racism. We therefore concentrate on the racism that one group, black people, have experienced and continue to experience. We now look at four different views of the origin of racism.

The idea of racial differences

Racism springs in the first place from the view that there are basic and unchangeable differences between races. This view gained widespread acceptance in the nineteenth century following the ideas of scientists, such as the Swedish zoologist Linnaeus. He divided humankind into Caucasian, Mongoloid and Negroid races. Such classifications were based on observable physical variations, colour being the most important one. Linnaeus thought that the cultural differences between races could be explained by their physical differences.

Other writers concluded that the 'superior' culture of the West was a result of the superior physical and mental features of the European races. Black people were seen as members of a biologically inferior race. While some people still hold these views, the modern science of genetics has made the idea of race meaningless. Our physical make-up depends on more than 100,000 genes and over 90 per cent of these are similar for all human beings. Physical differences between so-called races are few and superficial compared to physical similarities. A French person may be biologically more similar to an Inuit, for example having the same blood group, than to another French person.

Race is not really a scientific category. Race is more truly a social label. In some cultures ideas of race are passed on by socialisation. Sociologists prefer to use the term **ethnic group**. Membership of an ethnic group is based on shared cultural attributes, such as language, religion, diet and other customs.

Colonialism and slavery

The notion that races were unequal became popular at the same time that Europeans were settling in territories all over North and South America, Asia and, later, Africa. By the eighteenth century, Britain had larger colonies than any other empire in the history of the world and the British were transporting at least half of the 15 million West African slaves who were taken across the Atlantic Ocean. This trade in slaves flourished because of the demand for cheap labour in the West Indies and North America where huge profits could be made from cotton, tobacco and sugar plantations.

One view of racism sees it as a European invention which served to justify the slave trade and the colonising of Africa. Slavery and colonialism were held to be good things: they helped to civilise inferior black people by bringing them into contact with the superior way of life of the white man. In spite of the success of the popular campaign which abolished British slavery in the 1830s, racism remained a deeply entrenched part of British culture.

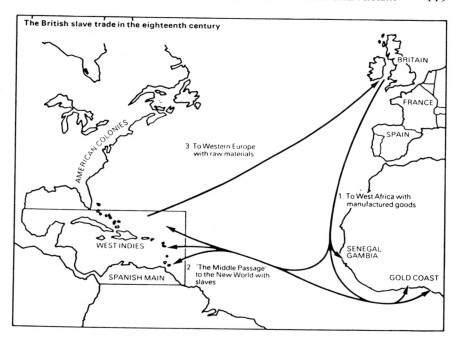

The British slave trade in the eighteenth century

3 To Western Europe with raw materials

1. To West Africa with manufactured goods

2 'The Middle Passage' to the New World with slaves

BRITAIN

FRANCE

SPAIN

SENEGAL GAMBIA

GOLD COAST

AMERICAN COLONIES

WEST INDIES

SPANISH MAIN

The British slave trade in the eighteenth century.

Scapegoating

In biblical times a ritual took place each year which involved loading a goat with objects which symbolically represented the sins of everyone in the community during the previous twelve months. The goat was then driven out into the wilderness and everyone felt better.

When a society is faced with difficult problems that threaten its stability, there is a tendency to blame distinctive and powerless minorities. In anxious times of crisis, people may readily accept simply but irrational explanations for complex problems. Blame may be easily directed at a minority because its distinctiveness arouses suspicion and its weakness prevents effective retaliation to hostility from the majority.

In the 1930s the Nazis made the Jews into scapegoats and succeeded in convincing millions of Germans that the Jews were the cause of their unemployment problem. Hitler knew that the Jews were not really to blame for Germany's economic problems but they provided a simple explanation which helped him to gain power by suggesting a simple cure – namely, the destruction of the Jewish community.

It is a familiar tactic for unscrupulous politicians to create scapegoats. In Britain, political parties like the National Front have tried to gain support by blaming black people for social ills such as unemployment, crime and poor housing.

Stereotypes and the media

To a certain extent, the media have had a harmful effect on race relations in Britain by reinforcing stereotyped attitudes about black people and by presenting them in a negative way; that is, the media tend to define black people as a problem.

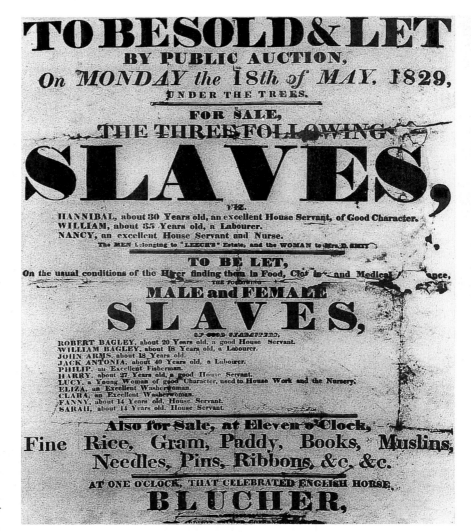

This advertisement, which appeared in the West Indies in 1829, offers three slaves for sale to the highest bidder and eleven more for hire.

A **stereotype** is a fixed image of a group of people and stereotyping is a process that involves the following stages: (a) taking some easily grasped features that a group is supposed to have; (b) making these features the dominant characteristics of the group; (c) suggesting that all members of the group possess these features. For example, the prevailing stereotype of Irishmen in jokes and cartoons has portrayed them as stupid.

White on Black (1992), by Jan Nederveen Pieterse, traces images of Africa and black people in Western popular culture:

- Early Christians used the colour black to denote sin and darkness, demons and the devil.
- The late Middle Ages saw positive images of historical black figures, such as the Queen of Sheba; Caspar, the King of the Moors (one of the Three Wise Men); the legendary Prester John, a Christian king in Ethiopia; and black saints.

A newspaper image: a suspect is taken into custody after a police raid.

- Scholars of the sixteenth century recognised the cities and civilisations of Africa, from the ancient Egyptian empire to the West African kingdom of Benin. Yet the slave trade was justified by arguing that all Africans were descended from Ham. Ham's father, Noah, had cursed Ham's son, Canaan, saying 'A servant of servants shall he be'.
- In the nineteenth century Africans were often portrayed as naked savages of the Dark Continent, cannibals who put white explorers and missionaries in their cooking pots. The wars of conquest of nations such as the Zulus brought images of savage warriors. The colonial missionaries gave Europeans images of evil witch doctors and simple, childlike people; civilising them was the 'White Man's Burden'.
- From the 1920s to the 1950s western fiction was populated with dumb and servile Africans, from *Tarzan* films to *Tintin* stories. Early films featuring black Americans showed them mainly as servants: the hotel bellhop, the train steward, the nightclub waiter or the shoeshine boy.
- Popular American entertainment from the 1890s to the 1920s featured a number of 'Negro' elements, such as the comic 'sambo', bawdy 'coon songs' and the 'darky melodies' of minstrel shows.
- Josephine Baker was a black American dancer who epitomised an exotic, sensual and erotic image of the jazz age when she performed topless in Paris in 1925. This tradition has been continued by Tina Turner.
- Sidney Poitier was Hollywood's 'token black' in the 1960s. Films usually showed him as a dignified underdog. There was little representation of the 1960s slogans of 'Black is Beautiful' and 'Black Power' until the *Shaft* and *Superfly* movies, in the 1970s, showed black heroes in powerful roles.
- The rag-doll golliwog was adopted as the emblem of Robertson's jam in 1930, and 1969 saw the publication of *The Three Golliwogs* by the popular children's author, Enid Blyton. *Doctor Dolittle* and *Mary Poppins* stories have now been produced in new editions with racist images removed.
- Fund-raising for famine relief in Africa has continually recycled images of starving people with flies in their eyes.

The stereotypes have changed over time, to modern images of the black athlete or the black criminal, such as the tabloid image of Jamaican drug gangs, the Yardies. These representations all tend to stress 'otherness', the idea that black people are essentially different.

3   Who are the ethnic minorities?

An **ethnic group** may be defined as a population who is regarded as sharing, and whose members believe that they share, a common descent and a common cultural heritage or tradition. In Britain, **ethnicity** often signifies people's allegiance to their country of origin. To be 'Asian' or 'Indian' or 'Sikh' may be an important part of a British citizen's identity.

Official statistics do not normally include every group having a distinctive culture. 'Ethnic minority' has generally only included people from the New Commonwealth (as described on page 111). Those in academic and policy research have used the term in a similar way. Some commentators suggests that to classify officially only non-white people as ethnic minorities is racist. They question whether 'ethnic minorities' should not also include those hundreds of thousands in distinctive communities, such as the Polish, Italian, Cypriot, Irish, Jewish and Ukrainian, who also have origins as immigrants to Britain, largely in the twentieth century. The 1991 Census was the first to include a question on ethnic group. The following figures show that 5.5 per cent of the population described themselves as belonging to an ethnic group:

Population of Great Britain: by ethnic group and age, 1991

	Total	Aged 0–15	*Percentage* Aged 60 and over
Black Caribbean	500,000	22	11
Black African	212,000	29	3
Black other	178,000	51	2
Indian	840,000	29	7
Pakistani	477,000	43	4
Bangladeshi	163,000	47	3
Chinese	157,000	23	6
Other Asian	198,000	24	4
Other	290,000	42	5
All ethnic minority groups	3,015,000	33	6
White	51,874,000	19	22
All ethnic groups	54,889,000	20	21

(Source: *Social Trends*, 1994)

Ethnic minority groups tend to have a younger age distribution than the population as a whole. Because of this, the ethnic minority population is expected to double and then stabilise within a generation.

The 1985 Swann Report gives the following approximate figures for some other ethnic minorities:

Italian 200,000
Cypriot 140,000
Travellers (including gypsies) 30,000
Ukrainian 25,000
Vietnamese 17,000

In 1984 the GLC estimated that the Irish community makes up 17 per cent of London's population.

A 1986 survey of Inner London Education Authority schools found that 20 per cent of the pupils spoke a language other than English at home. The total number of languages was 161 and the numbers of pupils speaking the most common of these languages were:

Bengali 12,000
Turkish 4,383
Gujerati 3,831
Urdu 3,642
Chinese 3,546
Spanish 3,210
Greek 3,033
Punjabi 3,015

Arabic 2,706
Italian 2,102
French 2,030
Portuguese 1,821
Yoruba (Nigeria) 1,120
Vietnamese 774
Tagalog (Philippines) 765
Twi (Ghana) 724

Seven per cent of the UK population were born outside the UK and of these over half are white.

Asian diversity

The diversity of the ethnic minorities may be seen by focusing on those labelled 'Asian'. Those who originate from the Indian sub-continent may speak a number of different languages including Bengali, Gujerati, Urdu and Punjabi. They may belong to different religions: in 1977, 40 per cent were Muslim, 29 per cent Hindu and 25 per cent Sikh. And they come from a number of countries: India, Pakistan, Bangladesh, Sri Lanka. There are also those of the East African Asian community who left Uganda, Kenya and Tanzania in the 1960s and 1970s.

The 1982 Policy Studies Institute (PSI) Survey found that 20 per cent of Asians aged over 25 left school before they were 10 years old. These might include Muslim peasants from Pakistan who were recruited by textile mills in Bradford and Blackburn in the 1960s to come and work the night shifts. In Indian restaurants 80 per cent of workers in fact come from Bangladesh, which was called East Pakistan until 1971. Other Bengalis work in the rag trade, cutting out and making up garments, in the Spitalfields and Brick Lane areas of Tower Hamlets in the East End of London. Another category, from the rural Indian state of Punjab, are the Sikhs. Many of these found work in the foundries of the West Midlands.

The 1982 survey found that another 20 per cent of Asians over 25 had stayed in full-time education past their nineteenth birthday – while less than half that proportion of whites had done the same. These Asians include businessmen and doctors. In a 1979 survey of heads of households in Greater London 21.5 per cent of Asians were in the category 'Professional, Managerial, Employers' compared to 20.8 per cent of whites and 3.6 per cent of West Indians. The 1991 Census found that 13 per cent of the Chinese in Britain were in professional jobs compared to 5 per cent of the white population.

The areas in which ethnic minority groups live

In 1991, the proportion of the population from ethnic minorities in rural areas was below 1 per cent, whereas the proportions for most London boroughs and other metropolitan districts were over 5 per cent. More than a third of the population in Brent, Newham, Tower Hamlets and Hackney belonged to an ethnic minority group. Outside London the main concentrations were in Leicester, Slough, the West Midlands and the Pennine conurbations.

4   The extent of racial discrimination

The 1976 Race Relations Act

This Race Relations Act strengthens the two previous laws of 1965 and 1968 so that every individual is legally protected against racial discrimination as a job applicant; as an employee; as a house-buyer; as a tenant; as a customer and as a pupil. The Act also outlaws 'incitement to racial hatred' and it has established the Commission for Racial Equality to give advice to complainants.

Despite laws against racial discrimination, it is still seen as widespread. The 1993 *British Social Attitudes* survey asked about the extent to which people of Asian and West Indian origin 'are not given jobs these days because of their race'. Sixty-four per cent thought that Asians suffered discrimination and 69 per cent thought that West Indians suffered discrimination. Forty-two per cent also thought that a black person was more likely to be found guilty of a crime they did not commit than was a white person. We now look at how widespread racial discrimination is in the key areas of education, employment, housing and policing.

Education

In 1985, the Swann Report found a number of reasons for the educational underachievement of children from minority ethnic groups. These included the lack of suitable pre-school provision, lack of relevance of the curriculum to the needs of pupils and poor communication between the school and the parents.

There is only one race: the human race.

The Swann Report also emphasised negative stereotyping and low expectations by teachers. The Report spoke of the 'unintentional racism' of teachers' attitudes and gave the following examples: 'West Indian children will be good at sports but "not academic"'; 'Asian children will be hard working and well motivated but likely to have unrealistically high career aspirations'; 'Chinese children will be reserved, well behaved, and likely to be "under pressure" at home from having to help in the family business in the evenings'.

Case study: racial discrimination in 'Jayleigh' Comprehensive School

In 1992, the commission for Racial Equality produced a report, called *Set to Fail?*, on the setting procedures in a north of England school where 41 per cent of the pupils were of Asian origin. This investigation found that teachers tended to put able Asian pupils in lower ability groups because English was not their first language. With rigid setting, these Asian pupils were unable to move into higher sets and so ended up less likely to be entered for exams than their white counterparts. The disadvantage caused in this way is an example of indirect or institutional discrimination.

By 1994 clear differences had emerged in the levels of educational success in the different ethnic minorities. More than a quarter of the 130,000 adult black Africans in Britain held qualifications higher than A-levels compared with about one in eight whites. More than one in seven Indians were educated above A-level. Together with the Chinese, these ethnic groups had a larger proportion than whites holding top professional jobs. Most black Africans in Britain come from highly qualified families. Zeinab Badawi, the Sudanese-born Channel 4 TV presenter, has degrees from Oxford and London Universities. She is one of six children who all have degrees.

In contrast, half of men and two-thirds of women of Pakistani and Bangladeshi origin have no educational qualifications. They are among the most recent immigrant groups and come largely from illiterate peasant communities. When they arrived in the 1970s, they had a strong 'myth of return' to their home countries. Their aim was not to get their children into British universities but to earn a target sum of money and then to return, with cash to purchase land or with a dowry for a daughter.

Activity

In 1989, a Pakistani sociology student at the University of Manchester interviewed fifty Muslim girls at a single-sex comprehensive school. She also interviewed their parents. About half of the parents were in favour of separate Muslim schools to help preserve their religion and culture. Only a quarter of the girls favoured such schools and these were mainly younger girls who disliked the teasing they received in multi-racial schools. The older girls were overwhelmingly against the idea because they did not want to be isolated from other ethnic groups and feared that separation would provoke racism.

Discuss whether the government should fund separate Muslim girls' schools.

The Islamia School in Brent was founded by the former pop singer, Cat Stevens, in 1983. Now known as Yusuf Islam, he is shown with the Schools Minister Stephen Byers, in 1998 when it became the first government-funded Muslim school (joining 24 Jewish and 7,000 Christian schools).

Highest qualification held by men and women aged 16–24, 1994 (percentages)

| | Degree | | A-level or higher | | None | |
	Men	Women	Men	Women	Men	Women
African Asian	9	17	50	51	22	17
Indian	12	13	46	54	27	21
White	6	3	46	43	22	26
Caribbean	5	2	38	53	31	18
Pakistani	4	10	34	31	44	40
Bangladeshi	2	5	19	19	42	52

(Source: *Ethnic Minorities in Britain: Diversity and Disadvantage,* Policy Studies Institute, 1997)

The above figures show a significant gender difference in most ethnic groups. One question which these figures raise is 'Why are young Caribbean men almost twice as likely to end up without qualifications as young Caribbean women?' The follow-up to the Swann Report, 'Recent Research in the Achievement of Ethnic Minority Pupils' (1996), focused on Caribbean boys. In 1994, black 5-year-olds outperformed white children in Key Stage 1 tests in Birmingham. But by their GCSE year, Caribbean pupils were on average about 5 exam points lower than white pupils. In the intervening years black pupils perhaps live up to their teachers' stereotype that they are more likely to misbehave and underachieve: they are 6 times more likely to be excluded than other pupils.

The 1996 report states: 'Irrespective of the teachers' conscious desire to help all pupils equally, the level of teacher-pupil conflict in the researched schools was such that, as a group, black pupils experienced school in ways that were significantly more conflictual and less positive than their peers. Teachers and schools may play an active, though unintended, role in the creation of conflict with African-Carribean pupils, thereby reducing black young people's opportunity to achieve.' In many local authorities the gap between the highest-achieving and the lowest-achieving ethnic groups was actually found to be growing.

Employment

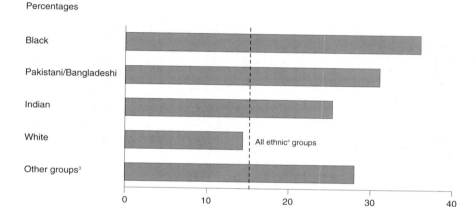

UK youth unemployment rates[1] by ethnic group, 1996–7[2]
(Source: Social Trends, *1998.)*

[1]Unemployment of 16 to 24 year olds based on the ILO definition as a percentage of all economically active. See Appendix, Part 4: Unemployment – ILO definition.
[2]Combined quarters: Spring 1996 to Winter 1996–97.
[3]Includes those of mixed origin.
[4]Includes ethnic group not stated.

Ethnic Minorities in Britain: Diversity and Disadvantage, the fourth Policy Studies Institute survey (1997), offers the following summary of the employment position of different ethnic groups:

- African Asians are as likely as whites to be in professional and managerial jobs. Chinese men are half as likely again to be so placed and Chinese women are twice as likely as white women to be in top jobs.
- Indians and Caribbeans occupy a middle position. Caribbean male employees average just over 90 per cent of the earnings of white men and Indians 85 per cent.
- Pakistanis and Bangladeshis are twice as likely to be in manual work as in non-manual work, whereas white men are evenly split between these kinds of jobs. Pakistanis and Bangladeshis experience severe and widespread poverty: 80 per cent of their households have incomes below half the national average, compared to 20 per cent of white homes.
- Since the 1960s, controlled tests have been conducted, whereby white

and ethnic minority applicants respond to advertised vacancies for which they are equally suitable. These tests continue to show that at least one-third of employers discriminate against non-whites.

- 20 per cent of ethnic respondents say that they have been refused a job on racial grounds. The number of complaints of racial discrimination made to the Commission for Racial Equality continues to rise every year.

Case study: the 'ethnic penalty' in well-paid, 'top jobs'

In 1994, Vandana Shah, a 33-year-old Kenyan Asian, was a partner with Bayer Rosin, a firm of London solicitors. She claims that when she qualified she had to make ten times more applications than white students to secure her first job. This is a piece of anecdotal evidence. Is it typical?

In 1993, Aneez Esmail, a senior lecturer in general practice at Manchester University, sent out forty-six false applications for twenty-three jobs to test whether doctors with foreign names suffered an 'ethnic penalty'. He found that those with ethnic names were half as likely to be shortlisted for interview. His study stemmed from his own attempts to get a job: 'I found that the only way I could get work was to go and visit the consultant in person and say, "Here I am. I speak better English than you do. Why don't you look at my application?"'

In 1994, Yuan Cheng, a researcher at Nuffield College, Oxford, published the following results showing the chances of different ethnic groups obtaining well-paid business, professional and administrative jobs:

- Thirty-one per cent of whites with only O-levels had these top jobs, compared to 7 per cent of Pakistani men with only O-levels.
- The percentages of graduates with these top jobs were:

Whites	90%
Chinese	90%
African Asians	68%
West Indians	68%
Indians	62%

Housing

When the 1974 study conducted test applications for rented property using black and white actors, the black applicants met with racial discrimination in over 25 per cent of cases. In the 1982 survey, 49 per cent of West Indians and 39 per cent of Asians reported that they had experienced discrimination in seeking privately rented accommodation from a white landlord.

The 1986 report on the allocation of council housing in the London borough of Tower Hamlets found the following pattern over sixteen months:

Type of housing	Percentage of offers to Asians	Percentage of offers to non-Asians
Has central heating	40	56
Built after 1969	23	34
Has access to garden	9	13
Built before 1945	10	5

The report found that housing officers tended to have unfavourable stereo-types of Bengalis and social security tenants which resulted in these groups being allocated to 'sink' or 'problem' housing estates: usually the oldest, most dilapidated and most inferior estates.

Ethnic Minorities in Britain (1997) found that ethnic minorities tended to live in areas with higher than average levels of unemployment, they were more likely than white people to mention graffiti, vandalism and vermin infestation, and they were more likely than white people to report problems of personal and property crime and nuisance from troublesome young people.

Case study: type of accommodation and housing tenure, by ethnic group, 1991 (column percentages)

| | | *Ethnic group of head of household* | | |
	White	*West Indian*	*Indian*	*Pakistani/Bangladeshi*
Detached house	21	4	15	4
Semi-detached house	33	22	31	18
Terraced house	27	31	36	60
Flat	16	42	15	17
Other	3	1	3	1
Owner-occupied	67	46	80	66
Rented	33	54	20	34

(Source: *Social Trends*, 1993 and 1994)

Data-response exercise: type of accommodation and housing tenure, by ethnic group, 1991

1 What is meant by the term 'column percentages'?

2 What proportion of West Indian households were accommodated in flats?

3 What proportion of white households lived in terraced housing?

4 Use the figures in the last two columns to describe some of the large variations between different Asian groups.

Sufia Bibi is a Bangladeshi. Her husband has worked in Britain since 1961. Her family of twelve share a damp, cramped flat in a graffiti-covered block in Stepney Green, Tower Hamlets. Net curtains are black with mould despite constant washings.

Policing

Following the Brixton riots of 1981, Lord Scarman's report recommended more community policing and more recruitment of black police officers. By 1988 there were 1,108 British police officers from the black and Asian communities. The Scarman Report also recommended that racially prejudiced behaviour by a police officer should be a disciplinary offence normally punished by dismissal. This last recommendation has not been implemented by the police.

In 1979 the Institute of Race Relations study, *Policing Against Black People*, identified seven elements of 'everyday, routine' police misconduct towards black people:

1 stop and search without reason;
2 unnecessary violence in arrests;
3 particular harassment of juveniles;
4 danger of arrest when suspects asserted their rights;
5 risk to witnesses and bystanders;
6 repeated arrests of individuals;
7 black homes and premises entered at will.

Ian Bennett, a community policeman, enjoying the St Paul's Festival in Bristol.

Researchers who spent two years carrying out participant observation with the police in London found that 'Racialist language and racial prejudice were prominent and pervasive ... racialist talk and racial prejudice are ... on the whole expected, accepted and even fashionable ... we cannot produce examples of police officers objecting to racialist language or arguing with others who express racialist views' (from the 1984 PSI Report on the Metropolitan Police).

Some see this racism as stretching to the very top of the force. In June 1982, shortly after he was appointed the head of London's police, Kenneth Newman told a journalist: 'In the Jamaicans, you have people who are constitutionally disorderly ... constitutionally disposed to be anti-authority ... It's simply in their make-up.'

Bangladeshi families protesting against Tower Hamlets Council outside the High Court in 1994.

Research reported in the *British Journal of Sociology* in 1992 found that black male youths had a high level of negative attitudes to the police due to their collective experience of a concentrated intensity of police surveillance. Over the course of a year, approximately one in three of the black adult male population under 35 were stopped by the police, resulting in formal police action, compared to only one in ten whites.

5   Racial harassment and violence

The following section is adapted from *Living in Terror: A Report on Racial Violence and Harassment in Housing* (1987), *Learning in Terror: A Survey of Racial Harassment in Schools and Colleges* (1988), both published by the Commission for Racial Equality, and *Under Siege: Racism and Violence in Britain Today* (1988) by Keith Tompson.

History

In 1919, there was a series of attacks on black people in the dock areas of the country where black people predominantly lived, among them Cardiff, Glasgow, Liverpool, Hull, Manchester and London.

In 1948 and 1949 there was a series of attacks in Liverpool, Deptford and Birmingham. In Liverpool, there were three nights of violence between black and white people.

The late 1950s saw attacks on black people by racist white youths. The 1960s saw the 'paki-bashing' phenomenon led by gangs of white skinheads. The 1970s saw further attacks, with the report *Blood on the Streets* describing the racial harassment suffered by Bangladeshis in the Spitalfields area of Tower Hamlets.

The 1980s

While racial attacks are not a new phenomenon, their scale and number are new. One reason is that racial harassment is now increasingly recognised and the police, for example, to some extent, attempt to record incidents in a structured way. Previously unrecorded and effectively 'forgotten' victims of racial attack are now increasingly public knowledge.

Another reason for public recognition of the problem in the 1980s was because of the sheer horror of the attacks. In 1981, Mrs Khan and her three young children lost their lives in a firebomb attack on their Walthamstow home. In 1985, Shamira Kassam, a pregnant woman, died with her three small sons in an arson attack on her home in Ilford.

In 1987, a young Asian boy was stabbed to death by a white pupil in a Manchester secondary school. He had been defending other Asian pupils from physical assault and his death after school in the playground was the outcome of a long period of racial conflict.

For years the effect of Newham Council's housing policy has been that the south of the borough is virtually white-only and that black people have been consigned to low-grade estates north of the Barking Road divide. The white Croydon Road gang patrols the frontier between the two territories. In 1986, a sister at Newham General Hospital's emergency department said that no black person was safe on a Friday or a Saturday night along the Barking Road – every night she was sure to get a case, some so badly hurt you couldn't recognise them.

Research findings

Newham Council's 1986 survey found that one in four of Newham's black residents had been victims of racial harassment in the previous twelve months. Two out of every three victims had been victims more than once. One hundred and sixteen victims reported 1,550 incidents of racial harassment, including:

- 774 cases of insulting behaviour;
- 188 cases of attempted damage to property;
- 175 cases of attempted theft;
- 174 cases of threats of damage or violence;
- 153 cases of physical assault;
- 40 cases of damage to property.

The Scottish Ethnic Minorities Research Unit carried out a survey of racial harassment of school children in south Glasgow in 1986. Within the sample, 25 per cent had suffered damage to property, 37 per cent had experienced personal racial attacks and 100 per cent had been subjected to racial abuse. In another Glasgow survey more than half of ethnic minority interviewees said they had suffered racist graffiti on their homes and almost half said they had been racially abused.

In 1987, the Commission for Racial Equality surveyed 107 council housing departments. Of these, 77 per cent said that they thought racial harassment was becoming a more serious problem. This was particularly the case in London, the South of England and the North, whereas the figure for the

Midlands was only 56 per cent. In a well-publicised case, Newham Council evicted the McDonnell family for racial harassment of other tenants. A number of councils now include a clause in their tenancy agreements which states that those who carry out racial harassment may be evicted.

The 1986 Runnymede Trust report *Racial Violence and Harassment* concludes by saying:

> Few areas in Britain can now be regarded as safe for black residents. As the section on arson showed, racial attacks have taken place in areas such as middle-class Hendon, North London and in Shrewsbury in rural Shropshire.

Young Asian women's involvement in football has been encouraged in Sheffield by FURD (Football Unites, Racism Divides).

Conclusion

Racial violence has continued in the 1990s. South-east London has had a particularly bad record with four men stabbed to death in racist murders: Rolan Adams in Thamesmead in 1991, Rohit Duggal in Eltham in 1992, Stephen Lawrence in Eltham in 1993 and Rafique Khan in Plumstead in 1998. The local race monitoring project recorded 139 race attacks in the borough of Greenwich in 1997. *Ethnic Minorities in Britain* (1997) found that, in the previous 12 months, 1 per cent of all non-whites had been racially attacked, 2 per cent had suffered racially motivated property damage and 12 per cent had suffered racial abuse or threats. These findings suggest that, between 1993 and 1994, 290,000 people were subjected to some form of racial harassment. In that year, the British Crime Survey identified 130,000 such incidents, whereas only 10,000 incidents were reported to the police.

Case study: the new racism

Some commentators have distinguished between the old racism and the new racism. The old racism was based upon the supposed biological inferiority of non-whites. This was used to justify prejudice, discrimination, oppression, slavery and colonialism.

The new racism of right-wingers in the 1990s claims that white people are now tolerant and not racist. White people are not the problem. The problem is seen to be those non-whites who do not try hard enough to fit in, who cling to their traditional cultural identity. Thus right-wing Conservatives can argue that they themselves are not racist, that they do not regard non-whites as inferior. Nevertheless, they see many of the ethnic minority population as alien, such as those who follow a strict Muslim way of life and those who 'fail' the 'cricket test' because they support India, Pakistan or the West Indies, rather than England.

GCSE question from Southern Examining Group 1990

Read Item A and Item B. Then answer the questions which follow.

Item A

Unemployment and ethnic minority groups

Percentage unemployment, 1984

within total UK population	12%
in specific ethnic minority groups	
West Indian/Guyanese	25%
Pakistani/Bangladeshi	35%
Indian	15%

(Source: adapted from *Labour Force Survey 1984*, HMSO)

Item B

Often minority ethnic groups do not have equal employment opportunities. West Indians are more likely to be found in manual than in white-collar jobs. Asians are less likely than Whites to be found in white-collar jobs although there are relatively more Asians than West Indians in these positions. Asians also tend to have high rates of self-employment but these are usually in small businesses.

(a) Study Item A and state:

   (i)   which of the minority ethnic groups shown have the greatest level of unemployment;

   (ii)   which of the minority ethnic groups shown has the least unemployment. (2)

(b) According to Item B,

   (i)   in which type of employment are West Indians more likely to be found;

   (ii)   in which type of self-employment are Asians likely to be found? (2)

(c) Identify and explain *two* factors, other than those given in Item B, for minority ethnic groups not having equal employment opportunities. (4)

(d) Identify and explain *two* ways, other than employment opportunities, in which minority ethnic groups may experience disadvantages. (4)

(e) How do sociologists attempt to explain racial discrimination? (8)

CHAPTER 8

Power and social stratification

A geologist uses the word *strata* to describe the layers of different rock formations. Sociologists use the term **social stratification** in analysing the power structure of a society. Social stratification refers to the division of society into superior and inferior groups. Such groups may differ from one another in terms of power, wealth, status and respect. People may find that their position in a society depends very much on their race, their religion, their sex and their age.

Most societies contain a number of different types of stratification. Sociologists try to identify these and attempt to pinpoint which one is the most important. Many sociologists claim that social class is the major basis of stratification in capitalist societies. The sections of this chapter look at a number of examples of different types of social stratification.

1 Stratification and skin colour

Brazil

About half of the population of South America lives in one massive country, Brazil. The people of Brazil are mainly descendants of black African slaves and white Portuguese settlers.

The indigenous peoples

The first European settlers arrived from Portugal in the sixteenth century. At that time there were probably several million native people already living in Brazil. These 'Indian' tribes were reluctant to serve as slaves or as soldiers fighting for the Portuguese against the French and Dutch settlers. Many died from European diseases, such as flu, measles and smallpox. Others were slaughtered in raids and massacres by the colonists. Survivors retreated to areas like the Amazon rain forests. By the 1990s, only 200,000 or so remained.

The black slaves
Slavery was abolished in Brazil in 1888. By this time, the slave trade had brought between 3 million and 4 million Africans to work as sugar-cane cutters, gold and diamond miners or domestic servants. The slaves mainly came from Nigeria and Angola.

The Europeans
In the last two hundred years over 5 million European immigrants have settled in Brazil. In 1822, Brazil ceased to be a Portuguese colony and became an independent nation. Since this time, the Portuguese settlers have been joined by Italians, Germans, Syrians, Lebanese and Eastern Europeans.

At a very early stage in Brazil's colonial history, the Portuguese mixed with the 'Indians' as well as the Africans, so that today most Brazilians have mixed ancestry. But one rule of stratification in modern Brazil seems to be that the rich elite tend to be the whitest people and those with the darkest skins are among the poorest part of the population.

Dancing in the streets at the Rio Carnival in Brazil.

In other societies, such as Jamaica, those with the palest skins tend to form the governing elite. In Bolivia, 80 per cent of the 6.3 million inhabitants are descended from the Incas, Aymara and other pre-Columbian tribes. In 1993, Victor Hugo Cardenas was elected Vice-president of Bolivia. He was the first Indian to be elected to high office anywhere in South America. The most famous recent example of ethnic stratification was the apartheid system in South Africa.

Apartheid in South Africa

Apartheid means 'separateness' and describes the system that the white minority government set up in South Africa in 1948. The non-white population was classifed as African, Indian or coloured (mixed race) and inter-marriage between these groups was made illegal. Each group had segregated residential zones, together with segregated schools, hospitals, buses, parks and bathing beaches. The stratification system of apartheid maintained a structure of social inequalities:

	Education spending by the government, per pupil in 1983–84	*Infant mortality rate, 1985*
White	1,654 rand	14 deaths per 1,000 live births
Indian	1,088 rand	18 deaths per 1,000 live births
Coloured	569 rand	59 deaths per 1,000 live births
African	234 rand	80 deaths per 1,000 live births

In 1983 there was one doctor for every 330 Whites, 730 Indians, 1,200 coloureds and 12,000 Africans.
(Source: *The Apartheid Handbook* by R. Omond)

The last apartheid laws were repealed in 1991 and the first multi-ethnic general election in South Africa was held in 1994.

Three examples of how apartheid affected people's lives

1   In 1979, five South African policemen were charged with criminal injury to a white woman. They had beaten her up because they suspected her of sleeping with an Indian South African in her Pretoria flat. The man produced a pass proving he was white. The policemen's defence was that the man had 'acted, talked and looked' like an Indian.

2   In 1984, a 23-year-old black New York dancer, Barry Martin, was on tour with the Hot Gossip dance group when his car crashed. An ambulance picked up his white driver but left him lying on the side of the road. A black passer-by took him to a local white hospital where he was seated on a hard bench and refused treatment while suffering from a fractured spine. A vertebra slipped forward and severed his spinal cord so that his arms and legs are now paralysed. He has since tried to sue the South African authorities for $130 million.

3   In 1984, 795 South Africans were reclassified, including 518 coloureds who became white; 2 whites who became Chinese; 1 white who became Indian; 89 Africans who became coloured; 5 coloureds who became African.

2   Feudal and religious stratification

Religion and stratification can be connected in two ways. First, religion can be the basis of stratification. This occurs where members of one religion have higher positions in society than members of another religion. Second, religion can support a system of stratification by providing persuasive justification for it.

The English feudal system

In England during the Middle Ages, the lower groups of the feudal social system, or **estates**, were tenants: villeins (villagers) or cottars (cottagers) and serfs (virtual slaves). They were socialised into accepting their place at the bottom of the social pyramid by their religion. Christianity taught that a good life would be rewarded in Heaven and that their position was fixed by God. This idea can be seen in one of the original verses of the hymn 'All things bright and beautiful':

> The rich man in his castle, the poor man at his gate,
> God made them high or lowly, and ordered their estate.

The traditional Hindu caste system

Scholars believe that the caste system originated with the Aryan invasions of India. Early castes represented the four main occupations in society: Brahmins (priests); Kshatriyas (warriors); Vaishyas (creators of wealth, such as farmers, traders and craftsmen); and Shudras (labourers). Over the centuries these castes have become a hereditary hierarchy, so that if you are born a Shudra you cannot move into a higher caste.

Outside this caste system is a further group, called the Untouchables. They have the filthiest and most menial occupations such as cobbling, cleaning toilets and burning the dead. These are considered to be tainted occupations and so Untouchables are strictly forbidden from polluting those of a higher caste by sharing a meal with them, praying in their temples, using their wells or touching them. They are the poorest and least educated villagers, often forced to live on the edge of villages.

Why have the lowest groups put up with their position over the centuries? The Brahmins have proclaimed that the caste system is divinely ordained and the Hindu idea of **reincarnation** has taught that if you lead a good life then you may be reborn into a higher position in your next life.

Social groups in modern India

In 1994, official figures divided the people of India into six social groups. This stratification is clearly based on religion. Apart from Muslims (12 per cent of the population) and other religions (6 per cent), the four main social groups are:

1   Upper castes (20 per cent)   These range from the priestly caste to the landed intermediate castes.

2   Backward castes (34 per cent)   These include the Kurmis. Many are small farmers; others are educated with government or professional jobs, although they are discriminated against by the upper castes. Also included are the Yadavs, the cattle herders.

3   Scheduled castes (16 per cent)   These include the Untouchables. Mahatma Gandhi called them Harijans, meaning 'Children of God'. But by 1994 they had rejected this name as patronising. They prefer to be called Dalits, meaning 'the oppressed', and they have become politically active.

4   Scheduled tribals (12 per cent)   These include most so-called tribal, or indigenous, communities across India. They are considered outside the Hindu caste system.

In 1990, the right-wing Bharatiya Janata Party (BJP) was elected in India's biggest state, Uttar Pradesh. But it was dismissed from the state government by the national government in 1992, after Hindu zealots tore down the historic Muslim mosque at Ayodhya. In elections in 1994 the BJP were confident of returning to power in Uttar Pradesh but they were defeated by a new coalition of Muslims, Dalits and other backward castes.

The message of the BJP is Hindu unity against others, notably Muslims. But Dalits and other backward castes are beginning to see that such unity merely prolongs the old repressive order, and that their vote can be crucial in radically reforming it – especially in alliance with the Muslims.

Northern Ireland: Protestants and Catholics

The main social division in Northern Ireland, apart from economic class or gender, is religion. Many areas of Northern Ireland are clearly split into Protestant and Catholic communities.

In the 1960s some of the Catholic minority were inspired by the success of the campaign by US blacks for **desegregation**. And so they copied Martin Luther King's tactic of civil rights marches to demonstrate peacefully for an end to injustice and discrimination in housing and jobs. In 1976 the British government passed the Fair Employment (Northern Ireland) Act. This made discrimination on religious or political grounds unlawful and it also set up the Fair Employment Agency to help Catholics get a fair share of jobs.

In the 1981 census 22 per cent of the people of Northern Ireland did not give their religion but it has been estimated that 36 per cent of the adult population is Catholic. If the Catholics had equal employment opportunities, then we could expect them to occupy roughly 36 per cent of the jobs in different occupational categories. We can see whether this is the case by looking at the following findings about the proportions of Catholics in different occupations:

- 3 per cent of management in the Northern Ireland Electricity Service
- 4 per cent of print workers on the Belfast Telegraph
- 7 per cent of (non-senior) policemen, firemen and prison officers
- 10 per cent of highest-grade civil servants, senior principal and above
- 14 per cent of managers in marketing, sales and advertising
- 16 per cent of scientists and engineers

(Source: *Research Papers of the Fair Employment Agency of Northern Ireland 1980–85.*)

A republican funeral cortège, Northern Ireland.

In her book, *In Search of a State: Catholics in Northern Ireland*, Fionnuala O'Connor writes: 'In June 1993, a league table of UK regional male unemployment showed Northern Ireland Protestants next to the bottom, at 10%, just above East Anglia. Catholics in Northern Ireland topped the list at 24.2%, double the rate for any other regions.' Male unemployment in the Catholic districts of Derry (Brandywell and Greggan) and Belfast (the Falls, Whiterock, New Lodge and Ardoyne) was between 50 and 60 per cent.

3   Gender stratification: women in China, Morocco and Britain

Women in China

Before he led the communist revolution to success, Mao Zedong said that the Chinese people were bound by 'four thick ropes'. He said that a man in China was dominated by three systems of authority: the political, state system; the family, clan system; and the religious, supernatural system. As for women, they were dominated by a fourth authority system: their husbands.

In the early years of the twentieth century Chinese women were still subjected to the traditions of foot-binding and arranged marriages. In 1950 the first article of the new marriage law in communist China abolished the 'compulsory feudal marriage system which is based on the superiority of men over women'. In giving women legal equality, the new communist government was trying to wipe out the centuries-old traditions of gender stratification.

Women in Morocco

In 1971, all but five of the 129 nations in the United Nations allowed women to vote. One of these five was the small state of Liechtenstein and the other four were Arab countries where the Muslim religion gives women an unequal social status.

For many years Morocco was one of the French North African colonies. When it became an independent nation, Morocco's new government passed the family laws of 1957 which was based on the Muslim traditions of the seventh century. These laws clearly give Moroccan women an inferior legal status: Article 12 states that a woman cannot give herself in marriage but must be given by a male guardian: Article 29 forbids her from marrying a non-Muslim partner, although a Muslim man may do so. Men are allowed more than one wife (polygamy) and Article 46 allows 'repudiation' which means that a husband can divorce his wife merely by saying 'I repudiate you' three times, in front of a witness.

Women soldiers in China.

While Arab girls may show their faces in Oman, many older women keep their heads carefully veiled.

Moroccan women have, however, to a certain extent been able to join in the modernisation of their society. Thousands have had access to secondary education but only 4 per cent of university graduates are women. In the service sector of the economy, Moroccan women have two main types of jobs. The 1971 census showed 27,700 working for the government (15,200 as teachers) and 100,200 working as maids.

We now consider how far equality of educational opportunity has given women job equality in Britain.

The occupational segregation of the sexes in Britain

There are two types of occupational segregation (or separation):

- **Horizontal segregation** refers to the way in which men and women are concentrated in different types of work. The following chart shows how women are concentrated in clerical and secretarial work.

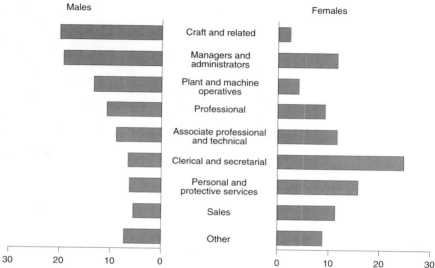

Employees and self-employed: by gender and occupation, 1997 (Source: Social Trends, 1998.)

- **Vertical segregation** refers to the way that women are concentrated in lower grades than men. The following chart shows how men are 4 times more likely than women to have professional job status and women are 3 times more likely than men to be in the lower, routine ('skilled') non-manual group:

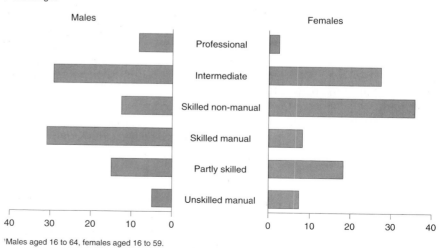

Working population[1]: by gender and social class, 1996 (Source: Social Trends, 1997.)

[1]Males aged 16 to 64, females aged 16 to 59.

With lower average occupational status in lower grades, women have lower average pay. The following chart, for seven major industry groups, shows how women's earnings ranged from 72 per cent of men's earnings in manufacturing to 90 per cent of men's earnings in the transport and storage industries:

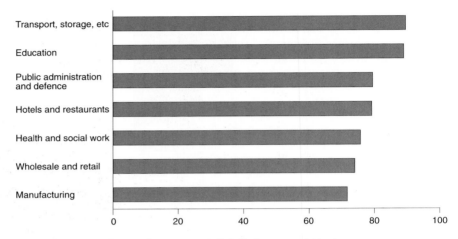

Women's earnings as a percentage of men's earnings[1]: by industry, 1997 (Source: Social Trends, 1998.)

[1]Full-time employees on adult rates whose pay was not affected for the survey period by absence.

Case study: women in banking

Captain Mainwaring in the TV sitcom *Dad's Army* is a comic stereotype of the traditional sober and reliable bank manager. In the 1940s, bank managers were expected to have these characteristics. They were paternalistic figures, males overseeing a largely male work force of young clerks.

In the 1970s, the labour force in banking was formed by relatively well-educated young women. They were expected to leave the employment of the bank when their first child was born.

In the 1990s, men can no longer expect eventual promotion to management as a reward for reliable, long service. Men have to apply if they want a managerial post. The key quality now is competitiveness. Managers must be innovative team leaders who can hit demanding sales targets. It is accepted that some women will want careers and promotion. (In 1996, 24 per cent of those on management grades in banking were women, compared to just 8 per cent in 1986.) But it is assumed that most female employees will wish to earn a 'component wage' which makes a substantial contribution to, but does not fully support, a household.

(adapted from *Women and Work in Modern Britain* by Rosemary Crompton, Oxford University Press, 1997)

4 Age stratification

I was born in Cyprus and lived there for ten years. In common with other Moslem countries the Turkish Cypriots bring their children up to have respect for others especially their elders. I believe Japanese people also have this exaggerated respect custom. As soon as a child is able to walk and talk it has to adopt certain ways of behaving such as the ceremonial kissing of elders' hands when visiting.

(Mike Aziz in *Changing Childhood*, edited by M. Hoyles)

In traditional societies the old are often the most powerful figures. There are no books to refer to, so people consult their elders for knowledge. The elderly are thought to have wisdom and the elders of the tribe or village are asked to settle disputes.

In fast-changing modern societies, youth and adaptability are given greater value. The mass media, such as advertising, and fashion equate good looks with youth. Magazines are full of tips on how to stay looking young and as a consequence respect for the old declines. The middle-aged in America feel that they suffer unfair job discrimination: inexperienced workers in their twenties are preferred by employers and this has led to campaigns for laws to combat **ageism**. In 1967 the US government passed the Age Discrimination in Employment Act. The purpose of this law was:

to promote employment of older workers based on their ability rather than age; to prohibit age discrimination in employment; to help employers and workers find ways of meeting problems arising from the impact of age on employment.

The UK does not have a similar law. In 1989, the House of Commons Employment Committee declared that a change of attitude might come 'if those who have the power to determine employment policies bothered to look in the mirror. If they are not too old at 50 neither are others.'

Case study: age discrimination in job advertisements

There have been many articles about the despair of older people who have been made redundant and find that employers are so unwilling to offer jobs to them that it seems unlikely they will ever work again.

This does not only apply to executives – anyone who looks, for example, at the advertisements for clerical and secretarial posts will know that permanent work is reserved mainly for people in the magic age range of 18–35 years. Occasionally one sees advertisements saying 'age up to 45' but not many.

There is a notice in the local Job Centre offering extra job services to people aged '18–35' who are 'looking for clerical or secretarial work'. The staff state that there is 'no prejudice' but 'most of the jobs are in that age range'. Exactly! We know that.

So there you have it. The Department of Employment, while demanding that everybody hunts unceasingly for work, has decided to offer extra help to the group of people who find it easiest to get work, but not, apparently, to those who find it difficult, through no fault of their own.

(Source: letter to the *Guardian*, January 1994)

From a survey in 1998, the Gallup poll organisation estimated that 18.5 million of the UK population have had personal experience of age discrimination, half of them when under the age of 45.

Both old and young alike tend to lack the status which comes from financial independence. Children depend on their parents for pocket money and pensioners may be entirely dependent on the government for their income, from the state pension. Housewives without a paid job may similarly depend on their husbands for a weekly allowance. Dependent groups such as these have to be supported from the earnings of the working population.

A gathering of village elders.

One way in which these groups lack power is that they often have no independent means of transport such as ready access to the family car. While they queue at the bus stop with students and the low paid, those who belong to the more powerful groups in society drive past in their own cars. British Rail and coach firms recognise that some groups have lower income by offering concessions such as Railcards which give cheaper fares.

5   People with impairment

The above section indicates that the status given to older people varies from society to society and has varied within many societies over the years. There is nothing 'natural' about the respect, or disrespect, shown to the elderly; age stratification is 'socially constructed'. In a similar way, the status of people with impairment, or their lack of status, is created by society. This section is adapted from an article by Tim Davies in the *Sociology Review*, April 1994.

Impairment means any loss or abnormality in the structure or function of the body or the mind. There are four types of impairment:

1   Physical impairment, e.g. paraplegia or multiple sclerosis.
2   Intellectual impairment, e.g. Down's syndrome or dyslexia.
3   Sensory impairment, e.g. visual or hearing impairment.
4   Hidden impairment, e.g. schizophrenia or epilepsy.

Disability refers to the resulting difficulties in performing 'normal' activities. **Handicap** is the resulting disadvantage, experienced by people with impairment, in performing 'normal' roles. Thus, for example, someone with a hearing problem (an impairment) may have difficulty following a conversation (a disability) which creates disadvantage when trying to be a worker or a friend (a handicap).

Here are two alternative views of what causes a person's degree of disability:

1   *Medical model*   (biological focus on the individual): the degree of impairment determines the degree of disability.

2   *Social model*   (focus on society): social attitudes and social arrangements determine the degree to which an impairment will be disabling. (Take, as an example, an impaired person who cannot run for a bus: this would not be a disability if bus drivers waited for their passengers!)

Disableism may be defined as the combination of social forces, cultural values and personal prejudices which marginalises people with impairments, portrays them in a negative way and thus oppresses them.

Common negative attitudes to people with impairment can be illustrated by considering the prejudice that stigmatises wheelchair-users. They are often stereotyped as ugly, dependent, bitter, asexual, intellectually impaired and unable to speak for themselves ('Does he take sugar?'). TV charity shows like 'Children in Need' and 'Telethon' have been criticised for portraying wheelchair-users as pathetic and pitiable. Disabled people want civil rights, not charity and patronising attitudes.

Research has shown that disabled applicants are six times more likely to be turned down for a job than non-disabled applicants and three times more likely to be unemployed. Prejudice also leads to discrimination in areas

Demonstrators outside the Houses of Parliament, protesting against the lack of civil rights for disabled people in this country.

such as education, housing, transport and leisure. The problem of access to buildings is illustrated by this story in which the tables are turned. Imagine a city designed for wheelchair-users. What would happen when the able-bodied came to visit? They would constantly find themselves knocking their heads on lowered door lintels and ceilings!

The 1996 Disability Discrimination Act made it unlawful to treat disabled people less favourably than other people in areas such as buying goods, using services, finding somewhere to live and getting a job. Here are two examples of unlawful discrimination:

- A newsagent says people with learning disabilities from a nearby training centre may not use his shop to buy snacks at lunchtime because the attention they need delays service to other customers. The shopkeeper is discriminating against them because of their disability.
- Martha has difficulty eating because of a disability. When she returns a second time to a restaurant, the waiter shows her to an out-of-the-way table, even though other customers are allowed to sit at unreserved tables with the sea view that she enjoyed last time. The reason that he is treating her less favourably is because of a disability.

6   Gays and lesbians

In Britain in the twentieth century, gay men and lesbian women have faced very considerable prejudice and discrimination. Gay and lesbian teenagers have had far higher suicide rates than the general population and many have been killed by 'gay-bashing'. In the 1990s, the situation may be changing with many celebrities 'coming out' as openly gay or lesbian. Chris Smith was the first openly gay cabinet minister.

A survey in 1996 found that 64 per cent of lesbians and gay men have concealed their sexuality from some or all of their colleagues at work. This is not surprising since the same survey also found that 21 per cent of gays and lesbians said that they had been harassed at work and 33 per cent of heterosexual employers said that they would be less likely to employ someone they knew was gay or lesbian.

According to the Sexual Attitudes and Lifestyles survey, the great majority of men (70 per cent) think that sex between two men is always or mostly wrong. Well over half of women (58 per cent) think the same.

Gay rights groups have pressed for new laws to ban discrimination against homosexual people. Another view is that their cause might be helped if gays and lesbians 'come out' at work, instead of 'staying in the closet'. Keith Cowan is a personnel officer for British Gas in Scotland. He is also chairman of his trade union's lesbian and gay group. His employer was among one of the first companies to include same-sex partners in its pensions plan, but he says that it is a change in attitudes that has made the most difference: 'We have a very young work force. Because of this, I have never faced any discrimination. The more people are willing to tell the truth about their sexuality, the easier it becomes. Once everyone realises that there are gay people all around them, there will be far fewer problems.'

Activist Peter Tatchell leads a demonstration by the militant gay group
Outrage, in 1998.

Case study: gay couple live in fear

Howard Llewellyn is a member of the National Union of Teachers Lesbian and Gay Task Group. For 20 years he has lived with his partner George, a maths teacher. They moved to the Cardiff area and George took a job in a local comprehensive school. Howard admits: 'We had fears about this which proved well founded; it's very unwise to live in the catchment area of a school. It wasn't long before we had hordes of kids surrounding our house, banging on our door and continuously ringing our bell.'

The situation rapidly deteriorated. Living in a close community, it became obvious that Howard and George shared a home together, and that was enough for the locals. Cries of 'Poof' rang after them on the street while youths shouted coarser filth. Their front window was smashed and a rose tree cut down. Graffiti displaying male genitalia were scrawled over their car bonnet and front door. 'Things worsened when a neighbour's child went to the school where George worked,' Howard continued. 'Word got round and soon a local gang of teenagers gathered on the corner and watched our every move. The verbal abuse and their behaviour worsened. They would dance up and down on our car. We counted 15 large dents.'

'While we were trying to cope with all this aggro and stress, George was suffering even more at school. I had got out of it, but he was having to face the taunts in school, the cocks drawn on blackboards, sarcastic comments from homophobic colleagues, no promotion prospects and being lumbered with poor classes.'

Like many gay people, George felt compelled to invent an imaginary wife and children to stave off homophobia in the staffroom. The incidents that have been part of George's and Howard's life continue: 'Recently a member of a gang threw a bottle at me which narrowly missed. And on another occasion, the gang blocked the road preventing me and George from driving away from the house. We have learnt avoidance behaviour and are both very anxious when stepping outside our front door. We are trapped. At night Geroge often has nightmares and wakes screaming like a wounded animal being hunted.'

(adapted from *The Teacher*, January/February 1998)

Out of the closet

Question: What do all the following have in common?
Answer: All have been in same-sex relationships.

W. H. Auden (Anglo-American poet)
Doris Day (American film star)
Angela Eagle (first openly lesbian British government minister)
Michel Foucault (French sociologist, died of aids)
Cary Grant (British film star)
Radclyffe Hall (British novelist, her lesbian novel *The Well of Loneliness*
    was banned in 1928)
David Hockney (British painter)
Sir Elton John (British singer)
Calvin Klein (American fashion designer)
T. E. Lawrence ('Lawrence of Arabia')
Daphne du Maurier (British novelist)
Sir Ian McKellen (British actor, gay activist with Stonewall group)
Harvey Milk (assassinated while Mayor of San Francisco)
Christabel Pankhurst (British suffragette)
Pam St Clements (Pat Butcher in *EastEnders*)
Skin (British singer, Skunk Anansie)
Chris Smith (Labour cabinet minister)
Sandy Toksvig (British comedienne)
Elizabeth Wilson (British sociologist and author)
Virginia Woolf (British writer)

7   Economic stratification: Marx and capitalism

Karl Marx, the founder of **communism**, put forward a view of history that has had a tremendous influence on the way that we think and live in the modern world. Communist states, such as China and Cuba, are supposed to be actually based on his ideas. And in non-communist societies there are a number of quite sizeable political parties that follow the teachings of Marx.

Ruling classes and subject classes in history

Karl Marx (1818–83) spent much of his life studying history. His studies led him to the conclusion that since ancient times all societies have consisted of two main classes whose struggle with each other has led to great social changes. As Marx said, 'All history is the history of class struggles.'

The two main classes are the **ruling class** and the **subject class** and although the nature of these two classes has changed, the basic division between those who have power and those who do not has always existed. According to Marx, in the ancient world the two classes were master and slave, in feudal times they were lord and serf and in modern capitalist society these two classes are **capitalists** and **workers**.

Class and economic production

For Marx, class is based on economic position. The ruling class is those who own the **forces of production**, things such as land, tools and machines which are used to produce wealth. The oppressed or subject class is formed from those who possess nothing but their ability to work.

The forces of production have changed in the past which is why classes have changed. In feudal times the forces of production consisted mainly of land, so the two rival classes were formed by those who owned land (the lords) and those who did not (the serfs).

In industrial societies the main forces of production now consist of factories and machines, which are known as **capital**. Marx believed that society would polarise so that everyone would end up on one of two sides:

- Capitalists: the ruling classes who own capital either as bosses and managers or as wealthy holders of shares in big companies – Marx called these the **bourgeoisie**.
- Workers: 'wage slaves' who live by selling their labour to the capitalist employing classes – Marx called these the **proletariat**.

Class confict and communist revolution

Marx claimed that a ruling class and a subject class would always be in conflict with one another. The reason for this is clear. The ruling class always want more wealth to be produced by the subject class, while the subject class always demand a fairer share of the product of their own labour. This explains why there are strikes and conflict in the workplace: the workers want higher wages while the capitalists or employers want to keep wages as low as possible so that their profits can be as high as possible.

One major event in the calendar of the rich is the Henley Regatta.

Marx believed that the end to this conflict would only come with the abolition of all classes and the creation of an equal, communist society. He predicted that in the near future the workers would overthrow the capitalist order and construct a communist world. This prediction has not so far proved to be correct.

Conclusion

Apart from nations with communist governments, there have in the past been a number of attempts to set up classless societies. Examples include the kibbutzim and communities inspired by the ideas of thinkers such as Kropotkin, Tolstoy, Robert Owen and William Morris. In striving for equality these societies have tried to abolish all types of stratification so that everyone is on the same social level.

Case study: a modern Marxist analysis of social class

Marx emphasised that the capitalist class consists of those who own capital, the means of production. One recent version of Marxist class analysis emphasises that the capitalist class also consists of those who have three sorts of power. The chart at the foot of the case study indicates how different occupations may possess one or more of these sorts of power:

We can draw several conclusions from this sort of structure:

1   The division between manual and non-manual workers is not as important as the division between company directors, the capitalist class, and those employees who have no power to control industry.
2   The second, third and fourth groups in the structure have **contradictory class locations** because they share characteristics with both the most powerful and the least powerful groups.
3   A major aim of socialists and trade unionists may be to alter this uneven distribution of power and control.

Details of these ideas can be found in *Class, Crisis and the State* by E. Wright (1978).

How big is the working class?
From asking employees how much power they have at work, Wright distinguishes between workers and semi-autonomous employees:

Semi-autonomous employees know how the production process is organized and they can use this knowledge in their jobs.

Workers are non-decision-making, non-supervisory employees, who have been 'deskilled'; that is, they perform simple, routinized tasks, under close supervision, and at a pace determined by machinery or by decision makers elsewhere, rather than by themselves.

According to these criteria, the working class includes the large majority of white-collar employees, especially clerical and secretarial employees, who 'have – at most – trivial autonomy (ie independence) on the job'.

From surveys in the 1980s, Wright concluded that the working population of Britain divides into the following class categories, based on power in the workplace:

	Percentage
Bourgeoisie	2.0
Small employers	4.5
Petite bourgeoisie	6.0
Managers and advisory managers	16.9
Supervisors	9.4
Semi-autonomous employees	11.6
Workers	49.6

(The issue of proletarianisation is discussed on pages 165–b.)

	Has control over the investment decisions of companies; the power to close old factories or open new ones	Has control over the machinery used in production; the power to speed up the production line	Has control over labour; the power to hire, fire and manage workers
Company directors	Yes	Yes	Yes
Senior executives	Only partly	Yes	Yes
Middle managers	No	Limited	Some
Foremen, supervisors	No	No	Limited
Low-level employees, manual and non-manual	No	No	No

Activities

1   What do you see as the main problems that would obstruct an attempt to create a society in which everyone is fully equal?

2   In *Animal Farm* George Orwell described a society composed of different types of animals.

   (a)   Find out how that society was stratified. In other words, which animals formed the top social strata and which strata did the other animals belong to?

   (b)   What was the basis of the system of stratification in *Animal Farm*?

GCSE question from Southern Examining Group 1990

Identify and briefly explain *two* forms of social stratification, other than social class.   (4)

CHAPTER 9 · Social class in modern Britain

Does social class matter?

This chapter looks at how social classes are defined, how they are changing, and at the movement of individuals and occupational groups from one class to another. We also consider whether there is any evidence to support the sort of generalisations made in the following chart.

Case study: stereotyped views of class

The middle classes

- live in detached or semi-detached houses which they own themselves,

- eat lunch, go to the loo, drink in the saloon or lounge bar,

- read *The Times, Telegraph, Mail, Express* and *Guardian,*

- enjoy tennis, rugger, squash, golf, sailing and bridge,

- breast-feed their babies,

- shop in Sainsburys, Mothercare, Benetton, Habitat and Laura Ashley,

- wear pure cotton and pure wool,

- enjoy drama and documentaries on BBC2 and Channel 4,

- undress in front of their children and don't lock the bathroom door,

- give their toddlers apple juice and whole-meal biscuits for snacks,

- eat cake with a fork,

- volunteer for the PTA.

The working classes

- live in terraced houses or flats rented from the council,

- eat dinner, go to the toilet, drink in the public bar,

- read the *Sun, Mirror* and *Star,*

- enjoy darts, football, boxing, dog racing and bingo

- bottle-feed their babies,

- shop in Tesco, the Co-op, and MFI as well as from catalogues,

- wear polyester and acrylic,

- enjoy soap operas and Benny Hill on ITV,

- turn out the light before they undress in front of their wives,

- give their toddlers sweets, crisps and fizzy drinks,

- turn their forks over to eat peas,

- keep away from Parents' Evenings.

1   Social class inequalities

The Office of Population Censuses and Surveys (OPCS) conducts a continuous General Household Survey using a sample of around 12,000 homes. This survey uses seven main socioeconomic groups, based on occupational categories. Occupations are allocated to these groups according to the income, status, skill, training and educational level of each type of job. These seven groups can be used to divide the population into the middle class and the working class:

Middle class, non-manual, white-collar:

1 **Professional**, e.g. doctor, lawyer, architect, accountant.

2 **Employers and managers**, e.g. company directors and executives.

3 **Intermediate non-manual**, e.g. teacher, nurse, journalist, farmer.

4 **Junior non-manual**, e.g. typist, clerk, shop assistant.

Working class, manual, blue-collar:

5 **Skilled manual**, e.g. bricklayer, plumber, printer, miner.

6 **Semi-skilled manual**, e.g. gardener, bar tender, sewing machinist.

7 **Unskilled manual**, e.g. cleaner, labourer, messenger.

Lifestyle and life chances

Lifestyle refers to patterns of behaviour, such as consumer spending patterns or the use of leisure time.

   Life chances refers to a person's prospects of living a long, happy and successful life. Lifestyle can influence life chances. For example, if a student's lifestyle includes regular and thorough completion of all his or her homework, then he or she may have a better chance of educational success.

Your lifestyle	can affect	Your life chances
for example:		for example, measured as:
diet		life expectancy
reading		educational qualifications
studying		adult income; type of housing
smoking		infant mortality rate
exercise		long-lasting marriage

The causes of unequal life chances

An important debate in sociology is the extent to which unequal outcomes are due to cultural, as opposed to structural factors. For example, why are the babies of unskilled manual mothers (infant mortality rate (IMR) of 7 per 1,000) far more likely to die in their first year than babies of professional mothers (IMR = 4.5)?

1　Cultural explanations　The right-wing answer blames the victim for their own condition. It is their own fault. We can blame their culture, their behaviour. For example, it can be argued that poor mothers are more likely to have ill babies because the poor mothers smoke more often than other mothers during pregnancy: 62 per cent of poor lone mothers smoke compared to 16 per cent of professional women.

2　Structural explanations　The left-wing answer blames the unfairness of the social structure. It is the fault of the unequal system and not the fault of the victim if their job is poorly paid, so that they live in worse housing and eat a worse diet.

A dangerous working-class job may affect a person's life chances.

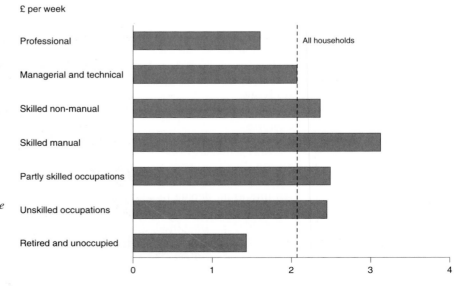

Household expenditure on the National Lottery: by social class of head of household, 1995
(*Source*: Social Trends, 1996.)

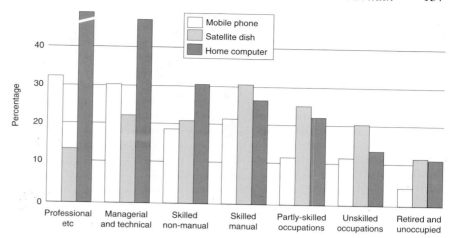

Percentage of households with new technology: by social class, 1997 (Source: Family Expenditure Survey, Office for National Statistics.)

Have class inequalities declined?

In *Repositioning Class* (1997), Gordon Marshall gives the example of social class differences in height. In 1900, it was recognised that working-class boys in London and Glasgow were on average 6.25 cm shorter than middle-class boys. Recent research shows that the differences in average height between the working and middle classes in Britain is still around rather more than 5 cm. This gap is largely established before the age of 7.

Marshall reaches the following overall conclusion: 'Like other investigators I have found that, despite such changes as the rising general levels of education, increased participation of women in paid employment, and the expansion of newer non-manual forms of work at the expense of traditional proletarian occupations, class inequalities in the industrialized countries have remained more or less constant throughout most of the twentieth century.'

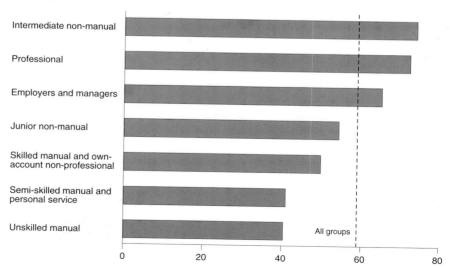

People covered by employers' pension scheme: by socio-economic group, 1991–93 (Source: Social Trends, 1995.)

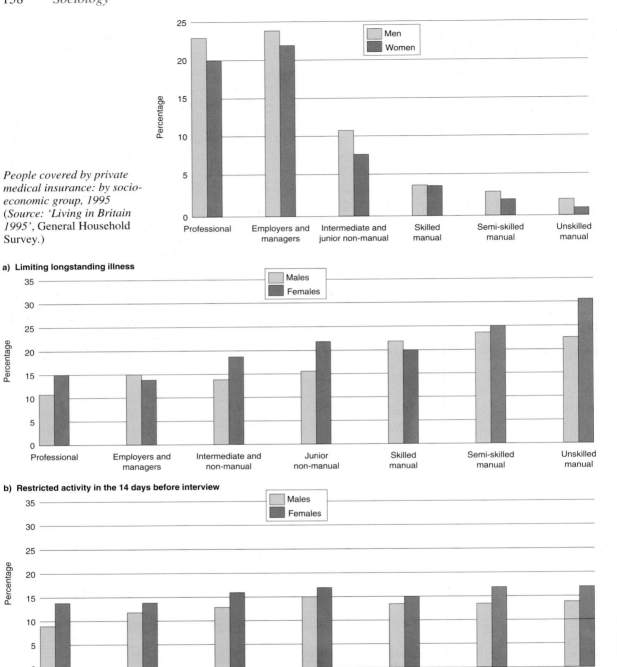

People covered by private medical insurance: by socio-economic group, 1995 (Source: 'Living in Britain 1995', General Household Survey.)

People reporting (a) long-standing illness, (b) being restricted by illness in the last 14 days: by socio-economic group, 1995 (Source: 'Living in Britain 1995', General Household Survey.)

A manual, working-class job, like milk deliverer, offers little chance of promotion into middle-class occupations.

Case study: accidents in childhood

In 1982 Penguin published *Inequalities in Health*, the report of a working party under Sir Douglas Black. This was set up by the Labour Government in 1977 to review differences in health between the social classes. The Black Report found that among child pedestrians the risk of death from being hit by a motor vehicle is about six times greater among the children of unskilled manual workers than among the children of professional parents. For accidental death caused by fires, falls and drowning, the gap between the classes is even larger. The following explanations were suggested for this pattern:

1 Parents in higher occupational classes are more likely to be able to let their children play safely within sight or earshot.
2 The children of semi-skilled and unskilled workers are more likely to be left to their own devices during school holidays and out of school hours.
3 Poorer homes are likely to have less safe furnishings and less safe domestic appliances such as heaters.
4 Poorer mothers lead more stessful lives which leave them less well equipped to provide continuous and vigilant protection for their children.

GCSE question from Southern Examining Group 1993

(a) State *three* factors which have been used by sociologists to define class.   (3)

(b) Identify and explain *two* ways in which children's lives might be influenced by the social class to which their parents belong.   (4)

(c) Surveys show that some people in Britain see themselves as belonging to a particular social class. Other people do not. How might sociologists explain these different views?   (9)

---

2   The upper classes

Government statistics, which divide the population into occupational categories, from professional to unskilled manual, lose sight of the aristocracy and the very rich. Most government figures thus refer just to the middle and working classes. To get an idea of the unequal rewards of the upper classes we can look at official data on income and wealth.

Income

After allowing for inflation, from 1976 to 1996 the average income of the richest 10 per cent has risen from about £300 to over £500 per week, whereas the poorest 10 per cent have stayed at about £60 a week net. Types of income can vary between different income groups:

The very rich	*The average household*	*The poorest*
often have	mainly has	often just rely on
rent from property dividends from shares interest from savings private pensions	hourly wage (working class) annual salary (middle class)	state benefits

In 1995, 73 per cent of all household income was earned income, 11 per cent was investment income and 16 per cent came from welfare state benefits. The 'idle rich' or 'super rich' might get most of their income from rent, dividends and interest which come from investment rather than employment.

Wealth

Wealth can come to people from very high earnings, large inheritances, a rapid rise in the value of the property or shares they own (or a large win on the National Lottery!). In 1996, the total wealth owned by all UK households was £2,992,000,000,000 or £2.992 billion. The main components were:

- 36 per cent pensions and life assurance policies;
- 25 per cent housing;
- 24 per cent shares and bank accounts;
- 15 per cent other assets.

The distribution of wealth in the UK in 1994, percentages

	Most wealthy 1%	Most wealthy 10%	Poorest 50%
Wealth possessed	19	51	7
Wealth minus the value of house(s)	28	65	6

Wealth is far more unevenly distributed than income. High earners may have an annual income of over £100,000 while poor people may have an annual income nearer £1,000. But if we take the example of wealth held as land, the inequalities are even greater. Most of the population own far less than an acre of land. But each of a handful of very wealthy landowners possesses well over 1,000 times more acres than the average person.

Case study: **The Sunday Times** *Rich List*

In 1998, *The Sunday Times* placed *Lord David Sainsbury* as the richest man in Britain, with his family's supermarket fortune estimated at £3,000m.

Of the richest 1,000 people in Britain 30 per cent inherited their wealth. Many are aristocrats from titled families with ancestral mansions full of valuable art treasures and with large holdings of farmland and property. The wealthiest aristocrat is the *Duke of Westminster*. He is the fourth richest person in Britain. It is mainly his 300 acres of properties in London's poshest areas, Mayfair and Belgravia, which make him worth £1,750m.

No. 14 is *Richard Branson*. His £1,000m business empire has grown from Virgin Records to 179 Virgin companies including Virgin Airways, Virgin Megastores, Virgin Cola, Virgin Cinemas, Virgin Rail, Virgin Hotels and Virgin Direct financial services.

Richard Branson: £1,000m.

No. 29 is *Sir Paul McCartney*. His £500m makes him the richest pop musician in Britain.

No. 40 is *Robert Earl* (£450m). After a degree in catering from Surrey University, he started the Planet Hollywood chain of restaurants.

No. 45 is *James Dyson* (£400m), the inventor of the bagless vacuum cleaner. Also at No. 45, with £400m, is Ronald Hobson who drives an old Vauxhall Cavalier. In 1948, he and a friend bought a bombsite for £200 and turned it into their first car park. In 1998, they sold their stake in the National Parking Corporation for £580m.

The Queen is placed at No. 94. Much of her £250m wealth comes from her private jewels and her estates at Balmoral and Sandringham. If the royal art collection belonged to her (rather than to the nation), her fortune would be between £5 billion and £10 billion.

No. 508 is the youngest multi-millionaire, 21-year-old *Reuben Singh*, who has £45m from his Miss Attitude fashion accessory company.

No. 668 is *Chris Evans* (£30m) with his radio and TV Ginger Media Group.

No. 769 are *Noel Gallagher* and *Liam Gallagher*, with £25m from their band, Oasis.

No. 837 is *Delia Smith* (£24m), Britain's top cookery writer and broadcaster.

No. 880 is *Terry Benson* who won £20m in the National Lottery in 1995.

Conclusion

Some argue that a marginal 'underclass' (the bottom 15 per cent?) exists at the bottom of the class system and is largely excluded from the rest of society. In a similar vein, it may be argued that an 'overclass' (the top 15 per cent?) exists which uses its wealth and influence to contract out of the world in which most people have to live.

This 'overclass' buys a different education for its children, pays for its own medical care and purchases elaborate home security systems. New fast-track transport developments, such as privately run toll motorways and the direct link from Paddington to Heathrow, will allow the 'over-class' to avoid the delays suffered by the majority of the population.

GCSE question from Southern Examining Group 1993

(a)   Identify *two* examples of wealth and explain how they can produce income for the owners.   (4)

(b)   Identify and explain *two* policies by which a government might reduce the income gap between the rich and poor.   (4)

GCSE question from Southern Examining Group 1990

Identify and explain *two* ways in which people can accumulate wealth.   (4)

3   The middle classes

The middle classes are divided in a number of ways. One division is between the old middle class and the new middle class. The old middle class includes self-employed partnerships, such as solicitors and vets, and owners of small businesses, such as shops and hotels. The new middle class includes newer occupations, such as planning inspector and youth worker.

The upper and middle middle classes

Government classifications distinguish between higher professionals, such as lawyers and doctors, and lower professionals, such as nurses and teachers. Sociologists stress how these categories are cross-cut by differences in chosen lifestyles. The cultural fragmentation in the middle classes can be seen in the consumption patterns of the following lifestyle categories:

- **Yuppies**   In the 1980s, young upwardly mobile professionals, such as rising advertising executives, were identified as a group who liked to show off and enjoy their high incomes through their consumption of status symbols such as Porsche cars, the first mobile phones and Filofaxes, opera and skiing holidays. Vote Conservative.

- **Young Fogies and Sloane Rangers**   With jobs ranging from city finance to public relations, these people like to emphasise their public school and high society connections. Essential accessories for weekends in the country include a Range Rover, a horsey headscarf, green wellies and a black labrador. Vote Conservative.

- **Sporters**   This name has been given to public sector professionals, such as university lecturers, who favour healthy living, with low alcohol consumption and high consumption of sport, activity and adventure holidays and high culture, such as theatre and classical music. May vote Liberal-Democrat.

- **Drabbies**   These are people, such as social workers and teachers, who care about the environment and world poverty. They favour second-hand clothes from Oxfam shops and travel to work by bike, Morris Minor or VW beetle. They are quite likely to be vegetarians and to be against tourism. Vote Green or Labour.

- **Undistinctives**   Managers or government officials who have high alcohol consumption scores and low consumption scores for exercise and high culture. Likely to enjoy holidays in country house hotels visiting cleaned-up heritage attractions like Stratford-upon-Avon. Vote Tory.

- **Drinkers**   Owners of small local businesses, such as car repair firms or building companies. Regular convivial drinking enjoyed: on package holidays, eating out at steak houses and in comfortably and traditionally furnished homes. Preferred entertainment would be a spectacular West End musical show. Vote Tory.

These categories suggest that the main social distinctions are no longer based on positions in the process of production, the workplace. Increasingly, social divisions involve consumption. Social class in the nineteenth century was symbolised by the factory and people's relations to the productive system. In the late twentieth century, our spending patterns in the shopping mall place us in lifestyle categories which perhaps modify the importance of occupational class. But the following figures show that the old class divisions are still to be found in the area of leisure; participation in active sports varies significantly between socioeconomic groups:

Percentage of women participating in the twelve months before interview, according to their current or most recent job, 1990

	Keep fit/ yoga	Skiing	Tennis	Horse riding	Climbing
Professional	42	20	14	9	8
Employers and managers	33	5	8	5	2
Intermediate and junior non-manual	33	3	6	4	2
Skilled manual	19	1	4	3	1
Semi-skilled manual and personal service	20	0	3	2	1
Unskilled manual	13	0	1	0	1

(Source: *General Household Survey*)

Upper- and working-class leisure activities: playing polo and playing pool.

The lower middle classes

Many routine white-collar jobs are low paid, such as working in shops or offices. In 1958 *The Black-Coated Worker*, by David Lockwood, gave a number of reasons for the decline in the social position of clerks since Victorian times:

Clerks in the mid-nineteenth century	*Clerks in the mid-twentieth century*
High status:	Low status:
• few offices and few clerical jobs;	• many offices and many clerical jobs;
• few able to read and write, so only the well-educated middle class could be clerks;	• due to mass education and mass literacy most school-leavers could do simple filing jobs;
• usually men, writing copper-plate script with quill pens at high desks which emphasised their importance;	• over 75 per cent of clerks were women, compared to 21 per cent in 1900;
• regarded as a 'good middle-class job'.	• a good middle-class job now means a university-educated profession.
Well paid; i.e. a good **market situation**, in the job market.	Clerks in a DHSS office often earn less than they pay out to many claimants each week.
A work situation allowing a fair degree of power. Often working independently, but in a close relationship with their employers.	Little power at work. Often closely supervised, in large, impersonal organisations.

Proletarianisation

Proletarianisation is the process whereby those with formerly middle-class jobs become increasingly like the working class. They may have a decline in their income and working conditions. They may become more likely to join trade unions and vote Labour. The Registrar-General has downgraded the following occupations from intermediate to skilled non-manual: clerks (in 1931) and draughtsmen (in 1961). Undertakers and waiters were reclassified from skilled non-manual to skilled manual in 1981.

Wright has argued that many routine non-manual workers lack power at work. Because of this, they should be categorised as proletarian workers. As a Marxist, he defines class location in terms of one's objective relationship to the 'means of production'. Marshall disagrees. He offers the following British figures from the International Sociological Association's research on social stratification, showing a significant difference between skilled non-manual and skilled manual workers, in terms of their subjective class consciousness:

	Self-assigned class Percentage describing themselves as:		Voting intentions Percentage intending to vote for:	
	Middle class	Working class	Conservative	Labour
Class I Professional occupations	84	16	43	14
Class 3N Skilled non-manual	53	47	49	24
Divide between middle and working classes				
Class 3M Skilled manual	26	74	28	50
Class 5 Unskilled manual	23	77	22	53

The class divide is more pronounced in Britain than in most European countries. Most British people know which of the two main classes they are in. British politics has also been very class based.

4   The working class

Images of the working class

What is your image of a typical working-class occupation? A coal miner (primary, extractive industry)? A factory worker (secondary, manufacturing industry)? A hotel cleaner (tertiary, service industry)? At the height of the factory era, in 1911, the 1.8 million manual workers in metal manufacturing were outnumbered by the 2.1 million female domestic servants. The working class has always consisted of a wide variety of groups.

In the nineteenth century Marx wrote of the proletariat as a single class but he recognised divisions within the ranks of manual employees. The 'labour aristocracy' were the skilled workers with the best pay. The 'lumpenproletariat' were the poorest group, unskilled labourers with casual and insecure employment.

Working-class culture

The British working class may cover a wide range of occupations, from skilled lorry drivers to unskilled labourers, but a unifying factor has been the common working-class culture built around working-class institutions, such as:

- trade unions, the co-operative movement and the Labour Party;
- working men's clubs, with darts teams and male voice choirs;
- workplace silver bands and allotments associations;
- non-conformist chapels, like the Methodists, and workers' institutes with reading rooms and evening classes;
- clubs for pigeon-fanciers, anglers and football supporters.

Two questions arise about this working-class culture. First, is it in decline? Sociologists often point to the decline of traditional working-class communities and the rise of mobile, nuclear families with more home-centred activities. Second, have these working-class organisations mainly included the 'respectables', sober and hard-working citizens, rather than the 'roughs'?

There have always been working-class people who have regarded themselves as more respectable than others. In the nineteenth century the 'roughs' were sometimes described as 'the dangerous classes'. Is there a lower working class who tend to be antagonistic to authority figures, such as teachers, social workers and the police? Part of this debate resurfaces in Chapter 15, on poverty, when we consider the use of the term **underclass**.

Essex Man

In the 1992 General Election the Labour Party looked set to unseat John Major's Conservative Government. On the election night, although a number of Tory MPs lost their seats, it was soon recognised that Labour would not win when an early result came through from a key marginal constituency: Basildon had stayed Tory. Essex Man had not deserted the Conservatives.

Essex Man was a term coined in the 1980s to describe the sort of working-class Tory who gave Mrs Thatcher her three election victories in 1979, 1983 and 1987. He represented the affluent, skilled manual worker of the new working class who differed from the old working class in the following ways:

Traditional working class	Essex Man
Collectivist, 'them-and-us' view: workers must stick together in trade unions.	Individualistic view: each person must get ahead on their own, e.g. by becoming self-employed.
Social life based around organisations and institutions in the community, e.g. the pub.	Privatism in leisure: activities shared with wife and children, social life revolving around the family.
Council tenant, reads the *Daily Mirror*, votes Labour.	Buying own house, reads the *Sun*, votes Tory.

Essex Man is a stereotype created by political and social commentators. It shows the thinking behind the Thatcherite strategy of creating a capitalist-minded 'property-owning democracy': by selling council houses to their tenants at a discount; and by encouraging the public to purchase shares through the privatisation of nationalised industries. This strategy was continued in the 1992 General Election with John Major declaring his aim of creating a 'classless society'.

Conclusion

The Essex Man stereotype overlooks other important groups within the working class, such as women, ethnic minorities and welfare claimants. In modern Britain social class divisions based on occupation are cut across by divisions based on gender, ethnicity, religion, region, disability, age and unemployment.

Some commentators have argued that modern British society is divided into three roughly equal-sized groups:

- The top third have secure jobs and are likely to own their homes outright.

- The middle third have jobs that are no longer as secure as they used to be in the recent past. Economic restructuring may cause redundancies and, if mortgage repayments are not kept up, house purchasers may find their homes repossessed by the banks and building societies who lent them money.
- The bottom third tend to be renting property owned by private landlords or renting 'social housing' owned by housing associations and councils. Many are heavily reliant on welfare benefits.

GCSE question from Southern Examining Group 1992

Identify and explain *two* ways in which the working conditions of non-manual workers are likely to be better than those of manual workers.   (4)

Non-manual and manual workers. Are they both proletarian?

At the end of the day, the following figures suggest a simple rule of thumb. Those earning below £300 a week are mainly working class and those earning more are the middle class:

Average gross weekly earnings, 1995
£764 doctor
£585 solicitor
£435 secondary teacher
£340 social worker
£329 nurse

£274 carpenter
£227 caretaker
£188 receptionist
£181 cleaner
£165 bar staff

---

5 Social mobility

Sociologists make a contrast between societies with very little social mobility and societies in which many people are able to move up or down the system of social stratification:

A closed society	*An open society*
Social status or position is generally ascribed, or fixed, at birth.	It is possible to achieve a higher position in society than one's parents.
Offers little chance for upward mobility.	Offers lots of scope for upward mobility.
e.g. 1 the caste system, 2 apartheid, 3 feudal England, where only a few peasants moved up the social pyramid by joining the army or the church.	e.g. 1 the USA, where the 'log cabin to White House' story is a part of the American Dream, 2 the UK, with self-made men such as Sir John Moores and Alan Sugar. Respectively, they left school at 14 and 15, to be a messenger boy and a barrow boy; they founded Littlewoods Pools and Amstrad computers; their personal fortunes, in 1989, were £1,700 million and £432 million.

Types of social mobility

Social mobility means movement within the class system. It should not be confused with geographical mobility, which means moving home to a different area. There are a number of different types of social mobility:

- **Group mobility**   This occurs when a whole occupational group moves within the system of stratification. For example, in 1961 all university lecturers were upgraded from intermediate to professional; in 1981 firefighters were upgraded from skilled manual to skilled non-manual and in 1961 postmen were downgraded from skilled to semi-skilled manual.
- **Individual vertical mobility**   This may be upward, such as the docker who becomes a restaurateur, or downward, such as the farmer who becomes a bus driver.

- **Horizontal social mobility**   This occurs when someone moves sideways rather than up or down. A carpenter who becomes a plumber still remains in the skilled manual group.
- **Inter-generational mobility**   'Inter' means 'between' and an example of mobility between the generations is D.H. Lawrence, the miner's son who became an author.
- **Intra-generational mobility**   'Intra' means 'within' and an example of mobility within one lifetime is Dennis Skinner, who has risen from being a miner to being a Member of Parliament.

Avenues of individual upwards social mobility

During the twentieth century there was a contraction of unskilled jobs. For example, 18 per cent of occupied men in 1921 were in unskilled manual occupation as against just 5 per cent in 1981. Much unskilled work, such as digging ditches, has been mechanised. Ditches are now usually dug by JCB excavators operated by skilled workers. There has also been a growth in non-manual work, from 24 per cent of male workers in 1921 to 40 per cent in 1981. As the class structure has changed shape, from a pyramid shape to a diamond shape, so there has been increased opportunity for upward inter-generational social mobility.

There are a number of ways in which an individual might ascend the social class ladder:

- **Marriage**   A bricklayer's daughter who marries a stockbroker moves from working-class origins to join the middle class.
- **Education**   A dustman's daughter who qualifies as a doctor has moved from an unskilled manual background to a professional position.
- **Promotion**   A semi-skilled manual factory worker might be promoted to become a non-manual supervisor or manager.
- **Luck**   A working-class pools winner might become a middle-class shop owner.

How much social mobility is there?

Studies have found a large amount of short-range mobility, such as manual worker to supervisor. But there is often a '**glass ceiling**' of gender discrimination, so that clerks promoted to middle management are more likely to be men than women.

The expansion of white-collar jobs and educational opportunities has also produced a degree of long-range mobility. In 1972, Goldthorpe found that 28 per cent of men in higher professional jobs had working-class fathers. But unfair relative chances of mobility were shown in the 1:4 ratio: sons of professional fathers were four times more likely to get professional jobs than the sons of working-class fathers.

Is openness increasing?

The 50 years from the 1940s to the 1990s were, overall, a period of considerable economic growth in Britain. During this half-century social reforms increased access to education and tempered the worst effects of poverty. As Goldthorpe wrote in 1978: 'The project of creating a more open society was undertaken, and in circumstances which might be regarded as highly favourable to it.'

Marshall (1997) has looked at the 'odds ratios' and found that boys and girls from professional homes are 5 or 6 times more likely to achieve professional employment (and to avoid-working-class destinations) than their peers who come from working-class backgrounds. He looks across a number of advanced societies and, with the exception of Sweden, concludes that, despite the attempt to minimise the influence of class on the processes of social selection, the degree of openness has remained unchanged over the last 50 years.

As an example of the continuing unfairness, let us take Marshall's data from the Essex Class Project of the mid-1980s. He examined the social mobility of people with similar qualifications:

People with medium-level educational qualifications (GCSEs and A-levels only)	Destination in:	
	Professional jobs	Working-class jobs
Origin in a professional home	39%	20%
Origin in a working-class family	17%	36%

These figures show that even when working-class children get the same sort of exam passes as children from professional backgrounds, they are almost twice as likely to end up in working-class occupations, whereas these from professional homes are more than twice as likely to enter professional careers.

Elite self-recruitment

A high percentage of top jobs in Britain are held by men who have been to 'public (fee-paying) schools' and Oxbridge (Oxford and Cambridge Universities). The elite seems to prefer new recruits who have a similarly privileged background to themselves. This is called the **old school tie network**.

In 1993, *The Sunday Times* researched the backgrounds of those with the top 100 jobs in the City, such as chairmen of banks. Forty-one were Oxbridge graduates and thirty-eight had been to the top eight public schools, sixteen to Eton.

The Economist surveyed the top 100 jobs in the UK in 1972 and 1992. The jobs held by women had risen from two to four. Those with public school educations had fallen from sixty-seven to sixty-six. Oxbridge graduates had risen from fifty-two to fifty-four.

GCSE question from Southern Examining Group 1996

Study Item A. Then answer all parts of the question which follow.

Item A

Comparison of Social Class and Feudal Systems		
	SOCIAL CLASS	**FEUDAL**
TYPE OF ECONOMY	Industrial	Agriculture
SOCIAL POSITION	Achieved	Fixed at birth
MARRIAGE OUTSIDE SOCIAL GROUP	Normally	Rare but possible

(a) (i)   According to Item A, in what type of economy is social class found?   (1)

 (ii)   According to Item A, is social position fixed at birth in a social class or in a feudal society?   (1)

 (iii)   State one example of social mobility given in Item A.   (1)

(b) (i)   Suggest *two* examples of weath in Britain.   (2)

 (ii)   Explain the difference between wealth and income.   (2)

(c) (i)   Outline *one* way of measuring social class.   (2)

 (ii)   Give *two* ways in which social class can affect an individual's life.   (2)

(d) (i)   Describe how the class structure has changed in Britain this century.   (3)

 (ii)   State **one** reason for the changes.   (1)

GCSE question from Southern Examining Group 1996

To what extent has social mobility become more common in Britain during the last fifty years?   (10)

In what ways might sociologists see life on a housing estate in a large city as similar to, and different from, life in a rural village?   (10)

CHAPTER 10

Education

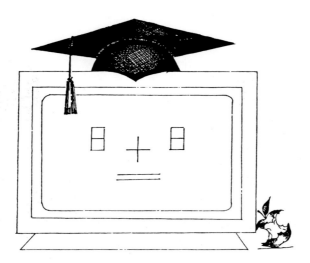

Case study: the response of the Indians of the Six Nations to a suggestion that they send boys to a college in Pennsylvania, 1744:

But you, who are wise, must know that different nations have different conceptions of things and will therefore not take it amiss, if our ideas of this kind of education happen not to be the same as yours. We have had some experience of it. Several of our young people were formerly brought up at the colleges of the northern provinces: they were instructed well in all your sciences; but, when they came back to us, they were bad runners, ignorant of every means of living in the woods ... neither were they fit for hunters, warriors, nor councillors, they were totally good for nothing.

We are, however, not the less obliged by your kind offer, though we decline accepting it; and, to show our grateful sense of it, if the gentlemen of Virginia will send us a dozen of their sons we will take care of their education, instruct them in all we know, and make men of them.

Education in the broadest sense means the process of acquiring knowledge and understanding. This occurs throughout our lives as a result of a large variety of influences. We learn from our parents, from our friends, from travel, from observing what goes on around us and we learn from all our experiences of life. All this learning and development of the mind occurs naturally, as an inevitable consequence of living, without any direct teaching. And until comparatively recently, this informal education was considered to be all that the average person needed.

During the nineteenth century, however, leading figures in British society increasingly felt that informal education was no longer adequate and that the government should provide compulsory schooling for all. Today, almost everyone in Britain experiences **formal education** – that is, learning particular subjects from qualified teachers in organised institutions called schools.

In 1992–93 government spending on education was £32,258,000,000. Schooling has become a central part of our way of life. In this chapter we will be looking at our educational arrangements and at their connection with other aspects of society. First we look at the origin of our state schooling system.

A lesson in a Victorian elementary school.

1   Why was schooling made compulsory in 1880?

Compulsory attendance in elementary schools was first introduced in Prussia in 1763. In 1870 a national system of basic schooling for every child was set up in England. By 1880 attendance was compulsory between the ages of 5 and 10. In 1893 the school-leaving age was raised to 11 and in 1899 it was raised to 12.

We will now look at the purposes of making this elementary schooling compulsory.

To meet the needs of industry

As the complexity of industry in the 1800s increased, factories needed literate and numerate workers who could read and count. By 1880 Britain was no longer so clearly the world's foremost industrial nation and its position was strongly challenged by Germany and the USA. As William Forster MP said in introducing the 1870 Education Act:

Upon the speedy provision of education depends our national power ... if we are to hold our position among the nations of the world, we must make up for the smallness of our numbers by increasing the intellectual force of the individual.

To 'mind' children while their parents go out to work

In 1948 T. Beggs complained (in his *Enquiry into the Extent and Causes of Juvenile Depravity*) that, with many working-class mothers out at work, 'Young children are left at home under very inadequate conduct and almost without restraint left to play at will and to expand into every lawless form.' The dual concerns of the authorities were to keep the children off the streets and to enable both parents to go out to work.

To prevent the exploitation of child labour

While the new factory system demanded the labour of both parents, reformers such as Lord Shaftesbury had severely restricted the employment of children with a number of Factory Acts since the early nineteenth century. But they called for schooling to be compulsory in order to stop the continued exploitation of young children who were employed, for example, to climb up inside and sweep chimneys.

To educate for democracy

Worried by the example of the French Revolution of 1789, observers such as Dr J. Kay-Shuttleworth wrote in 1832 that 'The preservation of internal peace ... depends on the education of the working class.' Six years later, he set up the first training college for teachers in Britain. In 1867 most working-class men were allowed to vote for the first time. They now formed the majority of voters which explains why Robert Lowe MP said, 'We must educate our masters.'

To civilise the 'heathen masses'

Lord Shaftesbury spoke in 1843 of girls in mining districts who 'drink, swear, fight, smoke, whistle, sing and care for nobody'. He urged the necessity of education for the children of the 'dangerous classes' whom he called 'a fearful multitude of untutored savages'.

The first schools for the urban poor in the early 1800s had been set up by the Bible Societies. These organisations saw their mission, not only across the Empire but also in Britain itself, to convert non-believers, or heathens as they were called, to Christianity and also to instruct them in the manners of civilised, polite society.

To enable individuals to develop fully

Teachers have always tried to help pupils develop their minds and bodies to their full potential. In other words, teachers want pupils to develop strength of character, individuality of personality and a range of hobbies and interests.

Summary: the functions of education

The above outline of the historical reasons for our state schooling system suggests the following functions of education:

1 socialisation: passing on culture and values;
2 preparation for work: teaching basic skills required by industry such as reading, writing and arithmetic and 'sifting and sorting' pupils by exams;
3 personal: developing individual potential;
4 political: preparation for adult citizenship;
5 social control: instilling respectable values into idle youth while their parents go to work.

2   The changing curriculum

The 1988 Education Reform Act

The 1988 Education Reform Act made a number of major changes to the education system, from testing for all 7-year-olds to new systems of financing for polytechnics and universities.

Activity

Read through the summary of the 1988 Education Reform Act below. Try to decide (a) how each of the changes relates to the general functions of education, as listed above, and

(b) which of the changes relate to the political ideas of the Conservative Party, such as competition and freedom of choice.

Open enrolment, opting out and control of school budgets

- Parents have the right to send their children to the school of their choice – as long as it is not physically full. Schools now have an incentive to compete for pupils since unpopular schools will decline and close.
- Parents can vote for their children's school to opt out from the control of their local education authority (the local council). Such schools will become **grant-maintained** (independent, with funding direct from central government).
- Governors are to control the running of their schools. They are to be free to use resources within their budgets according to their school's particular needs and priorities. Governors will thus be free to decide the numbers of teaching and non-teaching staff.

National Curriculum and testing

- All 5- to 16-year-olds in England are to take the **core subjects** of English, maths and science. The other compulsory **foundation subjects** are history, geography, technology, music, art and PE and, at secondary level, a modern foreign language.

- The government is to lay down attainment targets, programmes of study and assessment arrangements for these core and foundation subjects. Pupils must be assessed at the ages of 7, 11, 14 and 16.

Religious education

- Religious education is part of the basic, compulsory curriculum but it is not a foundation subject and so does not carry with it requirements for assessment and testing.
- Right-wing Conservatives in the House of Lords successfully amended the Act so that schools must have a daily act of collective worship which is 'wholly or mainly of a broadly Christian character'.

Vocational education (providing the skills needed for certain jobs)

- **City technology colleges** are to extend the choice of secondary schools in the inner cities. They are to have extra funds from industrial sponsors and to provide a curriculum with an emphasis on science and technology.
- **City technology colleges of the arts** are to specialise in arts technology, film and video and the range of technical skills that support the arts industry.
- Pupils are to leave secondary schools with **records of achievement** which cover all types of accomplishments, including practical and social skills, as well as more academic successes.

The Dearing Review

In 1994, the Dearing Review of the National Curriculum recommended pruning back on the compulsory content in Key Stage 4 to allow up to 40 per cent of time for a choice of courses. It recommended that vocational qualifications be taken alongside GCSEs from the age of 14. Sir Ron Dearing said, 'The main issue is the broadening of choice beyond the traditionally school-based academic subjects into more vocational areas.' Education Minister Tim Boswell added, 'We do not want to typecast children as "academic", "vocational" or "technical". Pupils should not be asked to burn their boats at age 14, or age 16 ... there is scope to take a GCE A-level alongside a vocational A-level – ensuring a smooth transition from 14 to 19 without any major discontinuity at age 16.'

The hidden curriculum

There are many things that pupils learn in school which are not directly taught or are not a part of the timetable of official lessons. The term **hidden curriculum** is used to refer to what pupils learn indirectly (and often unconsciously) from the manner in which the school is organised and from teachers' expectations of pupils.

In most schools this hidden curriculum includes:

1 punctuality: pupils are expected to arrive at lessons, assemblies and registration on time;
2 obedience to authority: pupils are expected to do what they are told without argument;

What aspects of the hidden curriculum are shown here?

3   the value of hard work: pupils are constantly reminded throughout their school lives of the importance of working hard and getting on;
4   appropriate dress: pupils are expected to dress suitably and 'respectably', especially when there is a school uniform;
5   co-operation: 'fitting in' and getting on with others is often impressed on pupils in school;
6   honesty: pupils are encouraged not to lie and steal.

These values and others, which make up the hidden curriculum, are communicated to pupils by lectures in assemblies, by remarks from teachers and by punishments and rewards.

Criticisms of the hidden curriculum

Most of us would accept that it is part of the job of schools to socialise the young into the sorts of values listed above. But some critics argue that the hidden curriculum goes much further, that it encourages pupils to become passive, unquestioning mental slaves. They argue that society directs schools to crush individuality because society needs an obedient workforce – workers who will do what they are told to do.

Hargreaves has explained how space and time are part of the hidden curriculum and we can note similarities with factory life. Of space he says:

It is only teachers who are free to move where they want and when they want. They have free access to what is the closest to being pupil territory, their lavatories. Even territory which is officially shared between teachers and pupils, the classroom, is frequently termed 'my room' by the teacher, who has complete control over entry, exits and movements within the room. In a very real sense, then, the pupils have no legitimate territory of their own. Wherever they are, they are subject to surveillance and control. Wherever pupils are in school, they must be ready to be called to account, to explain and justify their location. Thus pupils in corridors must always be 'going somewhere' lest they be accused of 'loitering' with or without intent. In the allocation, use and control of space in school, the teacher's power and authority are constantly represented and reinforced.

Of time he says:

> In school, as in the factory, time belongs to those who wield power and authority. And the idea of time conveyed in the school is the same as that conveyed in the factory – the idea that 'time is money'. Just as pupils own no territory, so they have little time they can call their own. Pupils must be ready to give an account of their use of time, for of all pupil sins *wasting* time is one of the most common, and the seriousness of the offence rises if the pupils waste not only their own time but that of the teacher as well. Good children, like good workers, do not waste time. In school, time belongs to the school; in the factory, time belongs to the factory.

(adapted from 'Power and the Paracurriculum' by D. Hargreaves)

Critics, such as I. Illich in *Deschooling Society*, argue that the organisation of the school is designed to produce passive individuals. Thus, for example, pupils are given little choice over the subjects available and little or no choice about learning methods and the structure of the school day.

Case study: 'Choosing to play their own tune' by Sally Ballard

There are estimated to be 5,000 children currently being taught at home. 'Many parents worry that their children don't seem to be doing anything at school,' says Jane Lowe of Education Otherwise, a charity that advises home-schooling parents. 'They say they learn more in the holidays than they do in term-time.'

I know of one mother who works evening shifts at a Little Chef in Humberside to help pay for books and outings for three primary-aged children she and her husband teach at home. They see school as a hotbed of bullying and bad behaviour and have no intention of sending their children there.

Another couple teach their four primary-aged children above their baker's shop in Suffolk.

They feel that if they sent their children to school all the moral values they have learnt at home would be undermined. The children work to an American Christian-based curriculum and learn Greek and French. After school, they play with friends who their parents feel have similar moral outlooks.

I know of a 15-year-old Norfolk boy who regularly travels with his father to take relief to the forgotten children in Romania. He does this and raises money for Romania between his GCSE studies at home. His parents feel he will have a richer education than will his counterparts hanging around the bicycle sheds.

(adapted from the *Daily Telegraph*, 9 February 1994)

Some parents choose to educate their children themselves, rather than put them through the school system.

3 The tripartite system and comprehensive schools

In 1900 only one in seventy pupils went to secondary schools. The 1902 Education Act allowed local authorities to provide secondary schools but it was not until 1944 that secondary education was proposed for all pupils. Before 1944 all pupils stayed at school up to the age of 14 but most were at elementary schools.

The 1944 Education Act

This Act set up the **tripartite system**, so called because it recommended three types of secondary school for all pupils to attend from the age of 11. The main points of the Act can be summarised by the 'three threes':

1   The three stages of education: **primary** from 5 to 11, **secondary** from 11, **tertiary**, meaning colleges of further education, polytechnics and universities.
2   The three types of secondary school: **grammar schools** for the most able, **technical schools** for training in practical skills, **secondary modern schools** for 70 per cent or so of pupils.
3   The three ways of deciding which type of educational institution a person should attend: **age**, **aptitude**, **ability**.

For example:

- Age: an 11-year-old would have to take the '11+' examination to be selected for one of the three types of secondary school.
- Aptitude: those who had shown a talent for 'working with their hands' might be selected for secondary technical schools with an emphasis on training workshops.
- Ability: those who failed the 11+ could not go to the grammar schools, unless there were spare places.

The 1944 Act was clearly a major step forward in the development of our education system because, for the first time, free secondary education was provided for all. Also, it genuinely aimed at creating 'equality of opportunity'. In other words, the Act set out to ensure that all pupils had a fair chance to develop their potential. But critics soon argued that selection by the 11+ examination was not fair at all. The 11+ examination, taken in the last year of junior school, usually consisted of an intelligence test based on questions in English, maths and general knowledge. Since those who passed the 11+ were mainly middle class, critics argued that the examination was in fact an obstacle to equality of opportunity.

Criticisms of the 11+ system

1 The whole basis of the 11+ examination has been rejected by those who claim that 'intelligence' cannot be defined and measured.
2 Even its supporters admitted that the 11+ had a 10 per cent margin of error and while late-developers were supposed to be able to transfer to grammar schools at the age of 12 or 13, few in fact did so.
3 Middle-class children of the same intelligence as working-class children had an advantage because of their home background. They were often coached for the examination by their parents as well as by the teachers in the primary schools in middle-class areas. 'Cramming' books could be bought which rehearsed typical 11+ questions such as 'What is the name for a family of lions?' (Answer: a pride).
4 The examination reinforced class divisions by providing two distinct types of education: academic grammar schools for mainly middle-class pupils and secondary modern schooling for mainly working-class pupils; very few technical schools were provided.
5 These two types of school were supposed to have **parity of esteem** or equal status but in fact grammar schools often had better teachers and facilities.
6 Seventy-five per cent or so were labelled as 11+ failures for the rest of their lives and their education was seen as inferior.
7 Before the introduction of CSE examinations in 1965 and before the school-leaving age was raised to 16 in 1972, most of the 75 per cent at secondary modern schools left with no qualifications at all.
8 Some areas of the country provided a higher proportion of grammar school places than others.

What do you think is meant by the term 'intelligence'?

The growth of the comprehensive schools

The mounting criticisms of selection by the 11+ examination led to a rejection of the whole tripartite system. One of the first councils to experiment with alternatives was Labour-run London which set up eight trial comprehensive schools between 1946 and 1949. These schools aimed to be **comprehensive** by taking all secondary pupils of all levels of ability in their areas.

In 1965 the Labour Government issued its famous circular '10/65' instructing councils to plan for comprehensive schools. This circular said: 'A comprehensive school aims to establish a school community in which pupils over the whole ability range can be encouraged to mix with each other, gaining stimulus from the contacts and learning tolerance and understanding in the process.'

Conservative Governments have since withdrawn this instruction to 'go comprehensive' but any council – such as Solihull in 1985 – that attempted to 'turn the clock back' and re-introduce the tripartite system would be very unpopular with most parents. This is because nobody wants to risk their children going to a secondary modern school for second-best pupils.

By 1984 the state secondary education system in England consisted of

> 3,300,000 pupils in 3,938 comprehensive schools,
>   171,470 pupils in 285 secondary modern schools,
>   117,187 pupils in 175 grammar schools.

Nevertheless, comprehensive schools have remained controversial and they still arouse a lot of opposition.

Three criticisms of comprehensive schools

1   The loss of the 'fine academic' grammar school traditions

Grammar schools were said to provide high standards of scholarly learning which met the needs of bright pupils. Critics claim that comprehensive schools fail to provide adequately for the 'gifted child' (although it can be argued that we all have 'gifts' of different kinds). Some parents feel that not enough is demanded of their children, that they are not 'pushed' or 'stretched' in comprehensives which attempt to cater for all abilities, often in mixed-ability teaching groups.

If comprehensives are accused of lowering educational standards, we can consider the following evidence about the qualifications of school-leavers:

	1969 (%)	1987 (%)
Percentage leaving with one or more A-levels	12	19
Percentage leaving with 5 or more O-levels (but no A-levels)	7	11
Percentage leaving with just 1, 2, 3 or 4 O-levels	18	28
Percentage leaving with O-level or A-level passes	37	58
Percentage leaving with no qualifications at all	50	10

These figures show that educational standards were higher in 1987, when less than 4 per cent went to grammar schools, than in 1969, when 21 per cent went to grammar schools. Therefore the abolition of grammar schools has not resulted in an overall decline in examination success.

2   The loss of the upward route for the able lower-class pupil   Prime
Ministers Harold Wilson, Edward Heath and Margaret Thatcher all rose
from lower-middle-class homes via success at their local grammar schools
and then at Oxford University. Part of the grammar school tradition was
that they enabled upward social mobility for a small proportion of bright
working-class pupils. It was for this reason that Harold Wilson once said
that grammar schools would only be abolished 'over my dead body', yet it

*Pupils at a grammar school
in the early 1960s.*

*Pupils with their form
teacher at a London
comprehensive school in
1986.*

was his government which sent out circular '10/65' asking local authorities to draw up plans to go comprehensive.

3   The size and anonymity of comprehensive schools   The pioneers in London in the 1940s reckoned that a 'real' comprehensive needed three forms of pupils who would have passed the 11+ to produce a viable sixth form. To get these three forms of able bright pupils a school in London would need an intake of thirteen forms. Thirty pupils in each of these thirteen forms would give a year size of almost 400 pupils and 400 pupils in each of the years from 7 to 11 gives a total of 2,000 pupils plus 200-odd sixth formers.

Schools of this size are said to have **economies of scale** such as being able to offer large libraries and sports halls as well as a wide range of special facilities and courses such as Photography GCSE with several darkrooms. But many critics believe that individual pupils are 'lost' in such massive schools where they do not know all the 150-odd teachers and where none of the staff can hope to know all the pupils by name. Such anonymity, it is argued, leads to indiscipline and poor results.

4   Home, social class and educational attainment

Educational under-achievement

Comprehensive schools were introduced to create greater equality of educational opportunity. But a large proportion of working-class talent and ability is never fully rewarded with examination success – this is called **under-achievement**. In the early 1990s the male workforce was 55 per cent working class and 45 per cent middle class. Did 55 per cent of university students come from working-class homes? In 1992, only 25 per cent of university entrants came from a working-class background. So the 45 per cent of families which were middle class took a disproportionate 75 per cent of new university places.

In this section of the chapter we will try to identify the aspects of home background which explain under-achievement and in the next section we will look at the aspects of school life which also contribute to this problem.

Case study: homes and schools in Hackney

Paul Harrison's 1985 book *Inside the Inner City* is a detailed look at life in the East London borough of Hackney. When we ask ourselves why it was that Hackney had the lowest examination success in all of London, we might consider the following factors:

- 69 per cent of parents were in classes IV and V (semi-skilled or unskilled manual workers)
- 33 per cent of pupils came from families poor enough to qualify for free school dinners
- 28 per cent came from one-parent families
- 27 per cent came from large families with five or more children
- 18 per cent spoke a first language other than English
- 20 per cent of dwellings in Hackney were 'unfit for human habitation'.

Harrison writes that family background affects schooling in two major ways:

The first is through educational performance. The typical Hackney home ... offers fewer toys and books; fewer outings and holidays; shortage of personal space for play or study; and shortage of attention from parents because of larger, less widely spaced, families, unsocial working hours or preoccupation with persistent housing and income problems.

The other main impact of family life on schooling is made through pupils' behaviour. The inner-city child is more indisciplined than average. Many children come from homes where arguments, disruption and instability, often involving violence, are everyday occurrences.

Truancy, delinquency and street life all offer counter-attractions:

All these influences are reflected in school in attention-seeking, insolence and inability to concentrate.

Activity

Children who experience the situations described by Harrison are often described as disadvantaged. Explain why a pupil from a working-class home which does not have these disadvantages may be more likely to succeed at school.

We now look at aspects of the material and cultural factors indicated in the Hackney case study.

Material disadvantages

1   Poverty   Pupils from poor families are less likely to remain in education after the school-leaving age and are more likely to try to get a job. In 1993, 67 per cent of English 16-year-olds stayed on in education, 12 per cent opted for training schemes and only 7 per cent went straight into jobs. Staying-on rates were over 85 per cent in prosperous areas such as Barnet and Harrow, while they were less than 50 per cent in poor areas such as Knowsley, Merseyside.

This family, in Manchester in 1986, were living on supplementary benefit. The children slept together with their parents, in the living room, to keep warm during the winter.

2   Poor health   Numerous studies have shown that children from classes 6 and 7 have a poorer diet and worse attendance at clinics (for example for immunisation). They also suffer more than the average from poor vision and impaired hearing and have higher rates of chronic illness which can obviously disrupt progress at school. The connection between diet, health and educational success was recognised as early as 1906 and 1907 when school medical inspections for all pupils and school meals for poor children were introduced.

3   Size of family   The number of children in a family can clearly be connected with

- less to spend on food per child;
- lack of space and quiet in which to do homework;
- lack of space and quiet in which to get a good night's sleep.

Cultural factors affecting educational attainment

Many of the material factors mentioned above build on each other or overlap; the 1967 Plowden Report on primary education described them as a 'seamless web of circumstance'. This Report also said: 'In a neighbourhood where the jobs people do and the status they hold owe little to their education, it is natural for children as they grow older to regard school as a brief prelude to work rather than as an avenue to future opportunities.' We now turn to the importance of attitudes and way of life in a pupil's home.

1 Parental support and encouragement J.W.B. Douglas conducted a longitudinal study of 5,362 British children born in the first week of March 1946. He managed to follow 4,720 of his original sample through to the age of 16. He concluded that the single most important factor relating to educational attainment was the degree of parents' interest in their children's education. Middle-class parents were more likely to attend parents' evenings and to encourage their children to stay on at school.

2 Preparation for school Compare these two mothers and bear in mind that *either* could be middle class or working class:

Mrs Targett	*Mrs Groom*
Treats her toddler to sweets at the supermarket checkout and lets her stay up late now and then.	Lays down clear discipline for her toddler with only two sweets from the sweets jar daily and regular bed-times.
Never takes the trouble to encourage language development by, for example, recounting the day's events or reading a story each bedtime. She smacks her toddler if she reaches up at the cooker and then just shouts at her.	When reaching up at the cooker her toddler is told about the painful consequences of boiling baked beans falling over one's head: a simple science lesson involving the abstract concepts of gravity, heat and time.
Emphasises the fun of treats and **instant gratification** or pleasure. The moral of this point is that we may enjoy smoking now or choose to leave school at 16 for a job to have money in our pockets, but we might regret both decisions later in life.	Uses practices like pocket money and a piggy bank to teach **deferred** (or postponed) **gratification**. The years of studying in the evenings and living on a low student grant at university may be endured for an eventual annual income which is three times as large as that of the early school leaver.

Activities

1 Do you think that Mrs Targett and Mrs Groom are totally unrealistic stereotypes or can you think of anyone who is like either of them?

2 Describe some other ways that parents can help to prepare their children for the demands that are made of them when they start school.

3 A survey using intelligence test results on 400,000 19-year-old male National Service recruits in Holland found that for all social classes there was a gradient in level of ability related to birth order. In other words, first-born children tended to be more intelligent than second children, and so on. A British survey of 7-year-olds found that first-born children were sixteen months ahead in reading compared to fourth or later-born children. The first-born 7-year-olds were also taller. What reasons would you give for these findings?

4 Professor Wiseman calculated for the 1967 Plowden Report that home and neighbourhood are 82 per cent responsible for difference in educational success while school itself is 18 per cent responsible. Recently sociologists have emphasised how aspects of school life can affect rates of educational attainment. Which set of factors do you think is more important in determining educational success?

5   The effects of schools on rates of educational success

This section of the chapter concentrates on four aspects of school life and organisation.

Creaming

In order to answer the debate about whether educational standards have fallen with comprehensive schools, a study by J. Gray and others surveyed 20,000 teenagers in Scotland (which went comprehensive earlier than most of England did and has far fewer private schools). They compared the results from two categories of schools:

1   **True comprehensives**, meaning schools with sixth forms which take *all* the pupils from a particular area without any bright children being **creamed** away (like the top of the milk) to local grammar or fee-paying schools.
2   Other secondary schools, including 'creamed', or false, comprehensives as well as grammar and secondary modern schools.

The survey found that middle-class children doing A-levels were better off in grammar schools but working-class pupils got better results at 16 in **true comprehensives** than in selective or creamed schools.

This need for a balanced intake was emphasised in the following case study of twelve South London comprehensive schools investigated by M. Rutter and others in the 1970s. They named their book after the number of hours we spend in school from the ages of 5 to 16.

School atmosphere

Case study: Fifteen Thousand Hours

Of the twelve schools studied, the best one had examination results four times better than the worst one. Similarly, after allowing for the different social backgrounds of the pupils, those from the worst school were three times more likely than those at the best to appear at Juvenile Court.

Rutter rejected the following causes put forward to explain the differences between the best and worst schools: single sex, not mixed sex; small, not big; spacious, not cramped; one site, not split; year system, not house system of pastoral care. Instead he pinpointed the following key factors which made the best schools best:

1   An 'ethos' or atmosphere which is well-organised, encouraging and caring with teachers showing not so much traditional methods of teaching but traditional values of dedication, commitment and preparation.

2   Frequent praise used rather than frequent punishment. (The schools using corporal punishment seemed to *produce* bad behaviour.)

3   A balanced intake: a fair proportion of high-ability pupils was shown to improve performance and behaviour of all pupils of all levels of ability.

Learning often depends on the atmosphere in the classroom.

Peer groups and self-fulfilling prophecy

Pupils may under-achieve at school because they 'run with the pack' and spend their evenings out on the streets with their gang (or peer group) rather than being kept in to do homework. Their lack of educational success is due to their home environment.

On the other hand a peer group can be based on the school environment. Turner has described how 'exam committed' pupils at 'Stone Grove' Comprehensive ended up getting poor results because they were sucked into a group which chose to be known as the 'dossers'. This peer group had an 'anti-school subculture' and obeyed 'work restriction norms'. In other words, they struggled to defeat the school's aim of making them work and promoted their alternative aim of 'messing about', while jeering at the hard-working pupils they called 'swots'.

Such a peer group subculture can be fostered by the way a school labels different categories of pupils, so helping to create groups of 'dossers' and 'swots'. Rosenthal and Jacobson conducted a famous experiment concerning this process of labelling which they described in their 1968 study called *Pygmalion in the Classroom: Teacher Expectations and Pupils' Intellectual Development*. They picked certain pupils at random and then lied to their teachers, telling them that the selected pupils were 'late-developers' who were likely to make good progress. As a result, their teachers treated these pupils differently. By the end of the year they had lived up to their teachers' expectations and had indeed scored somewhat better than their class mates in tests. This experiment shows that the expectations of teachers can result in a **self-fulfilling prophecy**, meaning that the teachers' predictions had come to pass.

In England, Lacey and Hargreaves have described how a similar process occurred with streaming in 'Hightown Grammar' and 'Lumley Secondary Modern'. Some comprehensives have compromised between fine streaming and mixed-ability grouping or setting by using broad banding (see below).

1   Fine streaming   In a school with a nine-form entry, pupils would be put into nine ability groups and be taught in these for all their lessons.

2   Setting   Pupils are put into different ability groups for different subjects. For example, a pupil might be in the top group for maths and the bottom group for French.

3   Mixed ability   In many comprehensive schools, pupils with a range of abilities are put into each form or tutor group and then taught in these same mixed-ability groups for a number of subjects.

4   Broad banding   In this case the nine forms in each year may be divided up into three broad bands of ability for teaching purposes. In his study of *Beachside Comprehensive* Stephen Ball uses the words of the teachers to show their stereotypes of the pupils in each of the three bands:

The Band 1 child

> has academic potential ... likes doing projects ... knows what the teacher wants ... is bright, alert and enthusiastic ... can concentrate ... produces neat work ... is interested ... wants to get on ... is grammar school material ... you can have discussions with ... friendly ... rewarding ... has common sense.

The Band 2 child

> is not interested in school work ... difficult to control ... rowdy and lazy ... has little self-control ... is immature ... loses and forgets books with monotonous regularity ... cannot take part in discussions ... is moody ... of low standard ... lacks concentration ... is poorly behaved ... not up to much academically.

The Band 3 child

> is unfortunate ... is low in ability ... maladjusted ... anti-school ... lacks a mature view of education ... mentally retarded ... emotionally unstable and ... a waste of time.

If teachers give greater encouragement to higher-band pupils and expect higher quality work from them, then such pupils may perform accordingly. In this way the performance of pupils may reflect the expectations of their teachers.

Social class and teaching groups

'Getting It Right: Selection and Setting in a 9–13 Years Middle School' is the title of some research by Troman. He found that pupils were not allocated to ability groups according to their school reports or their scores in tests. Instead of any objective, unbiased criteria, setting was based on subjective opinions derived from

> pupil performance in the class (behaviour, conformity to classroom rules, classwork), knowledge of siblings, knowledge of previous first years' sets and in some cases the physical appearance of the pupil.

Can setting pupils in this way lead to discrimination based on social class? In *The Happiest Days?* (1990), Peter Woods notes a number of studies which, like *Beachside Comprehensive*, have found that pupils in the top band or set tend to be mainly middle class, while lower ability groups tend to have more working-class pupils:

It is clear that the same kind of stratification by social class runs through all these schemes of school organization in some form or other – streaming, banding, setting, subject choice.

Regarding subject choice, Woods argues that teachers may be more likely to guide working-class pupils into taking the vocational qualifications of the **new vocationalism**. More traditionally academic courses, such as GCSE and A-level, may be seen as more appropriate for middle-class pupils.

Some would argue that the educational success of the middle-class pupil and the limited educational achievements of the working-class pupil are largely a matter of self-fulfilling prophecy. Teachers and parents expect most middle-class pupils to go to university – the large majority of university students are middle class.

Activities

1 In what ways might teachers show (a) positive, high expectations of pupils, and (b) negative, low expectations of pupils?

2 Why might Rosenthal and Jacobson's experiment be criticised as morally wrong?

Summary

We have seen how school life can affect a pupil's chances of educational success whatever his or her ability or background. Important aspects of school life include:

1 the school's catchment area and the balance of its pupil intake in terms of ability and social class;
2 the attitudes of teachers to different types of pupils and how far pupils are labelled by procedures such as streaming;
3 the atmosphere or ethos of the school in terms of its smooth organisation and the efficient dedication to learning of its teachers.

Case study: the 'third worst primary school in England'

In 1998, the Western Primary School in Grimsby came third from bottom in the National League tables. These tables recorded the percentage of 11-year-old pupils reaching target standards in tests for English, maths and science. The reasons for Western School's poor performance are partly to do with the social background of the pupils but are also partly due to the school itself.

The school is located on the Western council housing estate. In this deprived area, a large proportion of the 260 pupils come from unemployed families. Over half receive free school meals. Staff continually have to deal with 'social problems' and 'anti-social behaviour'. Many pupils have learning difficulties, such as needing special help with reading. Yet the school has average class sizes of 32. Staff have been demoralised by a shortage of essential resources, such as books and paper. Numerous staff have left in recent years and there has been a lack of leadership, with 7 head teachers in just 7 years.

6   Private, fee-paying, independent schools

*Malvern College, Worcester,
is an independent school
which became fully
co-educational in 1992.*

Case study: senior judges and the old school tie network

Percentage of senior judges from privileged backgrounds

	1987	1997
Public school	70%	82%
Oxford and Cambridge Universities	80%	88%

In 1998, out of Britain's top 149 judges only 8 were women and none were from ethnic minorities. How are lawyers promoted to become judges? The Labour Party has claimed that there is a 'system of secretive patronage'. The Lord Chancellor's Department makes 'soundings', consulting among the legal profession as to who should be promoted. Some see this as a grossly unfair 'old-boy network' where those who have been to exclusive schools merely promote their (white, male) old school chums. The chairman of the Home Affairs Select Committee, Labour MP Chris Mullin has said: 'There is strong circumstantial evidence that there is a glass ceiling beyond which lawyers who lack the appropriate background and contacts find it difficult, if not impossible, to progress.'

Definitions

The different names used for the two main types of secondary school can be confusing, but we hope that this makes it clear:

7 per cent of secondary pupils go to independent schools	*93 per cent of secondary pupils go to state schools*
These are all privately run and charge fees apart from some charity schools. In a few cases pupils' fees are paid by scholarships. Many are called 'public schools' because they are open to all the public (who can afford them). Many are boarding schools. The percentage of pupils who are privately educated increases with age. In 1991, 20 per cent of boys and 15 per cent of girls aged 16 and over went to independent schools.	These are funded by the government, either through the local education authorities of local councils or through grants to grant-maintained schools. In 1976, the Labour Government withdrew its funding of 174 direct-grant grammar schools and 119 of them became fee-paying, independent grammar schools.

Arguments in favour of fee-paying schools

1   They give parents greater freedom of choice. It would restrict the liberty of the individual if they were to be abolished. 'Adolf Hitler is the only man in Western Europe ever to have banned private schools' – David Malland, Headmaster of Manchester Grammar School.

2   Many of the private schools have centuries-old traditions behind them and so they are a precious part of our national heritage and culture. They also often have excellent records of academic and sporting achievement.

3   Pupils who are fortunate enough to go to fee-paying schools benefit from establishing social contacts which will help them in later life.

4   Parents who pay fees are in effect paying twice since they are also contributing to the costs of state schools through their taxes.

5   Schools outside the state system have the freedom to use experimental methods of schooling. Examples have included Dartington, Summerhill, Gordonstoun and the Rudolf Steiner schools.

Arguments against fee-paying schools

1   The rich and powerful who govern our country may never be fully concerned about the conditions in the schools attended by 93 per cent of the population as long as their own children join the privileged 7 per cent elite at private schools.

2   The ex-public school students dominate the top jobs of British institutions involving the government, the civil service, the church, the legal system, the armed forces and the financial system in the City. In other words, those who control these institutions come overwhelmingly from a few exclusive schools such as Eton, Harrow, Winchester and Westminster. Those who occupy the top jobs give their own children the unfair advantage of **sponsored mobility** by (a) sending them to these same

schools and by (b) choosing new recruits for their top jobs from among those who have been to these schools. This restrictive **elite self-recruitment** is known as the **old school-tie network**. The opposite of sponsored mobility is **contest mobility** where those with the most ability can get to the top through open and fair competition in a non-selective education system.

3   Comprehensive schools will not really be comprehensive and non-selective until 100 per cent of pupils attend them. At the moment they are creamed of those pupils with the most influential parents.

4   Fee-paying schools split British society into two and so they are socially divisive. Those who go to such schools are isolated from 'ordinary people'.

5   It is sometimes argued that the bus driver who goes without cigarettes, beer and foreign holidays could afford to send his children to private school. But a MORI survey in 1994 showed a marked drop, since 1989, in the number of families on incomes of less than £20,000 who were paying for independent schooling. Among all parents of pupils at private schools, the proportion earning over £40,000 had jumped from 36 per cent to 54 per cent.

Conclusion

Despite the criticism of private schools, in 1981 a survey by *The Observer* found that 72 per cent of parents would send their children to private schools if money was no problem and if they were unable to get their children into the state school of their choice. In 1982, a *Sunday Times* survey found that a 'significant minority' of the head teachers of comprehensive schools sent their own children to private schools.

GCSE question Southern Examining Group 1998

Study Items A and B. Then answer *all* parts of the question which follow.

Item A

> ### AN OPINION OF A PUPIL WHO LEFT SCHOOL IN 1991
>
> Once in my first year I walked out of school in the middle of a lesson because I was being picked on. My mum was amazed that no one came after me.
>
> I think streaming would have been good because those who didn't do well were left behind. People could get help if they wanted it but it was up to you. No one in school would force you to work for exams. That's hard if your parents aren't interested in education. In the school were those who got everything out of it and those who got nothing.

Adapted from an article in *The Independent* (9 June 1993)

Item B

> The broad statistics for children brought up by single parents are not good. Two longitudinal studies, one of children born in 1946 and another of children born in 1958, both following children through their lives, indicate that children of single parents do less well at school than children in two parent families. But that doesn't tell the whole story. The children who have never had a father do no worse than other children of the same social class. Since so many single parent families are poor, the figures are distorted.

Adapted from an article in *The Observer* (24 October 1993)

(a) Study Item A and state
    (i)   which children find it hard to work for examinations;

    (ii) a benefit of streaming in the view of the pupil.   (2)

(b) Study Item B and state
    (i)   what sociologists call the kind of studies mentioned in the passage;

    (ii) what factor distorts research findings about the educational achievements of the children of single parent families.   (2)

(c) State *three* benefits which may result from increasing the number of nursery school places available to children under five years old.   (3)

(d) Identify and explain *two* functions of schools in Britain today.   (4)

(e) A prominent politician once expressed his belief that Britain should be a classless society. To what extent is the education system likely to help to reduce class division and class inequality?   (9)

GCSE question from Southern Examining Group 1996

Study Items A. Then answer *all* parts of the question which follow.

Item A

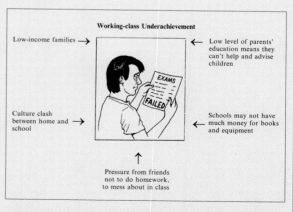

Adapted from Ken Browne, *An Introduction to Sociology* (Polity)

(a) (i) According to Item A, why might schools affect the working-class boy's underachievement? (1)

   (ii) According to Item A, how might the low level of parents' education affect the achievement of working-class children? (1)

   (iii) How can the hidden curriculum affect a working-class boy's achievement at school? (1)

(b) (i) State two purposes of schools in Britain. (2)

   (ii) Most children in Britain attend state schools. State *two* other ways in which school age children might be provided with their education. (2)

(c) (i) Explain what is meant by the 'National Curriculum'. (2)

   (ii) State *two* reasons why the Government introduced the National Curriculum into schools. (2)

GCSE question from Southern Examining Group 1996

To what extent can changes in education in the last twenty years be said to have increased educational opportunities in Britain? (10)

CHAPTER 11

Religion and society

1 The functions of religion

What personal needs does religion fulfil?

1 Religion can explain why we are here and what we should do with our lives. Without religion many of us would feel lost in a world and a universe without meaning.

2 Religion can help us to cope with the failures and tragedies that befall us. Most of us experience the death of relatives or friends and all of us face the prospect of death. Religion can provide us with an explanation of such events and help us to come to terms with them by giving them a meaning.

3 Religion can satisfy our need to know what is right and wrong and how we should act in certain situations. By providing a code of behaviour, religion can help us to form judgements about what is good and bad and about what we ought and ought not to do.

So religion can provide for our need to live in a meaningful world, our need to cope with personal disaster and our need for guidance about right and wrong. All the great faiths also recognise that humans are threefold beings of body, mind and spirit: religion attends to the spiritual aspect of our lives.

In 1998, only about 8 per cent of adults in England attended church regularly.

What social needs does religion fulfil?

Many sociologists have claimed that religion helps to create unity in society. It does this in a number of ways:

1   All religions provide shared values and standards of behaviour; without a general acceptance of some values between individuals a common way of life would be impossible and society would collapse. An example of a shared value is the Old Testament's Eighth Commandment, 'Thou shalt not steal'.

2   Religion gives further support (sanction) to the rules and laws of society. Thus individuals are fearful of breaking certain rules because they may be punished by God as well as society.

3   All religions have rituals and ceremonies which bring believers together and so strengthen their commitment to a common way of life.

We must be careful, however, not to exaggerate the unifying function of religion. Sometimes, far from acting as the cement holding the social structure together, religion can be a cause of disunity, as in the case of Northern Ireland. But for Durkheim, one of the founding fathers of sociology, religion has the essential function of binding communities together: religion is a system of beliefs and sacred rituals which unites people into social groups.

Marx saw religion as 'the opium of the people', as a sort of drug which distracted the working class from their exploitation and oppression, and Durkheim similarly wrote that 'religion instructed the humble to be content with their situation'.

Religion is by no means easy to define. One definition sees religion as any set of meaningful answers to the basic dilemmas of human existence such as birth, sickness and death. Another definition is that religion is any system of ideas, practices and rules of conduct that centre on belief in a god or supernatural reality.

Activities

1   If you were to break all of the Ten Commandments, in come cases you would be breaking the laws of the land but in other cases you would not. Which of the Ten Commandments are also part of the law in Britain today?

(You can find the Ten Commandments in Chapter 20 of the second book in the Bible, 'Exodus'.)

2   Name different ceremonies in either the Christian, Muslim or Hindu religions, apart from regular weekly services of worship, which help to bring the members of these religions together.

The Muslim religion in Iran

On 1 February 1979 the Ayatollah Khomeini returned from exile in Paris to become Iran's new leader after the overthrow of the Shah who had ruled for many years. The new regime was an Islamic dictatorship in which the Ayatollah Khomeini became both the religious and political leader.

The revolution which toppled the Shah of Iran from his throne had a number of causes, such as protest at the way Iran was dominated by American oil companies and disgust at the way that Muslim customs were threatened by modernisation which imposed a Western style of life.

Iran has now returned to strict Islamic practices; its new 1979 constitution enforced numerous **fundamentalist**, or traditional, measures such as:

1   rules for the veiling of women;
2   the abolition of modern divorce laws;
3   executions of homosexuals and adulterers;
4   prohibition of mixed public bathing;
5   a return to strictly Islamic schooling;
6   severe punishments for petty crimes such as theft.

Since the 1979 revolution, the Ayatollah's interpretation of the Islamic faith has been the only one permitted in Iran. Not only have believers in other

The Iranian leader, Ayatollah Khomeini, greeting soldiers at Qom in 1979.

religions, such as Christians and Baha'is, been severely persecuted but also those who belong to alternative Muslim sects. The Ayatollah died in 1989 and Iran's top religious leaders chose Ali Khamenei to follow him as faqih, or supreme leader of the Islamic Republic.

Summary   Children in modern Iran are socialised into accepting a view of the world and a code of conduct that conforms to the Ayatollah's Islamic teachings. This socialisation begins in the family and the school. It continues to be reinforced by peer group pressure, daily attendance at the mosque, a government-controlled mass media, compulsory military service and the laws of Iran's constitution.

There can be no doubt that in today's Iran religion is a central part of socialisation and a powerful means of social control.

2   Religious sects and denominations

How sects develop

Christians in Britain belong to a number of different organisations, such as the Baptist, Methodist or Catholic Church. These groups are called **denominations**. Many denominations started off as small **sects** which broke away from established churches. What usually happened was that someone disagreed with the teachings of the traditional church and set up a rival organisation with its distinctive doctrines.

When the beliefs of a new sect seem particularly strange, or when its leader has a very magnetic personality (called **charisma**), then a sect is sometimes called a religious **cult**. The followers of such groups are often idealistic young adults who are 'hot' with enthusiasm.

Sects often develop in one of two ways. They may cut themselves off from society and try to establish an alternative way of life, setting up an isolated 'perfect' community (a utopia). These world-rejecting sects often 'burn out' when the charismatic leader dies.

On the other hand, a sect may 'cool down' and become a well-established group with membership boosted by the children of the first generation of followers, rather than by new adult converts. Religious commitment may become less intense and the sect may evolve into a denomination with its recognised interpretation of a religious faith.

There is no hard and fast rule as to whether the groups in the list that follows should be properly called denominations, sects or cults. Some sociologists say that if a religious group demands unusual commitment which sets its members apart then it is a sect, no matter how long it has been established. An example would be the Jehovah's Witnesses. They usually forbid their children from attending school assemblies because they object to the teachings of conventional Christianity.

Some religious organisations in Britain, the USA and elsewhere

The Church of England (the C of E)
This began in 1534 when Henry VIII broke away from the Catholic Church. Membership in the UK has fallen below 2 million but there are churches

Members of the Hindu Hare Krishna sect.

across the world who are part of the Anglican Communion which is led by the C of E, including the Episcopalian Church in the USA.

Presbyterians

The English were not the only Christians to break away from the Catholic Church. In the 1530s, other northern Europeans broke away from the leadership of the Catholic Pope in Rome. They were led by Martin Luther and John Calvin. The process was called the Protestant Reformation because they protested at the way the Catholics had elaborate services in magnificent churches; they wanted reforms, such as simple worship in plain buildings. The Protestant Church in Scotland, set up in 1536, was called the Presbyterian Church.

Congregationalists

In the sixteenth century, Separatists broke away from the Church of England because they believed that the congregation in each parish should organise itself, following the authority of the Bible rather than obeying bishops. They came to be called the Congregationalists. In England, they joined with the

Presbyterians to form the United Reform Church in 1972, with 114,000 churchgoers in 1989.

Baptists

Martin Luther King was a Southern Baptist, from one of the southern states of the USA where there are 27 million Baptists. In 1989, there were 199,400 Baptists in England. The Baptist Church started in the seventeenth century, as part of the Puritan movement to purify Catholicism out of the C of E. Members must join as teenagers or adults and be baptised by total immersion in water.

Quakers (The Religious Society of Friends)

The Quakers were started in 1652 by George Fox. A famous Quaker was William Penn, who founded Pennsylvania. A service of worship at a Quaker meeting house consists of sitting in silent contemplation until someone feels moved by the inner spirit to get up and say something (usually about some verses from the Bible).

Quakers stress the need to practise social 'concern', such as pacifism. In the nineteenth century a number of Quakers were famous for encouraging social reforms, such as industrialists who set up model villages for their factory workers. There were 1,500 Quakers in England in 1989.

Methodists

In 1795, John Wesley broke away from the Church of England to form a new group named for the strict, methodical lifestyle of its members. Wesley wrote 6,000 hymns to spread the Gospel in an evangelical revival. Methodism became very popular among the respectable working class. Non-conformist chapels in areas like South Wales fostered self-improvement through reading rooms, libraries, evening classes and trade unionism.

Methodism also appealed to the lower middle classes, such as small shopkeepers. Margaret Thatcher was the daughter of a grocer from Grantham. She soon left the Methodists to join the more upper-class Church of England (the 'Tory Party at prayer'). In 1989, there were 396,000 Methodists in England.

The Mormons (The Church of Jesus Christ of the Latter-Day Saints)

In 1820 an American called Joseph Smith claimed that an angel had given him *The Book of Mormon* which said that the faithful will, like Adam, become gods. Smith was persecuted for advocating polygamy and eventually killed by a mob but the Mormon Church now has 4 million members across the world, including 150,000 in the UK. It is based in Utah where it dominates Salt Lake City.

Exclusive Brethren

The Plymouth Brethren were founded in 1825 by John Nelson Derby. The 10,000 UK members are strict and isolationist. Women must wear long hair, long skirts and no make-up. Sunday worship starts at 6 am and goes on all day. Brethren are not allowed to vote, join unions, watch TV, read newspapers or celebrate Christmas.

The Seventh-Day Adventists

Adventists believe that the Second Coming of Christ to this earth will soon come to pass. Seventh-Day Adventism began in 1831 when William Miller, an American, predicted the return of Christ in 1844. There are 3.5 million Seventh-Day Adventists in the world, three-quarters of them in developing countries where the idea of the Second Coming holds out the promise of escape from poverty. In 1989, there were 12,300 in England.

Spiritualists

In 1848, two American teenage sisters called Margaret and Kate Fox claimed that they had contacted the dead. Although they later denied this claim, there are now 40,000 members of the British Spiritualists Union.

Christadelphians

Most Christians believe in the Trinity, that God is the Father, the Son and the Holy Ghost or Holy Spirit. Unitarians reject the deity of Christ, believing that Jesus was not God. An example of non-trinitarians are the Christadelphians. They were started by John Thomas in 1848 in the USA and they have 20,000 British members.

The Jehovah's Witnesses

These began in 1874 when Charles Taze Russell, an American, predicted that 144,000 people would be Born Again when the final Battle of Armageddon occurred in 1975. There are 3 million Jehovah's Witnesses across the world, 130,000 in the UK. Their magazine, *The Watchtower*, teaches, among other things, that blood transfusions are wrong.

The Salvation Army

In 1878, William Booth set up The Salvation Army in England. Its members are well known for playing in brass bands and selling *The War Cry* magazine in pubs. As well as advocating abstinence from alcohol (teetotalism), salvationists run hostels for down-and-outs and our only national missing persons bureau. In 1989, they had 57,300 churchgoers in England.

Christian Scientists

In 1879, an American called Mary Baker-Eddy founded Christian Science which teaches that the Bible has errors, such as failing to recognise that humans are spiritual and part of God. There are 200,000 Christian Scientists worldwide, 12,000 in the UK.

Pentecostalists

Early in the twentieth century there was a Pentecostalist Revival on both sides of the Atlantic. Enthusiastic converts 'speak in tongues' and believe in faith healing. In Britain there are West Indian Pentecostalist churches and Pentecostalism has also inspired the Evangelical Alliance and the independent Free Church movement which has around two-thirds of a million followers (including Cliff Richard who worships at the Cobham Christian Fellowship). Many members give 10 per cent of their income to their church (called a 'tithe').

The Branch Davidians

In 1929 Victor Houteff broke away from the Seventh-Day Adventists in the USA to form the Branch Davidians. In 1984 David Koresh became their leader. In 1993, he died with seventy-four of his followers in a fire after the FBI's long siege of his ranch at Waco in Texas.

A Pentecostalist.

The Worldwide Church of God
In 1934, Herbert W. Armstrong started the Radio Church of God in the USA. This developed into the Worldwide Church of God which produces the *Plain Truth* magazine, with a circulation of 8 million. Heaven is condemned as a pagan doctrine and Anglo-Saxons in the UK and USA are called the ten lost tribes of Israel.

The Church of Scientology
In 1950, the American science fiction author L. Ron Hubbard invented Dianetics which teaches that humans are in fact Thetans, aliens who were banished to the Earth 75 million years ago by Xenu, an alien emperor. Followers, such as John Travolta, try to 'audit' away bad memories ('engrams') by the use of 'E-meters' (lie-detector machines). Between 1968 and 1980 foreign Scientologists were banned from entering Britain. The Church of Scientology employs around 500 staff in the UK.

The Moonies
In 1954 a Korean called Sun Myung Moon set up his Unification Church. He claims to be God, so his *Divine Principle* supersedes the Bible. By 1980, he had claimed 3,000 followers in Britain. After a 100-day court case in 1981, the longest ever English libel trial, a jury decided that the *Daily Mail* was justified in accusing the Moonies of breaking up families by brainwashing new recruits. This was not found to be true in the research of a sociologist called Eileen Barker, who wrote *The Making of a Moonie: Brainwashing or Choice*?

They tried to make me believe my sister was Satanic!

By ANDREW McEWEN

FRESH proof emerged yesterday that the Moonies s t i l l break up families — three years after a High Court jury ruled that the Daily Mail was justified in making that accusation.

It comes on the eve of a major conference designed to press the Government to break the power of the destructive cult. Angry parents will meet at the House of Commons today.

Sonia Martin, a 22-year-old travel agent from Falmouth, Cornwall who has just been rescued from the Moonies in America, said: 'They still break up families. They even tried to make me forget my twin sister. They wanted me to b e l i e v e she was Satanic.'

The process of separating Sonia from her past began soon after she was picked up during a visit to San Francisco.

Her aunt who lives there made persistent efforts to contact her at a Moonie indoctrination centre called Camp K. Sonia said: 'Myra Staneki, our leader, got annoyed that my aunt wanted to meet me. She said it was not fair because some members had not seen their families for years.'

When Sonia's twin sister Sara flew over to visit—but refused to accept the teachings of Korean prophet Sun Myung Moon—the Moonies tried to separate her, too, from Sonia.

'Myra said I should forget her. I was to treat her as a Chapter Two case. That's Chapter Two of the Divine Principle, the Moonies' scripture. They did not directly say she was Satanic, but I knew what Chapter Two said and that was what it meant.'

Kidnap dream

When her aunt succeeded in meeting Sonia at a restaurant, an experienced British Moonie woman accompanied her. 'She was my chaperone. She dominated the conversation. They had people outside sitting in cars in case my aunt tried to snatch me.'

By now Sonia was so indoctrinated that she even submitted letters to her mother for approval before posting them. A letter she wrote to her brother she had to re-write three times.

Sonia was strongly warned that her family might hire de-programmers' who could beat and rape her to break her faith. When a family friend, Phillip, flew over, and

'When I called my mother they said: Maximum two minutes'

Sonia warned her team, 'one of the team said she had a dream that Phillip was coming with people to kidnap me. They took it as a message from God. I never saw Phillip.'

Sara was allowed to see her three times, but always at Unification Church centres in the presence of Moonies.

When one meeting was set up for a restaurant, 'the team prepared paint bombs in freezer bags and put rocks in socks to pelt the car if she tried to kidnap me. Then they decided it was too risky and the meeting was switched.'

But the cruel separation from Sara was more than Sonia could bear. It led to furtive phone calls. Sara with her aunt and Phillip gradually drew her into a series of meetings — then held her against her will at a motel.

'A woman came past and I screamed "Get the police". We were all taken to the police station. I was handcuffed as my visa was out of date.'

During a five-day stay in prison she received advice from an immigration man and a prostitute. It proved a turning point. By the time the immigration man put her on a plane to London she was having doubts about the Moonies.

Sara and Phillip were on the plane too — but so was Myra, who bitterly attacked them for 'not respecting Sonia's religious freedom'. The British Moonie movement tried to arrange a getaway at Heathrow — but Sonia's family smuggled her away in a wheelchair.

With her consent Sonia was introduced to ex-Moonie Martin Faiers, a publisher's son, who until just over four years ago was public relations officer for the Canadian branch of the Moonies. Now he runs a counselling service to help ex-Moonies. She, Phillip and Sara spent weeks with Martin in Spain and France.

Sonia said that nothing more than persuasion was used to break her faith. Many members of FAIR (Family Action Information and Rescue), the main organisation for cult members' parents, believe that even this softly softly approach is risky.

Damnation

But Sonia has no doubts. 'I would advise parents to do it if they can afford it because I would still be a Moonie if my family had not taken action.'

In leaving the Moonies, Sonia had to cope with intense guilt feelings. 'They say that if you leave you are destined to eternal damnation.'

Mr Faiers's organisation COMA, which represents a vigorous approach to the cult problem, is at B.M. COMA, London, WC1 N3XX. FAIR, which has an information service, is at BCM Box 3535, PO Box 12, London, WC1 N3XX.

A story from the Sunday Mirror, *5 April 1984.*

The minister at St Paul's Pentecostal Church in Carlisle put this poster up in 1994 after MPs voted to lower the age of consent for homosexuals from 21 to 18.

The Jesus Children (The Christian Foundation)

In the 1960s, some 600 young adults worked on a ranch in the Californian desert owned by the preachers Tony and Susan Alamo. No TV was allowed and no books except the Bible. In a similar arrangement, recruits to the Jesus Army in the 1990s work for farms, Goodness Foods shops and other businesses in the Midlands run by Noel Stanton.

The People's Temple

This was set up in 1964 by Jim Jones (who predicted a nuclear war in 1967). Nine hundred and thirteen of his American followers drank cyanide and died in their commune in the jungle of Guyana in 1978.

Transcendental Meditation (TM)

In 1967 many young people, such as the Beatles, became interested in the teachings of an Indian called Maharishi Mahesh Yogi. Since then over 150,000 people in Britain have learned TM during a four-day course. The TM movement put up many candidates in the 1992 General Election. They claimed that we could achieve inner and world peace by chanting a mantra. None was elected. In 1995, a 1,000-acre former American air base in Suffolk was purchased to create a Natural Law University.

The Family of Love (The Children of God) (The Family)

In 1968 David Berg, an American known as 'Father Mo', started a cult which is now believed to have 7,000 members worldwide. A number of cults, such as the Moonies, make new members feel very special in a welcoming process known as 'love-bombing'. Berg encouraged his young female followers to go further and to prostitute themselves in order to gain male recruits. He called this process 'flirty-fishing'.

Following a policy of free love in secretive closed communities, the children of his followers have grown up not knowing the identities of their fathers. In the 1990s these communities have been raided by the police in

France, Australia and South America following accusations of the sexual abuse of children.

Osho

In 1974, hippies started visiting an ashram in Poona run by a guru called Bagwhan Rajneesh or Osho. Followers attempted to build utopia on a 126-square-mile site in Oregon but the project ended with a string of criminal charges, including tax evasion, wire-tapping and poisoning salad bars in the local town. Osho died in 1990 but his ashrams continue to offer courses, such as dynamic meditation.

Aum Shinrikyo

This was formed in 1987 in Japan by Shoko Asahara, and was blamed for the gas attack on the Tokyo subway in 1995 which killed 12 people. When police searched Asahara's office they found that he had amassed 10 kg of gold and 700 million yen (£5 million) from his 10,000 followers.

The Order of the Solar Temple

In 1994, 53 followers joined in a mass suicide in Switzerland. In 1997, 5 more committed suicide in Canada. Computer records seized in Montreal showed that some rich members had personally donated more than $1 million to the leader Joseph Di Mambro. In return he had made them knights and dressed them in Crusader-style robes at his Centre for the Preparation for the New Age.

Heaven's Gate

Dubbed the first Internet UFO (Unidentified Flying Object) cult. Founder Marshall Herff Applewhite and 38 followers committed suicide, in California, on the appearance of the Hale-Bopp comet in 1997. The time had come to shed their bodily 'containers' and board cometary spacecraft.

Conclusion

For many years there were laws that discriminated against those who did not belong to the official, state religion, the 'Established Church', the Church of England. A law in 1661 prohibited dissenters and non-conformists, such as Baptists and Methodists, from becoming Members of Parliament. This law was repealed in 1828 and Catholics were allowed to become MPs in 1829, Jews in 1858.

Many of today's respectable denominations started as sects which were persecuted for their revolutionary ideas. The early Mormons fought with the US cavalry and the early Quakers posed a revolutionary challenge to the state because of their pacifist refusal to join, or pay for, the army. Christians were themselves once a small, secretive group which the mighty Roman Empire tried to suppress.

In the past many sects have appealed to impoverished groups, such as the newly urbanised industrial working class in the nineteenth century. More recently, sects have attracted those who are not just mobile and rootless but also isolated and socially marginal, with a need to belong to communities offering certainties and hope. Examples of those who may feel themselves to be on the edge of society include immigrants, students, ex-drug-takers and those who are left single after failed relationships.

Case study: membership of new religious movements (NRMs)

While some earlier waves of new religions, and many of those emerging in Third World countries, have appealed to the poor and the oppressed, most of those who join the better-known of the present NRMs in the West come from the more privileged sections of society. By and large, Westerners who become involved in movements such as the church of Scientology, Transcendental Meditation or the Unification Church come disproportionately from the middle or upper-middle classes. They will have a better than average education and they will have had good prospects for their future careers.

There are exceptions. It is mainly disadvantaged black youth from the inner cities who join the Rastafarian movement. Not surprisingly, those who join movements that expect the kind of total commitment which involves living in a community and working full time for the organisation are likely to be young adults with few responsibilities; the average age of those becoming 'core members' of the Unification Church, for instance, is 23.

Movements that charge fees for their services tend to attract those in a slightly older age range – if only because such people are more likely to be earning enough to pay. In a survey of those visiting centres on the Greek island of Skyros, for holiday courses in yoga, 'holistic health' and 'personal development', it was found that the typical participant was 'single, over 30 and a *Guardian* reader'. Women outnumbered men by two to one.

(adapted from *New Religious Movements* by Eileen Barker)

Activities

1 Look in your *Yellow Pages* under 'Places of Worship' and 'Religious Organisations' and list the different groups in your area.
2 Apart from Christianity, what are the other main world religions which are represented in Britain's major cities and elsewhere?
3 Would you include the following elements of the New Age movement under the heading New Religious Movements?

- alternative and complementary medicine, such as acupuncture, aromatherapy, crystal therapy, herbalism and homoeopathy;
- psychotherapies of the human potential movement, such as rebirthing and primal therapy;
- occultism, witchcraft, neo-paganism, shamanism and satanism.

3   Religion today in Britain and the USA

Secularisation

Is Britain now a secular society? Secular means uninfluenced by religion. The process of the erosion and decline of the importance of religious beliefs, institutions and practices is called secularisation.

In order to answer the question 'How religious are the British people?', we might compare Britain with the USA. In 1991, the International Social Survey Programme (ISSP) used the same questions in both countries (details can be found in *British Social Attitudes: The 9th Report*). When asked 'What is your religion, if any?', the answers of the British sample were as follows:

Religious affiliation in Britain, 1991

% identifying with religious denomination

Church of England	39%
Roman Catholic	10%
Presbyterians (Church of Scotland)	5%
Free Churches (Baptist and Methodist)	4%
Other Protestant denominations	3%
Other faiths	3%

While only 7 per cent of Americans do not feel that they belong to any religion, the figure in Britain is 36 per cent (although only 6 per cent of British respondents say that they were raised and grew up without any religious affiliation).

One way to conduct further research (to 'operationalise' the secularisation theory) is to break religiousness down into different dimensions. For example, the ISSP asked questions about religious belief, experience and observance. The findings are summarised below.

Religious beliefs

		Britain	USA
Believe in:	God	69%	94%
	Heaven	54%	86%
	Life after death	55%	78%
	Religious miracles	45%	73%
	Hell	28%	71%
	The devil	28%	47%

The survey also found that belief in God was higher among women and the elderly.

Religious experience

	Britain	USA
Feel close to God most of the time	46%	85%
Ever felt close to a powerful spiritual force	28%	33%
Ever had a conversion experience, a turning point in life when you made a new and personal commitment to religion	17%	46%

Religious observance

	Britain	USA
Attend service two or three times a month	16%	43%
Pray weekly	27%	58%
Join church activities other than services	11%	31%

Activities

1 Which *three* of the above findings, from the 1991 ISSP research, would you select to compare religiosity in Britain and the USA?

2 From this evidence, would you conclude that most British people are religious?

3 Carry out a survey designed to discover the extent of people's religious knowledge.

Religion in Britain and the USA: a conclusion

The survey figures for Britain might be interpreted as showing that 40 per cent or so are seriously religious and 25–33 per cent are not religious at all, leaving some 30 per cent who are conventionally but not seriously religious.

The historical reason that churchgoing is higher in the USA may be because nearly all Americans originate from immigrants. A newly arrived settler may feel the need to belong and religion helps to give a sense of identity. This is shown in the use of descriptions such as Jewish American, Polish American and African American. (These are seen as less offensive than Yid, Polack or Negro.)

This church, in Winchester, has been converted into offices.

Case study: the Church of England is no longer the 'Tory Party at prayer'

The Church of England used to be known as the 'Tory Party at prayer' and was seen as a bastion of middle-aged, middle-class men. In 1996, 547 Church of England leaders (those who served on the General Synod from 1990 to 1995) were surveyed and most were Labour or Liberal Democrat supporters, with women for the first time in a majority among the laity (non-clergy).

Asked about the most important issues which they thought faced the Church of England, bishops put at the bottom of their list traditional areas of Christian morality, such as adultery, abortion, euthanasia and homosexuality. Their top priorities were more left-wing issues such as unemployment, politics, the environment, poverty and Third World problems. Two bishops went so far as to say that the Church should not speak out at all on adultery and one said that it should keep quiet on abortion. The Archdeacon of York, who was voted off the General Synod (the Church of England's own parliament, which decides its policies) said: 'Bishops are increasingly remote from ordinary people. It is the politically correct chattering classes who dominate, which is why ecological sins are seen as a greater sin than the ones against the family.'

Before the 1997 General Election, a survey of Church of England bishops found that 34 per cent said 'Yes' when asked 'Do you believe, as Tony Blair argues, that modern Conservatism is incompatible with Christianity?' The Bishop of Woolwich said: 'Some of the Conservatives' policies on refugees and law and order are distinctly unchristian. Under the economic policies followed by this government, 30 per cent of the population have done disasterously worse.'

---

4   Has Christianity declined in Britain?

The Christian Research Association gives the following figures for adult membership of the main Christian churches in the United Kingdom:

	1975	*1992*
Roman Catholic	2,520,000	2,040,000
Anglican (Church of England)	2,300,000	1,810,000
Presbyterian	1,640,000	1,240,000
Methodist	600,000	460,000
Baptist	240,000	230,000

These main Christian groups have all had a fall in membership. Total adult membership of Christian churches, at 6.7 million in 1992, represented only 15 per cent of the UK population aged 16 and over. Yet while overall membership of Christian churches fell from 8 million to 6.7 million, membership of independent evangelical Protestant churches rose from 510,000 to 660,000 over the same period.

However, a word of caution must be sounded about these figures. One priest might inflate his membership figures to avoid his church being closed down, while another might keep his membership low to avoid handing on a lot of capitation fees (subscriptions per head) to his bishop.

For the above figures, the Catholic Church counts as members those who attend mass, the Church of Wales counts those who attend Communion at Easter and the Church of England includes all those on its Electoral Roll who are qualified to vote on church matters.

The following figures, for membership of the Church of England in the Warwickshire parish of Hatton, were compiled as part of an A-level student's coursework project:

1929:	484	*1940*:	403	(most residents included)
1949:	165	*1983*:	77	(only active members included)
1993:	42			(irregular attenders excluded to cut the 'quota' paid to the diocese)

Religion in Britain in the past

The decline in religion may be seen in the fact that only 30 per cent of children were baptised in 1986, compared to 60 per cent in 1956. Also, there are only 10,000 Church of England priests now, compared to 20,000 in 1900. But was Britain really more religious in past centuries? Finke and Stark (1992) offer the following points to consider:

- The Middle Ages are sometimes seen as a golden age of religion. But scholars have noted that most medieval rural churches were far too small to accommodate all their local population.
- After the Civil War, Dissent (Congregationalism) declined rapidly from 5 per cent of the population in 1670 to less than 2 per cent in 1700. (This shows the way that sects flare up in times of social upheaval, such as England in the 1650s, 1830s and 1970s or post-Communist Ukraine in 1993 when thousands arrived in Kiev following a young woman's prophecy of the end of the world.)
- The real religion of the seventeenth century was magic and pagan superstition. The majority of the population, who were peasants, incorporated this in their own style of Christianity which was not acceptable to the church authorities.
- Figures for thirty Oxfordshire parishes show that in 1738 each church had an average of only thirty worshippers taking Communion at Christmas and Easter.
- The Potato Famine of the 1840s caused the Irish to turn to religion. (In 1992, 58 per cent in Northern Ireland and 78 per cent in the Irish Republic attended church regularly.) Or perhaps it was the less devout who died of famine or emigrated.
- Church membership, as a proportion of the population in England, has shown no great variation over the years:

1800	11.5%
1850	16.7%
1900	18.6%
1992	15%

The secularisation argument is not, however, about numbers. It concerns whether or not the *influence* of religion has declined in society.

Does the Christian Church have any real influence in modern Britain?

Yes	No

Yes

1   The Church of England is the state religion, the official church of the government.

2   Church of England bishops sit in the House of Lords where, for example, they have been able to protect the status of church schools.

3   The 1944 Education Act says that secondary schools should have daily collective acts of worship.

4   The 1944 Act also makes RE lessons compulsory.

5   Radio and TV include regular religious programmes, especially on a Sunday evening. (Can you name any of these programmes?)

6   Sunday remains a special day to spend with the family rather than working even if only a small minority actually go to church.

No

1   It is of only incidental interest that Prince Charles is unable to marry a Catholic.

2   The thorough 1985 Church report on inner-city problems called *Faith in the City* was scorned as 'Marxist' by members of the Conservative Government, which ignored its proposals.

3   Only seven out of 296 secondary schools surveyed by the *Times Educational Supplement* (20 December 1985) complied with this law; 30 per cent did not sing hymns in their assemblies.

4   Pupils in RE lessons often study world religions and social problems and do not learn much about Christian beliefs.

5   An increasing amount of media output verges on being blasphemous or sacrilegious, for example comedians such as Billy Connolly and Dave Allen.

6   Increasingly shift-workers have to work on Sundays and more and more shops are now open on Sundays.

To petrol companies, little seems sacred.

Conclusion

We can say with some certainty that the general influence of the Church over British social institutions has steadily declined over the centuries. In the Middle Ages, the Church had considerable political power and in Tudor times Cardinal Wolsey was Lord Chancellor in charge of Henry VIII's Government. In those days the Church controlled entertainment and festivals as well as sponsoring artists. Schools, hospitals and the care of the poor were all aspects of the role of the medieval Church. Since then many of these functions have been taken over by the welfare state.

The power of the Church to shape society may have declined but we now consider how far people's individual lives are still guided by Christian principles. Some see evidence for a decline in the Christian way of life in trends such as the increase in divorce, birth control, pornography, homosexuality and drug-taking. Yet if we look back in history we might question how 'Christian' English society was in past centuries. For example, the following practices might be considered *unchristian*: public hangings; slavery; cruel animal blood sports; the exploitation of child labour and the grossly unequal treatment of women.

It could be said that in so far as many of the above unchristian practices have ended, we are more Christian in our way of life today than we have ever been. Certainly large numbers of British people would consider that they live good, Christian lives.

Case study: secular funerals

Unlike weddings, anybody can legally conduct funerals. And an increasing number of atheists are paying for non-religious ceremonies carried out by members of the National Secular Society and the Humanist Association.

Jane Wynne Willson, in the Midlands, prefers a formal atmosphere with poetry and readings from such authors as Pasternak: 'I think the words used should be a little bit flowery ... there's a considerable need for ritual at this time. I try for a familiar kind of pattern that people would have been through with a Christian ceremony.'

In the London area, Barbara Smoker conducts one secular funeral a week on average. She is amazed by the British capacity for double-think. 'Sometimes I spend a long time finding out about the person who died. Then they'll suddenly come out with "Will you just say he is now in a happier place?" and I have to say no, I will not – it would be completely hypocritical.'

(adapted from *The Sunday Times*, 26 February 1989)

5   The Islamic faith in Britain

Adult membership of non-Christian religions in the United Kingdom

	1975	1992
Muslims	200,000	520,000
Sikhs	120,000	270,000
Hindus	100,000	140,000
Jews	110,000	110,000

(Source: *Social Trends*, 1994)

The above figures show that modern Britain is a multi-faith society. A number of non-Christian religions appear to be growing in Britain and a good example is Islam.

The Brick Lane Mosque in the East End of London has been used by different immigrant groups during its history. The building was originally the church of Huguenot refugees, French Protestants who fled from Catholic persecution at the end of the seventeenth century. It then became a Jewish synagogue before being converted, in 1976, into the largest religious centre for Bangladeshi Muslims in Britain, with 1,500 worshippers every Friday. In the same year, the large, new Regent's Park Mosque was opened in central London.

There are over a thousand mosques in Britain and the Islamic Foundation claims that there are some 2 million Muslims living in Britain. They are mainly from the Indian sub-continent but also include Arabs, Turks, Cypriots, Africans, Malaysians and Indonesians.

It is possible to see two contrasting trends in Islam in Britain: a weakening and a strengthening of the faith.

The weakening of Islam in Britain

If Britain is becoming an increasingly secular society with a predominantly secular culture, then this implies that the influence of all religions is declining in Britain. Many of the young people who live in British cities and who have little time for religion may have rural ancestors who, during the eighteenth century, regularly read their Bibles and attended church. In a similar way, many young British Asians have parents or grandparents who have grown up in peasant societies with strict Muslim traditions. Among the new generations brought up in Britain, many find themselves pulled in two directions and some find it difficult to continue with Muslim customs. One example is language. They may use English at school or college, use Arabic for prayers and speak Urdu, Bengali, Punjabi or Gujerati in the home.

Culture conflict   This can take two forms. First, culture conflict can arise because the customs of an ethnic minority differ from those of the majority population. For example, a Muslim may find it difficult to join in social activities with fellow workers because Islam prohibits all kinds of alcoholic drink. In her book, *Finding a Voice: Asian Women in Britain*, Amrit Wilson describes a Muslim student who never looked her cockney landlady in the eye because she had been brought up to consider this to be disrespectful, especially with an older person. The landlady then told her that in British culture if you don't look into somebody's eyes it means that you are telling a lie.

A second kind of culture conflict takes the form of role conflict. For example, a Muslim teenager may have a foot in both cultures. If a girl is to be a good daughter and a good Muslim, she may feel obliged to accept close parental supervision and rules about modest forms of clothing. But in her role as a teenage school pupil, she may be attracted by her peer group's social world of discos, parties and boyfriends.

A strengthening of Islam in Britain

Many Muslims in Britain want to strengthen their religion. These include older fundamentalists, who want a return to strict religious traditions, and younger political militants. Such radical groups have opposed Britain's war with Iraq and have supported the Iranian government's death threat to Salman Rushdie for insulting Islam in his book *The Satanic Verses*.

In 1994, officials of the Commission for Racial Equality warned that these radical groups were planting a time-bomb under harmony between Muslims and British society because the groups argued against social integration.

A Muslim imam leading prayers at a mosque in Norwich.

Case study: radical time-bomb under British Islam

The radicals say that British Muslims are a part not of British society but of the Islamic *ummah* – or world community – and must be fully involved in the struggle against Western 'oppression'.

The radicals are conducting a two-pronged offensive. First, they are challenging the management committees of Britain's mosques ('groups of local supermarket millionaires in the pay of Saudi Arabia'). They are critical of the ill-educated imams, from Pakistan and the Middle East, who cannot preach in English and who ban women from mosques.

Second, the Hizb ut Tahrir party has taken over nearly all the Muslim student societies at London University colleges and campuses in other areas where Muslims form a large part of the community. Many parents see this group as acting like a cult and they fear their children

coming under its influence.

The radical challenge to the older Muslim establishment comes at a time when many young British Muslims are wondering about their future in a Europe which has allowed the massacre of thousands of Bosnian Muslims and the cancellation of Algerian democracy, and is now enforcing what they see as an inadequate peace formula on Palestinian Muslims.

A Birmingham psychiatrist, Dr Farouk Hashimi, said he believed that the radical groups were providing many young Muslims with an identity. 'Instead of rituals which they can learn at the mosque, the radical groups function as clubs, providing support, friendship. They give them an identity which British society hasn't.'

(adapted from the *Guardian*, 7 February 1994)

GCSE question from Southern Examining Group 1998

Study Item A. Then answer *all* parts of the question which follows.

Item A

'The yobs have had their day'

Cleveland Police have pledged to tackle minor irritants like vandalism and yobbish behaviour in an attempt to bring crime rates down.

'We are a police force that means business and we want to hoodlums to realise they are not going to take the streets away from us,' says a senior police officer.

The police want to hassle the villains and thugs. They want the officer on the beat to stop his car and take action against the kids who shout abuse.

Top police officers argue that if you arrest a burglar urinating in a shop doorway you will curtail his chance of breaking into homes. These officers are of the opinion that when a kid starts with vandalism and abuse he can quickly turn to car crime, burglary and worse.

The police want to nip it in the bud. They say, 'Let the kid know we are there and will be waiting if he steps out of line, and then he will think twice about progressing his career in crime.'

Adapted from *The Evening Gazette*, 20 September 1996

(a) According to the information given,

   (i) identify *one* minor irritant that the Cleveland Police have pledged to tackle. (1)

   (ii) who will hassle the villains and thugs? (1)

   (iii) what would make someone think twice about a career in crime? (1)

(b) (i) the mass media are described by sociologists as *agents of social control*. Identify *two other* agents of social control. (2)

   (ii) Identify and explain *one* way in which the mass media act as agents of social control. (2)

(c) (i) Explain the difference between behaviour that is criminal and behaviour that is deviant. (2)

   (ii) Outline *one* reason why not all crimes are reported to the police. (2)

(d) (i) Identify *one* social group whose members are particularly likely to suffer from a fear of crime. (1)

   (ii) Fully explain why females are less likely to commit or to be convicted of crimes than males. (3)

CHAPTER 12

Crime and deviance

1 Deviance, crime and social change

The human cost of drug abuse

Which dangerous drug causes the loss of 8 million working days each year in Britain at a cost of more than £600 million? The answer is alcohol. The overall cost of alcohol abuse is difficult to calculate but it has been estimated that:

- 52 per cent of deaths from fire are linked with drinking;
- 50 per cent of murderers were drunk when they killed;
- 30–33 per cent of all road accidents, all accidents in the home, all drownings and all cases of child abuse are drink related;
- 25 per cent of all hospital beds are occupied due to alcohol-related illnesses.

Alcohol and tobacco kill about 400 people in Britain *every day*. (A quarter of all smokers kill themselves by smoking.) In contrast, illegal drugs kill about 400 people per year. In 1989, the government gave the Health Education Authority £22 million. Some of this was used to publicise the dangers of alcohol and tobacco. This is only a tiny fraction of the amount that is spent on advertisements to get us to buy cigarettes and alcoholic drinks.

Is it illegal to take a drug such as the tranquilliser called barbiturate? The answer is that it is legal to give yourself the dose prescribed by a doctor, but it is illegal to buy such pills in a club from a 'dealer' or 'pusher' who has stolen them from a hospital pharmacy. We could say that it all depends on whether society has sanctioned the use of a drug. Under certain circumstances the use of an allowed drug may be defined as abuse or misuse – for example, if tobacco is smoked by children.

The eco-warrior (tunnelling roads protestor) Daniel Hooper, alias Swampy, leaving court in 1998 after a £100 fine for possession of magic mushrooms.

Conceptions of deviance

Deviance refers to behaviour which deviates from or does not conform to accepted norms. It has been said that 'deviance is in the eye of the beholder'. Whether or not people label behaviour as deviant varies according to three questions: when? where? and who?

1 When? What is considered to be deviant changes over time. For example, drinking alcohol may have been considered deviant by many Americans during the Prohibition Era (1920–33) when alcoholic drinks were outlawed in the USA.

2 Where? Strict Muslim states such as Saudi Arabia still maintain a ban on all alcoholic beverages.

3 Who? Drinking alcohol may be considered appropriate in Britain during an evening out, with a meal, at a wedding reception or at a party, but it would be seen as deviant, or against the norm, for pupils at school or for police officers on duty.

Deviance and crime

A gang of youths might consider it normal to get drunk every Friday night but most people would regard drinking as socially unacceptable when a drinker's condition crosses the divide between 'merry' and 'paralytic'. Drunkenness may be deviant, but is it criminal? This would depend on whether a drunkard becomes disorderly or tries to drive a car.

Not all deviance is criminal, but is all law-breaking deviant? Many people may see it as socially acceptable to break certain laws such as parking briefly on a double yellow line. A large proportion of Americans considered it acceptable to carry on drinking during the Prohibition.

It was in the pub that he should have slowed down.

DERBYSHIRE
COUNTY COUNCIL
If you're drinking, don't drive.

Drinking and driving can be illegal, but is it deviant?

The 1996 *British Crime Survey* found that 42 per cent of 20–24-year-olds had used cannabis, 21 per cent had used amphetamines, 15 per cent had used LSD and 13 per cent had used ecstacy. Overall 49 per cent of young adults had taken illegal drugs.

Deviance and social change

Social change has often been inspired by those who have shown a new way of thinking and living but who have also, as a result, been persecuted as deviants. Jesus Christ was a deviant in that he opposed the religious beliefs and practices of his society. And for this he was crucified. But his life and teachings gave birth to the new religion of Christianity which has become the accepted faith in many societies.

The rest of this chapter looks at recent trends in crime and considers some of the causes of such crimes.

In 1998, campaigners to decriminalise cannabis organised a rally in London.

Case study: attitudes to 'wrongness' of various hypothetical actions

The following figures come from the 1991 *British Social Attitudes* survey.

	Nothing wrong	A bit wrong	Wrong	Seriously wrong	Very seriously wrong
	%	%	%	%	%
Paying cash to a plumber to avoid VAT charges	27	28	36	5	3
A milkman making £300 by slightly overcharging his customers	0	2	26	43	28
An employee making £75 by exaggerating travel expenses	3	15	50	21	10

Percentage answering 'yes'

Might you:		
	... pay a plumber in cash to avoid VAT	24%
	... exaggerate the value of burgled goods to make £150 from an insurance claim	71%
	... keep £5 extra change if given change for a £10 note when paying with a £5 note	25%

2   Patterns of crime

Notifiable, or **indictable**, **offences** are serious crimes, generally those for which an accused person may be sent to prison if found guilty. A defendant may decide to ask for trial by jury with a judge in a Crown Court in such cases.

Non-indictable offences are less serious crimes, such as parking offences, which may be dealt with by a 'ticket' or by a magistrate without a jury in a Magistrates' Court. Offenders in such cases often pay fines.

The following figures show that the total number of notifiable offences recorded by the police in England and Wales rose from just over 1.6 million in 1971 to just under 5.6 million in 1992.

Notifiable offences recorded by the police in England and Wales

	1971	1992
Theft and handling stolen goods	1,003,700	2,851,600
Burglary	451,500	1,355,300
Criminal damage	27,000	892,600
Fraud and forgery	99,800	168,600
Violence against the person	47,000	201,800
Robbery	7,500	52,900
Sexual offences	23,600	29,500
Other offences	5,600	25,600
Total notifiable offences	1,665,700	5,577,900

(Source: *Social Trends*, 1989, 1994)

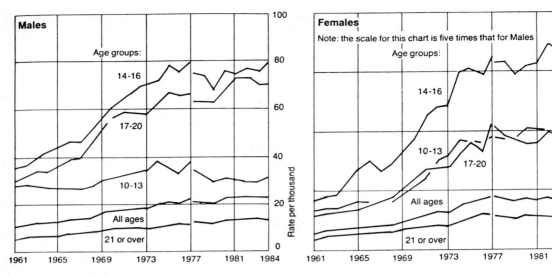

Offenders found guilty of, or cautioned for, indictable offences (by sex and age, in England and Wales).
(*Source*: Social Trends, 1986.)

Theft and burglary accounted for three-quarters of all notifiable offences recorded in England and Wales in 1992. The value of the property stolen was £3,771,000,000 and the value of the stolen property that was recovered amounted to £1,080,000,000 or 29 per cent of the total value stolen.

In 1992, 11 per cent of males and 3 per cent of females were known offenders by the age of 18, that is they had been found guilty of or cautioned for an indictable offence.

The graphs above show that teenagers have the highest crime rates (per thousands of their age groups) among the general population. Because of this, many of the theories of crime discussed in section 4 of this chapter focus on **juvenile delinquency**, or offences committed by youths.

In 1998, the *British Crime Survey's* 'Attitudes to Punishment' survey pointed out that 40 per cent of men have a criminal record of a non-motoring offence by the time that they reach the age of 40.

Data-response exercise: serious crime rates, by sex and age

1 Which male and female age groups, in the graphs, show the highest crime rates?
2 How do the scales differ between the charts for males and females?
3 Why do the scales differ between the charts for males and females?

4 Among 14–16-year-olds, 53,000 boys were sentenced for an indictable offence in 1984 compared to 5,400 girls. List possible reasons for the lower female crime rates.

A lot of criminal damage is not reported to the police.

Victims of crime

Is it the old who are most at risk from a burglary in their home? The *General Household Survey* found that in 1991, 5.6 per cent of 16–29-year-olds were burgled, almost twice as many as the 2.9 per cent of those aged 65 and over who were burgled.

Is it the rich who are most at risk of being burgled? In fact, those in rented property have a burglary rate 40 per cent higher than owner-occupiers.

The following figures come from the *British Crime Survey*:

Ethnic origin of victim	Percentage who were burgled in 1991
White	6
Asian	9
Afro-Caribbean	12

The chance of becoming a victim of crime depends upon a number of factors, such as where you live, how you live and who you know. Living in the countryside carries a far lower risk than living in an inner-city area. Those who live in middle-class areas of inner cities, such as Islington, have a high risk of becoming victims of property crimes.

There are two main types of violent crime: fights between young men and domestic assaults on women. Overall, the person who has most chance of suffering from violence is the young man who goes out frequently and drinks heavily. The next most common victim is the woman who suffers assault from her partner. Violent assaults by complete strangers are rare: strangers are only responsible for 14 per cent of female murder victims, 30 per cent of male murder victims and about 30 per cent of recorded rapes.

3   The interpretation of crime figures

Take two statements: 'the number of new university students increased by 10 per cent last year' and 'the number of burglaries increased by 10 per cent last year'. The first statement is probably reliable and can be checked by looking at figures for student enrolments. The second statement is likely to be less reliable and less easy to check since a large proportion of burglaries are not reported to the police. And some of the burglaries that are reported to the police might not be recorded in the official statistics, compiled by the police.

Crime statistics are socially created. The official crime figures depend on the actions of different groups, apart from the actions of criminals themselves:

- The total numbers of reported crimes depend partly on the willingness of victims to inform the police.
- The total numbers of recorded crimes depend partly on police procedures; crimes are only recorded if the police fill in the appropriate paperwork.
- Policing policies might lead to a crackdown on certain categories of offence, while the police might turn a blind eye to other infringements of the law.
- A media moral panic might demand not just action by the police but also new laws. When politicians create new laws, such as making it compulsory to wear seatbelts, this may add to the amount of law-breaking in society.

Unreported crime

The 'dark figure' refers to unreported crimes. These are hidden in the same way that most of an iceberg is concealed beneath the surface of the sea:

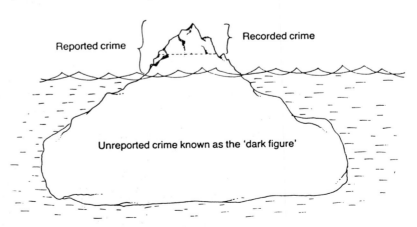

Reported crime   Recorded crime

Unreported crime known as the 'dark figure'

The 'dark figure' of unreported crime is like the huge mass of an iceberg hidden under the sea.

How can we estimate the size of the 'dark figure'?

1   Informed guesses   The most common non-indictable crimes are traffic offences and probably millions of these are committed every day by drivers breaking the speed limits. When the Metropolitan Police introduced the wheel-clamp, they estimated that 3 million cars are parked illegally every day.

As for serious offences, the dark figure is probably largest for sexual offences. For example, before the 1968 reform of the abortion laws there were reckoned to be about 100,000 illegal abortions per year of which only 250 or so were known to the police. In other words the police only recorded one in 400 cases and so the dark figure was 99.75 per cent.

More recently, Rape Crisis Centres, which offer a 24-hour hot-line and counselling service, have suggested that less than 10 per cent of rapes are reported to the police.

2   Crimes against shops and businesses   It may be impossible to know how much pilfering is done by people at work, but a shop that keeps accurate records of its stock can have a good idea of the extent of shoplifting. It may be difficult to know if the loss of 100 pairs of tights is the result of one theft or 100 thefts, but inside information suggests that about 99 per cent of cases are unreported. This is because store detectives may think that they are doing well if they catch 10 per cent of shoplifters and of these they may hand over only 10 per cent to the police for prosecution.

3   Self-report studies   A famous study called *Our Law-Abiding Law-Breakers* found that 90 per cent of a sample of adult Americans confessed to offences for which they could be gaoled (although one of these offences, 'malicious mischief', included the crime of opening your son or daughter's mail!).

4   Victim studies   The accident and emergency department at one Cardiff hospital found that 5 per cent of new patients, just over 3,000 a year, had been injured in violent crimes. Of these victims, who were seriously enough injured to need hospital treatment, only about a quarter reported the offence to the police.

The chart at the top of page 226 shows the results of the *British Crime Survey* which was carried out by interviewing a representative sample of 11,000 members of the population. They were asked about their experiences of crimes over the previous year and their readiness to report them to the police.

Such large-scale surveys are very costly. The results depend on the reliability of the victims' memories. They may forget about, or even be unaware of, offences such as criminal damage to their property – which might include the deliberate scratching of the bodywork of a person's car.

The offence that is most likely to be reported to the police is motor vehicle theft. Most people know when their car has been stolen and they need to report it to the police if they are to make an insurance claim. The *British Crime Survey* shows that, in 1991, 93 per cent of motor vehicle theft was recorded by the police, double the proportion for burglary and nearly three times that of theft from vehicles. Reasons for not reporting crimes varied from the incident being too trivial, to a belief that the police would not have been able to do anything about it.

Percentage of offences recorded by the police in England and Wales, 1991. (Source: Social Trends, 1994.)

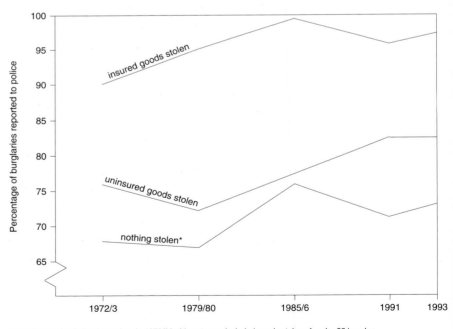

Percentage of burglaries reported to the police, Great Britain 1972–93 (Source: General Household Survey, 1993.)

*Includes goods of nil value stolen. In 1979/80, this category included goods stolen of under £5 in value

Unrecorded crime

The following chart, also from the *British Crime Survey*, shows that only half of all crimes are reported, only three in ten are recorded, and only 7 per cent are cleared up.

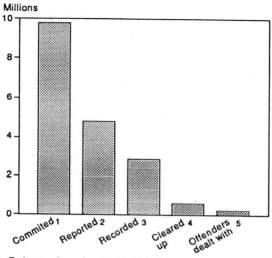

1 Estimates from the 1992 British Crime Survey.
2 Number of crimes reported by BCS respondents said to have been known to the police.
3 Estimates of a sub-set of notifiable offences recorded by the police also covered by the British Crime Survey.
4 Estimate of the proportion of offences commited which are cleared up.
5 Number of individual offenders dealt with for offences covered in bar 1.

Number of crimes committed and offenders dealt with, 1991.
(*Source*: Social Trends, 1994.)

Domestic violence is a crime where the decisions of the victims or the police may result in 'no-criming'. In 1984 and 1985, researchers found that the Metropolitan Police in Hounslow and Holloway filed crime reports of sixty-one cases of 'wife-battering'. Forty-eight of these assaults were then 'no-crimed'. In thirty-nine of the cases police dropped charges because the wife was unwilling to give evidence against her husband.

In 1996, a survey of 434 women in Surrey, the county with the highest divorce rate, found that:

- 33 per cent of women had been attacked in their homes;
- 24 per cent had been beaten up in their homes;
- 9 per cent had had their lives threatened;
- 5 per cent had been attacked with a weapon.

Domestic violence was found to cause:

- 16 per cent to live in constant fear;
- 7 per cent to suffer depression;
- 6 per cent to feel suicidal.

Almost two-thirds of the victims had not sought help because they were afraid, ashamed or considered it to be a private matter.

Policing policy

The police are unable to concentrate on all areas of law-breaking. A chief constable may decide to focus resources on particular criminal activities. The following example shows how a change in policing policy can affect criminal statistics. In Manchester in 1955 there was 1 prosecution for homosexual importuning, in 1956 and 1957 there were none. Following the appointment of Chief Constable McKay in 1958, prosecutions rose to 30 in 1959 and 216 in 1962.

Drink-driving is another example of an offence where policing policy may influence the number of recorded offences. If a police force in one county decides to deploy a lot of officers in making random breath tests on drivers over Christmas, then this county might have a big rise in prosecutions for drink-driving since a greater proportion of offenders are caught. But if the policing policy is widely publicised, then there may be a fall in prosecutions. This drop in cases might be because drinkers are deterred from driving or because they are careful to avoid busy roads where breath tests are likely.

Explaining the rise and fall in crime

Robert Reiner has argued that four ingredients are necessary for a crime to occur:

1   **Motive**   There must be a motivated offender.
2   **Means**   The offender must have the means to commit the crime.
3   **Opportunity**   A vulnerable victim must be available.
4   **Lack of control**   The offender must not be prevented by either external controls (police, security, closed-circuit TV, etc) or internalised controls (conscience, norms, the 'inner policeman').

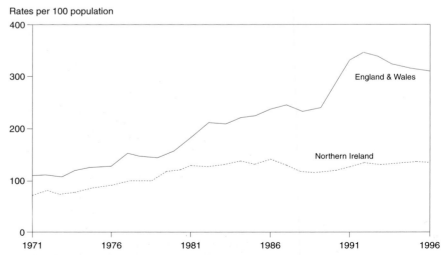

Rates per 100 population

Notifiable offences recorded by the police
(*Source:* Social Trends, 1998.)

[1] Indictable offences up to and including 1978. Excluding offences of criminal damagee of value £20 and under in England and Wales.

The steady rise in crime in the 1950s, 1960s and 1970s can be explained in terms of increased opportunities and less internalised controls. In an increasingly affluent society there was far more property to steal, such as cars, TVs and videos. There was also a gradual erosion of deference. This major change in British culture meant that there was far less automatic acceptance of authority. A more liberal and less deferential culture weakens both internal and external inhibitors of deviance.

The Conservative Government of the 1980s adopted free-market policies which increased poverty, inequality and long-term unemployment, especially among young people. These socio-economic factors, combined with the 'yuppie greed and materialism' of the Thatcher era, gave rise to an increase in the numbers of people with the motive to commit crime. And so the crime rate in England and Wales tripled between 1971 and 1992, peaking at 10.5 notifiable offences per 100 people.

The drop in notifiable offences from 1992 to 1997 was acclaimed by the Conservative Government as evidence that its law and order policies were working. But Robert Reiner suspects that the police may be recording a smaller proportion of the crimes reported to them, in order to improve their clear-up rates: 'The regime of policing by numbers has probably led to old and discredited techniques of massaging the figures creeping back in as an unintended consequence. The government has not so much got tough on crime, or on the causes of crime, as on recording crime.'

Is Britain becoming more violent?

The following chart shows a sixfold increase, over nineteen years, in the number of offences involving guns in England and Wales. But such offences remain only 0.25 per cent of all notifiable offences.

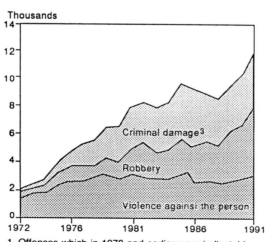

Notifiable offences[1] involving fire-arms[2] in England and Wales
(Source: *Social Trends*, 1993.)

1 Offences which in 1978 and earlier were indicatable.
2 Notifiable offences recorded by the police in which firearms were reported to have been used. Excludes offences of criminal damage estimated at £20 or less.
3 Includes "other offences" which were mainly burglary sexual offences and theft which numbered 345 in 1991.

Police involved in a siege in London.

The *British Crime Survey* suggests that police statistics may overstate the increase in crime. In the 1980s, recorded crime doubled, but the *British Crime Survey* suggests that crime increased by only a half. The pattern was different for different crimes:

Percentage rise between 1981 and 1991 for:	Burglary and theft	Vandalism	Violence
Crimes recorded by the police	192	105	190
Actual crimes reported by victims to the *British Crimes Survey*	192	0	22

The above figures show that most of the increase in recorded violent crime was due to an increased willingness to report it. We could say that this reflects an improvement in society. It shows higher standards of behaviour. Whereas a pub landlord in the 1860s might have expected a brawl at closing time every Friday night, his modern counterpart might show less tolerance of violence and greater willingness to call the police.

It is generally accepted that the police come to know about a very high proportion of all murders. This means that there is only a very small dark figure. The number of murders in England and Wales rose from 600 in 1974 to 676 in 1990. But before jumping to the conclusion that society is becoming ever more violent, we might consider the chart on page 231. This shows that the number of homicides recorded by the police, as a proportion of the population, was lower in the 1980s than it had been in the 1860s.

Going back further in history, research by Ted Gurr suggests that the murder rate has dropped dramatically in each century since the reign of King John in 1200. The murder rate in the thirteenth century was double

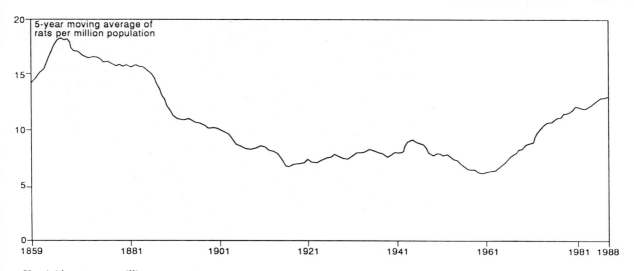

Homicide rate, per million population, England and Wales.
(Source: *Social Trends*, 1992.)

that in the sixteenth century. The murder rate in Elizabethan and Jacobean times was five times higher than it is today. Gurr comments that

> murderous brawls and violent death were everyday occurrences in medieval England. Most violent deaths resulted from fights with neighbours involving knives, cudgels and agricultural implements. Research sketches a portrait of a society in which men, but rarely women, were easily provoked to violent anger and were unrestrained in their brutality.

It should be noted that most crime is against property rather than people. Violent crime accounts for only one in twenty serious offences. Also, other countries and areas are much more violent than Britain. New York, for example, has a murder rate which is sixteen times higher than London.

4   Causes of crime

Biological theories of criminality

In the 1870s an Italian doctor called Lombroso published one of the first scientific theories that attempted to explain why some people commit crime. From his studies of convicts, Lombroso claimed that they had physical features in common, such as a flat nose, a narrow and low forehead and an arm span exceeding their height. Their primitive physiques caused them to lack a properly developed moral sense of right and wrong, thus explaining their criminality.

This theory of an inborn criminal nature has been rejected for the following reasons:

- Criminality does not necessarily 'run in families' from one generation to the next.

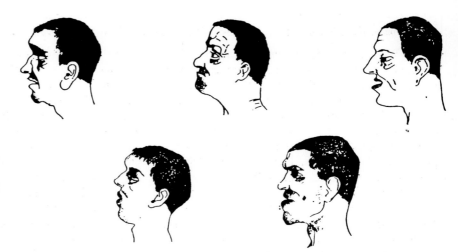

Victorian criminologists tried to identify deviants by their body type. These pictures are from The Criminals *by Havelock Ellis.*

- The convicts studied by Lombroso were by no means typical of the whole criminal population which includes businesspeople who commit frauds, evade taxes and break factory safety laws but are seldom imprisoned.
- Some of the apparent physical similarities between the convicts would have been due to the poor diet they received in prison.

Yet many of us still believe that we know what typical criminals look like and many police probably use certain stereotypes. For example, they may think that the typical football hooligan is a skinhead.

Psychological theories of criminality

Most psychological theories stress how events in early upbringing may lead to later criminality. In the 1950s, the idea of maternal deprivation was an influential psychological theory of crime. In extreme cases those who are deprived of the closeness of their mothers in their early years may develop into psychopaths. Since they have never been shown warm feelings, they are unable to feel consideration for others.

Maternal deprivation may be seen as a form of child abuse. Recent psychological theories have highlighted the significance of abuse in childhood. The gang leader who robs a teenager of his new bike is likely to have been bullied by his own father. A high proportion of the women in prison have, as children, been taken into care due to acute neglect or sexual abuse.

Case study: the childhood background of the 'nutters' who lead street gangs

In 1993, a Home Office survey studied 5,615 street crimes. A high percentage were committed by gangs who mugged and injured their victims. Nearly a quarter of these gangs carried knives.

Schoolkids in inner city areas live with a constant awareness of risk, expressed by 13-year-old Jason, from Battersea, who described gangs called 'The Killers' and 'The Demons' who, he says, 'are real nutters. They won't stop at anything.'

What explanations can psychologists offer? Nick Emler, who has done work on delinquency at Dundee University, says: 'Children who choose these gangs have a style of relating to others which has often developed over childhood, being reinforced by cold, uncaring parenting and the use of physical punishment. These children turn out to be bullies. They then relate to others in an aggressive, confrontational way and get the same response back. From this they develop the idea that being the meanest and toughest is the best thing they can achieve.'

The similar views of Felicity de Zulueta are indicated by the title of her book, *From Pain to Violence*. She says: 'A child who empathises with another will find it very difficult to be sadistic, but children whose emotional needs have not been met when they were young, who have been abused or brought up with physical violence as a way of control, children who have not felt valued and have split off their feelings, do not feel empathy. They can de-humanise victims and see them as "bad objects" which allows them to inflict the pain and abuse that was inflicted on them. This is what may be seen in street gangs in deprived working class areas, but sadistic behaviour coming from the same root is not exclusive to them. You see it manifested, for example, by prefects in public schools or middle class children who gain power by bullying.'

(adapted from 'Street Wars' by Angela Neustatter, the *Guardian*, 10 February 1994)

American sociological theories

1 The Chicago School, in the 1920, produced an **ecological** theory of crime. This focused on the inner-city slums which had the highest official rates of crime. The Chicago sociologists called these areas **zones of transition**. This is because such areas had cheap rooms to let which attracted poor migrants from the countryside and overseas. These new arrivals then struggled to move out to better parts of the city as soon as possible.

Those left behind in the zone of transition showed high rates of: poverty; broken homes; alcoholism; debt; illegitimacy; drugtaking; gambling; suicide; crime.

The rapid turnover of population meant that these areas lacked a stable community to exercise informal social control, for example stopping neighbours from stealing from each other. The zone of transition was thus seen as an area of **social disorganisation**.

2 Strain In 1938, Robert Merton put forward a very influential structural and cultural explanation of criminal behaviour. The dominant cultural goal in American society is to be successful in terms of wealth. But the position of the lower classes in the social structure means that many have limited prospects of becoming wealthy. There is a mismatch between legitimate means and cultural goals because many will never become wealthy by working hard in regular jobs. This mismatch creates a strain for individuals and they can respond in one of five ways:

- *Conformity* = accepting the legitimate means to such a goal, that is hard work (Laurie Taylor has likened this to working hard at playing a fruit machine).
- *Innovation* = using illegal methods to reach the accepted goal (like breaking into the fruit machine).
- *Ritualism* = accepting the means but losing sight of the object of the exercise (like playing the fruit machine mindlessly, forgetting what the aim is).
- *Retreatism* = dropping out and abandoning both the goals and the means (like leaving the fun palace to take drugs in the alleyway).
- *Rebellion* = rejecting society's values in favour of an alternative system, for example turning to communism or religious cults (like trying to build a different sort of amusement arcade).

In 1955, Albert Cohen developed a structural and subcultural theory of criminality from his study of delinquent boys. He claimed that the stratification structure generates criminal subcultures. This is because those from the lower classes are likely to fail at school and find themselves in dead-end jobs. In terms of society's values they have failed and are given a low status. In contrast to Merton's individual responses, Cohen describes how working-class lads may respond to their 'status frustration' in a collective way. They may reject society's values and create their own subcultures. These subcultures may turn mainstream values upside-down. The dominant culture condemns violence and vandalism, but the subculture rewards those who commit such crimes with high status.

We can illustrate this theory with the case of a youth who smashes up some public toilets. Local newspapers report such incidents with monotonous regularity. Why do young people commit such mindless destruction? Criminal damage cannot be seen as a form of 'innovation' to gain financial rewards. If teenage leisure activities were rewarded on a status scale, most people would give a high status to those who devote their time to team sports and voluntary community service. Toilet smashing would be given a very low status. But within a deviant subculture, such vandalism may be regarded as an heroic act. The vandal may earn high status in the eyes of fellow gang members.

British sociological explanations for crime

Section 5 of Chapter 3 outlines Stan Cohen's version of labelling theory. A media moral panic turns deviants, such as New Age travellers, into folk devils. They are isolated and persecuted by the police. Their peripheral deviance becomes central to their identity. Once labelled as outlaws, they may be more inclined to act like outlaws. Increased arrests feed back into the spiral. The media thus amplify the initial deviance.

More recently, Jock Young and John Lea have put forward three concepts which, taken together, are designed to give a full explanation of street crimes committed by young people:

- **Relative deprivation**   Poverty or deprivation will only cause crime when those who experience it feel deprived in relation to other groups. So, it is not deprivation by itself but the feeling of being deprived that is important. And, of course, in our society the media play a major part in creating this feeling of relative deprivation: unemployed youths are more criminal today than they were in the 1930s because today's consumer society gives them high expectations of owning expensive goods.

- **Marginalisation**   As a consequence of unemployment and poverty many individuals find themselves living outside mainstream society or on the margins of society. These 'marginalised' individuals do not have at their disposal established organisations through which to express their problems and aspirations and they are therefore prone to use violence as a means of self-expression. For example, rioting may be a form of political expression for unemployed youths who find themselves on the edge of society, with no community or workplace organisations to represent them.
- **Subculture**   If a group of people shares a sense of relative deprivation, they may create a way of life, a subculture, that helps them to deal with this problem. Thus, the subculture develops out of a common problem and a common desire to overcome it. But the subculture that develops may not be a criminal one: new religious cults often gain their followers from among the poor. For example, an inner-city Afro-Caribbean youth, facing racism and oppression, may turn to Rastafarian or Pentecostalist religious subcultures or the youth may turn to subcultures involving hustling and street crime.

In 1994, two studies highlighted the importance of unemployment. A survey by probation officers of 30,000 offenders found that 70 per cent of serious offences were committed by people out of work. Also, Dickinson reported a clear correlation between unemployment among young men and domestic burglaries. Both fell in the boom years of the late 1980s. Burglaries then rose as unemployment increased to 23 per cent of 16–19-year-olds and 17 per cent of 20–24-year-olds by 1993.

1994 also saw research that indicated the significance of expensive habits among those addicted to illegal drugs. Four studies in Liverpool, Lancashire, London and the Wirral found that more than 85 per cent of heroin addicts were funding their £600-a-week drug habits through property crime. This led to the claim that more than half of the £4 billion worth of property stolen each year is being sold to finance the habits of the growing numbers of drug users.

Criminality and educational underachievement

In 1998, the Basic Skills Agency sent a report to the Prime Minister's Social Exclusion Unit. The report was based on a study of 500 17–25-year-old offenders in Shropshire. In-depth interviews with these young adult criminals found a link between educational failure, truancy and turning to crime:

- 69 per cent had severe problems with basic literacy and were unable to fill in a job application form satisfactorily;
- 50 per cent had difficulty telling the time and giving the days of the week or the months of the year in the right order;
- 64 per cent had been habitual truants from the start of their secondary schooling.

Stephen Byers, the Schools Standards Minister, commented: 'These figures show how important early intervention is to ensure that every child has the ability to read and write. There is now clear evidence that for many youngsters the lack of basic skills leads to truancy and exclusion from school, ending all too often with criminal activity.' The Metropolitan Police has told the Social Exclusion Unit that children aged between 10 and 16 are responsible for 33 per cent of all car thefts and burglaries and 40 per cent of all street robberies in London.

Variations in crime rates between different groups in the community

Female crime

England & Wales

Percentages

Offenders[1] as a percentage of the population: by gender and age, 1996 (Source: Social Trends, 1998.)

[1]People found guilty or cautioned for indictable offences in 1996; excludes those whose age was not known.

Why is the male crime rate seven times higher than the female crime rate? It has been argued that the female crime rate is lower because female criminality, such as shoplifting and prostitution, is less visible. Other observers point to the 'chivalry factor': male police officers are more lenient with female than male offenders; women police officers are more likely to arrest female offenders than their male colleagues. But self-report studies, such as that done by Mawby in Sheffield, suggest that the 7:1 ratio of male to female crime in the official figures is about right. So why do females commit less crime?

Socialisation patterns

Males and females are socialised or conditioned differently. Girls are brought up in such a way that they come to possess qualities, desires and expectations that lead them to behave in a law-abiding way whereas boys are encouraged to possess qualities, such as aggressive assertiveness, that make them more disposed to commit criminal acts. A fuller account of gender and socialisation can be found in Chapter 2. Here are some notable differences:

- Girls have less chance to get up to mischief than boys because they are more closely supervised by their parents. In a similar way, men have more opportunity to commit crime at work since they are often free from supervision, for example driving lorries or working on building sites.
- Girls are less likely to learn the types of skill that are related to criminal

activity and they are less likely to have access to criminal networks to dispose of stolen goods, such as criminal subcultures in pubs.

- Much crime is caused by drunkenness, after the pubs close. Young women are less likely to abuse alcohol and hang around the streets in gangs late at night.

The gender deal

Feminists stress the way that girls are socialised into seeing marriage, child care and domesticity as their main goals. They are offered a 'gender deal': if they conform to the norms of respectable womanhood, they can 'enjoy a career' in the domestic sphere. The deal involves constant concern for maintaining a good reputation and this means the following:

- accepting stricter social control than males in the home, in public and at work;
- remaining in the family, as a daughter or a wife;
- avoiding any contact with criminality, in order to avoid being labelled unfeminine.

The women who are most likely to become criminal are the minority who have been brought up in care, or who have rejected 'normal' family life. A typical female prisoner is a young, poor mother who has committed cheque card fraud, benefit fraud or petty shoplifting.

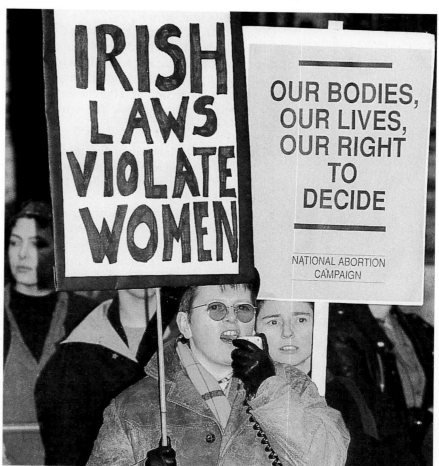

Why do feminists take issue with Irish laws?

Urban and rural crime rates

The crime rate has, in the past, been lower in rural than in urban areas. Three reasons for this are as follows:

- Quite simply there is less opportunity in rural areas to commit crime. There are fewer department stores and car parks, less to steal.
- There is a greater degree of informal social control in the countryside. Urban Neighbourhood Watch schemes try to imitate the situation in villages where folk are quick to spot strangers and soon know which youths are up to no good.
- The village bobby is less likely than an urban police officer to book first-time young offenders. An informal warning and a word with their parents avoids extra figures in the rural crime statistics.

All this is changing. Social mobility and newcomers to rural areas mean less stability and a more urban way of life in villages. Gangs of lager louts are common in market towns as are drug dealers. In 1992, recorded crime increased faster in rural than in urban areas. The highest rise in crime, over 20 per cent, was in Cheshire. The police have pointed to the improved motorway network – many rural areas are within an hour's drive of inner cities – but sociologists have noted the growth of a rural underclass.

Social class and crime

Official statistics suggest that most criminals come from working-class backgrounds. The last section of this chapter, on white-collar crime, shows that criminal activity is not confined to a particular class. The working class may be no more prone to commit crimes than other classes. Different groups in society tend to commit different sorts of crimes. The offences of working-class male youths dominate the crime statistics. This could be due to a number of reasons:

- their crimes are more public and visible than the crimes of others;
- they fit the police officer's stereotype of what a typical criminal is like and so they are labelled, subject to heavy surveillance and likely to be criminalised;
- society may be more concerned about vandalised public toilets than white-collar crimes, such as company fraud or industrial pollution.

The University of Edinburgh's *Survey of Young People* questioned 1,200 11–15-year-olds. Over a nine-month period, 35 per cent admitted to shoplifting, 30 per cent to vandalism, 18 per cent to drugtaking, 6 per cent to car crimes and 3 per cent to housebreaking. Little class difference was found: those admitting offences ranged from 75 per cent in the most deprived areas of Edinburgh to 62 per cent and 68 per cent in two of the most affluent parts of the city. The study was extended to 2,000 teenagers in industrial areas, rural areas and market towns. Again, the same patterns of offending were found in all classes and areas. Overall, 58 per cent admitted offences (compared to 66 per cent in Edinburgh), ranging from 62 per cent in council housing to 56 per cent in owner-occupier households.

5   White-collar crime

Edwin Sutherland produced the first major study of white-collar crime in 1949. He defined white-collar crime as offences committed by people of respectability and high social status in the course of their occupations. Researchers have suggested that white-collar crime involves at least ten times as much money as working-class crime. Tax evasion alone may 'rob' the Inland Revenue of around £20 billion a year. In 1991, the Serious Fraud Office indicated that the sum lost through household burglaries was only half the sum lost, mainly by small investors and pensioners, through management fraud. For example, eighteen thousand investors with Barlow Clowes lost £150 million. In *White Collar Crime* (1992), Hazel Croall outlines the following categories:

- *Employee theft*   A certain level of pilferage of stationery and 'theft' of phone calls for private use may be acceptable to the informal norms of the workplace. Firms may accept a certain amount of 'stock shrinkage' or fiddled time-sheets. Employees who are caught may be sacked or warned rather than handed over to the police for prosecution. In 1994, the Retail Consortium estimated that thefts by shop staff accounted for losses of £554 million a year.

- *Frauds*   Between 1992 and 1994, 30 per cent of large companies suffered at least one fraud of more than £50,000. The Serious Fraud Office only become involved where sums over £2 million are stolen. In 1991, they were investigating fifty-six cases involving over £1,600 million when the collapse of the Bank of Credit and Commerce International revealed a worldwide fraud of up to £15,000 million. Smaller frauds include the use of stolen credit cards, companies 'making off without payment' to suppliers and farmers illegally claiming subsidies.

- *Computer crime*   Computer crime may be costing up to £2 billion a year but organisations such as banks are reluctant to report offences for fear of losing public confidence. In one case, a bank employee transferred £45,000 from dormant accounts in Kuwait, to be placed in accounts of his own once he had left the bank. In order to prevent detection, he programmed the computer to delete all records of these transactions.

  Another type of computer crime is the 'electronic trespass' of a computer 'hacker' who may plant a destructive computer 'virus'. In the early 1990s British Airways employees hacked into the computer of their rival, Richard Branson's Virgin Atlantic, to obtain confidential flight data.

- *Tax fraud*   Income and spending that evades taxation is known as the black economy. This hidden economy is estimated to be worth between 6 and 8 per cent of total economic activity. In 1993, the black economy was around £50 billion. Those who do not fully declare their income for taxation range from drug dealers and professional traders at car-boot sales to multi-millionaire businessmen like Octav Botnar. Botnar's Nissan UK Ltd imported thousands of Japanese cars during the 1970s and 1980s, 'laundering' profits in secret Swiss bank accounts to evade corporation tax. In 1993, Botnar fled Britain, owing the tax authorities £177 million.

● *Crimes against consumers*   These include trade description offences, such as 'clocking' the mileage on second-hand cars; weights and measures offences, such as short measures in pubs; food and drug offences, such as the deaths caused by the Dalkon Shield contraceptive device. The deaths caused by the sinking of the *Herald of Free Enterprise* led to prosecutions for corporate manslaughter.

In 1994, the government decided not to prosecute the owners of the tanker Braer *for polluting the Shetland Islands with 87,000 tonnes of oil.*

- *Employee safety*   Each year there are around 1.6 million industrial accidents. These cause 5,000 people to leave work permanently and 16,000 to retire early. Five thousand people were killed in workplace accidents between 1984 and 1994 but, despite Health and Safety Executive investigations into negligence of safety procedures, no senior employees were jailed for their culpability.
- *Pollution*   When a lorry driver added aluminium sulphate to the water supply at Camelford, in 1991, 20,000 consumers suffered skin rashes, nausea and vomiting, even brain damage. The South Western Water Authority was fined £10,000. In England and Wales, there were over 22,000 reported water pollution incidents in 1991. These resulted in 356 prosecutions. In 1990 there were £54,000 of fines in 22 convictions for the 136 oil spills round the UK which had involved clean-up costs of £1,193,000.

A corporate crime: in 1998, the Environment Agency fined ICI £300,000 after 150 tons of the chemical chloroform leaked from its Runcorn factory.

Characteristics of white-collar crime

- **Complexity and low visibility**: these often hinder detection.
- **Diffusion of responsibility**: it is often difficult to tell whether senior management are to blame.
- **Diffusion of victimisation**: there may be no single identifiable victim.
- **Lenient sanctions**: few offenders are sent to prison and fines are often derisory. Roger Levitt's financial services company collapsed with debts of £34 million in 1990. At his trial, in 1993, the jury was told how one celebrity client, the thriller writer Frederick Forsyth, was duped out of £400,000 by Levitt. After pleading guilty to fraudulent trading, Levitt was sentenced to 180 hours of community service.

Roger Levitt after being sentenced to 180 hours of community service.

- **Ambiguous laws**: tax evasion is illegal but tax avoidance is not. In 1994, a report showed that thirty-seven Conservative MPs were advisers, consultants or partners in companies giving advice on tax avoidance via offshore tax havens.
- **Ambiguous criminal status**: shortly after his brief imprisonment Gerald Ronson, of the Heron Group, was shaking hands with royalty at a charity event. His fraud and false accounting during the Guinness affair also brought him a fine of £5 million to be paid by summer 1992. Heron helped Mr Ronson by paying him a bonus of £1.7 million in March 1992.

Case study: the McLibel trial

England's longest civil trial ended in 1997. It was a 315-day libel case. The McDonald's fast food empire was awarded £60,000 damages, to be paid by two penniless environmental campaigners. In a 1987 leaflet, they had accused McDonald's of 'crimes' under 7 headings: McDollars, McGreedy, McCancer, McMurder, McRipoff, McTorture and McGarbage. The judge found that some of the accusations were true but that others were false and libellous:

- 'McDonald's has destroyed rainforests by ranching' – false.
- 'McDonald's has caused starvation by evicting poor farmers to make way for ranching' – false.
- 'McDonald's only recycles a tiny part of its packaging' – false; the amount recycled is 'small'.
- 'McDonald's foods increase heart disease and cancer of the bowel and breast' – false; only those who eat at McDonald's several times a week have an increased risk of heart disease.
- 'McDonald's lies about the benefits of its food, which is high in fat and low in fibre, vitamins and minerals' – true; adverts, promotions and booklets 'pretended to a positive nutritional benefit which the food did not match'.
- 'McDonald's advertising exploits children' – true; 'It makes considerable use of susceptible young children'.
- 'McDonald's is responsible for cruel practices in the rearing and slaughter of pigs, chicken and cattle' – partly true; McDonald's is 'culpably responsible' for cruelty to battery hens and broiler chickens.
- 'McDonald's customers are at risk of food poisoning by the residues of antibiotic drugs, pesticides and hormone drugs in meals' – false; no evidence.
- 'McDonald's low wages help to depress wages in the catering trade' – true.
- 'McDonald's provides bad working conditions, exploits disadvantaged groups and prevents unionisation by getting rid of pro-union employees' – false.

During this epic David versus Goliath courtroom battle, the environmentalists' 'McSpotlight' website became home to 500 megabytes of evidence and comment and it was visited by 13 million readers from all around the world.

Children demonstrating, in 1998, against keeping hens in battery cages.

GCSE question from Southern Examining Group 1993

Study Item A and Item B. Then answer the questions which follow.

Item A

Victims of one or more crimes by ethnic origin and type of offence, 1987

England and Wales

| Type of offence | Percentage of ethnic group who were victims | | |
	White	*Afro-Caribbean*	*Asian*
	%	%	%
Household vandalism	5	4	8
Burglary	6	10	6
Assault	3	7	4
Threats	2	4	5
Robbery/theft from person	1	3	3

(Adapted from *British Crime Survey*, 1987)

Item B

A dramatic increase in the number of young men committing suicide was reported yesterday by The Samaritans. The organisation said that the figures were the 'tip of the iceberg' with many more cases concealed by coroner's courts in order to spare families further distress. 80% of the suicides among under 25s are male. However, 80% of those who *attempt* to kill themselves are women. 'Men tend to use more violent means. Women generally use means which may lead to the attempt being unsuccessful.'

(Adapted from an article in *The Independent*, 16 May 1992)

(a) Study Item A and state:

    (i)   the ethnic origin of those *least* likely to be victims of assault;

    (ii) the crime of which people of Asian origin are most likely to be victims. (2)

(b) Study Item B and state:

    (i)   why the suicide figures are likely to underestimate the number of suicides;

    (ii) whether men or women are more likely to attempt suicide. (2)

(c) State *three* reasons why a victim may not report a crime committed against him/her to the police. (3)

(d) According to official statistics, young men are more likely to commit crimes than are young women. Identify and explain *two* reasons for this. (4)

(e) The number of crimes reported in Britain increased between 1980 and 1990. What explanations might sociologists give for this? (9)

CHAPTER 13

The effects of the mass media

Are we manipulated by the mass media?

If I shout across the street to you then I am using my voice as a medium, or method, of communication. Letters and telephone calls are similarly **media**, or methods of individual communication. On the other hand, any methods that reach a mass audience are part of the **mass media**. These include: TV, radio, papers, magazines, films, videos, records and comics.

1 Research into audiences

National Readership Surveys

These surveys find out which social groups read different newspapers and magazines. Advertisers need this sort of information before spending millions of pounds on placing advertisements which might, for example, be targeted at rich young men who can be tempted to buy Porsche cars. The Institute of Practitioners in Advertising uses the following social class categories:

A = higher managerial or professional

B = intermediate managerial or professional

C1 = junior managerial or professional and supervisory or clerical

C2 = skilled manual workers

D = semi- and unskilled manual workers

E = pensioners, casual or lowest-grade workers, unemployed

In 1987 the National Readership Surveys found that 74 per cent of class A read a daily newspaper compared to 59 per cent in class E. A number of class and gender differences are shown in the following chart:

Percentage of adult readers in different groups, 1987

	Males	Females	A	B	C1	C2	D	E
Sun	28	23	5	10	20	32	37	27
Daily Telegraph	7	5	28	16	8	3	1	2
News of the World	30	27	9	12	23	36	40	30
The Sunday Times	9	7	35	22	10	3	3	2
Smash Hits	5	6	5	5	5	6	6	3
Exchange and Mart	6	2	3	3	4	5	4	2
Woman's Own	3	18	8	10	12	11	11	9
Good Housekeeping	2	9	15	12	7	4	3	2

(adapted from *Social Trends*, 1989)

Some magazines and newspapers vary widely in the sex and age of their readership:

Percentage of each group reading *Viz* and *Sunday Sport*, 1992

	Males	Females	15–24-year-olds	45–64-year-olds
Viz	14	5	29	2
Sunday Sport	5	1	7	1

(Source: *Social Trends*, 1994)

Television audiences

The average American sees a million television commercials by the age of 40. Compare your own viewing habits with the following figures:

Television viewing by social class, hours and minutes per week, 1992

AB = 19:56

C1 = 25:08

C2 = 27:30

DE = 31:54

(Source: *Social Trends*, 1994)

Case study: television viewing and gender

The following extracts are from *Family Television* by David Morley, 1986. It describes interviews which were conducted with eighteen families in South London.

Power and control over programme choice

Masculine power is evident in a number of the families as the ultimate determinant on occasions of conflict over viewing choices ... None of the women in any of the families uses the automatic control regularly. A number of them complain that their husbands use the channel control device obsessively, channel flicking across programmes when their wives are trying to watch something else.

Characteristically, the control device is the symbolic possession of the father (or of the son, in the father's absence) which sits 'on the arm of Daddy's chair' and is used almost exclusively by him ... The research done by Peter Collett and Roger Lamb in which they videotaped a number of families watching television over an extended period shows this to comic effect. On at least one occasion the husband carries the control device about the house with him as he moves from the living-room to the kitchen and then engages in a prolonged wrestling match with his wife and son simultaneously so as to prevent them from getting their hands on it.

Styles of viewing

The tapes made by Collett show the families concerned engaging in an almost bizarre variety of different activities; we eat dinner, knit jumpers, argue with each other, listen to music, read books, do homework, kiss, write letters and vacuum-clean the carpet with the television on.

... the men state a clear preference for viewing attentively, in silence, without interruption 'in order not to miss anything'. Moreover, they display puzzlement at the way their wives and daughters watch television. This the women themselves describe as an essentially social activity, involving ongoing conversation, and usually the performance of at least one other domestic activity (ironing, etc.) at the same time. Indeed, many of the women feel that to just watch television without doing anything else at the same time would be an indefensible waste of time.

Activity

Carry out your own research to check on the above findings about television viewing and gender.

2   The political effects of the media

Previous chapters have described the way that the media create stereotypes of sex roles, youth subcultures, single mothers, the 'typical family' and ethnic groups. Since so much of our information about the world is provided by the media, the question naturally arises of whether or not the media shape our political views and behaviour. The answer given by many left-wing commentators is a most definite yes, while the answer given by pluralist writers is that the media have little effect on us. We will now examine these opposing arguments about the political effects of the media.

The left-wing view

For the left wing, the media in the modern world act as an important agency of social control. This is done by transmitting an ideological view of the world that encourages us to accept the inequalities and injustices of the capitalist order. An **ideology** consists of a biased way of looking at the world that justifies the interests of a particular group. What the left wing are saying is that the media transmit an ideology that supports the interests of the group that benefits most from capitalism, namely the rich and powerful or the ruling class. The left wing see the media operating in the interests of the modern capitalist elite in the same way that the medieval Church supported the feudal ruling class:

- media rituals, like the televising of the Olympic Games, promote group identity, in a similar way to the rituals of the medieval Church;
- the witch-hunts of the early Church are matched by the moral panics about modern folk devils – both promote unity against a threat from outsiders;
- priests told the masses that the power structure was laid down by God – the modern media convince us that society is run in a democratic way;
- dissidents and protesters are stigmatised as 'extremists' who reject democracy, in the same way that 'infidels' and unbelievers were once condemned;
- the randomness of fate is a recurring theme in modern entertainment which, like the randomness of God's unseen hand, helps to explain away injustice and inequality;

The 1936 Olympic Games in Berlin were stage-managed as a vast exercise in Nazi propaganda.

- the masses used to find consolation in the promise that the meek would inherit the earth (via eternal salvation in heaven) – now we can escape into the glamour of the lives of showbiz stars.

The left wing have identified a number of aspects to do with the operation of the media that explain how the media act as a servant of the ruling class.

These aspects include ownership, censorship, gate-keeping and agenda-setting.

Ownership

Many commentators, across the political spectrum, have expressed great concern about the increasing concentration of ownership within the media. Concentration of ownership means that the media are becoming owned by fewer and fewer companies and individuals. The consequence of this is said to be that the range of political opinions expressed by the media is shrinking. This is because the power to decide what opinions the media express is held in the hands of fewer 'press barons' and 'media moguls'. Since the people who own newspapers and television companies tend to be supporters of the capitalist system, the media, especially the press, have become more biased in favour of capitalism. For example, Rupert Murdoch is able to use his many newspapers to express his right-wing view of the world. In 1994, Rupert Murdoch's News International owned 35 per cent of the UK's national press (the *Sun, Today, The Times, The Sunday Times* and the *News of the World*) as well as 50 per cent of BSkyB TV (*Sky One, The Movie Channel, Sky Movies Gold, Sky Sports, Sky News*). In the 1980s, Murdoch sacked the editor of *The Sunday Times*, Harold Evans, because he did not like the political tone of the newspaper under his editorship.

Censorship

Censorship refers to restrictions on what can be published or transmitted or portrayed on stage. Here are some of the landmarks in restricting freedom of speech in Britain:

1551　Theatre censorship was introduced.

1617　Blasphemy became a crime.

1792　The Libel Act gave a jury the right to decide on damages, to be paid by a liar who defames someone's reputation.

1968　Scripts of plays were censored by the Lord Chamberlain.

1857　Obscene Publications Act passed.

1898　Official Secrets Act passed.

1965　Race Relations Act outlawed incitement to racial hatred.

1984　Police and Criminal Evidence Act enabled police to demand unpublished confidential journalistic material from newspapers, broadcasters and freelance photographers.

1988　Clause 28 of the Local Authorities Act: no local council may 'intentionally promote homosexuality'.

Should video 'nasties' like
The Mutilator *be banned?*

1988   Removal of a 'public interest' defence by civil servants who disclose Official Secrets. (Two civil servants, worried that the Ministry of Defence was misleading Parliament, had leaked classified information: Sarah Tisdall's 1983 leak concerned the arrival of US Cruise missiles and Clive Ponting's 1984 leak concerned the sinking of the Argentinian battleship, *General Belgrano*, during the Falklands War.)

1988   No broadcasting of direct statements by representatives of Sinn Fein or the Ulster Defence Association.

1988   Broadcasting Standards Council set up.

The obvious complaint about censorship is that it is used by the powerful to cover up their devious and often illegal activities. Robert Maxwell was a multi-millionaire publisher. He is also alleged to have stolen £526 million, much of it from the pension fund of Mirror Group employees, to prop up his ailing business empire. Right up until his sudden death, he avoided close scrutiny of his £2.7 billion debts by intimidating and silencing investigative journalists. When BBC's *Panorama* accused him of fiddling the *Mirror's* spot-the-ball contest so that no reader could win the £1 million top prize, Maxwell issued four writs for libel and malicious falsehood.

Case study: the 1984 famine in Ethiopia

Democracy is not possible when citizens are deprived of information. In 1983, the military dictatorship in Ethiopia banned any reporting of famines by its own media. As well as the censorship of the Ethiopian government, the Western media imposed self-censorship by largely ignoring the starvation. All through 1983, international aid agencies warned of an impending disaster with millions threatened by starvation. A BBC TV news report from Ethiopia, in July 1984, was not given headline status and media coverage fizzled out.

In October 1984 the famine reached catastrophic proportions. The BBC finally treated the story as a major issue. A film report was prepared for the news bulletin and a full set of pictures was offered to the *Sun* newspaper. The *Sun*'s reply was 'We're actually not interested in famine.' Five days later, when the story had broken, the *Sun* ran two-inch headlines on 'RACE TO SAVE THE BABIES'. Bob Geldof's Band Aid record topped the charts that Christmas and in July 1985 1,500 million viewers in 120 nations watched Geldof's Live Aid concert.

Gate-keeping

Editors of newspapers and of TV news bulletins have the power to select some events for coverage while keeping the gate shut on other events. Left-wingers claim that the media often keep quiet about matters that threaten the interests of the powerful. An example is the way in which the American media kept the gate shut on the link between smoking and cancer. It was established as early as 1938 that smoking caused lung cancer. But for years this connection was played down and ignored by the media to such an extent that even as late as 1958, only 44 per cent of Americans thought that smoking was a cause of lung cancer. The American press did not want to publicise the scientific evidence because they did not want to threaten the interests of the powerful tobacco companies. Also, they relied on cigarette advertisements for revenue.

A less damaging example of gate-keeping is the way that editors are generally reluctant to allow items of foreign news 'through the gate'. In 1993, researchers at Goldsmiths College analysed five days of news coverage on BBC1, ITN, Sky News and Radio 4. This showed that ITN was competing with Sky in pursuing a more Americanised, downmarket presentation style. There was increasing use of live reports and 'two-ways' between newscaster and reporter to give pace and immediacy. Sky and ITN also pursued a more mainstream, domestic and tabloid agenda. ITN had the strongest bias towards sport, TV and showbusiness stories. BBC news had stronger international and business content, with twice as much foreign news as ITN and Sky.

Content of bulletins, 1–5 November 1993	Sky News Live at Five	ITN's Early Evening News	Six O'Clock News on BBC1	Radio 4
Foreign news	9%	11%	22%	20%
Showbiz and sport	23%	27%	15%	11%

In typical editions of daily newspapers you are likely to find the following amount of coverage of events overseas:

Average number of foreign news stories	Type of paper (with examples)
Fewer than ten	Downmarket popular tabloids (*Sun, Star, Mirror*)
Ten to twenty	Upmarket tabloids (*Mail, Express*)
Over thirty	Broadsheet quality 'heavies' (*The Times, Telegraph, Guardian, Independent*)

Activity

Check the amount of overseas coverage in a range of daily papers. List six other ways in which the three categories of newspaper differ in content. Select one or two foreign news stories from the quality press and rewrite them, with eye-catching headlines, for a downmarket popular tabloid.

Agenda-setting

The media help to determine which issues become the focus of attention. In this way, the media suggest to us which are the most important problems of the day. This power of the media is called agenda-setting.

In the mid-1980s the media highlighted heroin deaths but not fatalities from smoking and drinking; social security swindlers instead of tax evaders; black muggers in preference to racial attacks on black people. Issues like the abolition of the House of Lords or the monarchy may be kept off the agenda altogether.

Moral panics are dramatic expressions of the media's agenda-setting power, for they show how the media can make one issue dominate public debate and concern. The left wing claim that moral panics serve the ruling class in two ways. First, they direct our attention away from the real causes of society's problems which are inequality and injustice. Second, they strengthen the power of the state. Folk devils may be seen as a serious threat. This may lead to demands for greater police powers, harsher sentences and new laws. Moral panics have led to new laws to deal with the following folk devils: flying pickets (strikers who blockade workplaces at which they are not employed), all-night ravers, owners of pit bull terriers, New Age travellers and shopkeepers hiring out violent videos.

Here are some studies of moral panics:

- *The Drugtakers* by Jock Young (1971) describes a deviancy amplification spiral involving hippies.
- *Folk Devils and Moral Panics: The Creation of the Mods and Rockers* by Stan Cohen (1980) is discussed on pages 45–7.
- *Bad News* by the Glasgow University Media Group (1976) describes the negative portrayal of strikers in television news coverage.
- *Policing the Crisis: Mugging, the State and Law and Order* by Stuart Hall and others (1978) analyses a moral panic about black youth.
- *Images of Welfare: Press and Public Attitudes to Poverty* by Golding and Middleton (1983) discusses the phenomenon of **scroungerphobia**: hatred whipped up against social security claimants.
- *War and Peace News* by the Glasgow University Media Group (1985) claims that there was unfair coverage of the Greenham Common

There is a need to dance
There is a need to travel
There is a need to squat
There is a need for protest
There is a need for open spaces
There is a need to celebrate
There is a need for community
There is a need to communicate
There is a need for tolerance

There is a need

to be heard

Resist the Criminal Injustice Bill

Posters from the Oxford anarchist paper Oxfiend, *protesting at the measures in the 1994 Criminal Justice Bill against trespassers, squatters, New Age travellers and all-night rave parties.*

Women's Peace Camp and CND when they campaigned against the siting of American Cruise nuclear missiles in Britain.

- *Doctoring the Media* by Anne Karpf (1988) claims that the tabloid press promoted homophobic hysteria in its early coverage of AIDS as 'the gay plague'. (**Homophobia** means hatred of homosexuals.)

The pluralist view

The left wing claim that society is dominated by one group and by one political creed. The media are seen as biased in favour of capitalist interests. Pluralists reject this claim. They see our society as pluralist, with numerous political opinions and numerous competing interest groups, none of which is dominant. According to the pluralists, the media fairly represent the views of the many different groups in society. Pluralists claim that active audiences enjoy healthy competition between rival broadcasters and newspaper publishers. The demands of the audience dictate the news values that shape editorial priorities.

News values

Editors tend to value events as more newsworthy, more deserving of coverage, if the events are:

1 sudden (for example, murder) rather than slowly evolving (for example, pollution);
2 big – a small event may fail the size threshold;
3 unambiguous, clear in meaning;
4 familiar, relevant, close to home (for example, English-speaking USA may get more coverage than Europe);
5 able to fit our expectations ('most "news" is actually "olds"');
6 rare and surprising (an antidote to 4 and 5 above);
7 already established as news (a running story);
8 providing ingredients for a 'balanced diet' of bad, good and entertaining news;

9   about leading, elite nations;
10   about elite people (for example, presidents), famous personalities (for example, stars);
11   personal (for example, Nelson Mandela has personified the struggle against apartheid);
12   bad, with negative consequences.

The above list, drawn up by media sociologists, can be compared with the *Guardian*'s advice of news priorities (issued to new staff in the 1960s):

1   *Significance*: social, economic, political, human.
2   *Drama*: the excitement, action and entertainment in the event.
3   *Surprise*: the freshness, newness, unpredictability.
4   *Personalities*: royal, political, 'showbiz', others.
5   *Popular ingredients*: sex, scandal, crime.
6   *Numbers*: the scale of the event, numbers of people affected.
7   *Proximity*: on our doorsteps, or 10,000 miles away.

(from *News, Newspapers and Television* by Alistair Hetherington, 1985)

Healthy competition

Pluralists argue that there is no sinister political bias behind gate-keeping and agenda-setting. Rather, news values are dictated by the audience. The public gets what it wants. The media cannot impose an unwanted diet. The media must respond to public demand.

In 1969, Rupert Murdoch bought the *Sun* newspaper. It was a serious paper for working people, but with a falling circulation. By 1979, the *Sun* had overtaken the *Daily Mirror* with sales of 3.8 million. The *Sun* had offered a populist and entertaining diet of showbiz gossip and page 3 girls; it had also caught the political wind of change in the working class, taking a stand against trade union power and backing the radical ideas of the new Conservative leader, Margaret Thatcher. This shows that in changing the direction of the *Sun*, Murdoch was merely responding to public demand.

Active audiences

Pluralists like McQuail claim that the relationship between the media and their audiences is on equal terms. While the left wing see the media manipulating the audience, the pluralist view is that the audience is quite able to manipulate the media. We are not just passive dummies; we are active media consumers who can pick and choose. The political influence of the media is limited by three factors:

- **Selective exposure** means that we tend to choose newspapers that share our own political standpoint. We expose ourselves to a political bias which will reinforce, rather than change, our existing views.
- **Selective perception** means that we only perceive and accept information that fits in with our existing view of the world.
- **Selective retention** means that we conveniently forget any information that contradicts our viewpoint.

The left wing claim that the media in effect brainwash us and manufacture our consent to be ruled by the capitalist elite. The left wing may show that there is political bias in the media but this is not the same as demonstrating that the media shape our political views. The left wing are guilty of assuming that only they are untouched by the media's biased messages, while the rest of us are passive, unthinking slaves, at the mercy of the all-powerful media.

Pluralists maintain that we respond to the media's information in all sorts of ways. Our view of the world is shaped by other more important influences. **Political socialisation**, the process by which we form our political views, involves the influence of parents, friends, workmates and personal experiences.

Case study: the Sun and the 1992 General Election

The Sun *on the day of the General Election in 1992 and on the day after.*

The *Sun* carried a strong campaign against the Labour Party and its leader, Neil Kinnock, during the 1992 General Election. On voting day, the *Sun* had an eight-page 'Nightmare on Kinnock Street' feature. The *Sun* is Britain's most popular newspaper with 11 million readers. The following figures show a clear division in the voting patterns of the (mainly working-class) readership of Britain's two leading tabloids:

The Mori poll organisation has estimated that *Sun* readers showed a swing to the Conservatives which was 2 per cent greater than the national average. In a marginal seat like Bristol NW, where the Conservative majority was only 45 votes, this '*Sun* bonus' would have been worth a crucial 413 extra votes.

How readers voted in 1992	Conservative	Labour	Liberal Democrat
Sun	45%	36%	14%
Daily Mirror	20%	64%	14%

3   Media coverage of political protest

This section looks at the way that the mass media have reported three political protest demonstrations:

- the 1968 demonstration against the Vietnam War;
- the Greenham Common Women's Peace Camp (1982–83);
- the Battle of Westminster Bridge, 1988.

Case study: the anti-war demonstration and 'the Kick'

Graham Murdock has studied the press reporting of a massive demonstration which took place in London in 1968. Its purpose was to protest against the American government's escalation of the war in Vietnam and the British government's support for the Americans. About 70,000 people marched peacefully along an agreed route to a rally in Hyde Park. A breakaway march of some 3,000 people went to Grosvenor Square where about 250 of them attempted to break through a police cordon to demonstrate outside the American Embassy. This resulted in a number of violent incidents.

Next day the press all concentrated on the events at Grosvenor Square:

'Police win battle of Grosvenor Square as 6,000 are repelled'
(*The Times*)

'Fringe Fanatics Foiled at Big Demonstration – what the bobbies faced'
(*Daily Express*)

'The Day the Police were Wonderful'
(*Daily Mirror*)

All except *The Times* carried a front-page picture of 'the Kick'.

Murdock's first point is that the press coverage 'characterised' the demonstration as full of violence and streetfighting. The small print might have mentioned the 70,000 peaceful marchers, but the picture and headlines alone created a false and distorted impression.

Murdock's second point is that by concentrating on the violence the press not only ignored the 'message' of the demonstration but also undermined it. As a result of the papers' reporting of the event, the message or cause of the demonstrators would be associated in the public's mind with violence and lawbreaking. In other words, the press had given the demonstrators and their cause a bad name.

Verdict on Demo-Day:

Yes, our police ARE wonderful!

'WELL DONE, LADS.' MR CALLAGHAN CONGRATULATES POLICEMEN IN GROSVENOR SQUARE AFTER THE DEMONSTRATION

By
HARRY LONGMUIR, JAMES
LEWTHWAITE, MICHAEL
O'FLANERTY, BERNARD JORDAN
and OWEN SUMMERS

THE MAN who won the day in yesterday's big protest demonstration in London was the ordinary British bobby.

He kept his head, his humour and his self-control. He kept the peace and sanity as well.

And at the end of a day in which 30,000 demonstrators marched, only eight policemen were injured.

There was only one point on the long march through London when there was an attempt at violence. That was Grosvenor Square

But at five past four, just before the marchers arrived, a senior police officer broadcast a 16-word message to his men: 'Your job is to maintain police lines, according to instructions. There are to be no incidents'.

And the police maintained their lines —magnificently—when, five minutes later, a group of militant followers of Chinese Communist leader Mao Tse-tung led some 3,000 demonstrators away from the main body of 30,000 marchers and into the square. Their target: The U.S. Embassy.

For more than three hours the protesters were forced back by the police.

Persuasion

In spite of rushes from the hard core of 300 Mao-militants, who hacked with poles from their banners and showered the police with fireworks, the police held firm, refusing to be provoked. The police horses stood firm, too, as firecrackers exploded under their hooves.

Home Secretary Mr James Callaghan later went among the police and said: Well done, lads. Thank you.'

Behind the triumph for police tactics and behaviour was Deputy Commander John Lawlor.

Commander Lawlor, 62-year-old softspoken trouble-shooter of Scotland Yard's riot department, pressed for an outwardly soft approach to the demonstration at a secret conference several weeks ago.

Despite some senior officers' opinions that a harsher line should be taken, his persuasion won through.

It was Commander Lawlor's wish that no tear gas or water cannon should be used and that demonstrators if they wished should be allowed to squat in streets.

Commander Lawlor's plan—and he got backing to the hilt from Mr Callaghan and Metropolitan Police Commissioner Sir John Waldron—was: 'Don't antago-

THE boot goes in. One demonstrator holds PC John Alliston down as another kicks him. PC Alliston, 37, attached to Limehouse Police Station, was pulled out of the cordon and attacked in one of the few outbreaks of real violence. He was rescued from the mob by a police baton charge and taken to hospital. Later he was said to be comfortable.

nise the demonstrators—they've got a right to demonstrate.'

Two thousand hand-picked bobbies were on duty in Grosvenor Square—all men who had attended crowd-control courses at Hendon Police College.

Last night the police were reluctant to discuss their crowd control course. One senior officer commented: 'The methods, which appear to be pretty successful, will be used again. We are learning and improving every time.'

Significantly the use of water, gas or gas masks played no part in the course schedule.

It all ended successfully, with police morale high. An inspector in Grosvenor Square said: 'I'm a proud policeman tonight. The eyes of the world were on us, and we've proved it can be done without the police getting violent.'

And a sergeant joked: 'I think the worst thing about all this is that I'm missing *The Forsyte Saga* on television.'

The front page of the Daily Mail, *with 'the Kick'.*

Case study: the Battle of Westminster Bridge

Compare and contrast the coverage of a national demonstration by the National Union of Students in the following four sources:

Source A: from the front page of the *Guardian*, 25 November 1988.

Clash as 25,000 protest over loans scheme

ADRIAN BROOKS

Students battle with police

By Staff Reporters

Mounted police wielding batons yesterday dispersed a student demonstration after thousands of protesters broke away from a march, brought central London to a standstill for hours and confronted police as they tried to reach Parliament.

Missiles of bottles and sticks were thrown by protesters as police officers on horseback fought to clear Westminster Bridge.

Source B: from the front page of *The Times*, 25 November 1988.

Source C: from the *Hornsey and Muswell Hill Journal*, 1 December 1988.

Pupils in police charge alarm

FIFTY sixth formers of Fortismere comprehensive school, Muswell Hill, went on the national students' demonstration last Thursday – and a number were horrified when they were unwittingly caught up in the "pitched battles" with police near Westminster Bridge.

The police charged on horseback during the protest against Government plans to bring in loans to replace grants for students gaining college or university places.

Fortismere head Mr Andrew Nixon was disturbed by stories of violent police action which pupils brought back.

"I acceded to a request to take part. This is because they are going to be concerned about grants and loans when they go to university. They also got parents' permission," he said.

"For many it was the first time they had seen what happens when demonstrators and police get into conflict.

"It does seem that some of the police lost their tempers. At one time, police were having to pull colleagues off students. My youngsters got frightened.

"I know of no instances where youngsters from here misbehaved." Some of his pupils might have got the odd bruise (he had been given no details) but none was off sick.

Joanna Simons (17) a Fortismere sixth former said: "They charged at the students on the embankment. They were completely unreasonable."

Source D: from the *Hampstead and Highgate Express*, 2 December 1988.

Students 'wanted to kill us'

POLICE from Hampstead station, who helped form a cordon across Westminster Bridge during last Thursday's student demonstration, spoke this week about the "appalling levels of hostility" they encountered.

One sergeant said: "I thought that some of the demonstrators wanted to kill us; it was very frightening."

Two women constables and nine male officers from Hampstead were injured during the demonstration. WPC Judith Taylor, 21, who has been with the force for 18 months, was rushed to Westminster Hospital by ambulance after being crushed unconscious when people fell on top of her. Another 20-year-old WPC spent two days in hospital, after being bitten in the hand by a protester and punched in the face. She suffered concussion and shock, and is still on sick leave.

A 32-year-old sergeant was brutally kicked in the testicles.

Inspector Keith Walmsley said the officers were accompanying the front of the march when some of the demonstrators decided to turn right towards Westminster Bridge instead of continuing on to the Imperial War Museum.

"We ran along with them to try and stop them and stuck our arms out. But the group, about 3,000 strong, were determined to go on".

At Westminster Bridge the officers from Hampstead met up with horses and vans and helped to form a cordon across the bridge to stop the protesters demonstrating outside Parliament, which is illegal.

"The demonstrators were 60 yards deep from our position on the south side of the bridge. People were pushing and throwing full beer cans and glass bottles and using banners as spears," said Inspector Walmsley. "It was very frightening."

Officers at the front of the cordon lost gloves and ties, had watches ripped off and badges torn from their helmets, he said.

He added that the official NUS stewards on the demonstration had done a "marvellous job".

Data-response exercise: the Battle of Westminster Bridge

Use the four sources on pages 59–60 to answer these questions.

1 What was the demonstration about?
2 Which sources mention the purpose of the demonstration?

3 Sources C and D are both from local newspapers. Both offer local angles on the event. Which local participants are highlighted?
4 How do the descriptions in Sources C and D differ?

Case study: the Greenham Common Women's Peace Camp

In December 1982, 30,000 women protesters joined women who had been camping outside the American Air Force base at Greenham Common in Berkshire for over sixteen months. They were protesting against the use of the base for a new type of nuclear weapon: Cruise missiles.

The Glasgow Media Group analysed TV coverage of six women's peace demonstrations between December 1982 and December 1983 from a sample of thirty-eight news broadcasts. These were compared with other reports to assess the fairness and accuracy of the TV news. Their observations, described in *War and Peace News*, include the following:

1   One BBC2 reporter said: 'If all goes well ... by the end of the year, Greenham will be a fully active nuclear weapons base.' Is this neutral language?

2   The bulletins portrayed the peace campers as an unrepresentative minority and only once did they refer to opinion polls. These polls mostly showed an absolute majority against siting Cruise missiles in Britain – for example the January 1983 Marplan Poll showed 61 per cent against and only 27 per cent for.

3   On one demonstation women started to work the perimeter fence rhythmically with their hands. The fence posts swayed and one knocked a policeman unconscious. TV reports then focused on this incident and three other slight injuries. The BBC2 headline was 'The Greenham women attack the camp's perimeter fence, nearly sixty are arrested and four policemen are hurt.' Compare this with the account given in the feminist paper *Outwrite* (January 1984): 'GREENHAM WOMEN FACE VIOLENT ATTACK ... Soldiers armed with huge wooden sticks and metal bars reached out across the barbed wire and started bashing women's hands, some had their fingers crippled.'

4   Violence on television

Moral panics about the effects of the mass media on children are by no means a new phenomenon. In 1879, the Religious Tract Society launched the *Boy's Own Paper*. It was designed to lure young readers away from the enticements of the 'penny-dreadful' magazines which were popular at the time. The Children's and Young Persons (Harmful Publications) Act of 1955 tried to ban American horror comics. New media, such as videos, create new panics. In 1996, a survey of 2,258 children aged 9–11 found that 60 per cent had a TV in their bedroom and 25 per cent had their own video recorder. Two-thirds had watched 18-rated videos. The most popular included *Nightmare on Elm Street, The Silence of the Lambs* and *Pulp Fiction*.

In 1989 a book by Maire Messenger Davies was published with the provocative title of *Television is Good for Your Kids*. This is provocative because there has been widespread concern about the effects of TV violence on children. One problem in any debate about violence on TV is that it is not as easy as one might think to define violence. If you were surveying scenes of violence on TV, would you include scenes of violent anger where the violence was verbal rather than physical? Would you include a car chase that ended in a collision? Would you include the multiple bodily mutilations seen in every Tom and Jerry cartoon?

The *Broadcasting Standards Council Monitoring Report II* gives the following figures for violence on TV in 1993:

	Terrestrial TV	Satellite TV
Percentage of programmes containing violence	52%	73%
Average number of violent scenes per programme	4.3	7.5
Average length of violent scenes, in seconds	28	41

The average rate of violence had increased from 2.9 scenes per hour in 1992 to 4 scenes per hour in 1993. This was attributed to a greater proportion of violence in news, factual programmes and American films.

When the child in the *Home Alone* films wreaks terrible revenge on the intruders, is it harmless fantasy, like the revenge of cartoon mouse Jerry on the cat Tom? Are the *Robocop* and *Terminator* films also harmless fantasy? What about the effects of horror films on children? Is it more disturbing for children to see a domestic verbal row than a goodie shooting a baddie dead?

We are clearly affected in some ways by TV, otherwise advertisers would not spend so much on TV commercials. But how are children affected by scenes of violence? Three possible effects of screen violence are sensitisation, catharsis and de-sensitisation.

Sensitisation means the process by which people are made more sensitive. In the late 1960s and early 1970s the American people found themselves watching close-up action shots of real killing virtually every night on their TV news bulletins. They were shown the war in Vietnam in a way that no war had previously been seen. Some argue that the Americans became sensitive to the sufferings of the civilians and soldiers involved

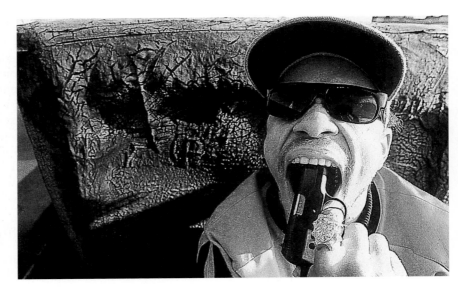

Ice-T: how much influence do controversial gangsta rappers have on their audiences?

and that this shock and revulsion helped to fuel the popular protest which led to the American withdrawal. On one of his visits to the troops in Vietnam, Bob Hope told them: 'If your TV ratings don't improve, we'll have to cancel this war.'

Catharsis refers to the process by which we are purged of an emotion. Some people argue that watching screen violence is good for us because it helps to purge or get rid of our violent emotions in a harmless way. We live them out in fantasy when watching, say, Clint Eastwood brutally eliminating his enemies.

De-sensitisation describes the process by which an experience makes us less sensitive to human suffering. The experience of watching violent programmes may have this effect on us. We may lose our sensitivity to human suffering and come to believe that the use of violence to get what we want is acceptable and normal. The debate on screen violence mostly revolves around this particular effect. Research into the effect of desensitisation takes three forms: clinical case studies, laboratory experiments and surveys.

Clinical case studies

Clinical case studies involve examining the biographies of individuals who have been convicted of particularly dreadful violence to discover whether or not they were influenced by screen violence. One example is the killer who committed the Rambo-style Hungerford massacre in 1987. Many concluded that he was influenced by his large collection of video nasties.

When two 10-year-old boys were found guilty, in 1993, of the murder of the toddler James Bulger, the trial judge said that the manner of their attack bore 'some striking similarities' to the horror film *Child's Play 3*. This film is about a demon doll which attacks a military cadet, and it is possible that the boys had seen it on video.

In the 1990s there has been much public debate about whether parents are aware of which video films their children are watching, unsupervised.

After the murder of James Bulger, *Child's Play 3* was shown on Sky Movies, in October and November 1993. Even though it was broadcast after 10 p.m., the Broadcasters' Audience Research Board estimated that it had been watched by 181,000 children, 42,000 aged 9 and under. Sky's Head of Programming described *Child's Play 3* as a 'typical Hollywood horror film, produced by the studio that gave us the rather more frightening *Jurassic Park*'.

The problem with case studies is that the very few people who directly imitate very violent films are only a tiny proportion of the total number of viewers. This suggests that factors other than screen violence cause such crimes.

Laboratory experiments

Psychologists have attempted to study the effects of screen violence by conducting experiments that test reactions in laboratory conditions. One example is the Bozo Doll experiment. Pre-school children were shown a film of other children in a playroom attacking a large blow-up doll with a hammer. The children were then shown into the playroom. It was full of toys and in the middle was the Bozo Doll and a hammer. The children were then observed and, before long, they copied the film and attacked the doll. They were later compared with a control group who had not seen the film. None of the second group carried out such an attack in the same way, sitting on the doll as they hit it.

Does the Bozo Doll experiment prove that screen violence leads to violent behaviour? There are obvious objections to this experiment and to the experimental method in general. First, it could be argued that the children attacked the doll because they thought that this was what the experimenters wanted them to do. This points to a general problem with experimental settings. Subjects may behave in ways that they think are expected of them. A second objection is that such experiments never tell us how people will behave in the real world. They only tell us, at best, how people behave in the artificial conditions of a laboratory.

Surveys

There have been numerous surveys into the effects of screen violence but they have produced very mixed conclusions. The US Surgeon General's report, *TV and Growing Up*, concluded that TV violence does increase the degree of aggression among young audiences. This report claimed that as many as 25 per cent of young children may be seriously affected. British sociological studies tend to show no direct harmful effects. They deny that TV can be the prime cause of violence and give far greater emphasis to family background and upbringing.

In 1997, in the USA, Michael Carneal shot three fellow students who were in a prayer circle in his school corridor. He later said that he was re-enacting a scene from *The Basketball Diaries*, starring Leonardo DiCaprio.

In 1994, the Policy Studies Institute report on Young Offenders and the Media compared the viewing habits of seventy-eight persistent young offenders with 500 12–18-year-olds. The survey found that the offenders had not watched a greater number of violent films. In both groups the favourite film was Terminator 2. The offenders had had less access to videos and satellite TV. The interviewers gained the overriding impression that the offenders had 'lives that were full of chance, chaos and deprivation, in which the media were of less significance than was the case for non-offending peers'. One of the researchers has said, 'We found all sorts of disruption and chaos at home, and a disproportionate amount of loss. There has nearly always been family bereavement: a fatal accident, a parent suicide or the loss of a sibling. On the whole I was overwhelmed by the sadness of their lives rather than the badness of them.'

In 1998, the results were reported of a Home Office backed two-year study which involved 122 males aged 15 to 21. Of these, 54 were violent offenders, 28 were non-violent offenders and 40 were non-offenders. Their viewing habits were monitored and their reactions to films compared. The report found:

- Violent offenders are more likely to have a taste for violent videos: 11 per cent of non-offenders chose a violent film as their favourite, compared with 25 per cent of non-violent offenders and 64 per cent of violent offenders.
- Offenders spent more time watching violent films and they remembered their plots for longer than non-offenders.
- Almost three-quarters of violent offenders admitted that the aggressive parts of the films excited them most.
- Offenders were more likely to identify with macho actors such as Jean-Claude Van Damme, Arnold Schwarzenegger and Sylvester Stallone.
- Violent films 'may reinforce distorted perceptions about appropriate means of resolving conflict and responding to frustration and provocation'.

- 'Offenders were more likely to prefer actors who typically play characters whose use of severe violence appears positive and successful – a dangerous role model for young people, particularly those disposed to crime and delinquency.'

The report concluded: 'The implication is that both history of family violence and offending behaviour are necessary preconditions for developing a significant preference for violent film action and role models.' In a chicken and egg argument, this implies that children who are already violent are more likely to choose violent films. Rather than such films making them violent, they are already violent because of growing up in violent homes. 'The research points to a pathway from having a violent home background, to being an offender, to being more likely to prefer violent films and violent actors.'

One of the joint authors of the report is Dr Kevin Browne, a psychologist from Birmingham University. He has commented that the report could not prove whether or not video violence caused crime. But he has also said, 'People who come from violent families and commit violent offences are more likely to lock into violent scenes, remember violent characters ... This may go on to make their own violent behaviour more frequent ... Once the taste for video violence is developed, that diet can nurture increasingly anti-social behaviour.'

Other studies have led to greater concern about the direct effects of video violence. Dr Greg Philo, of the Glasgow University Media Unit, conducted a study which found children who repeatedly watched the same violent material from 18-rated films. These children thought it 'would be really cool to pull the trigger on someone'. He concludes that such film and video images encourage 'a children's culture which neglects the victim and celebrates power, violence and control over others'.

Case study: video violence and the protection of children

In 1994, psychologist Elizabeth Newson wrote: 'Many of us hold our liberal ideals of freedom of expression dear, but now begin to feel that we were naive in our failure to predict the extent of damaging material and its all too free availability to children. It now seems that professionals in child health and psychology underestimated the degree of brutality and sustained sadism that film-makers were capable of inventing and willing to portray ... and we certainly underestimated how easy would be children's access to them. It is now clear that many children watch adult-only videos on a regular basis, with or without their parents' knowledge, and that many parents make less than strenuous attempts to restrict their children's viewing.'

Violence in the context of entertainment is dangerous because the 'viewer receives the implicit message that this is all good fun – something with which to while away one's leisure time. The child viewer receives distorted images of emotions that he has not yet experienced, so must accept – especially dangerous when love, sex and violence are equated ... The ingenuity with which brutality is portrayed has escalated.'

Conclusion

Newson calls for systematic research 'to keep pace with the growth of violence in children and the growth of violence visual material available to them'. The problem that confronts all such research is that in order to measure the influence of the media we must first isolate it from all the other influences that shape our behaviour. This is difficult, if not impossible, to do. As a consequence, firm conclusions regarding the effects of the media are unlikely to be forthcoming in the future.

GCSE question from Southern Examining Group 1995

Study Item A and B. Then answer *all* parts of the question which follow.

Item A

It is very difficult to estimate how much crime there is in society. We can see the amount of crime rather like an iceberg. The amount above the waterline represents the official figures about the amount of recorded crime. The amount below the waterline represents the unrecorded amount we do not know about officially, and is called the 'dark figure of crime'.

Item B

PUBLIC CONFIDENCE IN THE POLICE COMPARED TO THREE YEARS AGO
(percentages)

	All	Men	Women	16–24	25–54	55+	White	Black
More confident about the police	7	6	9	6	6	12	8	5
Same confidence	46	52	40	41	44	54	46	48
Less confidence in the police	31	26	36	38	34	18	32	25

Adapted from *Sociology Review*, April 1992 (Philip Allan)

(a) Read Item A.

   (i) According to the passage, what is represented by the 'amount above the waterline'? (1)

   (ii) According to the passage, why is it difficult to estimate the real amount of crime in society? (1)

(b) Study Item B.

   (i) According to the table, in which age group was there the greatest fall in confidence in the police in the previous three years? (1)

   (ii) According to the table, what percentage of females had more confidence in the police in 1992? (1)

(c) Identify and explain *two* reasons why the official figures for the number of crimes are likely to be different from those actually committed. (4)

(d) Identify *two* methods used by the police and the courts to encourage most people to conform to the law. In *each* case, explain how these methods may lead to conformity. (4)

(e) Identify and fully explain *one* way in which the mass media influence people's view of the amount of crime in society. (4)

(f) Identify and fully explain *one* way in which the mass media create stereotypes of the role of men in society. (4)

CHAPTER 14

Politics

Political activity is usually associated with government. Governments take decisions that affect the organisation of a society and in order to do this governments need to exercise **power**. Generally, therefore, politics is concerned with the exercise of power. Governments vary considerably regarding the source of the power that they exercise. **Democracy** and **dictatorship** are terms that primarily refer to different sources of power. Before examining the processes of the political system in Britain, we will look closely at these two important terms.

1 Democracy and dictatorship

Direct democracy in ancient Athens

The word 'democracy' means 'rule by the people' and it was invented by the Ancient Greeks. They not only originated the word 'democracy' but actually practised it. Ancient Greece consisted of a number of independent city-states. For a period of about 200 years, in the fifth and fourth centuries BC, the city-state of Athens was governed directly by regular meetings of the assembly. This assembly numbered potentially 30,000 male citizens. A quorum for important business was 6,000 and all decisions were taken by a majority vote. As well as women, non-citizens such as slaves and foreign residents were excluded. This pure, classical type of democracy, in which the citizens are the government, approximately fits Theodore Parker's famous definition of democracy as 'government of all the people, by all the people, for all the people'.

Representative democracy in modern Britain

In modern Britain citizens do not participate directly in decision making (apart from when a **referendum** is held – a vote by all the people on a single issue), but this does not necessarily mean that British political arrangements are undemocratic. It is true that, unlike the citizens of ancient Athens, British citizens do not actually exercise political power. Rather, the power to make decisions is passed on to an elected group. These representatives meet in the assembly called the House of Commons and they are called Members of Parliament. If the government, formed by the party that has a majority of MPs, fails to satisfy the electorate it can be removed at the next general election. So, as in ancient Athens, the source of political power in Britain is the citizen.

The British type of democracy is called **representative** or **parliamentary democracy**. The central part of such a democracy is the process of elections where the voters give their decision-making power to a group of representatives. The party that has the majority of these Members of Parliament then forms the government. It is at elections, therefore, that citizens give their permission or consent to be governed in a particular way by a particular group.

Democratic rights

We have defined democracy as rule by the people and emphasised the importance of elections. Yet a democratic society consists of more than this. The democratic way of life in modern Britain also consists of the following rights which give the individual a degree of freedom and security:

1   Equality before the law   This right is designed to ensure that, while no one has the right to break the law, all citizens are treated equally by the courts, regardless of race, religion, sex or class; so that no one is 'above the law'.

Prime Minister John Major at the 1992 Conservative Party Conference.

2   Personal freedom   In 1215, Magna Carta established the principle that an individual's property or liberty can only be removed by the courts in accordance with the laws of the land. The 1679 Act of Habeas Corpus (which is Latin for 'you must have a body') confirmed that an individual cannot be arrested and detained without being charged for an offence.

3   Freedom of speech and writing   This right is limited by laws such as the Official Secrets Act and the libel laws, but in the main we cannot be punished for expressing our opinions and ideas.

4   Freedom of religion and public worship   This right ensures that citizens can practise any religion without fear of harassment and persecution.

5   Freedom of association and assembly   This right enables any number of citizens to meet and discuss whatsoever they wish, apart from criminal conspiracies.

6   Free and fair elections   Any individual can form his or her own political party and compete as an election candidate in a secret ballot of all registered electors who wish to vote.

We should note that there is a difference between the theory and practice of rights (for example, Rastafarians would argue that their right to practise their religion is restricted by the law that bans the use of cannabis), but in any discussion of the extent of democracy in Britain we should remember the existence of these rights. The possession of such rights creates notable differences between British society and other societies. In Communist China and North Korea, for example, the majority of citizens do not enjoy the right to free elections, the right to freedom of assembly, and so on.

Democracy can be seen as a matter of degree. Although the actual exercise of political power by the British people may be small, it is

On election days, party workers sit outside polling stations to check if supporters need reminding to come and vote.

certainly greater than in many countries. The claim that Britain is a democracy therefore is not based on a blindness to the imperfections of British democracy. Rather, the claim is based on the view that the word 'democracy' usefully expresses some of the notable political differences between a society like Britain and one like Communist China, where the majority of the people have no control over who governs them or how they are governed.

Dictatorship

A dictatorship is a type of government that does not rule with the known consent of the people. Dictators often claim the support of the majority but such claims are questionable because the majority are denied the opportunity to show which leader or party they support. Some dictatorships only affect people's lives to a limited extent, to the extent necessary to stay in power. But **totalitarian dictatorships** are not merely content to stay in power, they aim to control every important aspect of people's lives.

A totalitarian dictatorship: the USSR under Stalin, 1928–53

Under Stalin's dictatorship, the USSR was transformed from an economically backward country into a modern, industrial nation. In the process, the Soviet people paid the terrible price of 20 million deaths. In the early 1930s, Stalin forced 100 million peasants into collective farms. The clash between their resistance and his ruthlessness led to 5 million deaths from grain famines. Another 2 million were killed by machine-gunnings or died from privation after expulsions from their homes. A further 3 million died in labour camps. These gulags, or forced labour camps, were spread across the USSR like an archipelago, or sea full of islands. This **gulag archipelago** killed another 9 million and a further million were shot in prisons before Stalin's dictatorship was over.

Under Stalin, there were no free trade unions. Political parties other than the Communist Party were banned. Stalin tried to control totally every aspect of Soviet life. His secret police had agents spying on the people in factories, offices, the armed forces, schools and apartment buildings. Peasants who refused to help the government take over their farms were sent to labour camps as well as managers and workers who failed to reach industrial production targets.

In Stalin's periodic 'purges' thousands of people who were even remotely suspected of opposing him disappeared and were executed or sent to labour camps. Army officers, Communist Party officials, managers of factories and even leaders of the secret police were 'purged' from time to time.

There was complete censorship. Art, literature, films, entertainment, music, newspapers and broadcasting were all strictly controlled by the state. Much publicity was given to the confessions of innocent leaders at 'show trials'. Such leaders were caught in the purges and then tortured so that they would confess to crimes against the state. Schoolchildren were indoctrinated with Stalin's version of communist beliefs.

Mass propaganda in a totalitarian dictatorship: portraits of leading communists are held high during the 1982 May Day parade in Red Square in Moscow.

Active citizenship

A healthy democracy needs the active involvement of its citizens in political processes. When we ask ourselves 'What should an active citizen do?' we might come up with the following activities:

- Obey the law and assist the police whenever possible.
- Defend the rights of minorities and campaign against unjust laws.
- Register to vote and use our votes in all local, national and European elections.
- Join or try to influence political parties.
- Support and join pressure groups.

Roy Hattersley, together with regional newspaper editors, hands in petitions at 10 Downing Street. They were against any imposition of VAT on newspapers in the November 1993 budget.

*Arms trade protesters from
the Campaign Against
Militarism.*

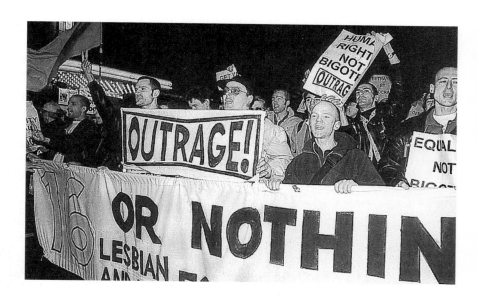

*In 1994, 250 police officers
using vans blocked off an
attempted march from
Piccadilly to Parliament by
800 supporters of the gay
activist group Outrage!*

2   The role of pressure groups in Britain

Totalitarian dictatorships, such as Communist China, are **monolithic** because politics and society are dominated by the single creed of a single party. Democratic societies, in contrast, are **pluralist**, meaning that they contain many competing centres of power and influence. For example, in Britain, the Hunt Saboteurs' Association and the League against Cruel Sports are opposed by the British Field Sports Society; anti-abortion groups such as LIFE and the Society for the Protection of the Unborn Child are opposed by the Abortion Law Reform Association and the National Abortion Campaign.

Lobbying your Member of Parliament

In a democracy the individual is free to try to influence local and central government in numerous ways. For example, people who feel strongly about an issue can write to their councillors or MPs, write to newspapers, or ask others to sign a petition. Also, we all have the right to **lobby** our MPs directly. There are two ways to gain personal contact. Most MPs hold Saturday morning 'surgeries' where constituents can queue up to see them. Alternatively, you can visit the central lobby or hallway in the Palace of Westminster and fill in a card requesting to see your MP. Messengers are employed in the Houses of Parliament so that these lobby cards can be swiftly delivered to MPs.

Such individual action is not likely, however, to be as effective as action carried out by an organised group. Organisations that aim to influence the views of the public and the government are called **pressure groups**. These are different from political parties because they do not try to win power by standing in elections.

Sectional and promotional pressure groups

Many observers have divided pressure groups into two categories. **Sectional groups** are concerned with protecting the interests of their members and so their membership is usually restricted to a particular section of the population, such as those in a certain occupation. **Promotional groups** campaign to promote a particular cause and so their membership is usually open to as many supporters as possible.

The *Directory of Pressure Groups and Representative Associations*, by P. Shipley, lists well over 600 organisations. There are also thousands of pressure groups that have no formal structure. These range from a group of parents asking for a school-crossing patrol, to the bankers and stockbrokers who constitute 'the City'.

Factors determining the methods used by pressure groups

1   Type of membership   A group that is composed of influential members is likely to be taken seriously by the government. The British Medical Association (BMA), for example, has established means of communication between doctors' representatives and the Department of

Health. While **ministers** have overall responsibility for different government departments, such as the Foreign Office and the Department of Environment, Transport and the Regions, the day-to-day running of these ministries depends on **civil servants**. When the officials in the Department of Health were drafting regulations requiring doctors to retire at the age of 65, they almost certainly consulted the BMA.

2   Financial resources   A rich pressure group can pay MPs for their services or make donations to a political party. In 11972 the Labour MP Brian Walden entered into a five-year contract to act as a paid parliamentary consultant to the National Association of Bookmakers. Another example is the 'Flexilink' consortium of ferry companies and ports which was formed in 1985 and unsuccessfully opposed the proposal to build a fixed link across the Channel. This group spent large sums hiring MPs and professional lobbyists to organise a public relations campaign and to wine and dine as many MPs as possible.

Examples of different types of pressure groups

Types of sectional pressure group	Example of organisation	Example of one of their aims
Professional	British Medical Association	Better working conditions for doctors
Trade union	National Union of Miners	No more pit closures
Industry	Solid Smokeless Fuels Federation	Clean air regulation
Commerce	Road Haulage Association	More motorways
Finance	Building Societies Association	Changes in the banking system
Consumers	Automobile Association	Prevent big increases in road or petrol tax

Types of promotional pressure group	Example of organisation	Examples of one of their aims
International	Amnesty International	Release all political prisoners and all prisoners of conscience
Political	Campaign for Nuclear Disarmament	Removal of US nuclear bases from UK
Child welfare	Child Poverty Action Group	Research on how to improve the social security system
Animal rights	Animal Liberation Front	Rescue animals from laboratories and factory farms
Cultural	British Humanist Association	End religious school assemblies
Recreational	Ramblers Association	Extend the number of coastal paths
Environmental	Greenpeace	Close all nuclear power stations
Health	Action on Smoking and Health	Ban tobacco advertisements

Hillgrove Farm breeds cats for animal experiments. In 1998, Thames Valley police spent over £500,000 keeping out animal rights protestors.

3   The need for public support   In his book on *Pressure Groups and Government in Great Britain*, Geoffrey Alderman has described how the need to mobilise widespread support may lead pressure groups to use a variety of methods. Some of the ways to gain publicity and influence public opinion are listed below:

- *Public meetings*: the Clean-up TV Campaign was launched by Mary Whitehouse in 1964 with a meeting at Birmingham Town Hall which brought instant nationwide publicity.
- *Advertisements*: as part of their campaign against the THORP nuclear reprocessing plant at Sellafield, in 1994 Greenpeace placed advertisements in the press showing an infant with a grossly enlarged head with the caption 'Kazakhstan nuclear test victim'.
- *Reports*: in 1994 the Runnymede Trust published *A Very Light Sleeper: The Persistence and Dangers of Anti-Semitism*, describing increased attacks on Britain's Jewish community.
- *Petitions*: in 1994 the World Wide Fund for Nature delivered a petition with 155,000 signatures to the government. It called for the laws that protect rare habitats and species to be strengthened and a new law to protect marine habitats.
- *Demonstrations*: in 1993 disabled members of the Block Telethon campaign demonstrated against the passive and needy images of disability portrayed by ITV's charity fund-raising programmes.
- *Publicity stunts*: in 1993 three people were arrested for stripping off and carrying a banner round their waists saying 'We'd rather go naked than wear fur!' They were publicising the opening of the London office of an animal rights group called PETA.
- *Mass lobbies*: in 1994 over 2,000 disabled people held a mass lobby of Parliament in support of the Civil Rights (Disabled Persons) Bill.

- *Direct action*: in 1994 dozens of roof-top protesters held up the demolition of some of the 350 houses in Wanstead which were cleared for a £250 million 3.5-mile six-lane link road to the M11.
- *Hunger strikes*: in 1994 the junior health minister, Baroness Cumberledge, brought forward a meeting with thalidomide campaigners in response to a hunger strike by two women victims of deformity caused by the drug.
- *Legal action*: in 1994 the Tower Hamlets Housing Campaign challenged the allegedly racist housing policies of Tower Hamlets Council in the High Court.

M11 link road protesters demonstrate on the roof of Transport Secretary John MacGregor's house as the Cabinet Minister leaves his home.

Greenpeace protest against a secret deal, in 1998, to accept nuclear waste from the former Soviet Union.

The role of pressure groups

MPs are not supposed to represent just those who voted for them. (In 1992, the Conservatives won a 21-seat majority in the House of Commons with only 14 million votes from Britain's 44 million electors.) MPs should try to represent the interests of *all* their constituents. Powerful pressure groups, which only represent particular sections of the population, may make it difficult for MPs to serve the community as a whole.

While those who are poor, badly educated and lacking in organisation might lack an effective voice, influential groups, such as the National Farmers' Union, may routinely help to shape government policy and **deep-pocketed lobbies** may be able to afford expensive campaigns. For example, the tobacco companies can afford to pay over £100,000 per year to FOREST, the Freedom Organisation for the Right to Enjoy Smoking Tobacco.

But without pressure groups, citizens would have to rely on political parties or individual contact with MPs and the media. A democracy should not merely be a tyranny of the majority, it must listen to the voices of all minorities. Pressure groups provide the channels of communication through which governments can be made to change their mind.

Post-modern politics

Some observers have suggested that there has been a shift of emphasis in political life as Britain has become a post-modern society:

Characteristics of modernity *(the modern era = 1870–1970)*	*Characteristics of post-modernity* *(which have emerged since 1970)*
The nation state	Globalisation
Identity based on one's position in the production system, based on class	Identity based on consumption and lifestyle choices
Politics centred on political parties	Importance of new social movements
Parties based on class	Issue-based politics, e.g. animal rights, environmental and anti-racist movements
Politics centred on class	Life-politics, linking the personal and the political, e.g. gay rights, feminism, green/vegetarian lifestyle

Case study: Des Wilson – a master campaigner

Des Wilson has a reputation as a master media manipulator and a veteran of a number of pressure group campaigns. In 1966 he started Shelter, a campaign for the homeless. He went on to found the Campaign for Lead-Free Petrol and the Campaign for Freedom of Information. He chaired Friends of the Earth and ran election campaigns for the Liberal Democrats.

In 1994, Des Wilson was earning over £100,000 a year working for Burson-Marsteller, one of the world's most successful public relations companies. Burson-Marsteller represented Union Carbide after the disaster at its chemical plant in Bhopal, India, and it did its best to 'greenwash' Exxon after the *Exxon Valdez* oil spill in Alaska.

Burson-Marsteller has a separate lobbying wing to whisper in Westminster ears. Its client list includes tobacco giant Philip Morris, the Glaxo drug company, L'Oreal cosmetics group, the Ford Motor Company and Scottish Nuclear. In 1994, Des Wilson was using his skills to promote Richard Branson's bid to run the new national lottery and, in a six-month £50,000 contract, to promote the relaunch programme of the Trades Union Congress.

Activities

1 In 1986, opinion polls showed that most people supported 'deregulation' of Sunday opening hours and yet groups representing shop-workers and churchgoers persuaded enough Conservative MPs to vote with the Opposition to defeat the proposed reforms of the Sunday Trading Bill. Was this outcome a victory for democracy?

2 Give examples of five of the following types of pressure groups and in each case say what their main aims are: (a) local, (b) national, (c) successful, (d) unsuccessful, (e) short-lived, (f) permanent, (g) small but rich, (h) poor but with mass support.

3 During the campaign for votes for women, in the early years of this century, public attention turned from the 'suffragists' (National Union of Women's Suffrage Societies by Millicent Fawcett) to the 'suffragettes' (Women's Social and Political Union led by Emmeline Pankhurst). Compare the moderate methods of the former with the militant methods of the latter.
or Compare the moderate methods of the RSPCA with the militant methods of the Animal Liberation Front.

4 How would you plan a campaign to attract publicity and supporters in order to (a) prevent the council from building a rubbish incinerator in the field behind your house, or (b) improve the toilet facilities in your school or college?

5 Name four famous personalities who are associated with four different pressure groups.

3   The main British political parties

The results of General Elections since 1945

Year of General Election	Party forming the government
1945	Labour
1950	Labour
1951	Conservative
1955	Conservative
1959	Conservative
1964	Labour
1966	Labour
1970	Conservative
1974 (February)	Labour
1974 (October)	Labour
1979	Conservative
1983	Conservative
1987	Conservative
1992	Conservative
1997	Labour

In terms of providing the main means of political recruitment, representation, communication and participation, the established political parties are more important than pressure groups. It is parties which form governments and oppositions. We now look at the main ideas that underlie their differing policies.

The Conservative Party

As their name implies, Conservatives (or Tories) are concerned that any reforms of society should not sweep away historic institutions and traditions. They wish to conserve important parts of the British way of life such as the monarchy, the House of Lords, the Church of England and the public schools. The basis of their policies is expressed by the following comments, from the Conservative manifesto 1997:

- 'We do not believe there is a case for more radical reform that would undermine the House of Commons. A new Bill of Rights, for example, would risk transferring power from parliament to legal courts ... opposition proposals on the House of Lords would be extremely damaging. We will oppose change for change's sake.'
- 'The free market is winning the battle of ideas the world over ... Free competition is important for free markets. Our aim is nothing less than tariff free trade across the globe by the year 2020.'
- 'For enterprise to flourish, the state must get out of the way of the wealth creators ... High taxes and rates deter enterprise.'
- 'Self-reliance underpins freedom and choice. Families are stronger if they have the money to look after themselves ... our aim will be to achieve our target rate of a 20p basic rate of income tax.'
- '... the nation state is a rock of security ... We want to be in Europe but not run by Europe ... We will insist that any new Treaty recognises that

our opt-out from the Social Chapter enables Britain to be exempt from the Working Time Directive.'
- 'Firm, but fair, immigration controls underpin good race relations.'

The Labour Party

The Labour Party is, to a certain extent, the political arm of the trade union movement. It grew out of the Labour Representation Committee formed by the Trades Union Congress in 1900 and so its purpose is to represent the ordinary worker. Here are some of the Labour Party's ideas, from their 1997 manifesto:

- '… tough on crime, tough on the causes of crime ….'
- '… we will face up to the new issues that confront us. We will be the party of welfare reform ….'
- '… no increase in the basic or top rates of income tax.'
- 'National minimum wage to tackle low pay.'
- 'Our values are: the equal worth of all, with no one cast aside; fairness and justice within strong communities.'
- 'We will get 250,000 under-25-year-olds off benefit and into work by using money from a windfall levy on the privatised utilities.'
- 'Cut class sizes to 30 or under for 5, 6 and 7-year-olds.'
- 'Nursery places for all 4-year-olds.'
- 'The House of Lords must be reformed.'
- 'Reform of party funding to end sleaze.'
- 'A Scottish parliament and a Welsh assembly.'
- 'There will be no return to flying pickets, secondary action, strikes with no ballots or the trade union law of the 1970s. There will instead be basic minimum rights for the individual at the workplace, where our aim is partnership not conflict between employers and employees … The key elements of the trade union legislation of the 1980s will stay.'

This Labour Party poster appeared during their European election capaign in 1994.

Help the Joneses keep up with the Schultzes, the Georgious the Henricks, the Berouches, the Anvers, the Depardieus, the Van Dammes, the Fratinis, the De Witts, Tell the Tories you've had enough the Müllers, the Galassis, Vote Labour the Devitos, the Schiffers, In Europe June 9th the Kotters, the Borgs, the Ackermanns, Labour

Politics in the 1980s

In the early 1980s, the Labour Party shifted to more left-wing, socialist policies while the Conservative governments of Mrs Thatcher introduced right-wing, free-market, pro-capitalist measures:

More left-wing Labour policies of the 1980s	Con-Lab consensus of the 1950s and 1960s, agreed on:	More right-wing Tory policies of the 1980s
Main aim to reduce unemployment	Need to keep both unemployment and inflation low	Main aim to reduce inflation
Unilateral nuclear disarmament	Need for nuclear weapons	Support new nuclear weapons such as Cruise and Trident
Replace sold council houses by building more	Need for large numbers of council houses to be built	Sell off council houses and create a nation of owner-occupiers
Extend nationalisation – for example in the area of banking	Need for a fair-sized public sector with basic industries nationalised	Privatise, or sell off, industries such as Telecom, gas and water
Leave the European Economic Community (EEC)	Need for UK to join EEC	Get tough with the Common Market
Abolish private education	Need for expansion of state education	Support public schools
Abolish House of Lords	Need for life peers	Create new hereditary viscounts

The two main parties drew apart in the early 1980s. This left the middle ground of politics open for an alliance, in the 1983 election, of the old Liberal Party and the new Social Democrat Party. This new party had been formed by a breakaway group of right-wing Labour MPs. The two-party alliance evolved into the Liberal Democrat Party.

The Liberal Democrat Party

Here are some of the distinctive policies from the Liberal Democrat 1997 manifesto:

- 'We will invest an additional £2 billion per year in education, funded by an extra 1p in the pound on the basic rate of income tax.'
- 'We will begin a long-term shift in taxation, reducing taxes on jobs, wealth and goods and shifting them to pollution and resource depletion.'
- 'We will set tough new targets for the reduction of traffic pollution and carbon dioxide emissions.'
- 'We will safeguard individual liberties by establishing a Bill of Rights.'
- 'We will break open excessive government secrecy, by passing a Freedom of Information Act.'

- 'We will introduce a fair system of voting (proportional representation).'
- 'We will expand local youth services.'
- 'We will tackle any discriminatory use of police powers, such as stop and search, and enhance police action to deal with racial attacks.'

The social background of party members

A survey in 1996 showed that, on average, Labour Party members are younger and earn more than members of the Conservative Party:

	Labour Party members	*Conservative Party members*
Average age	43	62
Percentage in households earning over:		
£20,000 p.a.	57	45
£30,000 p.a.	30	25
Total number of members	365,000	300,000

The survey showed that 86 per cent of Labour's full-fee members are home owners. Professor Patrick Seyd of Sheffield University commented that 'New Labour is recruiting the crucial group of young and affluent voters to its ranks'. But the left-wing Labour MP for Derbyshire North East, Harry Barnes, reacted with dismay: 'It's disturbing we are not growing likewise in working-class areas. Trade union and working-class support should be the bedrock that we should not abandon.'

4   Opinion polls

Newspapers and TV programmes pay for opinion polls to predict the outcome of elections. Pollsters claim that with their scientific techniques they only need to interview a few thousand voters to predict with accuracy how 31 million people will vote. This is because they carefully select samples of different groups in proportions that represent the composition of the whole adult population.

In the 1992 election 54 per cent of the middle class voted Conservative and 22 per cent Labour. An opinion poll in 1994 showed the middle-class vote evenly split with 37 per cent for both parties. How was this figure arrived at? MORI conducted face-to-face interviews with a representative quota sample of 1,936 adults at 146 constituency sampling points across Britain. Data were weighted to match the profile of the population. Voting intention figures were added up, excluding the 10 per cent who said they would not vote, the 7 per cent who were undecided and the 2 per cent who refused to name a party.

Australia and other countries ban the publication of the results of opinion polls in the final stages of an election. A party with an increasing lead in the polls may benefit from a bandwagon effect and so gain a commanding lead. Campaign strategists often talk down such a lead for fear that many of their supporters may not bother to vote if they think that the outcome of the election is a foregone conclusion.

Polls in the 1992 General Election

Fifty-seven opinion polls, carried out by eight different polling organisations, were published during the 1992 General Election. On the eve of election day these polls, on average, showed Labour one point ahead. On the day, the Tories won by 8 per cent. How can we explain this nine-point error? It has been estimated that a third of the 'error' was not the pollsters' fault: the Tories' lead grew by three points during the final twenty-four hours of the campaign. That leaves a six-point error to explain. The polls seem to have inflated Labour support by three points and underestimated Tory support by the same amount. We now look at five possible explanations.

The shame factor
The 'shame factor' may lead people to say that they support the caring, welfare policies of Labour when in fact they selfishly vote for the tax cuts of the Tories in the secrecy of the polling booth. Research by ICM has shown that 33 per cent of Tories would avoid revealing their party allegiance to a friend or colleague who asked how they intend to vote, compared to only 23 per cent of Labour supporters. To avoid the shame factor ICM have used a secret ballot in their polls since September 1992. This has cut Labour's poll rating by five points.

Refusers
Around 3 per cent of the public refuse to be interviewed for polls. In 1992 this rose to 5 per cent. Pollsters usually replace them with someone of the same age, sex and class to fit their quota. But during Conservative unpopularity in 1993, ICM found that 'refusers' were more likely to be Tories. Recall polls after the 1992 election found that 60 per cent of 'don't knows' and 'won't says' had voted Tory.

Unregistered
Many people may have avoided registering to vote in 1992 in order to avoid paying the poll tax, which preceded the council tax. One survey showed that 51 per cent of those not on the electoral register supported Labour, while only 17 per cent supported the Conservatives.

Abstainers
Exit polls ask voters leaving the polling station to fill in another ballot form for the pollsters. In the 1992 election, these exit polls estimated that the Tory share of the vote was 40 per cent (BBC/NOP) and 41 per cent (ITN/Harris) whereas it was actually 43 per cent. These exit polls were more accurate than other polls because they excluded abstainers. The exit polls showed a 'differential turnout' with certain groups less likely to have bothered to vote. These included council tenants, semi-skilled and unskilled manual workers and welfare claimants. Many of these may have told pollsters before the election that they were registered and intending to vote Labour.

Protesters
Some voters may have stayed reluctantly loyal to the Conservatives but may have told pollsters that they would vote Labour in order to register a protest, to show their dissatisfaction with the Tories during the depths of an economic recession. On the day they may have been too scared to switch to Labour.

5   The social factors that influence voting

During the day of the General Election on 1 May 1997, the BBC commissioned the National Opinion Poll (NOP) organisation to conduct an exit poll. Voters exiting from a sample of polling stations were polled on how they voted. From their answers we can study the social factors that influence voting patterns.

Age and voting

As we get older we tend to get more conservative (wanting to keep things the same and to avoid change) and so older people are more likely to support the Conservative Party. Younger voters may tend to be more radical, wanting major reforms and changes, and so they may be more likely to support the Labour Party. This contrast is shown in the 1997 voting figures from the BBC/NOP exit poll: 57 per cent of first-time voters voted Labour compared to only 34 per cent of voters aged over 65, whereas 44 per cent of these older voters voted Conservative compared to only 19 per cent of first time voters.

Party support by age in the 1997 General Election (percentages)

	Conservative	Labour	Lib. Dem.
First-time voters	19	57	18
All voters aged:			
18–29	22	57	17
30–44	26	49	17
45–64	33	43	18
65+	44	34	16

Gender and voting

Party support by gender in the 1992 and 1997 General Elections (percentages)

	Conservative		Labour		Lib. Dem.	
	1992	1997	1992	1997	1992	1997
Men	39	31	38	44	18	17
Women	43	32	34	44	18	17

The above figures show how women were more likely to vote Conservative in 1992. This is usually the case and is explained in a number of ways. Women live longer than men. So, among the elderly, there are far more female than male voters and, as we have seen, the elderly are more likely to vote Conservative. Another factor is that women are less likely than men to spend their working lives in manual jobs where trade unionism and Labour support is strongest. It has also been suggested that female roles in the domestic sphere, housewife and mother, are likely to make them more conservative in outlook. On the other hand, Labour can often project a more caring image than the Conservatives and this may have helped Labour to gain more ex-Tory votes from women switching to them in 1997 than from men.

On page 167 we discussed how 'Essex Man' helped the Conservatives to power in the 1980s. In 1997, commentators spoke of the importance to Labour of capturing the votes of the composite female voter named 'Worcester Woman'. We compare the characteristics of these 'ideal types' below:

Worcester Woman	*Essex Man*
Routine white-collar occupation	Skilled manual job
Married to skilled manual worker	Buying his council house
Lives in the southern half of England	Lives in the southern half of England
Floating voter in Tory seat winnable	Ambitious to be self-employed (e.g. a
for Labour (a key marginal seat)	plumber who wants a Dyno-rod franchise)

101 women Labour MPs were elected in 1997.

Class and voting

There are strong class differences between the parties in terms of their origins and funding, their past policies, their membership and the social background of their MPs. So it is not surprising that social class is the main social factor to influence voting in Britain.

Party support by social class in the 1997 General Election (percentages)

	Conservative	Labour	Lib. Dem.
All voters in Great Britain	31	44	17
AB voters (professional and managerial)	42	31	21
C1 voters (routine non-manual)	26	47	19
C2 voters (skilled manual)	25	54	14
DE voters (less skilled manual and jobless)	21	61	13

Both Conservative and Liberal Democrat Parties have their strongest support among the highest paid, the AB voters. Labour support is strongest among the poorest, the DE voters.

Class dealignment

In 1966, 70 per cent of the working class voted Labour. But in 1992, only 44 per cent of the working class voted Labour. In the 1980s, Ivor Crewe noted the characteristics of the 'new working class' who were losing their traditional class alignment (loyalty) to Labour:

The new working class	*The old working class*
Growing in size	Shrinking in size
New owner-occupiers	Council tenants
Jobs in the private sector	Jobs in the public sector
Not in trade unions	Trade union members
Live in the South	Live in the North
Switching to the Conservatives	More loyal to Labour

From the 1997 election, we can see that the strongest predictor of Labour voting is when a voter lives in a council house, while the second strongest predictor of Conservative voting is home ownership.

Class-related social factors and party support in the 1997 General Election (percentages)

	Conservative	Labour	Lib. Dem.
AB voters	42	31	21
Home owners	35	41	17
All voters	31	44	17
Trade union members	18	57	20
DE voters	21	61	13
Council tenants	13	65	15

Region and voting

In which area did each of the parties have their strongest support in 1997 and why?

- **Liberal Democrat**: the South West (31 per cent of voters) – a long tradition of support for the old Liberal Party and home of the Liberal Democrat leader, Paddy Ashdown.
- **Conservative**: the South East (41 per cent of voters) – largest concentration of middle-class and new working-class voters.
- **Labour**: the North (61 per cent of voters) – heartland of male manual working-class trade unionism, without loss of votes to Welsh or Scottish Nationalist Parties.

The following figures are arranged in order, from Labour strongholds to Conservative strongholds.

Party support by region in the 1997 General Election (percentages)

	Labour	*Conservative*	*Lib. Dem.*	*Nationalist*
North	61	22	0	
Wales	55	20	12	10
North West	54	27	14	
Yorks and Humberside	52	28	16	
London	49	31	15	
East Midlands	48	34	14	
Scotland	46	18	13	22
East Anglia	38	39	18	
South East	32	41	21	
South West	26	37	31	

Tony Blair campaigning in the 1997 general election.

Activities

Which social characteristics do you think most influence voting in your local constituencies?

GCSE question from Southern Examining Group 1992

(a) Identify and explain *two* ways in which voting intentions may be influenced by the published results of opinion polls. (4)

(b) There are very few non-white MPs in relation to the number of non-white people in the population. Identify and explain *two* reasons why this is so. (4)

(c) A political party will be more successful in winning votes in some parts of the United Kingdom than others. Why is this? (8)

GCSE question from Southern Examining Group 1992

(a) Identify and explain *two* actions which pressure groups may take in an attempt to influence political decision making. (4)

(b) Identify *two* types of pressure group and explain the reasons why they are formed. (4)

(c) Democracy is said to exist when political power is in the hands of the people. Identify and fully explain *one* reason why the view of ordinary people might *not* have an effect on the actions of those who represent them. (4)

(d) Power is said to be the ability to influence the behaviour of others.

   Identify and fully explain *one* way in which an individual may become powerful in society and influence the behaviour of others. (4)

GCSE question from Southern Examining Group 1997

Study Items A and B. Then answer *all* parts of the question which follows.

Item A

The right to stand for Parliament is an important aspect of citizenship: candidates are guaranteed financial support in the form of free postage and hire of rooms. They are certain to get attention, particularly in by-elections. At the Christchurch by-election in the summer of 1993 there were fourteen candidates. 'Lord' David Sutch, Britain's longest-serving party leader, has based his entire career on this constitutional right.

Adapted from Frank Conley, *General Elections Today*

Item B
Percentage share of the vote gained by four parties in Scotland

	1992 General election	*1994 European election*	*1995 Local election*
Conservative	26	15	12
Labour	39	43	48
Liberal Democrat	13	8	11
Scottish National Party	22	23	29

From *Politics Review, Autumn 95*

(a) Read Item A. According to the information given,

  (i) what financial help is guaranteed to all parliamentary candidates? (1)

  (ii) who is the longest-serving party leader in Britain? (1)

(b) Study Item B. According to the table,

  (i) what share of the vote in Scotland did the Liberal Democrats gain in the 1994 European election? (1)

  (ii) how did the trends in the Conservative and Scottish National Party results over the three elections differ? (1)

(c) State *two* rights of citizenship other than the right to stand for Parliament. (2)

(d) (i) What is meant by 'democracy'? (1)

  (ii) Explain why Britain might be described as a democracy. (3)

(e) (i) Identify one factor which influences the way in which an individual votes. (1)

  (ii) Explain how this factor might have become more or less influential in the last 30 years. (3)

CHAPTER 15

Poverty and the welfare state

1   The welfare state

The history of the welfare state

The idea of a welfare state is that the government should provide for the welfare of all citizens from cradle to grave, or 'womb to tomb'. Our social services date back at least to the Elizabethan Poor Law of 1598 which provided for **parish relief** for the destitute. This meant that officials in each village could collect a poor rate from every household and distribute the funds among the needy.

The 1870s saw a number of advances, under both Conservative and Liberal Governments, on the road to our modern welfare state. These included:

- the first national system of elementary schooling;
- the start of slum clearance and council housing;
- Public Health Acts which forced every area to have a Medical Officer of Health and a Sanitary Inspector.

The 1906–14 Liberal Government made further advances in the provision of welfare, such as:

- old age pensions;
- contributions by employees, employers and government to a national insurance scheme which gave benefits for disability, maternity, sickness and unemployment;
- clinics for children;
- free school meals and medical inspections;
- labour exchanges for the unemployed;

- wages councils which laid down minimum wages for low-paid workers in certain industries;
- probation officers.

The 1942 Beveridge Report laid the basis for the next stage in the development of the welfare state. Sir William Beveridge wrote of conquering the 'Five Great Social Evils' and the 1945–51 Labour Government took a number of appropriate measures:

1 **Poverty** This was tackled by providing the 'safety net' of **national assistance** which was replaced by **supplementary benefit** in 1966. This is a means-tested benefit payable to people with no other income, or to top up other benefit payments such as **family allowances** (since renamed **child benefit**) which were introduced to help large families.

2 **Ignorance** New secondary schools were built providing free secondary education for all in the tripartite system of grammar, secondary modern and secondary technical schools.

3 **Disease** The National Health Service was set up to ensure free medical treatment for all.

4 **Squalor** One focus for the rehousing of families from slums was provided by the string of new towns built beyond the 'green belts' around certain cities.

5 **Idleness** The 1950s saw successful 'full employment' policies which kept the proportion out of work below 3 per cent.

Rowntree's York surveys found that the proportions of the total population in poverty had fallen from 28 per cent in 1899 to 18 per cent in 1936 and to only 1.5 per cent in 1950. But poverty was 'rediscovered' in the 1960s. The TV drama *Cathy Come Home* highlighted the plight of the homeless and led to a new campaigning group called Shelter. And *The Poor and the Poorest* by Abel-Smith and Townsend estimated that 14 per cent, or 7.5 million people, were in relative poverty in 1960. Their cause was championed by a new pressure group called the Child Poverty Action Group, started in 1965.

The 1970s saw some new social security schemes such as **invalidity benefit** for the long-term sick and disabled and **family income supplement** available for low-wage families according to the number of children. Benefits not only became more widely available in the decades after 1945 but they also increased in value. The state retirement pension paid to a married couple, for example, rose in value between the 1950s and 1978 from a third to almost a half of average earnings.

Case study: the redistribution of income by the welfare state

The following figures show how, in 1996, the welfare state was a
'Robin Hood' taking taxes from the rich and giving benefits to the poor:

	Bottom 20% of households £	Top 20% of households £
Average original income from earnings, investments, pensions, etc	2,430	41,260
Plus benefits in cash	4,910	1,200
= gross income	7,340	42,460
Minus direct taxes:		
income tax	540	9,660
council tax	590	820
= disposable income	6,210	31,980
Minus indirect tax (e.g. VAT)	1,930	5,090
= post-tax income	4,280	26,890
Plus the value of benefits in kind (e.g. education and health services)	3,950	2,310
= final income	8,230	29,200

The average original income of the top earners was almost 17 times
greater than that of the poorest fifth of the population. But after
redistribution, by taxes, benefits and services, the top group only had 3.5
times as much 'final income'.

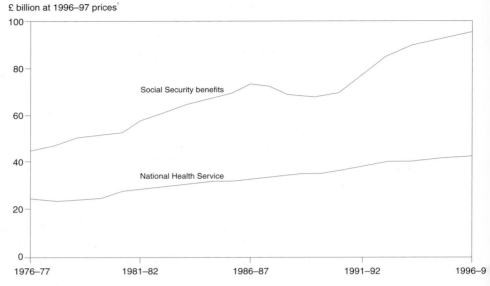

£ billion at 1996–97 prices[1]

Social Security benefits

National Health Service

1976–77   1981–82   1986–87   1991–92   1996–9

[1]Adjusted to 1996–97 prices using the GDP market prices deflator.

Growth (after inflation[1]) of social security benefits and NHS spending (Source: Social Trends, 1998.)

The new mixed economy of welfare provision

Welfare services can be provided by:

- **central government** (e.g. centrally funded hospital trusts or employment training);
- **local government** (e.g. council-funded schools or old people's homes);
- **profit-making businesses** (e.g. private nursing homes or private nursery schools);
- **the voluntary, charity sector** (e.g. Salvation Army hostels for the homeless or housing association flats);
- **informal carers** (e.g. family, friends and neighbours).

The Conservative Governments of the 1980s and 1990s have encouraged a system of purchasers and providers. For example, your family GP may become a 'fundholder' able to purchase treatment from different hospitals and the council Social Services Department may purchase help for a disabled client from a private firm which provides 'home helps'.

The Conservatives saw advantages in moving to a more mixed system of welfare services:

- Clients prefer choice (e.g. 'social housing' can be rented from the council or a housing association).
- Government services are often 'captured' by trade unionists and run in the interests of the workers rather than in the interests of the clients (e.g. the prison service is said to be run for the prison officers and not for the prisoners).

- Competition leads to improved standards of service (e.g. private firms competing for schools meals contracts).
- Profit-seeking management means less bureaucracy, more efficiency and lower costs for the taxpayer.

Others have seen disadvantages in moving away from state-run services:

- lower quality of service (e.g. hospital wards cleaned in a hurry);
- lower morale among staff (e.g. social workers forced to cut costs);
- higher charges for users (e.g. more expensive school meals);
- care in the community (e.g. after the closure of large mental asylums) too often leads to the neglect of the most vulnerable (e.g. schizophrenics living on the streets).

Those who live on the streets may have difficult claiming social security benefits.

2   What is poverty?

Case study: the growing up in poverty

In the early hours of Monday morning, 3 January 1994, five small boys from Leeds were taken into care. They were brothers, aged between six months and 6 years and their mother was only 22. The national newspapers reported the case as part of a 'Home Alone at Christmas' moral panic about neglected children.

In an average week, Leeds social workers deal with 50 cases of children in need of protection, 2,500 of them a year. The city's Social Services chairman, Michael Simmons, said: 'We have seen a steady increase in poverty and a steady dismantling of the benefits system. The whole system has got tighter. They now get no benefits at all for their children aged 16 to 18. If their cooker blows up, they used to get a grant to replace it. Now all they get is a loan and they have to pay that back out of income support, which is, by definition, already at the level of poverty. This is deprivation. And I am afraid deprivation and neglect go hand in hand.

'People in these circumstances become depressed – clinically depressed. Their physical health suffers: they eat bad food and wear inadequate clothing. They all suffer stress, children as well as adults. We have a young boy now who is literally chewing the ends off his fingers, breaking the flesh, drawing blood.

'We have numerous homes without electricity or gas, because the newly privatised companies have put them on meters and they simply don't have the cash to pay for fuel. In a few cases, we find they don't even have water; they're running a hose pipe from the house next door.

'Their kids can't afford to go to school because they can't afford school meals or proper clothing, and they don't even have the know-how or the money or the energy to drag five children across Leeds to fill in complicated forms to get help.

'And now the schools have started turning them away. Since schools have been compiling league tables, there are headteachers who are deliberately excluding children like this to avoid damaging their statistics.

'There was one family who simply couldn't communicate. The children just cried all the time. Why? They were extremely unhappy. And who could blame them?

'It all flows from this extraordinary idea that we have to give rich people an incentive to work by giving them more money and poor people an incentive to work by taking money away from them. These people are not evil. If they're bad parents, it's not because they don't care about their children. It is because they cannot cope.'

(adapted from 'I want my kids' by Nick Davies, the *Guardian*, 19 January 1994)

Three definitions of poverty

1   Absolute poverty   Rowntree defined absolute poverty as the condition of those unable to afford 'the minimum provision needed to maintain health and working efficiency'. How did Rowntree decide on his first 'poverty line' in 1899? He consulted the work of a nutritionist called Dr Dunlop who had experimented on the diets of Scottish prisoners. Rowntree estimated that the basic foods needed by parents and three children could be bought for just under 13 shillings per week. He then added amounts to cover the costs of clothing, fuel, rent and 'household sundries'. Any families whose income fell below this poverty line were in absolute poverty.

The United Nations defines absolute poverty as 'a condition characterised by severe deprivation of basic human needs, including food, safe drinking water, sanitation facilities, health, shelter, education and information. It depends not only on income but also on access to services'.

2 Relative poverty   In 1899 Rowntree decided that the minimum clothing needs of a young woman were: one pair of boots, two aprons, one second-hand dress, one skirt made from an old dress, a shawl, a jacket, two pairs of stockings, one pair of old boots worn as slippers and a third of the cost of a new hat. What would you regard as the decent minimum nowadays?

Left: Angela and Ricky Pulhofer with their children in their bed-and-breakfast room in a hotel where seventy families share one cooker. In 1986 the Guardian *reported that Hillingdon Council was paying £187 per week for this room.*

Right: Squatters protesting about local housing policy.

Townsend has defined relative poverty as applying to those who cannot afford the amenities and activities that are customary. Cultural norms, or socially approved minimum standards of decency, vary over time and so they are relative. In 1992, 11 per cent of households had no phone and 12 per cent lacked washing machines: we could say that, relative to the expectations of the majority at the time, they were deprived of what most people consider to be essential.

The following comments come from an article by David Donnison (the *Guardian*, 30 September 1992):

> The lack of separate bedrooms and three meals a day for children will seem odd measures of poverty to people in the Third World. But every generation reinvents poverty by transforming some of their predecessors' luxuries into necessities. These necessities are created by the economy in which we live and the life styles it supports. Needs are real and unmet needs really hurt.
>
>   The process continues relentlessly. Already there are places in Britain where central heating is a necessity because all the houses have it and there is no other reliable source of heat; where you have to have a refrigerator because the house is warm and there are no shops for miles; where without a car you cannot get readily to work, to shops, to a doctor or a post office. This is the 'rising tide' of economic growth. It lifts those

who are doing well but drowns those who cannot afford these new necessities – all of which were luxuries not long ago.

Those in relative poverty tend to be powerless as well as poor. 'Exclusion' might be a more revealing description of their plight. They are likely to feel excluded from a wide range of normal activities, from enjoying trips to the cinema to feeling involved in the political life of the community, feeling able to influence the political process.

3   Environmental poverty   Using a broader definition, it has been argued that poverty is not just a matter of money. A family with both parents in full-time jobs might be well above the poverty line, yet they might live in a damp flat in a neglected council block. Their local public services and amenities (such as parks, schools, hospitals and public transport) might be inadequate or 'poor'. Are they living impoverished lives because of their deprived environment?

In his 1968–69 survey, *Poverty in the United Kingdom*, Townsend found that 34 per cent had no safe place for their children to play; 27 per cent suffered from dirty, smelly or smoky air and 22 per cent (or 13 million) lived in defective housing.

The United Nations definition of 'overall poverty' includes 'ill health; lack of access to education and other basic services; inadequate housing; unsafe environments and social discrimination and exclusion'.

A boy begging on the street –
a case of absolute poverty?

Case study: the 'Breadline Britain' survey

In 1983, MORI (Mass Opinion Research International) conducted a survey for London Weekend Television's documentary series called *Breadline Britain*. The survey tried to uncover a definition of relative poverty as 'the minimum standard of living laid down by society'. In order to get popular agreement on this, 1,174 interviewees were asked to select which out of thirty-five items they considered to be necessary for all families or adults. The following fourteen indicators of poverty were among those most frequently selected by the interviewees. The figure on the right is the percentage of the sample describing the items as necessary:

Heating to warm living areas	97
Public transport for one's needs	88
A warm waterproof coat	87
3 meals a day for children	82
2 pairs of all-weather shoes	78
Toys for children	71
Celebrations – e.g. at Christmas	69
Roast joint or chops once a week	67
New, not second-hand, clothes	64
Hobby or leisure activity	64
Meat or fish every other day	63
Presents for friends or family once a year	63
Holidays away for one week a year	63
Leisure equipment for children – e.g. bicycles	57

Those interviewed were then asked which items they themselves lacked which they wanted but could not afford. From the results to these questions it was estimated that:

6 million people cannot afford some essential items of clothing;

3.5 million cannot afford carpets, washing machine or fridge;

3 million cannot afford to heat the living areas of their homes.

Taking the total in poverty as those unable to afford three or more of the twenty-two 'necessities', *Breadline Britain* calculated that 7.5 million people (or 13 per cent of the population) are in poverty. A simple subjective measure of how many people feel that they are poor was also given in the survey's findings. In 1983, 12 per cent of people said that they were poor all the time (compared to 8 per cent in 1968) and 28 per cent said that they were sometimes poor (18 per cent in 1968). The details of the survey were published in 1985 in *Poor Britain* by J. Mack and S. Lansley.

Children in Newcastle – growing up in a deprived environment?

3   Who are the poor?

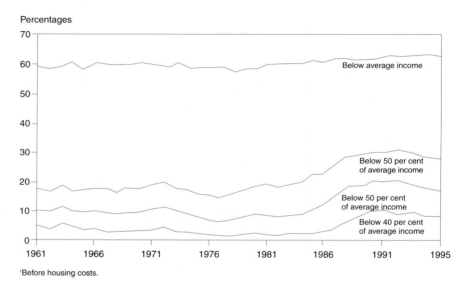

Percentages

*Percentage of people whose income is below various fractions of average income[1]
(Source: Social Trends, 1998.)*

[1]Before housing costs.

The above chart shows that the proportion of people with less than half of the average income doubled in the first half of the 1980s. In the early 1990s those below this poverty line fell back to less than 20 per cent of the population. The figures below show how the absolute numbers of poor people rose with the increased inequality of the 'Thatcher Decade', the 1980s:

Children and adults in the UK below 50 per cent of the average income of 1979

	1979	1993
Adults	3,850,000	4,100,000
Children	1,430,000	1,940,000

Two particularly vulnerable groups are the long-term sick and disabled and non-working single parent households. These make up a tenth of the whole population but almost a quarter of the poor. Another large group in poverty are pensioners. In 1998, almost 2 million pensioners relied on income support. A further 1 million were entitled to income support but did not claim it. In 1998, the average weekly income for the bottom 10 per cent of pensioner households was £69.90 a week, compared with £602.50 for the top 10 per cent.

Economic status of those in the poorest 20 per cent of UK households, 1996

24 per cent were those on benefits, such as long-term sick or disabled or non-working single parents
20 per cent were categorised as unemployed
23 per cent were old age pensioners
33 per cent were in households with only part-time work and/or low pay

Low pay

In 1997, the areas with over 25 per cent of employees earning less than £4 per hour were Wales and the North East and the South West of England. Only 11 per cent in London and 18 per cent in South East England earned less than £4 per hour. In all other areas of Britain between 20 and 25 per cent were on less than £4 per hour.

Ethnicity

Some ethnic groups are far more likely than others to be poor.

Percentage of each ethnic group in the poorest 20 per cent of UK households, 1996

19 per cent of the white population
26 per cent of the Indian population
30 per cent of the black population
66 per cent of the Pakistani/Bangladeshi population

Homelessness

6 per cent of households experienced homelessness between 1986 and 1996. This experience varies with age: 20 per cent of those aged 16–24 had been homeless, compared with only 1 per cent of those aged 55 and over. 4 per cent of households had been accepted as homeless by the council.

Homeless households placed in temporary accommodation by local councils, Great Britain

Year	
1982	10,000
1992	68,000
1996	46,000

The average life expectancy of single homeless people is 42.

Income dynamics

The final section of this chapter raises the issue of the extent to which there is an 'underclass' who may be permanently trapped in a 'cycle of deprivation'. In 1997, the new Labour government set up a Social Exclusion Unit to co-ordinate policies, such as the welfare-to-work programme. Government research has shown that almost half of those in the poorest 20 per cent in 1991 were no longer in the poorest 20 per cent in 1995. Three-quarters of those who ceased being unemployed left the poorest 20 per cent.

Another factor affecting income dynamics is the stage of the family life cycle. In any one year 14 per cent of households change their composition. Government research divides the population into fifths or 'quintiles', from the highest earning 20 per cent to the poorest 20 per cent. This research shows that more than half of the children who leave home and more than half of the women who leave their partners move to a lower income quintile.

4   The causes of poverty

'The poor are to blame': the culture of poverty and the cycle of deprivation

In the nineteenth century it was widely believed that people were poor because of their own inadequacies. Poverty was caused, it was held, by defects of character such as idleness, indiscipline and an inability to plan for the future. A modern sociological variation of this explanation of poverty is the idea of the **culture of poverty**.

This idea was first put forward by Oscar Lewis, in the late 1950s, and it arose from his research among the urban poor of Mexico and Puerto Rico. Briefly, Lewis found that the poor had developed their own subculture in response to the difficult circumstances in which they found themselves. The following four features of this subculture explain why the subculture has the effect of keeping the poor in poverty:

1 a sense of fatalism, feeling that one's destiny cannot be altered;
2 a strong inclination to live for the present and an unwillingness to plan for the future;
3 a feeling of worthlessness and isolation from the rest of society;
4 a lack of interest in joining political parties, trade unions or pressure groups which campaign for social change.

Poverty passes from generation to generation in a **cycle of deprivation** because the children of the poor are socialised into the subculture of poverty. President Johnson's 'War on Poverty', in the USA in the 1960s, tried to break this cycle by intervening with programmes of compensatory education and help for small businesses starting up in deprived areas. Some would argue that such policies are misconceived since the real cause of poverty is to be found in the way that our society is organised.

Some people have to scavenge for their food.

Claimants waiting in a DSS office in Marylebone, London, in 1993.

'Poverty – it is the fault of the capitalist system'

Marxists claim that poverty is an inevitable feature of the capitalist economic system. A laissez-faire or **free market economy** allows capitalists who own businesses to make huge profits while paying low wages to their workers. This argument leads to a number of conclusions:

1   Those who are unable to sell their skills in the market place and those with few skills to sell (such as the disabled, the old and the unemployed) will become 'casualties' of the market economy.

2   Poverty will never be eliminated until a communist system distributes wealth according to need rather than on the basis of skills or inheritance.

3   Conservative governments with free-market ideas will increase incentives to work for the rich by cutting their taxes and increase incentives for the unemployed to work by cutting their benefits – so that they will 'price themselves back into work' by accepting low rates of pay.

The way in which the free-market policies of the 1980s have helped the rich to get richer can be seen in these figures:

Shares of pre-tax income received by top income groups

	Top 1 per cent	Top 5 per cent	Top 10 per cent
1979	5%	15%	24%
1994	8%	20%	30%

This shows that the share of total national pre-tax income going to the top 1 per cent increased by 60 per cent between 1979 and 1994. This top group have clearly benefited from the squeeze on the incomes of the bottom two-thirds of the population who, in 1994, lived in households with below-average incomes.

The life-cycle view of poverty

The culture of poverty theory is not only rejected by the Marxists who blame the inequality of the capitalist system, it is also rejected by the view that emphasises the importance of the **life-cycle of the family**. This view stresses that many of the poor are not so very different from the majority of the population.

The idea of the family life-cycle shows that a young married couple or a couple in late middle-age may be fairly well off financially since both partners may be working full-time with no children to support. In contrast, the couple starting a family may struggle financially due to the burden of high mortgage repayments and the loss of the wife's income.

Because the average family has insufficient income to accumulate significant wealth by saving, there is a predictable fall in living standards again when income is reduced by retirement – in the same way that many are vulnerable to any loss of income by sickness, unemployment, divorce or widowhood.

This view points out that many of us may, at some stage in our lives, depend on the 'safety net' of the social security system. Much poverty can be seen then as due to the inadequacies of the welfare system or the way that some people 'fall through the net'.

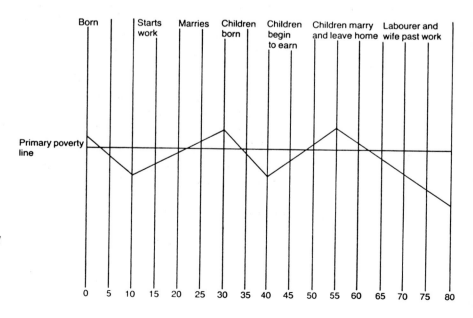

The life-cycle of the low-paid (Source: M. O'Donnell, Age and Generation, Tavistock, *1985; adapted from Rowntree, 1901.)*

Case study: the benefits of tax changes

During the 1980s the Conservative Governments cut income taxes (for example, cutting the top rate from 60 per cent to 40 per cent in 1988) while increasing indirect taxes, such as VAT (8 per cent in 1979 and 17.5 per cent in 1994). Many of those in poverty have no earned income and so gain no benefit from cuts in income tax. But the poor are hit from rises in indirect taxes on their spending, such as VAT on domestic fuel (introduced in 1994). Tax changes that have such an unfair impact are called 'regressive'.

If we consider the top 1 per cent of earners, they received 30 per cent of the benefit of all the tax cuts between 1979 and 1994, worth around £75 billion. In 1994, this top 1 per cent had average annual incomes of £120,000 and their average reduction in income tax since 1979 was worth £35,000 per year.

An analysis of tax changes between 1985 and 1995, by the Institute for Fiscal Studies, found that the richest 10 per cent of households gained an average of £125 a month while the bottom 40 per cent were worse off.

Those in the second poorest 10 per cent were not as badly hit by the 1985–95 tax changes as those in the third poorest 10 per cent. This was because the second poorest 10 per cent contained a heavy concentration of pensioners. These pensioners smoke and drive less than others and so were less badly hit by increases in excise duties, such as cigarette and petrol taxes. Pensioners were also more generously compensated for the imposition of VAT on domestic fuel than others on benefit.

---

5   The underclass

In the early 1990s there were a number of connected moral panics. These concerned persistent truants, unmarried mothers, and joy-riders and rioters on 'peripheral' council estates, on the edges of cities like Newcastle, Cardiff, Oxford and Coventry. These concerns were often linked with the idea of *The Emerging British Underclass* (the title of a book by Charles Murray in 1990).

What is meant by 'the underclass'?

In the 1960s, the term 'underclass' was used by left-wing (socialist) thinkers to analyse the position of ethnic minorities. In the 1990s, 'underclass' has been used by right-wing (conservative) commentators, such as the American Charles Murray, to describe those who have made living on welfare benefits their way of life. This idea of **welfare culture** or **dependency culture** echoes earlier American theories of the culture of poverty.

Murray's underclass is like the 'lumpenproletariat' identified by Marx. It consists of those who are outside the class system because they have no job on which to base their social class position. Murray's definition does not include those in the 'secondary labour market', with jobs that offer poor security and low pay and are often part-time.

Many people have periods in their lives when their jobs are insecure. Unemployment rises during recessions and falls in economic booms. A faster pace of economic change also leads to redundancies, such as bank employees losing jobs due to cash dispenser machines. But is there a group who stay outside employment? One characteristic of a social class is that it has a fairly stable membership. For the underclass to be a true class it would have to have members who have little chance of employment throughout their lives. Pensioners who have had jobs would have to be excluded. The underclass is thus another name for long-term or frequent claimants of income support. Nick Buck has estimated that this underclass grew from 5 per cent of the working population in 1979 to 10 per cent in 1986.

Structure versus culture

Why is there a growing underclass outside the world of work? Murray argues that these people have lost the will to compete in the labour market due to their culture. They have adapted to a way of life surviving on welfare benefits.

Many sociologists would argue that Murray is blaming the victim when he should blame structural factors: a section of the population is denied the opportunity and resources to compete for jobs due to the following:

- **changes in the economic structure:** there are fewer simple manual jobs on offer;
- **institutional structures:** poor education and training provision, especially in declining urban areas;
- **the lack of appropriate facilities**, such as nursery schools accessible to single mothers.

Murray argues that it is largely cultural factors, such as the increase in illegitimate births and criminal behaviour, that have contributed to the growth of the underclass.

Gender and the underclass

William Wilson is an American with a theory that ties together the two main groups within the underclass, the long-term unemployed (mainly male) and young single mothers (by definition, female). He compares the Harlem area of New York in the 1940s and 1950s with the Harlem of the 1980s and 1990s.

In the 1940s and 1950s Harlem was a traditional black ghetto, in the classic European Jewish sense: it was a complete community, with community leaders and a whole set of community roles, which was trapped by systematic discrimination from outside.

By the 1980s and 1990s less discrimination and more opportunities had led to outward mobility. Those who could get out did get out, leaving behind a much more hopeless group than before, without the same community structure. This left a shrinking 'marriageable pool' of wage-earning men. A lot of the available men are either unemployed, or casually employed, or engaged in crime and in and out of jail. Men cannot offer to be reliable, bread-winning husbands. So young women bring up their families alone, on welfare. Their sons then grow up without positive role models of how to be responsible fathers.

Murray has argued that the same pattern is being repeated on deprived, problem council estates in areas of high, long-term unemployment in Britain.

Welfare and social security

If 'social security' is a mutual insurance against adverse life events, then we all pay in and we all expect to take out again at various stages in the life-cycle. Those on social security, in this sense, would include pensioners and claimants of contributory unemployment insurance. But Murray does not include these in the underclass. He speaks only of long-term claimants of 'welfare', something which *we* give to *them*.

There are as many low-paid people as unpaid people among Britain's poor. But we do not know how much movement there is between these two groups. The theory of the underclass argues that as high unemployment persists, it becomes concentrated in particular families, and among particular groups. In time, these groups become increasingly isolated from contact with employed people and the world of work; they begin to adopt a new style of life.

Is there an underclass?

We will have to wait for the results of a longitudinal study, by Essex University, to see whether there is a distinct group of people who are likely to be the long-term recipients of income support: an underclass largely detached from paid employment, having an increasingly separate culture and way of life.

Polarisation of married couple families

	1983	1997
Male only working	43%	26%
Two earners ('work-rich')	46%	63%
No earners ('work-poor')	11%	11%

Ray Pahl's research on the Isle of Sheppey, in the 1980s, suggested that there is a polarisation between two groups in the working class, a widening gap between 'work-rich' and 'work-poor' households. Work-rich families have two or more incomes. Wives may have full- or part-time jobs while working husbands are often able to earn money on the side at evenings and weekends. Such work in the 'hidden economy' often depends on the skills, tools and contacts of the workplace. This type of casual work may not be so easily available to the long-term unemployed men in work-poor homes. Also, their benefits may be cut if their wives work. So their families tend to have no earned income.

There are two reasons that the USA has a large group of the population who are 'outside society', lacking security and protection. First, there are huge numbers of illegal immigrants in the USA. Second, a significant proportion of Americans are not covered by health insurance. In 1994, the Clinton government was planning to introduce a universal health-care system. If there are similarities between the poorest in Britain and America, there are differences too.

Case study: poor smokers

In 1994 a PSI report on *Poor Smokers* included the following findings:

- In the late 1940s almost 80 per cent of men were smokers.
- Between 1976 and 1990 smoking became less socially acceptable among higher social classes: among the better-off, the top quarter of the population, smokers fell from 40 per cent to 20 per cent.
- In the bottom quarter, by income, there was no fall in smoking: 62 per cent of lone mothers and 48 per cent of men with children were smokers. 'What appears to have happened is that the concentration of unqualified school-leavers in the council estates of the 1970s became a protected social habitat for high levels of smoking not seen elsewhere since the early 1960s.'
- A typical low-income couple in 1991 might have had a weekly income of £160 a week, with fixed costs, such as housing, of £80. If both smoked twenty cigarettes a day, their habit would cost £22 a week: over a quarter of their disposable income.
- Among couples on income support, parents who both smoked were twice as likely as non-smokers to say that their children lacked food, clothes, coats and other necessities.
- If married couples have only modest qualifications and low income but are owner-occupiers, then they have only average levels of smoking. Owning your own home brings optimism and self-esteem.

Two of the report's conclusions are as follows:

1 'All modern research on how people give up smoking shows that they do so for reasons connected with optimism. Britain's lowest income parents are not people with great cause for optimism, or for self-esteem.'

2 If the government is to achieve its target of cutting the prevalence of smoking to 20 per cent by the year 2000, doctors should prescribe free nicotine patches or gum for those on benefits.

GCSE question from Southern Examining Group 1997

Study Item A. Then answer *all* parts of the question which follow.

Item A

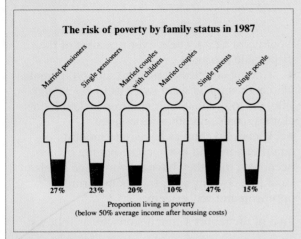

The risk of poverty by family status in 1987

Married pensioners — 27%
Single pensioners — 23%
Married couples with children — 20%
Married couples — 10%
Single parents — 47%
Single people — 15%

Proportion living in poverty
(below 50% average income after housing costs)

Adapted from Carey Oppenheim, *Poverty, The Facts* (CPAG) 1990

(a) According to the information given,

   (i)   which type of family was most likely to be living in poverty in 1987?   (1)

   (ii) which percentage of married pensioners were living in poverty in 1987?   (1)

   (iii) was the risk of falling into poverty higher for people with children than for those with no children?   (1)

(b) (i)   Explain what is meant by a 'means-tested benefit'.   (2)

   (ii) Identify *one* advantage and *one* disadvantage of means-tested benefits.   (2)

(c) (i)   Identify *one* group not named in *Item A*, members of which are at risk of falling into poverty. Explain why these people are at risk.   (3)

   (ii) Name *one* voluntary organisation which operates in Britain to help people in poverty.   (1)

(d) (i)   Suggest *two* reasons why poverty still exists in Britain.   (2)

   (ii) State *two* ways in which governments have attempted to reduce poverty in Britain in the last 50 years.   (2)

GCSE question from Southern Examining Group 1997

What explanations might sociologists offer for the existence of poverty in Britain in the 1990s?   (10)

CHAPTER 16

Work, unions, unemployment and leisure

Collective bargaining?

1 Changing patterns of work and technology

In *The Future of Work*, C. Handy has described some new patterns of work which clearly emerged in the 1980s:

- Britain no longer seems to be a society that can guarantee full employment, with jobs for all who want to work.
- While many workers (often men) have been made redundant from full-time jobs, many others (often women) have been employed in new part-time jobs.
- Knowledge-based skills, such as data processing, have been replacing manual skills, such as welding.
- Jobs in service industries have been replacing jobs in manufacturing industries.
- The life-time career in one organisation is becoming rarer. An increasingly common pattern is for workers to be occupationally mobile, changing careers as well as employers.

These changes will sweep away many of the patterns of work of previous generations. As Handy says:

> to our grandchildren the massive organisations of this industrial age may look as bizarre as trench warfare does to today's military commanders. The idea of the 100,000 hours, 47 hours per week for 47 weeks per year that everyone used to work, and many still do, may seem as unnatural to them as child labour in the mines does to us.

In facing an uncertain future, Handy reminds us of the following precedents:

1   We have created jobs before. Between 1932 and 1937 we increased the number of jobs by 2.25 million and reduced unemployment by 1.25 million.

An automated assembly line at Ford.

2   We have lived with a growing labour force before. In the 100 years from 1860 to 1960 the labour force nearly doubled, but so did employment.

3   We have survived structural change before. Agricultural jobs fell from over 25 per cent of the labour force to under 3 per cent in the same 100 years but were all absorbed into new industries and occupations.

4   We have seen technological change before. Between 1860 and 1960 the capital machinery employed per worker doubled, the output trebled. Automobiles replaced horses and society adjusted.

Three stages of production technology

1   The division of labour   The specialisation of occupational roles and production tasks is called the division of labour. There has always been a degree of specialisation in human societies. Among Stone Age groups, for example, the young might have gone out hunting while the old kept the home fires burning. In medieval times craftsmen and merchants specialised in different tasks. When textiles were produced by a cottage industry some homes concentrated on spinning or weaving and others on bleaching or dyeing.

But the factory system, which accompanied the Industrial Revolution in the eighteenth century, broke jobs down into simpler, more repetitive tasks. In 1776 Adam Smith noted how, in a pin factory, 'One man draws out the wire, another straightens it, a third cuts it, a fourth points it, a fifth grinds it and prepares the top for receiving the head ... ten persons could make among them upwards of 48,000 pins in a day'.

The historian E.P. Thompson has described how, before the Industrial Revolution, Pennine farmers were also weavers; northern leadminers were also smallholders; servants also joined in with the harvest and Cornish tinners also joined in the pilchard fishing during the peak autumn season.

The factory system largely put an end to such irregular labour patterns – where occupations had been mixed and where workers had alternated bouts of intense labour with long periods of leisure.

2   Mass production on assembly lines   In 1911 an American, F.W. Taylor ('Speedy Taylor'), wrote *The Principles of Scientific Management*. He claimed that for any job there was a single best method for organising the work which could be established by careful study of the time and motion involved in each task. Efficiency could be increased by standardising tasks, tools and equipment as well as by offering productivity bonuses.

Specialisation by simplification offered the following advantages:

- inexperienced, unskilled workers could be employed;
- efficiency could be gained by mastery of repetitive routines;
- foremen could monitor work more effectively;
- individual tasks could be better synchronised with one another and with machines, allowing smoother and more intense production.

These ideas were first linked with the use of a continuous assembly line, before the First World War, by Henry Ford. This new method of **mass production** was so successful that by 1921 Ford had 60 per cent of the world car market and every other car on the road was a Model T Ford.

The conveyor belt method was soon applied to other industries. Audrey Swann has described how televisions were assembled at Pye factories in the 1950s:

> The sets came along on runners. We each did our own little bit of wiring, and soldering, and then it went on to the next person, and it was rushed. If you wanted to go to the toilet you had to call a float so that she could take your place, otherwise the sets piled up.
>
> (From *All Our Working Lives* by P. Pagnamenta and R. Overy)

3   Automation

> 'I'm a machine', says the spot-welder. 'I'm caged', says the bank teller and echoes the hotel clerk. 'I'm a mule', says the steel worker. 'A monkey can do what I do', says the receptionist. 'I'm less than a farm implement', says the migrant worker. 'I'm an object', says the high-fashion model. ... Nora Watson may have put it more succinctly: 'I think most of us, like the assembly line worker, have jobs that are too small for our spirit. Jobs are not big enough for people.'
>
> (From *Working* by Studs Terkel)

Several of the soul-destroying jobs mentioned above are now being automated. Automation involves machines which work by themselves, automatically, with little human supervision. In recent years robots have replaced many spot-welders and paint-sprayers in car factories and the need for bank clerks has declined because of 'hole-in-the-wall' cash-dispensers.

In supermarkets the check-out assistant 'wipes' the bar code on goods across a detector and the linked computer system (a) gives the customer an itemised bill, (b) automatically re-orders stock from the warehouse and (c) reports to supervisors on the speed and efficiency of the till worker. One can see that the work done by the check-out assistant has become so 'deskilled' that it could well be done by a robot.

Deskilling

Let us suppose that a worker uses great knowledge and skill to select pieces of wood and transform them into an individually designed and crafted table. If this production process comes to involve a simple, repetitive job, assembling prepared parts, then the worker has been deskilled.

The way in which new technology can reduce the traditional skill of a job has been described in an international study of *Microelectronics and Office Jobs: The Impact of the Chip on Women's Employment*, by D. Werneke:

> Some jobs have been made better by the use of new technology. Tedious, repetitive tasks have been eliminated by machines which have allowed some employees to take on more responsible and satisfying work. However, many more instances have appeared where clerical jobs became poorer as a result of introducing new technology. The traditional skills of the clerical workforce in many cases have been made redundant by machines with the result that many jobs have been deskilled. If, for example, a typist's speed and accuracy are no longer as important when using a word processor, the job has become less skilled unless higher level functions are added to the work. Deskilling not only results in a less satisfying job but it also has a serious impact on career progression as it eliminates traditional paths to promotion.

Keyboarding skills may soon be redundant because voice recognition technology has developed so that advanced word processors can take direct dictation without the need for a human operative with the manual skills of keying in words.

Three examples of how new technology can polarise skills

Low skill	*High skill*
1 Mundane machine-minding on an automated assembly line.	Highly skilled maintenance work involving systems control and fault diagnosis.
2 Low-level technicians supervising automatic testing or using computer-aided design.	High-level technicians undertaking non-routine testing or complex design draughting.
3 'Marginal' word processor operatives with easily replaceable skills – like the 'temp' copy typist in the typing pool.	Personal secetaries with complex multi-function roles which cannot be standardised.

How far do the findings below support the idea of deskilling?

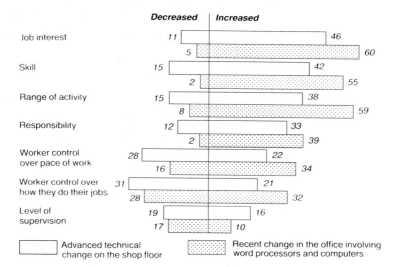

The impact of advanced technical change on jobs (percentages). (Source: W.W. Daniel, 'Workplace Industrial Relations and Technical change', PSI Bulletin, 1988.)

2 The changing workforce

One way of describing the trends in changing patterns of work is to use the term **post-Fordism**. Whereas old-fashioned Fordist production involved a steep hierarchy of specialised workers in large-scale mass production, newer post-Fordist production involves a flatter hierarchy of workers and is characterised by flexibility. Post-Fordist production is driven by ever-faster innovation in products and the greater variety demanded by consumers. Production needs to be flexible, with shorter production runs of more varied products. The post-Fordist employer also wants a more flexible workforce.

The two-tier workforce

Post-Fordist firms increasingly organise their production with two types of workers:

1 Core workers These are **functionally flexible**. They will do a range of tasks, whatever the company demands of them, in return for a secure full-time contract with good conditions, such as company pension scheme and high wages.

2 Periphery workers These are **numerically flexible**. A company can increase the number of these workers and then lay them off again easily, without having to give redundancy payments. They are often on temporary, part-time contracts and are self-employed or employed by sub-contractors. They are less likely than core workers to be protected by trade union membership.

Many organisations, from insurance companies and factories to schools and hospitals, no longer keep canteen, cleaning and caretaking staff on their direct payroll. Instead, these workers are often hired from the cheapest contractor and they are often women and/or from ethnic minorities.

In 1994, nearly 50 per cent of the available workforce were effectively 'outside the organisation': 23 per week were part-time or temporary, 12 per cent were self-employed and 12 per cent were unemployed (looking for work or given up searching). Also, for the first time, 50 per cent of the national workforce were women. In the 16–19 age group, more young women had jobs than young men. And in certain countries, such as Essex, women outnumbered men in the workforce.

Fordist and Post-Fordist economics

The Fordist modern economy (which has declined since the 1970s)	*The Post-Fordist post-modern economy of the 1990s*
Growing demand for consumer goods	Extra income spent on services
Large manufacturing sector	Most new jobs in service industries
Mass marketing of standard product	Niche marketing of range of products
Changes in production technology	Changes in information technology
Steep hierarchy of command	Delayered middle managers stripped out
Lots of skilled, semi-skilled and unskilled manual jobs for men	More job opportunities for women than men, in non-manual rather than manual work
Secure full-time 'jobs for life', with one employer	Insecure part-time jobs, short-term contracts with different employers
Apprenticeship providing skills to last a lifetime	Flexibility via reskilling, retraining for a number of different jobs within one career
Predictable, stable life-patterns (e.g. large peer groups working together in large local factories from the ages of 16 to 65)	Individualisation of the life-course (e.g. everyone who leaves the same school now has different, unique experiences of work and family life)
Strong trade unions	Laws to cut union power
Lots of nationalised industries	Privatisation (selling) of state-owned firms
High taxes and high welfare spending	Tax cuts and welfare cuts
Increasing mobility of labour	Increasing (global) mobility of capital

In 1994, more young women had jobs than young men in the 16–19 age group.

The increasingly rapid transfer of capital refers to the movement of both investment funds and employment from one country to another. This is one aspect of the globalisation of social life. We consume world brands (e.g. McDonalds, Sony, Virgin, Nike) and we work for worldwide companies (e.g. McDonalds, Sony, Virgin, IBM).

The dual market

A similar idea to the two-tier workforce is the dual labour market theory which divides the workforce into the following:

- **The primary labour market**   This consists of jobs with high wages and good career prospects.
- **The secondary labour market**   This consists of insecure, low-paid employment where there is little chance to acquire skills.

Government policy and flexible labour markets

The government has encouraged flexibility for employers by a policy of deregulation, for example reducing the employment protection rights of part-time workers – their rights to redundancy pay and maternity leave. In 1993, the government encouraged flexibility in rates of pay by abolishing the Wages Councils. For over eighty years the Wages Councils had set minimum rates of pay for many of Britain's lowest-earning workers. By 1993 Wages Councils covered 2.4 million people working in hairdressing, shops, hotels, catering, agriculture and clothing manufacture.

In 1994, the Low Pay Network reported on a survey of 2,000 job advertisements in forty-five Job Centres. It found that 20 per cent of jobs in hairdressing were advertised at less than the £2.88 per hour minimum previously set by the Wages Council. One vacancy offered £2.56 an hour for a stylist with a Vocational Qualification and three years' experience. A greengrocer was found to be offering £65 for an assistant working a 37-hour week. Under the Wages Councils it would have been illegal for the greengrocer to pay less than £119 a week for the same job. The most significant change in the area of low pay is likely to come about with the introduction of a National Minimum Wage. However the level this wage should take is the subject of much debate in Parliament. Opponents argue too high a figure will cost people their jobs by making it inefficient to employ them. Supporters claim companies will be able to handle the small extra cost.

In 1994, the last government's policies of flexibility and deregulation suffered a reversal when the House of Lords ruled that part-time workers must receive the same compensation for redundancies as full-time employees. Since 85 per cent of part-timers are women, the Equal Opportunities Commission (EOC) had spent four years fighting for equal rights in the courts. After losing in the High Court and the Court of Appeal, the EOC won its case when four out of five law lords agreed that discrimination against part-timers was in breach of European Union laws.

The rise of the service sector

In 1994, Charles Handy wrote that 'the servant society will be re-born, but this time it will be servant businesses, not servants; independents, not employees'. He gave three examples of areas of work that will grow, in the future, for self-employed workers in the service sector:

1 'More education will take place outside schools and universities than inside, and education uses a lot of people, be they producers of new media, software programmers, coaches, trainers or writers.'

2 'As society ages, we will take more care of our bodies and will pay for help in doing that ... The young-old will not, most of them, be poor. The over-55s will actually have more money to spend than any other category, but they will be buying time not things – time to travel, time to eat and drink, time to watch and time to play. That sort of expenditure is people-intensive.'

3 'On the other hand, the busy ones inside the organisations will be spending money to save time, on cooks and gardeners, nannies and chauffeurs.'

The extent of the recent shift in employment from the manufacturing to the service sectors of the economy can be seen in the following figures:

Employees employed in:	1971	1992
Agriculture, forestry and fishing	450,000	283,000
Energy and water supply	798,000	403,000
Other minerals and ore extraction	1,282,000	635,000
Construction	1,198,000	839,000
Transport and communication	1,556,000	1,324,000
Shrinking jobs in manufacturing:		
Metal goods, engineering and vehicles	3,709,000	2,030,000
Other manufacturing industries	3,074,000	1,924,000
Service sectors with growth in jobs:		
Distribution (shops), catering and repairs	3,686,000	4,605,000
Financial services (e.g. banking, insurance)	1,336,000	2,639,000
Other services (e.g. health, education)	5,049,000	7,076,000
All industries	22,139,000	21,758,000

(Source: *Social Trends*, 1993)

The 1980s also saw a rapid increase in self-employment. The self-employed numbered 3,212,000 in 1992 and over 60 per cent worked in services.

Part-time work and gender

The following figures show the way that women have gained most from the growth in part-time employment:

	1984	1993
Male employees:		
full-time	13,240,000	12,769,000
part-time	570,000	886,000
Female employees:		
full-time	5,422,000	6,165,000
part-time	4,343,000	5,045,000

(Source: *Social Trends*, 1994)

In 1994, the Mintel study *Men 2000* summarised trends in the following way: 'The overall effect of the changes which are coming about can be summed up as "more flexibility, less security". On the whole this less structured working environment is more suited to women than men.'

The growing underclass

The increase in numbers of those who are long-term claimants, dependent on benefits, is largely due to rising male unemployment (13.4 per cent in 1994 compared to female unemployment of 5.3 per cent). There has been a decline in male full-time employment. There has also been a decline in unskilled manual jobs. These trends have particularly hit unqualified male school-leavers and areas that have had a steep decline in traditional male jobs in manufacturing, construction and other heavy industries.

Rising male unemployment leaves some young mothers without the support of employed young fathers. Flexible labour markets may offer lone mothers part-time work during school hours. However, benefits may be more predictable than income in the insecure flexible workforce, where flexible employment practices may involve hiring and firing staff more readily than in the past.

The 1994 Policy Studies Institute report *Lone Parents and Work* noted that:

> Getting into work, paying travel costs, re-budgeting to cope with a differently structured income, all present difficulties and uncertainties. The likelihood of making such an adjustment only to be flung back on income support is a threat, especially if it involves the surrender of long-term benefits such as full payment of mortgage interest.

Conclusion

The following predictions come from the Institute of Employment Research at Warwick University:

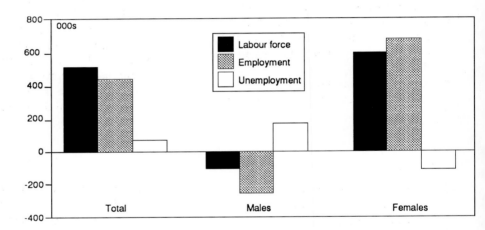

Changes in labour force, employment and unemployment, 1991–2000.

3   Dissatisfaction at work

Symptoms

In 1985, a MORI/*Sunday Times* survey found that 76 per cent of workers were 'very' or 'fairly' satisfied with their jobs. This compared with 83 per cent in 1976. All managers must be concerned with this issue because the dissatisfaction of employees can lead to any of the following consequences:

- low-quality goods with more faults due to poor workmanship;
- high labour turnover with many recruits leaving the job after a short while;

- high absenteeism with large numbers of workers off sick with 'backache';
- open industrial conflict such as strikes;
- industrial sabotage with workers 'accidentally' dropping spanners in the works of conveyor belts. The expression comes from the French word *sabot*, meaning wooden clog, because French workers threw these into machines which were taking away jobs. At the same time, 1812–14, the English 'Luddites' were destroying new textile machines for the same reason;
- each of the above can cause low productivity, meaning low output per worker.

Case study: dissatisfaction and domestic labour

The following findings are from Ann Oakley's classic 1974 survey of forty housewives with at least one child under five, *The Sociology of Housework*:

- Hours spent on housework ranged from 48 to 105 per week, with an average of 77.
- 57 per cent reported a high level of dissatisfaction with housework and 84 per cent a medium or low level of dissatisfaction.
- The housewives were more likely to experience monotony, fragmentation and loneliness in their work than the assembly-line workers in Goldthorpe *et al.*'s *Affluent Worker* studies.
- 70 per cent of the middle-class housewives disliked housework compared to 30 per cent of the working-class housewives.
- The most favoured tasks (in order) were cooking, shopping, washing, cleaning, washing up and ironing.
- Only 20 per cent of the working-class mothers said that they liked looking after their children 'very much', compared to 70 per cent of the middle-class mothers.

Activities

1 Carry out a survey of a sample of housewives designed to test some of Ann Oakley's findings.
2 Outline some arguments for and against the following development: In 1985 the Post Office employed 8,000 part-timers. They were mainly doing sorting in the evenings and 85 per cent were women. The Post Office aimed to increase the number of part-timers to 20,000 in order to cut the eight-hours-a-week average overtime of postal workers in 1985.

Alienation

To be human is to possess certain needs, such as the need to be creative, to exercise initiative and the need to achieve something worthwhile. When people's work fails to fulfil such needs we describe their working experience as one of **alienation**. Individuals who are alienated at work may feel like alien inhabitants of a world that has little meaning or purpose in relation to their needs. The four classic aspects of **alienation** at work are:

1 **powerlessness**: no control over the work that you are expected to do;
2 **meaninglessness**: unable to see any point in the product of your labour;

3 **isolation**: cut off from others;
4 **self-estrangement**: prevented from realising your full potential.

Presenteeism

Presenteeism is the opposite of absenteeism. It means putting in extra hours at work. June 21 1996 was the first national 'Go Home On Time Day'. It was organised by Parents at Work, a charity which campaigns against long working hours, saying that they damage family and personal relationships. Between 1992 and 1996 there was a jump of more than 585,000 people with a working week of more than 48 hours. By 1996, almost 30 per cent of UK employees were working more than 48 hours a week, compared to less than 10 per cent in the rest of Europe.

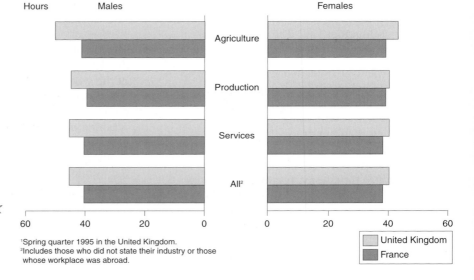

Usual weekly hours worked by full-time employees, in UK and France: by gender and sector, 1995[1]
(Source: Social Trends, *1998.)*

[1]Spring quarter 1995 in the United Kingdom.
[2]Includes those who did not state their industry or those whose workplace was abroad.

In 1996, the Gulbenkian Foundation published the results of a survey of 2,000 white collar workers, mostly women. The survey found that almost two-thirds of respondents said that they routinely work longer than their contracted hours. In busy periods, 42 per cent worked more than 50 hours a week and 27 per cent worked more than 60 hours a week. Asked why they were working such long hours, the pattern of reasons was:

- 96 per cent: 'pressure of workload';
- 55 per cent: 'workplace culture';
- 35 per cent: 'direct pressure from management';
- 18 per cent: 'fear of losing job'.

Among the effects of working overlong hours:

- 64 per cent said that they did not see enough of their children;
- 72 per cent of working mothers said that they were exhausted at the end of the day;
- 20 per cent said that the pressure put a strain on their marriage.

A similar 1996 survey of fathers, by the Family Policy Studies Centre, found that 'more than one in four fathers worked 50 hours a week or more, and those who did so were less involved in family activities'. One in 10 fathers worked 60 hours or more a week. Two-thirds sometimes worked in the evenings and 60 per cent sometimes at weekends.

Overwork can clearly lead to tiredness. The slogan of the campaign to cut working hours is 'less excessive, more effective'. We work better if we are fresh rather than tired. Shattered people are more likely to make mistakes. Human fatigue has contributed to a number of catastrophies in recent years, including the US space shuttle *Challenger* crash and the Clapham Junction railway crash. Several of the most notorious man-made disasters have occurred in the last few hours before dawn, when even the most practised night worker has trouble staying awake. These include the *Exxon Valdez* oil spill, the explosion at the Bhopal chemical works (India) and the nuclear leaks at Three Mile Island (USA) and Chernobyl (Russia).

Stress

Overwork can also lead to stress. Stress becomes a medical problem when it is experienced as an intolerable pressure that causes both serious physical and mental problems. In a 1996 survey by the Industrial Society, more than half of the UK's top 700 companies said that stress levels have increased during the past 3 years. The following related factors have contributed to the increase in occupational stress:

1   Weaker trade unions are less able to protect the working conditions of employees.
2   Workers feel more insecure and vulnerable to losing their jobs.
3   Stronger, more aggressive managements demand more flexibility in hours and tasks.
4   Employers also demand that staff work harder, faster and more productively.

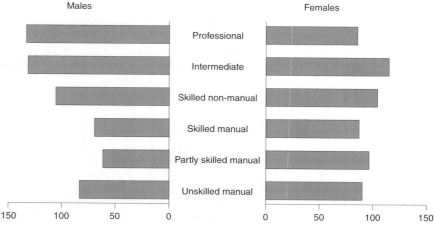

Adults[1] who had experienced high stress levels: by gender and social class of head of household, 1993. A ratio of more than 100 indicates a greater likelihood of suffering stress.
(Source: Social Trends, 1996.)

[1]Aged 16 and over.

In 1996, a third of Britain's workforce was employed in 'flexible work' (part-time, temporary or contract work). By the year 2000, almost half of all workers may be in these insecure types of work. As a consequence of these factors, many employees find that, despite working long hours, they have insufficient time to complete all the tasks related to their job. They may also find themselves without any opportunity to express complaints or exercise influence over the running of their workplace. Added to this, for many workers recognition or reward for good job performance is often not forthcoming, whilst criticism for mistakes always is.

These circumstances produce not only deep dissatisfaction with work, but also a hopeless feeling that one cannot cope with work. There are many symptoms of stress, such as tiredness and irritability, loss of sense of humour and inability to concentrate, excessive use of alcohol and tobacco, irritable bowel syndrome and eating disorders, insomnia and depression, and nervous breakdown.

Among the effects on businesses are decreased productivity, high staff turnover and absenteeism. Each year 24 million days are lost due to stress-related problems, at a cost to employers of some £1.3 billion. The TUC has said that stress from work is the most serious health hazard facing the British workforce. Government figures suggest that £16 billion a year is lost through work-related accidents and illness.

Intrinsic and extrinsic satisfaction at work

Three main motives for working have been suggested. First, some are influenced by the **Protestant work ethic**, a religious tradition which says that we should lead sober, devout and hard-working lives to gain our rewards

In 1998, Shaun Dent returned from work at 7 p.m. and Hannah Marie Dent left at 9 p.m. for her night shift at the Scunthorpe Golden Wonder factory.

in the 'next life'. Some people are still influenced by this centuries-old theory in that they believe that it is *right* to work hard and *wrong* not to work, even if they don't need to work.

Second, some jobs allow people to express themselves; they offer the **intrinsic satisfactions** of interest and involvement; they are meaningful or sociable. These might include the work of skilled craftsmen, such as stonemasons, or the 'caring professions', such as nursing or teaching.

Third, many people see work as an instrument or a means to an end rather than as an end in itself. The objective is usually to earn as high a wage as possible. This **instrumental orientation** to work might mean that a worker's main satisfactions from work are **extrinsic** to, or outside, the job itself. Such extrinsic factors are the contractual conditions of a job: the pay, the hours, the holidays and the pension scheme.

Many of the suggested cures for dissatisfaction at work aim to give employees more involvement, interest and responsibility – in other words to increase the amount of intrinsic, rather than merely extrinsic, satisfaction.

Activity

Interview six working adults about their jobs. Ask them the following questions:

(a) What is your occupation?
(b) How do you usually spend your working day?
(c) What are the three best aspects of your work?
(d) What are the three worst aspects of your work?
(e) How could your job be improved?
(f) What job would you like to be doing in ten years' time?
(g) What job do you expect to be doing in ten years' time?

---

4   Trade unions

It was when I got interested in the union, that's when my life took off. It changed my life, it became my life. What excited me? Well, it was the thought of the workers taking part in their lives, workers having a say, the idea that you'd got the right to argue with the gaffer. I felt the blokes weren't going to go back to the old days, they were going to have their say.

(A Coventry car worker who took early retirement at the end of the 1970s, quoted in *Wigan Pier Revisited* by Beatrix Campbell)

Trade unions aim to provide a voice for employees in a number of different ways. Some of the ways in which they represent their members' interests are mentioned below.

Reasons given for belonging to a trade union, 1989

	Very/fairly important	Not important/does not apply to me
To protect me if problems come up	93%	6%
To get better pay and working conditions	80%	20%
To get members' benefits	71%	29%
To help other people I work with	76%	23%
I believe in them in principle	67%	33%
Most of my colleagues are members	55%	45%
It's a condition of having my job	38%	62%
It's a tradition in my family	15%	84%

(Source: *Social Trends*, 1993)

The four main benefits of trade union membership

1   Collective bargaining for better pay and working conditions   As well as higher wages and safer, cleaner workplaces, unions press for a shorter working week, longer holidays and better sickness, maternity and pension schemes. In order to press such claims, union members can take a number of forms of **industrial action**. These include the all-out withdrawal of labour, or strike action; the go-slow; the overtime ban; and the work-to-rule (for example, teachers refusing to supervise pupils at lunchtimes because it is not ruled in their contract).

Other weapons used by trade unions are:

- The **closed shop**: a workplace where all employees must belong to the union.
- The **picket line**: a group of strikers demonstrating outside a workplace. They might be trying to persuade non-strikers ('strikebreakers' or 'scabs') to join them. Or they might be aiming to get lorry-drivers to 'black' the firm by turning away without making deliveries.

In 1996, 320 Magnet Kitchens workers were sacked for striking for a 3 per cent wage rise. After more than a year of round-the-clock picketing at the Darlington factory, they picketed the mansion of one of the bosses and then accepted £8,500 compensation each in 1998.

A union can also call on the support of other unions through the Trades Union Congress (TUC). Most unions belong to this organisation which, for example, can channel funds to a union that faces a crisis. (The employers' equivalent institution is the Confederation of British Industry, or CBI.)

The strength of a union in a particular factory or office often depends partly on the energy of the worker who is elected by members to be their **shop steward**. This local leader has to recruit members, collect subscriptions, distribute union information, take up grievances with the management and call meetings.

2　Legal and financial assistance　Unions originally developed from **friendly societies** which offered payments to members if they were off work due to sickness. The main form of support now is **sustentation** while on strike. Since 1980 the government has cut social security payments to strikers on the assumption that they will get some strike pay from their union. In 1984–85 many miners held out on strike against pit closures for over a year even though (a) the National Union of Miners was unable to afford strike pay and (b) the government still made deductions from their supplementary benefit payments.

3　Courses and training　An example of the eduational role of the unions can be found during the 1974–79 period when the Labour Government passed a number of laws for which the unions had long campaigned. These included the Sex Discrimination Act, the Health and

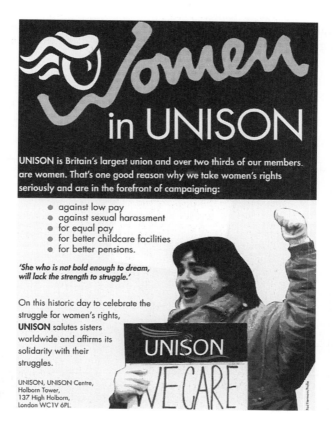

This advertisement appeared in newspapers on International Women's Day in 1994.

Safety at Work Act and the Redundancy Payments Act. The unions held
numerous conferences and courses, as well as distributing many thousands
of booklets, in order to educate their members about their new legal rights.

4   Research and government policy   Unions are not only concerned
with issues that directly affect their members at work, such as the dangers
of asbestos. They also campaign on more general issues such as
unemployment, nuclear disarmament and better schools and hospitals. The
Labour Party is largely paid for by the unions and the unions have a large
share of the votes at Labour Party Conferences. At these conferences, trade
union delegates propose many of the resolutions which may become
Labour Party policy.

Case study: the 24-hour union

After round-the-clock banking and shopping,
the 24-hour trade union arrived in 1998 for the
300,000 members of the Royal College of
Nursing (RCN). After raising subscriptions from
£98 to £114 per year, members were offered
RCN Direct, a helpline offering advice and
information at any time of the day or night.
RCN Direct is based in Cardiff where a team of
30 telephone advisers answers queries on
employment, professional and legal issues. The
Transport and General Workers' Union has a
24-hour telephone legal advice service called
T & G Care Express.

Some see a clear contrast between the
characteristics of old-style and new-style trade
unionism:

Old-style unionism	*New-style unionism*
Branch meetings	24-hour helpline
Union card	PIN number
Sickness pay	Financial services
Workers education	Professional development
Strikes	Lobbying

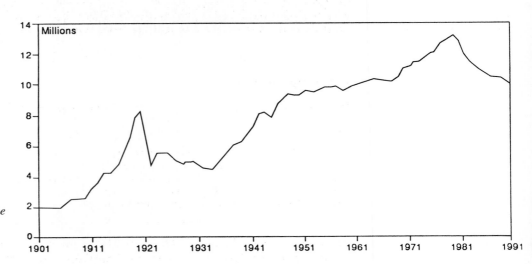

Trade union membership in the UK. (Source: Social Trends, 1993.)

Rates of trade union membership, 1996 (percentages)

All employees	31
Women in professional occupations	63
Men in professional occupations	44
Health, education, public administration	52
Transport and communication	47
Manufacturing	31
Construction	25
Banking, finance, insurance	21
Women in sales occupations	12
Men in sales occupations	10
Farming and fishing	9

Nurses protesting outside Guy's Hospital in 1994.

Industrial disputes

Number of working days lost due to labour disputes, 1926–96

Year	
1926	160 million (year of the General Strike)
1972	24 million (45 per cent due to a miners' strike)
1979	29 million (just over half due to engineering workers' strike)
1984	27 million (over 80 per cent due to miners' strike)
1996	1.3 million (the highest level since 1990)

In the recession of the early 1990s redundancy issues were one of the main causes of strikes. Lay-offs of unwanted workers caused strikes involving

60 per cent of all lost working days in 1993. As the economy recovered, disputes centred more on pay: 82 per cent of all working days lost in 1996 were as a result of pay disputes.

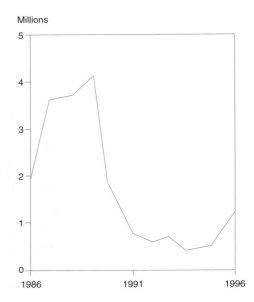

Working days lost in strikes
(*Source:* Social Trends, *1998.*)

Case study: a strike over working on Sunday

In 1993, 4 million workers (16 per cent of employees) were involved in working unsocial hours on shift work, at weekends or on night shifts. In 1994, there was a 24-hour strike of shift workers among the 1,500 employees at Tesco's giant distribution centre near Northampton.

Management was demanding that shift workers put in at least three Sundays out of every seven Sundays (and work four out of seven to get overtime). Representatives of the Union of Shop Distributive and Allied Workers said that workers, who earned £4.23 an hour, had been repeatedly assured that Sunday working would not be introduced.

One warehouse worker with three primary-school-age children said: 'I have been told I will get Mondays and Tuesdays off instead. But the children are at school then. On Sundays we often go fishing or to speedway matches as a family. I will not get to see my kids if this goes through.'

Conclusion

In 1994, a Policy Studies Institute survey looked at the evolution of worker-management relations. If modern companies like to dispense with trade unions, do they do more to involve their workers? The report's gloomy conclusion was that we are:

moving towards a situation in which non-managerial employees are treated as a 'factor of production'. Britain is approaching the position where few employees have any mechanism through which they can contribute to the operation of their workplace in a broader context than that of their own job ... The recent growth in inequality in wages and earnings ... is being matched by a widening in the inequalities of influence and access to key decisions about work and employment.

In 1994, the RSA interim report from its inquiry on *Tomorrow's Company* criticised British industry's 'heavy emphasis on adversarial transactions', with an atmosphere of confrontation and conflict between bosses and workers. The report commended the Japanese practice of building 'long-term trust relationships' and quoted haunting words from a speech by the Japanese industrialist Konoke Matsushita to American businessmen in 1979:

We are going to win and the industrialised West is going to lose out. There is nothing you can do about it because the reasons for your failure are within yourselves. With your bosses doing the thinking while the workers wield the screwdrivers, you are convinced deep down that this is the right way to do business. For you the essence of management is getting the ideas out of the heads of the bosses and into the hands of labour ... For us the core of management is the art of mobilising and putting together the intellectual resources of all employees in the service of the firm.

The extent of worker participation or democracy at work is very limited in Britain. Unions are mainly only able to exercise negative power, such as blocking the demands of employers, rather than positive power, such as contributing to company policies. The 1979 TUC Report called *Employment and Technology* contained many positive ideas. It predicted that new technology will mean far fewer jobs and proposed that these be shared out among as many workers as possible by giving priority to:

- a shorter working week;
- longer holidays;
- earlier retirement;
- a reduction in systematic overtime;
- more provision for **sabbatical leave**, such as taking a year off for retraining.

These proposals would give more jobs to more people and would create more leisure for all workers. The rest of this chapter looks at the two related topics of leisure and unemployment.

Activities

Interview six adults about trade union membership. If they belong to a union, ask how much it costs them and what benefits do they get for their subscription. If they do not belong, ask them why not. In all cases ask for their general views about trade unions: 'Do unions have too much power?'

A rally organised by the TUC in 1994.

5   Work, non-work and unemployment

What is work?

Since 1965 Jimmy Savile, the disc jockey, has worked as a voluntary porter at the Stoke Mandeville Spinal Injuries. In the early 1980s, he raised £10 million from public donations to rebuild the Unit. He has his own room there so that he can work from 10 a.m. to 3 p.m. on the five days he spends there every fortnight.

Most people need to use some portion of their spare time on housework such as washing dishes or ironing shirts. In 1980, British households spent the following amounts on **self-provisioning**, that is on products to be used for work in and around the home:

Home decorating products	£1,035 million
Products for car maintenance	£950 million
Tools and wood products	£890 million
Gardening equipment	£600 million
DIY repairs and improvements products	£325 million

All these sorts of work (voluntary work, housework and self-provisioning) are, however, 'non-work' if we define work as time spent earning a living, time that has been sold to an employer and so is no longer our own to do with as we like.

Rock star Bob Geldof takes a standing nap after Live Aid at Wembley in July 1985. It was the world's biggest ever rock concert, seen by 1.5 billion people in 160 countries, and raised millions of pounds for famine relief in Africa. Geldof had worked continuously, and voluntarily, for four months to mastermind the project.

Cricket hero Ian Botham walked the length of Britain, from John O'Groats to Land's End, in November 1985. His purpose was to raise a million pounds for leukaemia research.

The psychological meaning of work

In *The Forsaken Families: The Effects of Unemployment on Family Life*, L. Fagin and M. Little have listed the following seven positive aspects of work:

1 Work as a source of identity When adults meet for the first time at a party, one of the first questions is 'What do you do (for a living)?' A bricklayer or a doctor is defined in many people's eyes by the job that he or she does.

2　Work as a source of relationships outside the nuclear family　One wife in their survey said of her unemployed husband: 'What got me was that him being at home, he didn't see no one, we had nothing to talk about after tea.'

3　Work as a source of obligatory activity　An unemployed person lacks the routine of a worker who is obliged to pursue regular and purposeful activities. Unemployed people lose a framework that regulates how they spend their time.

4　Work as an opportunity to develop skills and creativity　Apart from simple, dead-end jobs, most occupations give workers the chance to learn new skills and to create new ways of carrying out tasks.

5　Work as a factor that structures psychological time　Fagin and Little's study found that unemployed men spent more time in bed but felt more tired than when they were at work.

6　Work as a sense of purpose　Fagin and Little were told: 'I'm surplus to requirements'; 'I'm marginal, a nobody, and nobody gives a bugger'; 'I'm on the scrapheap at fifty-five, with a lot of working life in me yet'.

7　Work as a source of income and control　Many workers only earn poverty wages and so are below the 'breadline', but most people who earn a living find that income from working provides independence and freedom of choice – for example in how to spend leisure time.

There is an old Haitian proverb that says: 'If work were a good thing, the rich would have found a way of keeping it to themselves.' It is true that many people have jobs that are boring or stressful, dirty or dangerous. But surveys have found that less than 10 per cent of workers who lose their jobs report an improvement in their mental or physical health. Most suffer a deterioration.

Unemployment figures

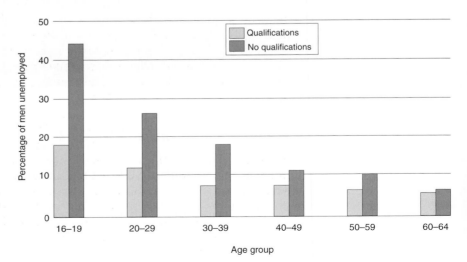

Percentage of men unemployed: by age and qualifications, Great Britain, 1994
(Source: 'Living in Britain, 1994', General Household Survey.)

A CAREER AS A CHEF, HOUSEKEEPER, CONCIERGE OR...

Mark
I enjoy cookin...
and this has
helped to sta...
my career
prospects.

Joh...
It gave...
opportu...
get h...

Doris
This programme
built up my
confidence about

Chancellor Gordon Brown launching the New Deal national network of training centres for young people entering the hotel, catering and leisure industry, in 1998.

The effects of unemployment

Someone who loses their job usually goes through a number of phases: first, shock; second, refusal to accept the situation and even optimism; third, anxiety and longing for the past; finally, resignation and adjustment. These phases are similar to the process of mourning the death of a close relative or friend.

In his study of *White Collar Unemployment: Impact and Stress*, S. Finneman found that all those he surveyed 'felt a stigma in being unemployed. It was associated with considerable shame, degradation and inferiority.' Those who sought in vain for jobs suffered desperation and despair, chronic self-doubts and anxiety. Some found new jobs but felt unsuited to them, mainly because they had to accept a drop in pay and status. 'Their stress, strain and self-esteem were worse than when they were unemployed.'

The most common consequences of unemployment are poverty and cigarette and alcohol abuse. These in turn contribute to a deterioration in health. M. Harris also found the following patterns from different studies of the unemployed: 'They are up to 19 times more likely to attempt suicide. They are six times more likely to batter their children and twice as likely to get divorced.' Also, '40 per cent of the people appearing before English courts describe themselves as unemployed' (from 'How Unemployment Affects People', *New Society*, 19 January 1984).

Social Change and the Experience of Unemployment (1994), based on 6,000 interviews with employed and unemployed people, paints a picture of poor psychological health among the unemployed. They were more likely to be depressed, less likely to mix with people in work and had little access to social support. Richard Lampard pointed firmly to the conclusion that unemployment directly increases the risk of marriage break-up. The chances of an unemployed person's marriage ending in the following year were found to be 70 per cent higher than those of a person who had never been out of work.

6   Patterns of leisure

The separation of work and leisure

In pre-industrial Britain the line between work and leisure was not so sharply drawn as it is today. When work was carried on in the home, people had greater freedom to choose when to work and when to relax. Also, work and leisure were more integrated. For example, going to a fair was both an opportunity to trade and a chance to enjoy games and good company. Another example is the use of taverns in pre-industrial times; people went to taverns not only for entertainment but also for business reasons such as making and repaying loans.

Industrialisation led not only to a separation of home and work but also to a separation between work and leisure. Work for many became an activity that took place outside the home in factories, shops and offices. It became an activity over which the ordinary worker had little control. The employers regulated the beginning and end of the working day, the breaks in between and the number of working days per week and year.

Case study: leisure patterns in early retirement

One definition of leisure is that it is **discretionary time**, spare time which can be used at your own discretion for rest, recreation or self-development. Ann McGoldrick has studied 1,800 men who took early retirement and divided them into nine categories according to how they used their spare time:

1   'Rest and relaxers': content to read papers, watch TV and do some gardening and walking.
2   'Home and family men': enjoyed looking after and helping in the home.
3   'Good timers': chose social life, travel and evenings out.
4   'Committee and society men': 24 per cent devoted time to positions such as treasurer of a sports club.
5   'Volunteers': 19 per cent helped charities or friends and neighbours.
6   'Hobbyists': many concentrated on pastimes such as birdwatching, golf, music or fishing.
7   'Further education men': 9 per cent enrolled in courses such as those of the Open University.
8   'Part-time jobbers': 24 per cent got part-time jobs.
9   'New jobbers': one had started a new, 'easy job' – he closed his new business down for each cricket season.

Activities

1   Describe which of the nine options above are available to young people who are unemployed. In what other ways can they usefully spend their time?

2   If you were offered an average yearly income for the rest of your life, on condition that you never took up paid employment, would you accept the offer? Give reasons for your answer.

A teacher marking books at home: some people's work extends into their leisure time.

The effects of work on leisure: opposition and extension patterns

Three contrasting ways that a person's type of job can influence leisure have been described. **Opposition-type leisure** has been found among workers with dangerous and hard jobs such as steelworkers, miners and trawlermen. Among these male-dominated occupations the worlds of work and leisure are both men's worlds. The loyalties needed for teamwork during the day are carried over into the friendships of the male drinking groups in the evening. And the main leisure activity, drinking in pubs and working men's clubs, is done to relax and forget about the strains of work. Such escapist leisure is in contrast, or opposition, to work.

At the other extreme, professional gardeners may spend their evenings and weekends digging their own gardens and many teachers spend their spare time marking books or organising clubs and outings for pupils. In both of these cases work extends into leisure. Workers in the City of London who are involved in their jobs and get intrinsic satisfaction from their work might spend their spare time reading *The Financial Times*. Their leisure is then an **extension** of their work.

A third possibility is that people such as office workers may be fairly indifferent to their work and their work may have little effect on their leisure. This has been called **neutrality-type leisure**.

How do we spend our leisure hours?

The following figures show that class, age and sex all have a bearing on the way that individuals spend their leisure time:

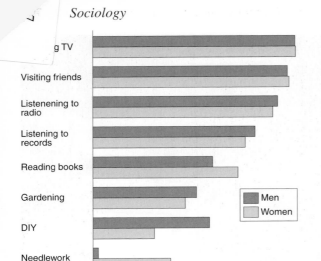

Participation in selected leisure activities in the 4 weeks before interview: by gender, Great Britain, 1993 (Source: General Household Survey, 1993.)

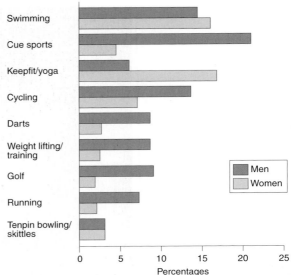

Participation in sport in the 4 weeks before interview: by gender, Great Britain, 1993 (Source: General Household Survey, 1993.)

Participation in sport by women, 1990

		Percentage engaging in each activity in the twelve months before interview	
	Professional	*Intermediate and junior non-manual*	*Unskilled manual*
Swimming	70	48	21
Keep fit/yoga	42	33	13
Skiing	20	3	0
Badminton	16	9	2
Tennis	14	6	1
Golf	10	7	2
Horse riding	9	4	0

(Source: *General Household Survey*, 1990)

The Saracens' captain during the 1998 women's rugby cup final.

'Top six' sports by gender and age, Great Britain, 1993

Persons aged 16 and over

Rank order for the percentage of men or women participating in the activity in the 4 weeks before interview

Aged 16–19	Aged 25–29	Aged 45–59	Aged 70+
Men			
Snooker/pool/billiards	Walking	Walking	Walking
Walking	Snooker/pool/billiards	Snooker/pool/billiards	Cycling
Soccer	Cycling	Swimming	Bowls
Cycling	Swimming	Cycling	Golf
Weight lifting/training	Weight lifting/training	Golf	Keep fit/yoga
Swimming	Soccer	Darts	Snooker/pool/billiards
Women			
Walking	Walking	Walking	Walking
Keep fit/yoga	Keep fit/yoga	Swimming	Keep fit/yoga
Swimming	Swimming	Keep fit/yoga	Swimming
Snooker/pool/billiards	Cycling	Cycling	Cycling
Cycling	Snooker/pool/billiards	Golf	Bowls
Running	Tenpin bowls/skittles	Darts	Golf

(Source: *General Household Survey*, 1993)

One in eight football supporters is female.

Time use in a typical week, 1985

Weekly hours spend on:	Full-time employees		Housewives	Retired people
	Males	Females		
Employment and travel	45	41	–	–
Essential activities	33	45	77	50
Sleep	56	57	59	60
Free time	33	25	32	58
Free time per weekday	3	2	4	8
Free time per weekend day	10	7	6	9

(Source: *Social Trends*, 1986)

On average, women who work full-time have less free time than men because they spend more time on essential activities such as housework, essential shopping and child care. (Eating, washing, getting up and going to bed are counted as 'personal care' and are also essential activities rather than free time.)

Activities

1   Ask two adults how many hours they spend each week on major categories of activity such as eating, travelling, active and passive leisure (for example, participating or spectating). Compare their figures with an analysis of your own typical week.

2   Select four of the following possible trends and in each case explain why you would, or would not, welcome them:

- an increase in the proportion of people who change careers during the course of their working lives;
- an increase in the proportion of mothers returning to full-time work while their children are still toddlers;
- increasing automation of production processes; for example, in bakeries and biscuit factories;
- increasing automation of service industries such as banking and petrol retailing;
- a polarisation of the workforce into core or periphery workers;
- more widespread shiftwork;
- more widespread home-working;
- more widrespread flexi-time working;
- more widespread non-strike agreements between trade unions and management;
- a shorter working week and a shorter working life.

Work and leisure in the era of the telecommunications superhighway

In 1994, it was predicted that our living rooms would soon be dominated by a 'smart box' consisting of interactive television, computer and VCR, with a credit-card swipe for home shopping and purchasing movies. It would be linked with the outside world via satellite, modems to telephone lines and fibreoptic cable to the information superhighway.

It was predicted this smart box will:

- take you shopping: 'walk' down the on-screen images of aisles in shops, clicking with the mouse on whatever you want delivered;
- take you to the rest of the 'electro-mall': visit fast-food outlets, your bank, travel agent and doctor;
- educate your children: via access to vast libraries and the bulletin boards of networks like Internet;
- entertain you: all the latest games, music and films plus interactive TV which allows you to choose the camera angles and replays at sports events;
- allow telecommuting by on-line employees from their 'electronic cottages': using fax machines and teleconferencing.

Will we become couch-potatoes? Will we be able to spend more time with our families and less time stuck in traffic jams? Will there be a growing divide between a technological elite, communicating across the globe, and a disenfranchised, unplugged underclass denied access to cyberspace?

An American trend-predicting company, called Brain Reserve, has forecast the following:

- cocooning: more home-based leisure;
- burrowing: work and schooling also based in the home;
- clanning: friends moving into enclave communities, isolated by electronic surveillance security systems.

GCSE question from Southern Examining Group 1997

Why might the experience of leisure time for unemployed 18 year olds differ from that of retired 65 year olds?   (10)

CHAPTER 17

Research methods

Participant observers may not find it easy to fit in.

1 Doing scientific research

A typical piece of scientific research involves six stages. Let us take as an example two botanists who are interested in the effects of light on plant growth:

1 Observation   The botanists notice that beans that germinate in a cupboard, with very little light, grow into tall, pale and weak plants.

2 Hypothesis   Our scientists then put forward a proposition to be tested. Their theory is that extra light can improve plant growth.

3 Selection of methods   Two groups of bean plants are grown in similar conditions, with the same amounts of water, except that one group is left on a windowsill with sun-lamps above them which are turned on at night. The other group is a **control group**, growing on a similar windowsill but without any sun-lamps.

4 Collecting data   The growth of the plants is systematically observed. Measurements are taken daily.

5 Analysing and interpreting data   From the information that they have recorded, our botanists try to establish how far the **dependent variable** (sturdy growth) is influenced by the **independent variable** which has been altered (extra light under the lamps).

6 Making conclusions   In the report of their experiment, they might claim to have proved that too much light is harmful to young bean plants.

The problem of objectivity

In conducting research, scientists try to follow two general rules:

1   Researchers should use standard scales of measurement and should describe their methods fully. This allows others to test their findings by repeating their research.

2   Researchers should remain unbiased and objective. Being objective involves not taking sides and not making judgements as to whether what one has observed is good or bad. It also involves not allowing personal values and preferences to influence the conclusions of one's research.

If sociologists were alien beings it would be relatively easy for them to remain **objective** while studying human society. But sociologists are, of course, very much part of the social world that they are studying. This makes it difficult for them to maintain an objective, neutral stance. Like everyone else, sociologists have their own particular beliefs, moral preferences and political opinions which can all too easily affect their research.

Total objectivity is an impossibility and it cannot be obtained by any discipline. But a high degree of objectivity can be achieved if certain habits of mind are adopted:

1   Patience is needed so that the sociologist will take the time to consider all of the evidence.
2   Open-mindedness is needed so that the sociologist is receptive to different viewpoints and interpretations.
3   The sociologist needs to be reasonable and only prepared to offer explanations that are based on the evidence.

2   Conducting a survey

The **survey** is a method that sociologists frequently use to collect evidence. It plays a similar part in sociology to the part played by the laboratory experiment in the natural sciences. A survey about pupils and smoking is a typical piece of research that might be carried out by some sociology students. Like researchers in the natural sciences, such as biology or physics, the social science students would follow the same six stages of research:

1   Observation   They notice that fewer 14- and 15-year-old girls take part in sports than boys. It also seems that more female pupils take up the habit of smoking in Years 10 and 11 at secondary school.

2   Hypothesis   Our researchers may test the proposition that active teenage sports enthusiasts are more likely to be non-smokers and male.

3   Selection of methods   It might be decided to interview some pupils from Years 10 and 11.

4   Collecting data   A sample of pupils are interviewed using a standard schedule of questions.

5   Analysing and interpreting data   The answers show whether there is a correlation, or connection, between smoking and gender. There may be a significant difference between the proportions of males and females who smoke.

6   Making conclusions   It might be clear that fewer girls take part in sports and that these same girls are more likely to smoke.

Choosing a sample

It is important that the sample of pupils from Years 10 and 11 chosen for the survey is a **representative cross-section** of *all* pupils from Years 10 and 11. If general conclusions about a group under study are drawn from findings about an unrepresentative sample, then we cannot be sure that these generalisations are accurate.

How can we try to make sure that those selected for the sample are typical? First, the **survey population** must be defined and, second, a **sampling frame**, or list of the survey population, must be drawn up. In our case, the survey population is all pupils from Years 10 and 11 in our school and a suitable sampling frame could be compiled using up-to-date form registers. We can now choose between three sampling procedures:

1   A systematic, or quasi-random, sample   If we want to select a 20 per cent sample, then all we have to do is take every fifth name on the list of all pupils from Years 10 and 11.

2   A random sample   In a truly random sample everyone listed on the sampling frame has an equal chance of selection. We can ensure this by picking the names out of a hat or by numbering the list and then getting a computer to select numbers at random. If there are 200 pupils in Year 10 and 200 in Year 11, then we take the first eighty random numbers in order to get a 20 per cent sample.

3   A stratified random sample   We are interested in comparing boys and girls and we might also want to ensure equal numbers of Year 10 and Year 11 pupils. In this case we would stratify, or layer, the survey population into four separate sampling frames: for example 100 Year 10 girls, 100 Year 11 girls, 100 Year 10 boys and 100 Year 11 boys. We then select twenty names at random from each group to get our 20 per cent overall sample. A stratified sample reflects accurately the major characteristics, such as age and gender, of the survey population.

Having selected a sample of pupils from Years 10 and 11, information can be collected from each pupil using a number of different methods. Each method has its weaknesses as well as its strengths.

Collecting information by using interviews

●   **Structured interviews**   In a structured interview all those who are interviewed, the **respondents**, are asked the same questions in the same order. The main advantage of this method is that the interviews can easily by repeated by others in order to verify the results. This is because the

Pupils conducting interviews.

interviews are standardised and the role of the interviewer is kept to a minimum.

The chief disadvantage of structured interviews is that they can only yield limited, superficial information. The respondent has little opportunity to give information that may be useful but is not prompted by the questions.

● **Unstructured interviews**   An unstructured interview is more like an informal, relaxed discussion. Rather than use a list of fixed questions, the interviewer might hope to raise a number of topics, in any order, during a fairly natural conversation. Since the questions are not imposed on the respondent, the interview may reveal what he or she actually thinks. This type of interview therefore allows the interviewer to probe beneath the surface and acquire deeper knowledge than can be gained in a formal, structured interview.

The main problem with this type of interview is that because it is unstructured and personal, the information gained from it cannot be easily checked by others. That is, the interview cannot be precisely duplicated.

● **Interviewer bias**   A major problem with both types of interview is that of interviewer bias. This occurs if the interviewer influences the answers of respondents. The age, sex, class, race or other aspects of the accent or appearance of the interviewer may influence respondents so that they give answers that are not genuine.

The problem of interviewer bias can be minimised by the use of trained and skilled interviewers. But interviews remain artificial situations. If the respondent does not act 'typically' then the findings of the interview may be unreliable.

Collecting information by using self-completion questionnaires

This method asks respondents to fill in their answers to printed lists of questions. The questions may be 'closed' or 'open-ended':

- **Closed questions**   A closed question allows only a limited response. For example, the question 'Do you like to take part in sporting activities?' might only allow respondents to answer 'yes', 'no' or 'don't know'. An example of a pre-coded question is: 'How many cigarettes do you usually smoke each week? (Please tick a, b, c, d, or e.)

(a) none   (b) less than 20   (c) 20 to 40   (d) 41 to 60   (e) more than 60'

The answers to such questions may be easily analysed by computers.

- **Open questions**   A wide-ranging discussion may be invited by an open-ended question such as 'Why did you take up smoking?' If the response to this type of question is likely to be a ten-minute-long answer, then a tape-recorder may be used. Unstructured interviews generally employ open questions.

Self-completion questionnaires are likely to be cheaper and faster than using interviewers. Postal questionnaires allow coverage of a wide geographical area. And the information from questionnaires with closed questions may easily be quantifiable so that it can be presented in figures and percentages.

- **The problem of response rates**   A major problem with self-completion questionnaires is that a large number of respondents may not fill them in and return them. If there is a **low response rate**, then those who have completed the questionnaire may not be truly representative of the sample as a whole.

- **Loaded questions**   Questions should not contain any bias. For example, the following question was asked in an opinion poll of black South Africans in 1986: 'President Botha is totally opposed to the imposition of economic sanctions by other countries. Are you in favour of such sanctions?' The majority answered 'no'. Many were probably influenced by the wording of the question.

- **Pilot surveys**   Another problem in composing a questionnaire is that of ensuring that the questions are clear and likely to elicit the information required. Investigators often try to overcome this problem by conducting a small-scale pilot, or test, survey. Weak and ambiguous questions may then be altered before the main survey is conducted. A further measure, which is used by the census survey, is to collect self-completion questionnaires and check them through on the doorstep so that any misunderstood questions can be explained.

Overall problems of using surveys

There are two main problems that all surveys face:

1 Reliability This refers to whether a survey is representative, whether its findings are dependable and not distorted by the researcher. A survey is reliable if its findings are confirmed when others repeat it.

2 Validity Research is valid if it gives a true picture of social reality.

Quantitative research, such as self-completion questionnaires, tends to have more reliability than validity. A survey may yield a vast quantity of data but it may fail to give a true and valid account. Quantitative surveys tend to impose the sociologists' views of what is important on the world of those being surveyed and thereby fail to understand people's lives.

For example, a questionnaire or structured interview investigating football hooliganism might concentrate on questions about the amount of alcohol that fans drink, ignoring the role of the police or the point of view of the fans themselves. Unstructured interviews and participant observation, such as Peter Marsh's research at Oxford United, have revealed that the behaviour of fans is informally organised by a complexity of rules and roles.

Aggression among football fans may be seen as a ritual which allows young men to gain status which compensates for their failure at school and the way that they are denied dignity in employment. Those who establish reputations as violent leaders may be grateful that the traditions of the ritualised confrontations, and the control exercised by other fans, usually restrains them from inflicting or incurring injury. This delicately balanced control, which is exercised by the crowd, may be quickly undermined if the police over-react to the threatening displays of rival fans.

The informal rules that govern such ritual behaviour may be invisible to outsiders so that they can only be uncovered by careful participant observation. This method, which gives the 'feel' of complex social situations, may be called **qualitative** research. The problem of this type of research is that its findings are difficult to check and it therefore lacks reliability.

3   Some examples of different types of survey

An in-depth survey

The book entitled *From Here to Maternity: Becoming A Mother*, by Ann Oakley, describes a research project conducted between 1974 and 1976. Oakley first spent six months as an observer in a London hospital. She then selected a sample of sixty-six women who were expecting their first babies and attending the hospital. Fifty-four of these were interviewed on four occasions: twenty-six weeks and six weeks before delivery as well as five and twenty weeks afterwards. All interviews were tape-recorded and they lasted an average of 2.36 hours each. Oakley also observed six of the births.

Case study: the sample used by the 'Breadline Britain' survey

The fieldwork was carried out in February 1983 with a quota sample of 1,174 people from throughout Britain ... The sample was designed, first, to enable a view representative of the population as a whole to be gained and, second, to ensure that a sub-group of the poor was large enough to enable their living standards to be examined. The first of these aims has been achieved. The checkbacks made on the weighted sample as a whole – whether on, for example, age of the respondents or housing tenure – show that the sample is in line with Britain's population profile. The survey's findings that refer to the sample as a whole can be taken to be representative of the adult population of Britain.

The second aim was more difficult to achieve within the cost constraints of the survey ... the analysis of the living standards of the poor is based on a sub-group of about 200 households ...

It was decided to use the ACORN sampling method to produce a sample of some 200 poor households. ACORN (A Classification Of Residential Neighbourhoods) is an analysis of the social characteristics of small areas throughout Great Britain ... For the purposes of the Breadline Britain survey, the oversampling was confined to three ACORN groups: urban areas with local authority housing, areas with most overcrowding, and low-income areas with immigrants ... Although ACORN sampling does have various disadvantages, it controls fieldwork tightly – unlike conventional quota sampling, which allows a fair amount of interviewer choice – and can be used for sampling purposes.

(*Poor Britain* by Joanna Mack and Stewart Lansley)

Data-response exercise: the 'Breadline Britain' sample

1 (a) How many people were surveyed in the overall quota sample?
   (b) How large was the sub-group of poor households?
2 Why was it difficult to examine thoroughly the living standards of the poor?
3 How was the overall quota sample checked to ensure that it was representative of the total population?
4 Why is ACORN sampling better than conventional quota sampling?
5 Which three types of residential neighbourhoods provided the areas for the extra sub-sample of poor households?

Market research: a quota sample

If a brewery wants to find out whether a 'special offer' of free cigars might help sell more beer, then they might hire a **market research** company. Interviewers might be sent out to twenty different shopping centres around the country to ask people which beer they drink and whether they enjoy cigars. Each interviewer might be told to use his or her judgement in select-ing fifty men in their twenties, fifty in their thirties, fifty in their forties or fifties and fifty aged 60 or over. If the interviewers do not find fifty elderly men who agree to reply, then they will have failed to 'fill' their quotas.

Three longitudinal age-cohort studies

In 1982 the Channel 4 series *Citizen 2000* started filming a number of babies born into a variety of British homes. The series has continued to show how their lives have varied as they have grown up and they will be filmed regularly until they become adult citizens in the year 2000. Because they were all born in the same year, they all belong to the same **age-cohort** and this sort of follow-up research is called a **longitudinal study**.

In *How Voters Decide*, Himmelweit and others describe how they first interviewed a cross-section of over 600 London boys aged between 13 and 14 in 1951. Since there was an election that year, they asked the boys how they would have voted if they had been old enough. In 1962, 450 of the original sample were followed up and interviewed again. Further questionnaires were sent the day after each of the following General Elections:

Year	Numbers sent	Numbers returned	Response rate
1964	450	371	82%
1966	371	325	88%
1970	325	246	76%
1974	246	178	72%

The 178 of the original sample who were successfully contacted in 1974 were now aged about 37. Notice how the non-response rate in the different survey years eroded the number of respondents.

The most famous longitudinal survey is the National Child Development Study. This has followed all 17,000 people born in the first week of March 1958. It has also studied the children of a third of this sample. Among the study's findings, it has shown that babies of mothers who smoke heavily in pregnancy are 30 per cent more likely to die and that adults have less risk of heart disease if they were breast-fed as babies.

Self-selected samples

In 1994, the *Hite Report on the Family* was published. Its findings were based on questionnaires completed by 3,208 respondents on three continents. And the findings were dramatic and shocking: 31 per cent of girls and young women reported sexual harassment or abuse by a male family member.

But were these findings typical? Were they representative of the general population? The author, Shere Hite, had distributed 100,000 questionnaires via outlets such as *Penthouse* magazine in America, Women Against Fundamentalism in Britain and Nouvelles Questions Féministes in France. Only 3 per cent had bothered to return the lengthy and personal questionnaires.

The dangers of unreliable self-selected samples were demonstrated in 1936 when an American magazine, the *Literary Digest*, issued a mailshot to 10 million people asking them how they would vote in the presidential election. Two million replied and their answers pointed to a heavy defeat for Franklin Roosevelt. But he won by a landslide.

Gladys Engel Lang, professor at the University of Washington, defended Hite's research methods. She argued that large non-random samples were preferable for this type of study, which offered rich data in people's own words about their intimate feelings and experiences. Lang also pointed out that so-called random samples are never perfect as long as they have a non-response rate, when not all those chosen respond.

Peter Kellner agreed that the *Hite Report on the Family* contained 'a compelling variety of voices', obtained by 'a valid and underused technique for probing below the surface of touchy issues'. But Kellner took issue with the Report's statistics:

Hite says that her American respondents – half the total sample – 'quite closely mirror' the American population by age, occupation and religion. This is beside the point. What matters is whether they mirror the general population according to their family and sexual experiences. Self-selecting groups do not suddenly become accurate yardsticks of, say, domestic violence merely because they contain the right proportion of Christians, students and non-working mothers.

The National Survey of Sexual Attitudes and Lifestyles

The findings of the 1948 *Kinsey Report*, based on 8,000 interviews, suggested that 10 per cent of American men were practising homosexuals. Some gay rights campaigners have since claimed a higher figure. In 1994, the results were published of a carefully representative survey of nearly 19,000 people which had been financed by a £1 million grant from the Wellcome Trust. This *National Survey of Sexual Attitudes and Lifestyles* found that only 6 per cent of British men said that they had had some homosexual experience in their lives and only 1.1 per cent had had gay sex in the past year. This led to newspaper headlines like 'Only 1 in 90 gay.'

Critics said that the method used by the researchers, home interviews, was likely to have underestimated the number of gay men. Peter Tatchell, of the gay rights group Outrage, said: 'Closeted gays are very unlikely to admit their homosexuality to a total stranger who turns up on their doorstep and asks them personal questions about the intimate details of their private life.'

In fact, the researchers guaranteed anonymity and they interviewed respondents in private, away from other members of the family. Some of the most intimate questions were printed in booklets; respondents placed their answers in envelopes which they then sealed. But of those the researchers tried to contact, only 65 per cent were interviewed.

The leading gay rights campaigner, Sir Ian McKellen, noted:

Only 1.1% of men surveyed said they had had a homosexual 'partner' in the past year. However, 'partner' is widely used by gay men to mean a long-standing relationship. The authors of the report recognise that the wording of their question could well have affected the answers ... The respondents, of course, were not under oath. Had I been asked such questions before I came out I might have lied.

1   Give five possible reasons for the following occurrence: the answers from a carefully selected national sample lead an opinion poll in a newspaper to confidently predict that 40 per cent will vote for Labour; but, in a General Election a week later, Labour candidates only attract 30 per cent of the votes cast.

2   Give reasons for each of the following surveys having a poor response rate:
(a) a postal questionnaire to teachers asking for their views concerning a new syllabus;
(b) a truancy survey of school pupils;
(c) a questionnaire to be conducted with drug users.

3   Why might there be a problem of representativeness with:
(a) a postal questionnaire that has a low response rate?
(b) a self-selected sample, such as the 25,000 women who replied to the 1986 *Woman's Own* survey on rape? (Twelve per cent of them said that they had been raped and of these 76 per cent had not reported it to the police.)

Case studies using mixed methods

A **case study** is a piece of research that focuses on a single good example. It is somewhat artificial to argue whether one research method is better than another because many case studies that focus on a particular community or group, such as a religious cult, in fact use a mixture of methods. Well-known case studies which have analysed documentary evidence, such as media coverage, as well as using interviews and observation, include Tunstall's study of the trawlermen of Hull and Cohen's study of mods and rockers in the 1960s.

In *Beachside Comprehensive: A Case-Study of Secondary Schooling*, Stephen Ball describes how he used the following methods during his three-year study of one school:

1   He interviewed pupils and teachers.
2   He carried out several small-scale questionnaire studies.
3   He worked through and analysed school records and registers.
4   He also used **participant observation** to find out about the school.

In 1985, health and police authorities in the Portsmouth area decided that there was a need for research into the local drugs scene. In 1986, the independent Policy Studies Institute began its study of *Illicit Drug Use in Portsmouth and Havant*. From a national point of view, this research may be regarded as a case study. The following mixed methods were used to collect primary and secondary data:

- Discussions with those who come into contact with the drugs problem in the course of their work, including probation and police officers.
- Official statistics, such as the number of drug addicts notified to the Home Office by doctors and prosecutions under the 1971 Misuse of Drugs Act.
- Questionnaires filled in by 1,063 pupils and students in twenty-three schools and colleges. One of the nineteen structured questions asked:
  – Have you ever sniffed glue or other substances?
  – IF YES: Have you had any in the last week? ... in the last month?

- Informal interviews with forty-one drug users, covering topics such as their housing, employment, family history, health and diet.

Eleven per cent of 16–19-year-olds reported having smoked cannabis and 44 per cent of them knew a cannabis user. There was a strong correlation (connection) between those who smoked cigarettes and those who took drugs. A quarter of the regular smokers had used an illicit drug. The proportion of women among users registered at a local drug advice centre was 20 per cent. Many of the habitual heroin users admitted in interviews that they had at some time been involved in shoplifting, burglary or cheque and credit-card frauds; many of them had been prosecuted.

4   Participant observation

Participant observation means that the researcher actually joins the social world of those whom he or she wishes to study. In his case study of Beachside Comprehensive, Ball observed many different lessons and he also participated in the daily life of the school in a number of ways. He taught three or four periods per week for two years and he also did some supply teaching. He joined forms on school visits, went on one school trip, invigilated examinations, took registers for absent teachers, played in the staff-against-pupils cricket match, and so on.

Why use participant observation?

1   Participant observation may be the only way to collect information about a particular group, such as a religious cult.

2   Joining a group of people and experiencing how they live may offer the opportunity to gain a deep and accurate understanding of their lives. Other methods might not have this potential to provide detailed and valid data.

3   The participant observer just observes and records. The participant observer does not impose hypotheses and ideas on to the social reality of those under study. Researchers using interviews and questionnaires have already decided what they want to know and, as a consequence, social reality is shaped to fit their questions.

4   Whereas a survey may offer a snapshot picture of people's lives, participant observation may provide a changing picture of how their lives develop.

In 1990, *Villains* by Janet Foster was published. Her eighteen months of participant observation enabled her to gain access to petty offenders in South East London: two groups of 'streetwise' teenagers and a middle-aged group of men and women who socialised in the Grafton Arms pub. She was able to show how deviant careers typically develop from a highly visible and public juvenile street life to the private, institutionalised, adult exploitation of the black economy, for example using the pub to sell stolen goods pilfered from work.

In a study entitled *Hooligans Abroad*, Williams and others joined English football fans travelling to three matches in Europe during 1982. This is their explanation for using participant observation:

A standard survey methodology using questionnaires and/or interviews is, of course, a means of gaining information about the social composition of a crowd. It is also a useful way of obtaining quantitative data about the attitudes and opinions of its members. But, in the context of crowd research, questionnaires are difficult to administer and, in some respects, unreliable. Moreover, the survey method cannot tell one anything in a direct sense about the dynamics of disorderly incidents. For that, direct observation is required. In particular, the presence at such gatherings of a trained participant observer is a useful way of providing information of a richer and more reliable kind than that to which we have been accustomed hitherto. Here, too, of course, one encounters problems. How, for example, can one be sure that one's observations are accurate and would not be disputed by another participant observer or by the 'ordinary' participant in the event?

Some problems of participant observation

Laurie Taylor's study *In the Underworld* describes how he used an ex-convict, John McVicar, as a **key informant** who helped him to gain access to professional criminals in secret drinking and gambling clubs:

> He usually introduced me as 'Laurie', accompanied by a single nod of the head, which I took to mean 'not one of us, but all right'. Not that there was ever any chance of me being confused with the usual clientele. Wherever we went, I stood out ... My greatest embarrassment was always reserved for the moments when I attempted to buy a round of drinks ... I would keep fiddling with single pound notes in order to assemble the heavy cost of the round – sometimes £10 or more could disappear with one order – while everyone else seemed to deal exclusively in twenties and fifties.

On one occasion McVicar took Taylor to interview two con-men who were busy practising the signatures needed to cash a wad of stolen travellers' cheques. Did Taylor, a professor of criminology, aid and abet the con-men by his presence? Taylor answers:

> Look, they'd have committed the crime anyway. Whether I'd been there or not. They completely ignored me. Looked through me. I couldn't have stopped them if I'd wanted to. And if I had reported the matter to the police, it wouldn't have led to their detention. I had no idea where they were going or whose cheques they were carrying. By the time they were found, they'd have been clean. What's more, any such call to the police would have meant the end of the project. Absolutely no more introductions by John and so no chance to discover anything of interest about the tactics and style of a group of criminals about whom we know so little.

Some criticisms of participant observation

1   Participant observation is usually carried out on small groups. This limits the method's usefulness because sociologists often want to make general statements about large sections of the population. Such statements may be better supported by surveys of large, representative samples.

(Taylor's sampling technique, where one respondent introduces the researcher to new contacts, is called **snowballing**.)

2   Those who use participant observation often face moral difficulties. If they are observing covertly, without revealing their true intentions, then it may be difficult to record data with note-books or tape-recorders. They will also be involved in deception: lying to and cheating those whom they observe. They may also find themselves getting involved in dangerous and illegal activities.

3   It can be an expensive and time-consuming method of collecting information. If participant observation is to be done properly the researcher may need to spend two or three years with the group under study.

4   It is a very personal and subjective method of research. The findings of participant observation depend to a great extent on the researcher's powers of observation and interpretation. But how do we know whether such findings are accurate and true? It is not easy to repeat a participant observation study.

5   Secondary data

The information that researchers gain from their own surveys is called **primary data. Secondary data** refers to information that has been collected by others. The study of male voters conducted by Himmelweit and others over a period of twenty-three years led them to construct a 'model' or general explanation of how voters decide to cast their votes. In order to test this theory they analysed the results of some secondary data. In other words, they compared their hypothesis, based on their own observations, with the findings of other people's surveys. In fact, they examined six separate British election surveys carried out between 1970 and 1983 which had involved over 15,000 voters.

Types of secondary data

Historical sources
In his research on the connection between *The Protestant Ethic and the Spirit of Capitalism*, Max Weber examined the ideas of the eighteenth-century American writer Benjamin Franklin. Maxims such as 'Time is money, so do not idle' were taken to be ideal-types of the puritan business ethic. Gordon Marshall tested Weber's theory by looking for the aims of early capitalists in the company documents of the Newmills Cloth Manufactury which began in Scotland in 1681.

In their research on household size in the past, Laslett used parish records and Anderson used the 1851 census figures for Preston. Researchers at Leicester University have found reports of violent football hooliganism in 1903 editions of the *Leicester Mercury*.

Personal documents
Letters, diaries and autobiographies have the advantages and disadvantages of qualitative data. They may give a rich and detailed picture but they might not be representative. Thomas and Znaniecki used the letters sent by immigrants to study *The Polish Peasant in Europe and America* (1919).

Official records

Young, Female and Black (1992) describes research at two South London comprehensive schools by Heidi Safia Mirza. As well as interviews and observation, Mirza used pupil records to find out details about punctuality, attendance and conduct.

Content analysis

'STRAIGHT SEX CANNOT GIVE YOU AIDS – OFFICIAL' was a headline in the *Sun* in 1989. While the *Sun* portrayed AIDS as a 'gay plague', the *Daily Express* reported on 'AIDS fear for women' in 1990 and 'AIDS despair that knows no barriers' in 1991. Press coverage of AIDS has been analysed by Peter Beharrell of the Glasgow University Media Group. He examined each of the national newspapers over a 34-month period, from November 1988 to August 1991. (If you have access to a library that has newspapers stored on CD-Rom, it can be easy to find stories on a particular subject by just keying in a topic title and using the search facility.)

T.A. van Dijk's study of *Racism and the Press* (1991) was based on content analysis of all articles on ethnic affairs in five national newspapers from 1 August 1985 to 31 January 1986; 2,700 articles were analysed and one of van Dijk's conclusions was that 'law and order reporting in the British press during the mid-1980s continues a long tradition of media criminalization of the black community'.

Content analysis has also been widely used to study sex role stereotyping, for example in children's books and advertisements. Such research can be both quantitative, measuring the percentage of female roles, and qualitative, describing the types of female roles. Women may be portrayed as passive or active, in the workplace or in domestic situations.

Official statistics

Government figures for the incidence of crime, suicide or marital breakdown all suffer from a dark figure of unrecorded, hidden cases. A controversial example of this problem is the official total for unemployment. In 1992, the Unemployment Unit noted that Conservative Governments had made more than thirty changes to the way that unemployment was defined since 1979. All but one of these changes had resulted in lower figures.

Rates per 100,000 population

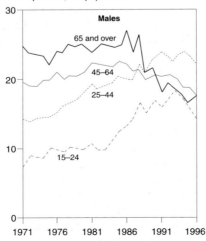
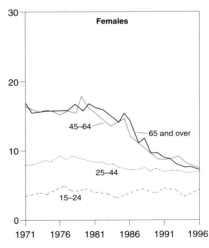

Death rates from suicide[1]: by gender and age (Source: Social Trends, 1998.)

[1]Includes deaths undetermined whether accidentally or purposely inflicted.

Case study: child suicides

Experts estimate that at least one child commits suicide every week. But official figures recorded only three suicides by under-15s in 1991 and two suicides by under-15s in 1990. Each year up to sixty deaths of under-15s are recorded as due to 'injury undetermined whether accidentally or purposely inflicted'. Researchers say that coroners frequently record open verdicts – often ignoring persuasive evidence that a child has taken his or her life – to spare the feelings of distraught parents.

Over a five-year period, researchers in Oxford monitored the progress of teenagers admitted to hospital for drug overdoses. Of sixteen who died within a year of admission, four had verdicts of suicide although others had died from unnatural causes such as hanging, drowning or injuries sustained on a railway line. One London coroner's officer recalls a case in which a suicide note was found in the pocket of a teenager killed by a train. The family insisted that the note was not in his handwriting and an open verdict was recorded.

6 Experiments

We began this chapter by looking at an example of an experiment. Researchers in the natural sciences, such as botanists, often use experiments in which they alter variables in a laboratory and compare outcomes. Sociologists at work might be found collecting primary data, in living rooms or court rooms, in gangs or cults; or sociological research may involve examining secondary data, existing sources such as diaries, newspapers and statistics.

Sociological research does not take place in laboratories (although social psychologists sometimes observe and measure social interaction, such as conversations and 'body language', in controlled laboratory conditions). But sociologists sometimes conduct experiments in which they artificially control variables to obtain constrasting results. We have already described the Skeels experiment (page 7), a sex roles experiment (page 15). Here are two more examples of sociological experiments.

An experiment on wife-batterers

In recent years organisations like the National Women's Aid Federation have pressed for the police to take tougher action against husbands who beat their wives. But many sociologists might argue that the police have been correct in their traditional 'softly, softly' approach which tries to patch up any domestic affray. Sociologists might be concerned that 'labelling' violent husbands by pressing charges may damage marriages irrevocably by **criminalising** the husbands and **amplifying deviance**.

Two American sociologists, Sherman and Berk, tested these ideas with an experiment which depended on the co-operation of the Minneapolis police department. Officers agreed to deal with domestic assault in one of three ways, on a strict rota basis, without reference to their own judgement. The three options were: arrest; asking the suspect to leave for eight hours; and trying to patch things up between the partners. Between March 1981 and August 1982, Sherman and Berk followed up 314 cases by monitoring whether the police intervened during the subsequent six months and then interviewing the victims. Their conclusions support the feminist argument for a tougher line because domestic assaults were more likely to be repeated where partners were merely separated and were less likely to recur when husbands were arrested. Prompt arrest proved to be a strong deterrent against re-offending.

An experiment on coroners

W.M. Atkinson, N. Kessel and J. Dalgaard were suspicious that suicide rates were 'socially constructed', created by the judgements of coroners. Their experiment was to send the details of forty cases to a sample of English and Danish coroners, asking for their verdicts. The English coroners, who have to find evidence of 'definite suicidal intention' to record a suicide, on average gave nineteen suicide verdicts to the forty cases. In Denmark suicide can be recorded when it seems likely 'on the balance of probability'. The Danish coroners on average declared twenty-nine of the forty cases to have been suicides.

7   Theoretical perspectives

A sociologist's choice of research methods is also influenced by their theoretical perspective:

Theoretical perspective	*Macro*	*Micro*
	Structural theory	*Social action theory*
In the tradition of	Durkheim: functionalism, structural consensus theory and Marx: structural conflict theory	Weber: interactionism
Outlook on methods	Positivist (scientific, objective)	Interpretive (subjective)
Favoured methods	Quantitative, numerical 'hard facts'	Qualitative, descriptive 'soft data'
Primary data	Large surveys via questionnaires and structured interviews	Informal interviews or participant observation
Number of respondents	High	Low
Involvement of researcher	Low	High
Secondary data	Statistics	Life documents (letters, diaries)
Representativeness	High	Low
Validity, truthfulness	Low	High
Examples, study of	Correlation between poverty and smoking Patterns of domestic division of labour	Why more poor people smoke What it feels like to be a a housewife
Advantages	Broad and reliable Can test to check and can generalise Can repeat and establish a 'law' (e.g. the poor smoke more)	Find motives and meanings Easy to follow up new ideas In-depth understanding of the rich texture of social lives
Disadvantages	Shallow, superficial, skims surface, bland, boring	Narrow, non-typical, unique, one-off, hard to verify by replication

Theoretical models

The main theoretical perspectives in sociology offer models, or pictures, of how society works. The Marxist tradition sees class conflict as the main feature of the social structure. Hence, the Marxist perspective is known as the **structural conflict view**.

Followers of Durkheim, or functionalists, study the functions of social institutions. All the parts of society are seen as working together, like parts of the body. This is called an organic analogy. Because functionalists stress harmony, agreement and consensus, their perspective is called the **structural consensus view**.

Positivism

Auguste Comte first coined the word 'sociology'. He also developed the idea of 'positivism'. This maintains that the only true knowledge is 'empirical'. This means knowledge which is based on systematic observation. If we say 'God is a woman', this is a speculative assertion, a subjective belief which cannot be proved. But if we say '79 per cent of people believe in God', then, according to positivists, this is an objective empirical fact which can be scientifically tested (for example, by repeated surveys).

Durkheim's research

Emile Durkheim developed Comte's new science of sociology, the scientific study of society. In *Suicide* (1897), Durkheim used a quantitative approach, studying official statistics. He found social patterns in suicide figures. For example, he found a higher suicide rate among Protestants than among Catholics.

Marx's research

Karl Marx also had a quantitative approach. He spent most of his working life in the Reading Room of the British Museum in London. He collected masses of facts and figures on the economic relationships in capitalist society. His analysis appeared in the volumes of *Das Kapital* (1867–95).

The Weberian tradition

Max Weber inspired the social action approach. This approach aims to uncover the motives and subjective meanings which guide us in our social interaction with others. For example, one might undertake observation in coroners' courts and carry out in-depth interviews with coroners. This might reveal their 'taken-for-granted assumptions' or stereotypes. One might discover that suicides by children do not fit their preconceived picture of a 'typical suicide'. This might explain their motive in giving open verdicts in such cases. Only some self-deaths get officially 'labelled' as suicides. If this interpretive research discovers that suicides by children are seldom recorded in the official statistics, or that Catholic families are more likely than Protestants to cover up suicides, then the 'hard data' favoured by positivists, such as Durkheim, no longer looks so reliable.

Macro and micro

The structural approaches of Marxism and functionalism have a macro approach because they are concerned with the analysis of whole societies. This approach favours quantitative research. On the other hand, the social action approach of microsociology uses qualitative data to gain meaningful understanding (Weber called this *verstehen*) and explanation of the face-to-face interactions of individuals in everyday life.

Feminist research

Feminists, such as Ann Oakley, have argued that feminist researchers should avoid the assumptions and approaches of traditional 'malestream' sociology. Rather than being superior to interviewees, they should try to establish an equal relationship with respondents. Instead of trying to be objective, impartial, neutral, detached and value-free, they should take the side of the women that they interview. All should be part of the 'women's struggle' which challenges and ends the oppression of women.

Practical limitations

A sociologist's choice of research methods is influenced by his or her chosen theoretical perspective. It is also partly dictated by the amounts of time and money that are available. For example, Hannah Gavron's study of *The Captive Wife: Conflicts of Housebound Mothers* (Penguin, 1966) was carried out while she was a postgraduate student, working as a single researcher without large funds or a supporting organisation. These practical limitations meant that she was only able to conduct a small-scale survey of forty-eight working-class wives and forty-eight middle-class wives, all living in North London. She acknowledged that large-scale generalisations could not be made from such a sample.

A student doing research for a GCSE project should also be aware that time and resources are limited. It is advisable therefore to plan a project that is not too broad in scope. This point is discussed further in the next chapter which takes up the issue of project work for the GCSE examination.

GCSE question from Southern Examining Group 1997

Read Item A. Then answer *all* parts of the question which follows.

Item A

The researchers carried out an investigation into the extent of poverty. It was based on whether or not individuals had a range of articles or possessions and, if they did not have them, whether this was because they could not afford them or by choice. They interviewed 91 people between November 1989 and May 1990. They used a 'quota sample', selecting possible interviewees to obtain the groups they were looking for. All the interviews with the Asian families were conducted in their mother tongue of Urdu or Pakistani by Asian researchers. The interviews were lengthy and were tape-recorded. The interview schedule was piloted in two areas similar to those in which the final study was conducted.

Adapted from R Cohen, J Coxley, G Craig and A Sadiq-Sangstar *Hardship Britain: Being Poor in the 1990s*

(a) With reference to Item A, identify the kind of sample used by the researchers. Indicate why they used this technique. (2)

(b) With reference to Item A, what were the two ways in which the researchers attempted to make the Asian families feel comfortable and able to communicate easily? (2)

(c) Suggest *one* reason why the researchers piloted their interview schedule. Why might they have used areas similar to those in the final study? (2)

(d) (i) Suggest *one* reason why it might be better to use a relative rather than an absolute definition of poverty in this kind of study. (1)

(ii) Identify and explain *one* advantage to the researchers of tape-recording the interviews. (3)

(e) What advantages might face-to-face interviews have over postal questionnaires in this type of study? (8)

CHAPTER 18

Coursework project

BUT COULD I
JUST ASK YOU
A FEW........

1   General advice on coursework

The advice in this chapter applies to the coursework component of the **Southern Examining Group**. Candidates are required to submit a project undertaken in the twelve months preceding the written examination. This project carries 20 per cent of the total marks for the examination and assesses a candidate's ability to apply critical understanding to the Syllabus Subject Content while demonstrating the following skills:

1   to acquire information for different purposes by direct collection of information (primary data) and by acquiring information from existing sources (secondary data);

2   to interpret information presented in different forms and to analyse and evaluate its relevance and accuracy;

3   to use information to examine issues and construct and evaluate arguments and conclusions.

The purpose of the project is to enable candidates to:

1   pursue a topic of personal interest in some depth;

2   show by practical application to a topic of their own choice, that they understand the nature of sociological enquiry and are able to select and adapt research methods appropriate to a specific study;

3   learn by experience some of the problems of sociological investigation and to examine their chosen topic of study in a critical manner.

Here is some further advice from the Southern Examining Group:

- **Aims**   The aims should be expressed clearly and explicitly, usually with an accompanying hypothesis.

- **Collaboration**   Students may collaborate in the early stages of planning and collecting data but the analysis and writing up of the topic must be the work of each individual candidate.
- **Length**   The recommended length is between 1,000 and 2,500 words. Credit will be given for clear and concise work. The emphasis is on quality rather than volume.
- **Copying**   Findings should be presented in the candidate's own words. Work consisting largely of copied extracts is inadequate. Any copied extract should be identified by quotation marks, if text, and by reference to the source of the material (author, title, date).
- **Presentation**   The work should be presented in written form and should include the following features:
  - table of contents;
  - clear separation of chapters;
  - good layout and clear use of language;
  - clear labelling of any diagrams, graphs, photographs, recorded tapes or cassettes;
  - all sources of information listed in a detailed bibliography.

2   The coursework marking criteria

Although the examination weighting for coursework is 20 per cent, it is marked initially out of 30 raw marks. To reach the top band of marks in each of the five elements of the Southern Examining Group's marking scheme, you should meet the following criteria.

A   *Knowledge and understanding (9 marks)*

Knowledge is presented in depth using diverse sources. It is explicitly relevant to the aims of the project and relates closely to the social structure of modern Britain (although a research topic could include a cross-cultural or historical approach).

Shows clear understanding of the relationship between the chosen social issue and related social processes with clear examples in several parts of the project.

B   *Methodology (3 marks)*

Applies an appropriate sociological method in depth and shows clear understanding of its effectiveness for the chosen project.

C   *Sources (6 marks)*

Uses primary and secondary sources, at least one of which will be treated in depth. All sources will be clearly and explicitly relevant to the stated aims of the project.

D   *Analysis (6 marks)*

A clear logical interpretation of all information used is made in the candidate's own words: description of findings, comparison and contrast of data, questioning of secondary source material.

Critical judgements of the accuracy and relevance of the information to the precise aims of the project are explicitly presented.

E   Evaluation (6 marks)

Relevant conclusions are drawn which refer to both the findings of the research and the method used. These conclusions are explicitly relevant to the precise aims of the project, are explored in depth and show some insight and perception.

3   Some ideas for a coursework topic

Here are some possible topics from each section of the Southern Examining Group's syllabus.

Section 1 – What is Sociology?

- Any chosen topic. Construct and use a questionnaire. Assess its usefulness.
- Any sociological study. Look at the method(s) of research used and assess alternatives.

Section 2 – The Sociology of the Family

- Study of family relationships using interviews with three generations.
- Study of the structure of the family in modern Britain or in another culture (e.g. kibbutzim), using secondary sources.
- Study of kinship networks, contacts with members of extended family.
- Study of domestic division of labour, conjugal roles.

Section 3 – The Sociology of Education

- Study of subject choices within student's school or college, including work on how choices are made. Specific reference to gender or race.
- Study of educational achievement, e.g. examination performance in relation to social class, using secondary sources.
- Study of socialisation and gender, e.g. sex role stereotyping in text book illustrations or advertisements.

Section 4 – Social Differentiation

- Study of attitudes to social class using questionnaire/interviews with peer group.
- Comparison of the social class system in modern Britain with an alternative form of stratification.
- Social class differences in consumption patterns (e.g. housing, leisure, newspaper readership) or attitudes (replicate part of the annual *British Social Attitudes* survey).

Section 5 – The Welfare State and Poverty

- Study of the use made of a health clinic by different social groups using questionnaire and/or interview.
- A study of poverty in Britain or in a Third World country, using secondary sources.
- A study of a local voluntary welfare organisation.

Section 6 – The Sociology of Politics

- Study of media presentation of either specific issues or news during one week.
- Study of one pressure group, mostly secondary sources.
- Carry out a political opinion poll.

Section 7 – The Sociology of Work

- Study of the role of a trade union in a specific place of work of which the student has experience.
- Study of the effects of technology on specific occupations, using secondary sources.
- A study of how work affects the leisure of an occupational group, e.g. teachers.

Section 8 – Social and Demographic Aspects of Population

- A study of population movement in student's own area – local secondary sources.
- Study of specific trend, e.g. de-urbanisation and its consequences, using secondary sources.
- Survey of attitudes towards the provision of asylum for refugees.

Section 9 – Social Control and Deviance

- Study of specific 'problems', e.g. social effects of unemployment in student's area. Secondary sources plus interviews.
- Study of the changing role of the police. Secondary sources plus interviews.
- Study of workplace fiddles and pilfering, using participant observation and informal interviews.
- Study of a media moral panic about folk devils, e.g. New Age travellers, ravers, owners of pit bull terriers.

Access: using contacts

You may already have access to a particular group that you can study. It could be your family or peer group, a club or religious organisation to which you belong, or your school or college. Access to a workplace, a shop or a nursery school, may be possible through any of the following:

- voluntary work, e.g. community placement;
- work experience;
- a weekend or holiday job;
- a parent's or neighbour's employment.

Index

Acknowledgements

We are grateful to the following for permission to reproduce copyright material:

Philip Allan Publishers Ltd for an adapted extract from pp.15–19 in *Sociology Review*, April 1994; Blackwell Publishers Ltd, for an extract from *Youth in Britain Since 1945* by Bill Osgerby (1998); Causeway Press Ltd for an adapted extract from *The Sociology of Youth* by Simon Frith (1984); Central Statistical Office; Child Poverty Action Group for an extract adapted for SEG from *Hardship Britain: Being poor in the 1990s* by R.Cohen, J.Coxley, C.Craig & A.Sadiq-Sangstar; Guardian Newspaper Ltd; for an adapted extract from the article 'I Want My Kids' by Nick Davies in *The Guardian* (c) 19.1.94, an adapted extract from the article by Kathy Evans in *The Guardian* (c) 7.2.94.; an adapted extract from the article 'Commentary' by Jonathan Freedland in *The Guardian* (c) 29.10.97, and an extract adapted for SEG from an article in *The Observer* (c) 24.10.93.; the author, Janey Hulme for an extract from an article in *The Teacher* Jan–Feb 1998; an extract from an article by Jill Joliffe in *The Guardian* (c) 12.6.80, and adapted extracts from the articles 'Street Wars' by Angela Neustatter in *The Guardian* (c) 10.2.94, and 'New Tribes of England' by Alix Sharkey in *Guardian Weekend* (c) 11.12.93; Hampstead & Highgate Express; Hornsey & Muswell Hill Journal; Independent Newspapers Ltd for an extract adapted for SEG from the article 'Holland Park: What's school got to do with it? No one pushed you: Student-Eighties' by Celia Dodd in *The Independent* (c) 9.6.93; Ladybird Books Ltd; North Eastern Evening Gazette for an extract adapted for SEG from an article in *The Evening Gazette* (c) 20.9.96; Policy Studies Institute Publications; Polity Press Ltd for a Table from *Working Lives of Women Managers* by C.Cooper & M.Davidson; SEG for questions from past *Foundation Tier and Higher Tier* 'Sociology' examination papers; Tavistock Publications; Times Newspapers Ltd for adapted extracts from the article 'Women Fall Behind in Degrees of Excellence' by Charles Hyams from *The Sunday Times* (c) 23.5.93; Wharfedale Newspapers Ltd for an extract adapted for SEG from an article by Louise Auty in *Wharfedale Newspapers* (c) November 1993.

We have been unable to trace the copyright holders of the article 'Choosing to Play Their Own Tune' by Sally Ballard in *The Daily Telegraph* (c) 9.2.94, an article by Frank Conley in *General Elections Today* and a letter by J. Elliot in *The Guardian* (c) 4.2.94, and would appreciate any information that would enable us to do so.

We are grateful to the following for permission to reproduce the following photographs and copyright material:
Allsport, p.16 (Rick Stewart) (above); Associated Press, p.116 (above); Barnaby's Picture Library, pp.6, 47, 73, 105,151, 183 (top), 224, 232; Stewart Bonney (News) Agency, p.206; Bridgeman Art Library, p.33; British Library, p.72; Camera Press, pp.16 (both), 61 (Snowdon), 142 (both); City Art Gallery and Museum, p.110; Derbyshire CC, p.220; Environmental Images, p.213; Ford Motor Company, p.312; Format, pp.37, 56 (Maggie Murray); Richard Gardner, p.28; Sally & Richard Greenhill, p.86; *The Guardian*, pp.9, 131 (Graham Turner), 201 (Graham Turner), 250 (David Sillitoe), 259 (top), 270 (Richard Olivier), 273 (E.Hamilton West), 288 (Sean Smith), 297 Mark Argles (left), 326 (Graham Turner); Guzelian, p.324; Hutchison Picture Library, p.146 (Sarah Errington); The Hulton Deutsch Collection Ltd, pp.65, 96, 120, 174; INS, p.276; *The Independent*, p.50 (Robert Hallam), 157, 241 (Andrew Buurman), 159 (Nicholas Turpin), 220 (Nicholas Kurtz) (below), 243 (John Voos) (below), 265 (Centre for the Study of Cartoons & Caricature, University of Kent), 278 (Peter Macdiarmid); Katz, p.12 (John Reardon); Labour Party, p.281; London Features, p.262 (Glen E. Friedman); Magnum, p.199 (A. Abbas); Kippa Matthews, p.129; Mirror Syndication International, pp.46, 80 (John Frost Newspaper Library), 205; Sam Morgan Moore, p.219; Network, pp.19 (Paul Reas) (both), 108 (John Sturrock), 130 (Barry Lewis), 140 (Christopher Pillitz), 164 (Homer Sykes) (top), 168 (both) Roger Hutchings, left, Mike Abrahams, right), 186 (Mike Abrahams) 197, 204, (Mike Abrahams), 269 (John Sturrock) (right), 299 (Paul Lowe), 302, 304 (Neil Libbert), 317 (Neil Libbert); Oxfiend, p.253 (both); Press Association; p.126 (Peter Jordan) 277, 334 (Tony Harris); Photofusion, p.149; Popperfoto, pp.26, 39, 129, 248, 272, 332; Tony Prime, p.192; Report/Derek Speirs, p.84; Rex Features, pp.6, 121, 136, 161 (left), 240, 242, 273, 286, 298 (bottom), 329; Rex Features and John Frost Newspaper Library, p.255 (both); Peter Sanders, p.217 Trevor Smith, p.133; Suddeutscher Verlag, p.42; David Swindells, p.48; Syndication International, p.333; Times Newspapers, pp.339, 340 (Gill Allen); Topham Picture Source, pp.116, 147, 210, 237; Tropix, p.58; Unison, p.327; Geoff Ward, pp.2, 164 (bottom), 263, 295, 298, 303. The following pictures were provided by the author: pp.54, 83, 124, 178, 189, 337.